READINGS IN THE
WESTERN HUMANITIES

READINGS IN THE WESTERN HUMANITIES

VOLUME I

Third Edition

Edited by

ROY T. MATTHEWS
F. DEWITT PLATT

Michigan State University

MAYFIELD PUBLISHING COMPANY
Mountain View, California
London • Toronto

Library of Congress Cataloging-in-Publication Data

Readings in the Western humanities.—3rd ed. / edited by Roy T. Matthews,
   F. DeWitt Platt.
     p.   cm.
   Designed to accompany Matthews and Platt's textbook, Western
humanities, 3rd ed.
   ISBN 1-55934-577-2 (v. 1).—ISBN 1-55934-578-0 (v. 2)
   1. Civilization, Western—History—Sources.   I. Matthews, Roy T.
II. Platt, F. DeWitt.   III. Matthews, Roy T.   Western humanities.
CB245.R39   1997   96-52519
909'.09812—dc21   CIP

Manufactured in the United States of America
10   9   8   7   6   5   4   3   2   1

Mayfield Publishing Company
1280 Villa Street
Mountain View, CA 94041

Sponsoring editor, Holly J. Allen; production editor, Julianna Scott Fein; manuscript editor, Darlene Bledsoe; design manager, Susan Breitbard; text and cover designer, Susan Breitbard; manufacturing manager, Randy Hurst; cover art, *Dante*, by Signorelli, © Scala/Art Resource, NY. The text was set in 9/11 Palatino by Archetype Book Composition and printed on acid-free 45# Amherst Matte by Malloy Lithographing, Inc.

Acknowledgments and copyrights continue at the back of the book on pages 235–236, which constitute an extension of the copyright page.

For Dixie Leigh

"Many women have done excellently, but you surpassed them all."
— *Book of Proverbs 31:29*

FDP

—⁓—

For Randy and Elizabeth

We taught them the past, and they have brought us happiness.
Now, they show us the future by making the world a better place.

RTM

PREFACE

―――――――――――――――― ∽ ――――――――――――――――

We are pleased to present the third edition of *Readings in the Western Humanities*, an anthology of literary and philosophic writings. This is the first edition of this work for which we have had sole responsibility, although we have been associated with it since its inception. The anthology began as a complementary resource for our textbook *The Western Humanities* (and so it remains today); but concurrent time constraints—seeing our book through press and teaching courses at Michigan State University—kept us from assuming the initial editorship. Members of the editorial staff at Mayfield Publishing Company—Julie Wildhaber, Kate Engelberg, and C. Lansing Hays—stepped into the breach and, working from a tentative Table of Contents drawn up by us, as well as from suggestions by a number of experienced humanities faculty, produced the first edition of the anthology. This proved to be a useful collection, which was adopted at many colleges and universities around the country.

. . .

The selections in this anthology reflect the educational ideal expressed first by the nineteenth-century poet and critic Matthew Arnold and adopted by us in *The Western Humanities*—that to be truly educated, students need to be exposed to "the best that has been thought and said." We think that this ideal can be an effective bulwark against the twin dangers of the late twentieth century: a cyberspace culture divorced from history and a mass culture catering to the lowest common denominator. We have assembled this anthology with the hope that it will give students an understanding of the West's literary and philosophical heritage and thus empower them to greater heights by expanding their horizons.

Starting in about 3000 B.C. and ranging over five thousand years, Western philosophy and literature have left a vast, diverse, and complex record. To keep this anthology to a manageable length, we adopted two principles of selection: Include works that have significantly influenced Western culture, and offer as many diverse and representative voices as possible. The readings are presented in chronological order, arranged into twenty-one chapters, just as is *The Western Humanities*, and divided into two volumes. Volume I covers ancient Mesopotamia through the Renaissance; Volume II, the Renaissance through the twentieth century.

The application of our principles of selection to Volume I led us to keep most of the time-honored works that appeared in the first edition and are discussed in *The Western Humanities*, such as selections from *The Epic of Gilgamesh*, Homer's *Iliad* and *Odyssey*, Plato's *Phaedo*, Aristotle's *Poetics*, Sophocles' *Oedipus the King* (complete), Vergil's *Aeneid*, St. Augustine's *Confessions* and *The City of God*, Einhard's *The Life of Charlemagne*, Chrétien de Troyes's *Lancelot*, Chaucer's *The Canterbury Tales*, Christine de Pizan's *The Book of the City of Ladies*, and Castiglione's *The Book of the Courtier*.

In some instances in Volume I, we changed the readings in the first edition to include new material that we thought better represented an author's viewpoint, such as replacing the rather uneventful

Book XVIII of Homer's *Iliad* with Book I, which establishes the central theme of Achilles' anger. We added some pages from Plato's *Republic* in order to demonstrate the author's feminist sympathies; we also deleted one of Horace's *Odes* and added one of his *Satires* ("The Bore"), thus offering another Roman literary genre. Other changes included choosing new verses from the *Song of Roland* to make the climactic scene more dramatic; selecting a more forceful episode from Comnena's *The Alexiad* to illustrate Byzantine impressions of Western Crusaders; omitting Book XIII, on suicides, in Dante's *Inferno* and replacing it with the more critically important Canto XXXIV. We also augmented the excerpt from Boccaccio's *The Decameron* by including one of the stories (Filomena's Tale, Day 1); clarified Pico's *On the Dignity of Man* by adding his vision of the soul's unity with the divine; and gave a balanced overview to Machiavelli's *The Prince* by including chapters showing both moral and immoral arguments.

Furthermore, we revised Volume I to take advantage of translations that we considered better than those represented in the first edition. Because the Old Testament is the creation of the Jewish experience, we thought that a Jewish version of the Bible would be appropriate; so after surveying the field, we chose *The Holy Scriptures*, published by the Jewish Publication Society. Similarly, for the Christian writings we chose *The Revised Standard Version of the Holy Bible* because of its popularity. We then placed the selections from Judaism and Christianity together in Chapter 6, "Judaism and the Rise of Christianity," as this is the same chapter in *The Western Humanities* in which the two faiths are introduced. Other new translations in Volume I include Sappho's poems and selections from Aristophanes' *Lysistrata* and Alberti's *On Painting*.

The most drastic changes to Volume I occurred when we added authors excluded from the first edition, which in turn caused us to eliminate other writers because we were restricted in the length of text we could assemble. We added the complete poem *The Exaltation of Inanna* by Enheduanna, the Akkadian priestess who is the world's first known author, and we introduced chapters from Eusebius's *The History of the Church*, since this work established the genre of church history, a genre not otherwise found in the anthology. We also corrected a major omission by adding passages from *Scivias* by Hildegard of Bingen, the most important medieval writer to be rediscovered and restored to the West's literary canon. Deleted from this edition are the Unas Pyramid Texts, St. Francis of Assisi's "The Canticle of the Sun," *Sir Gawain and the Green Knight*, and *Everyman*.

. . .

We want to thank the faculty around the country who adopted earlier editions of this anthology, because that demand has warranted the publication of this edition. We especially want to thank the humanities teachers who acted as readers and gave us helpful advice in making these selections: Camille Weiss, West Virginia University; Bertha Wise, Oklahoma City Community College; and Martha Durant Kirchmer, Grand Valley State University. We also express our appreciation to Holly Allen, our sponsoring editor, who made this project possible, and to Darlene Bledsoe, the copyeditor, whose eagle-eyed concern has saved us from many mistakes. Special thanks must go to Julianna Scott Fein for shepherding the manuscript through the various production stages. To our former humanities students at Michigan State University who served as guinea pigs for most of the anthology's selections, we offer our gratitude; their informed responses helped hone the way we interpret literature and philosophy. If our headnotes are clear and apposite, then part of the praise must be shared with those students.

CONTENTS

Chapter 11   THE EARLY RENAISSANCE: RETURN TO CLASSICAL ROOTS, 1400–1494   221

Chapter 12   THE HIGH RENAISSANCE AND EARLY MANNERISM: 1494–1564   227

1

PREHISTORY AND NEAR EASTERN CIVILIZATIONS

Selection from *Inanna: Queen of Heaven and Earth*

Inanna: Queen of Heaven and Earth illustrates the problems of understanding Mesopotamian literature. Like other stories from this civilization, it probably was told thousands of times before it was ever transcribed onto a clay tablet. Its survival is more a matter of chance than the result of a deliberate act; and what remains may be only a small fragment of a long and complex tale. Adding to the difficulty in understanding this story is that its purpose, whether as a moral lesson or as pure entertainment, cannot be fully determined. Since Mesopotamian civilizations borrowed tales from one another over long periods of time, stories played a variety of roles across kingdoms and centuries and often found their way into other folk tales. Furthermore, Akkadian, the language of Mesopotamian literature, differs so much from English that the precise meaning of words is often impossible to determine; the more subtle aspects of language, such as puns or alliterations, are lost in either the translation or our lack of knowledge of ancient vocabularies.

Within the past thirty years, however, the discovery of more cuneiform-inscribed tablets, the intense study and scholarship brought to deciphering and interpreting the findings, and the willingness of scholars to view artifacts in new ways have all enhanced the understanding of the stories. Also, scholars now know much more about myths and their meaning and appreciate that myths can be interpreted in various ways.

Reading the Selection

This passage from the full text describes the stages Inanna (the goddess of love, also known as Ishtar) goes through to prepare herself for entry into the underworld, what happens to her once she is there, and her rescue from the "Great Below." The verses that describe her dress and jewelry reinforce the image of Inanna's power and wealth; ordinary humans would not have worn such splendid clothes and precious beads and rings. Other verses dwell on the creative aspects of the divinities, as in the case of Enki, Inanna's father, who is known as the god of the subterranean waters and is associated with wisdom and magic. Enki, deciding to bring Inanna back from the underworld, fashions two creatures to assist in her rescue.

While some of the terms, such as *shugurra* (Inanna's crown), are identified, others, such as *me*, a vague term whose meaning shifts according to context, remain unclear. For example, when Inanna

1

gathers the seven *me* into her possession, she seems to be collecting the powers ascribed to deities that allow them to perform certain tasks. *Me* is elsewhere understood to be the powers of gods and goddesses that permit them to carry on the basic activities identified with civilization. In another story, Enki and Inanna gamble for the *me*, and she wins all of them from her father.

Inanna's journey into the lower region is a common theme found in many ancient stories. In Homer's *Odyssey*, Odysseus descends into Hades, and in Vergil's *Aeneid*, Aeneas goes into the land of the shades. In both these works, the heroes are given prophecies about the future; however, Inanna's descent appears to be more of an adventure spurred on by her own curiosity. Her explanation that she wants to attend the funeral rites for her brother-in-law obviously does not convince the Queen of the Underworld, who, for whatever reason, decides that Inanna must die.

—m—

From the Great Above to the Great Below

From the Great Above she opened her ear to the Great
   Below.   1
From the Great Above the goddess opened her ear to the
   Great Below.
From the Great Above Inanna opened her ear to the Great
   Below.

My Lady abandoned heaven and earth to descend to the
   underworld.
Inanna abandoned heaven and earth to descend to the
   underworld.
She abandoned her office of holy priestess to descend to
   the underworld.

In Uruk she abandoned her temple to descend to the
   underworld.
In Badtibira she abandoned her temple to descend to the
   underworld.
In Zabalam she abandoned her temple to descend to the
   underworld.
In Adab she abandoned her temple to descend to the
   underworld.   10

In Nippur she abandoned her temple to descend to the
   underworld.
In Kish she abandoned her temple to descend to the
   underworld.
In Akkad she abandoned her temple to descend to the
   underworld.

She gathered together the seven *me*.
She took them into her hands.
With the *me* in her possession, she prepared herself:

She placed the *shugurra*, the crown of the steppe, on
   her head.
She arranged the dark locks of hair across her forehead.
She tied the small lapis beads around her neck,
Let the double strand of beads fall to her breast,   20
And wrapped the royal robe around her body.

She daubed her eyes with ointment called "Let him come,
   Let him come,"
Bound the breastplate called "Come, man, come!" around
   her chest,
Slipped the gold ring over her wrist,
And took the lapis measuring rod and line in her hand.

Inanna set out for the underworld.
Ninshubur, her faithful servant, went with her.
Inanna spoke to her, saying:
   "Ninshubur, my constant support,
   My *sukkal* who gives me wise advice,   30
   My warrior who fights by my side,
   I am descending to the *kur*, to the underworld.
   If I do not return,
   Set up a lament for me by the ruins.
   Beat the drum for me in the assembly places.
   Circle the houses of the gods.
   Tear at your eyes, at your mouth, at your thighs.
   Dress yourself in a single garment like a beggar.
   Go to Nippur, to the temple of Enlil.

   When you enter his holy shrine, cry out: 40
   'O Father Enlil, do not let your daughter
   Be put to death in the underworld.
   Do not let your bright silver
   Be covered with the dust of the underworld.
   Do not let your precious lapis
   Be broken into stone for the stoneworker.
   Do not let your fragrant boxwood
   Be cut into wood for the woodworker.
   Do not let the holy priestess of heaven
   Be put to death in the underworld.'   50

   If Enlil will not help you,
   Go to Ur, to the temple of Nanna.
   Weep before Father Nanna.
   If Nanna will not help you,
   Go to Eridu, to the temple of Enki.
   Weep before Father Enki.
   Father Enki, the God of Wisdom, knows the food
      of life,

He knows the water of life;
He knows the secrets.
Surely he will not let me die."   60

Inanna continued on her way to the underworld.
Then she stopped and said:
    "Go now, Ninshubur—
    Do not forget the words I have commanded you."

When Inanna arrived at the outer gates of the
        underworld,
She knocked loudly.   .

She cried out in a fierce voice:
    "Open the door, gatekeeper!
    Open the door, Neti!
    I alone would enter!"   70

Neti, the chief gatekeeper of the *kur*, asked:
    "Who are you?"

She answered:
    "I am Inanna, Queen of Heaven,
    On my way to the East."

Neti said:
    "If you are truly Inanna, Queen of Heaven,
    On your way to the East,
    Why has your heart led you on the road
    From which no traveler returns?"   80

Inanna answered:
    "Because . . . of my older sister, Ereshkigal,
    Her husband, Gugalanna, the Bull of Heaven,
        has died.
    I have come to witness the funeral rites.
    Let the beer of his funeral rites be poured into
        the cup.
    Let it be done."

Neti spoke:
    "Stay here, Inanna, I will speak to my queen.
    I will give her your message."

Neti, the chief gatekeeper of the *kur*,   90
Entered the palace of Ereshkigal, the Queen of the
        Underworld, and said:
    "My queen, a maid
    As tall as heaven,
    As wide as the earth,
    As strong as the foundations of the city wall,
    Waits outside the palace gates.
    She has gathered together the seven *me*.
    She has taken them into her hands.
    With the *me* in her possession, she has
        prepared herself:

    On her head she wears the *shugurra,* the crown
        of the steppe.   100

Across her forehead her dark locks of hair are
        carefully arranged.
    Around her neck she wears the small lapis beads.
    At her breast she wears the double strand of beads.
    Her body is wrapped with the royal robe.
    Her eyes are daubed with the ointment called 'Let
        him come, let him come.'
    Around her chest she wears the breastplate called
        'Come, man, come!'
    On her wrist she wears the gold ring.
    In her hand she carries the lapis measuring
        rod and line."

When Ereshkigal heard this,
She slapped her thigh and bit her lip.   110
She took the matter into her heart and dwelt on it.
Then she spoke:
    "Come, Neti, my chief gatekeeper of the *kur,*
    Heed my words:
    Bolt the seven gates of the underworld.
    Then, one by one, open each gate a crack.
    Let Inanna enter.
    As she enters, remove her royal garments.
    Let the holy priestess of heaven enter
        bowed low." . . .

Naked and bowed low, Inanna entered the throne room.   120
Ereshkigal rose from her throne.
Inanna started toward the throne.
The Annuna, the judges of the underworld,
        surrounded her.
They passed judgment against her.

Then Ereshkigal fastened on Inanna the eye of death.
She spoke against her the word of wrath.
She uttered against her the cry of guilt.

She struck her.

Inanna was turned into a corpse,
A piece of rotting meat,   130
And was hung from a hook on the wall.

When, after three days and three nights, Inanna had not
        returned,
Ninshubur set up a lament for her by the ruins.
She beat the drum for her in the assembly places.
She circled the houses of the gods.
She tore at her eyes; she tore at her mouth; she tore at
        her thighs.
She dressed herself in a single garment like a beggar.
Alone, she set out for Nippur and the temple of Enlil. . . .

Father Enki said:
    "What has happened?   140
    What has my daughter done?
    Inanna! Queen of All the Lands! Holy Priestess
        of Heaven!
    What has happened?
    I am troubled. I am grieved."

From under his fingernail Father Enki brought forth dirt.
He fashioned the dirt into a *kurgarra,* a creature neither
    male nor female.
From under the fingernail of his other hand he brought
    forth dirt.
He fashioned the dirt into a *galatur,* a creature neither
    male nor female.
He gave the food of life to the *kurgarra.*
He gave the water of life to the *galatur.*   150
Enki spoke to the *kurgarra* and *galatur,* saying:
    "Go to the underworld,
    Enter the door like flies.
    Ereshkigal, the Queen of the Underworld,
        is moaning
    With the cries of a woman about to give birth.
    No linen is spread over her body.
    Her breasts are uncovered.
    Her hair swirls about her head like leeks.
    When she cries, 'Oh! Oh! My inside!'
    Cry also, 'Oh! Oh! Your inside!'   160
    When she cries, 'Oh! Oh! My outside!'
    Cry also, 'Oh! Oh! Your outside!'
    The queen will be pleased.
    She will offer you a gift.
    Ask her only for the corpse that hangs from the
        hook on the wall.
    One of you will sprinkle the food of life on it.
    The other will sprinkle the water of life.
    Inanna will arise."

The *kurgarra* and the *galatur* heeded Enki's words.
They set out for the underworld.   170
Like flies, they slipped through the cracks of the gates.
They entered the throne room of the Queen of the
    Underworld.
No linen was spread over her body.
Her breasts were uncovered.
Her hair swirled around her head like leeks.

Ereshkigal was moaning:
    "Oh! Oh! My inside!"

They moaned:
    "Oh! Oh! Your inside!"

She moaned: 180
    "Ohhhh! Oh! My outside!"

They moaned:
    "Ohhhh! Oh! Your outside!"

She groaned:
    "Oh! Oh! My belly!"

They groaned:
    "Oh! Oh! Your belly!"

She groaned:
    "Oh! Ohhhh! My back!!"

They groaned: 190
    "Oh! Ohhhh! Your back!!"

She sighed:
    "Ah! Ah! My heart!"

They sighed:
    "Ah! Ah! Your heart!"

She sighed:
    "Ah! Ahhhh! My liver!"

They sighed:
    "Ah! Ahhhh! Your liver!"

Ereshkigal stopped.   200
She looked at them.
She asked:
    "Who are you,
    Moaning—groaning—sighing with me?
    If you are gods, I will bless you.
    If you are mortals, I will give you a gift.
    I will give you the water-gift, the river
        in its fullness."

The *kurgarra* and *galatur* answered:
    "We do not wish it."

Ereshkigal said: 210
    "I will give you the grain-gift, the fields in harvest."

The *kurgarra* and *galatur* said:
    "We do not wish it."

Ereshkigal said:
    "Speak then! What do you wish?"

They answered:
    "We wish only the corpse that hangs from the
        hook on the wall."

Ereshkigal said:
    "The corpse belongs to Inanna."

They said: 220
    "Whether it belongs to our queen,
    Whether it belongs to our king,
    That is what we wish."

The corpse was given to them.

The *kurgarra* sprinkled the food of life on the corpse.
The *galatur* sprinkled the water of life on the corpse.
Inanna arose. . . .

Selections from *The Epic of Gilgamesh*

The Epic of Gilgamesh is now considered by most scholars to be the oldest known epic in Western literature. This work predates Homer's *Iliad* and *Odyssey* by some fifteen hundred years, appearing about 2200 B.C.

Like other epics, *The Epic of Gilgamesh* went through several variations before reaching its final form. It is based on a historical figure who quickly passed over into folklore. Gilgamesh reigned as king of the Sumerian city of Uruk around 2700 B.C., and soon after his death, his ordinary experiences were turned into stories of heroic deeds and dangerous journeys. Civilizations that succeeded the Sumerians infused into the epic new episodes and characters, different sets of deities, and issues reflecting the concerns of their own time. Nonetheless, despite its evolution through various civilizations, this epic recalls similar events that appear in other cultures' histories. In *The Epic of Gilgamesh*, the tale of a devastating flood that killed all animals and humans except those who took refuge in a boat resembles stories from other societies, in particular the biblical narrative of Noah, his family, and God.

Another reason why *The Epic of Gilgamesh* evolved from its original form was that it, like all epics, was sung long before it was written, and storytellers adapted the episodes and characters to fit their new audiences. The earliest written form of *The Epic of Gilgamesh* uncovered by archaeologists dates from about 600 B.C., a time when many Middle Eastern societies were disappearing and just before many others would fall under the influence of Greek civilization, later to become provinces of the Roman Empire.

Reading the Selections

This excerpt deals with two themes: one, that mortals cannot insult the gods and goddesses without punishment, and two, that humans are destined to die. Ishtar, the goddess of love, attempts to seduce Gilgamesh, who spurns her overtures by recalling how she ruined other humans. Furious at Gilgamesh, Ishtar asks her father to send the Bull of Heaven to kill Gilgamesh. Gilgamesh and Enkidu, the former wildman who had become civilized and had fought Gilgamesh before becoming his close companion, kill the bull. The gods and goddesses decide that Enkidu must die for this transgression. As Enkidu lies dying, he dreams of walking through the "house of dust," where he encounters dead kings and priests and various deities. Homer and many other writers later copy this device of transporting their heroes into the world of the dead to speak with the great men and, sometimes, women of history, as a way to glorify the past and allow the characters to be told of future events by the dead.

Gilgamesh's grief over the death of Enkidu reveals the Sumerian way of death. As king, Gilgamesh orders his artisans to memorialize Enkidu with a statue—one that may very well have existed at some time in Sumerian history. Touched by Enkidu's death, Gilgamesh recognizes his own mortal nature but refuses to accept his final fate, at least not yet. Through a series of adventures, he comes close to possessing immortality only to see it stolen by a serpent—a creature often associated with cults of immortality. Saddened by this turn of events, Gilgamesh returns home to serve others and to die.

—❦—

Ishtar and Gilgamesh, and the Death of Enkidu

Gilgamesh washed out his long locks and cleaned his weapons; he flung back his hair from his shoulders; he threw off his stained clothes and changed them for new. He put on his royal robes and made them fast. When Gilgamesh had put on the crown, glorious Ishtar lifted her eyes, seeing the beauty of Gilgamesh. She said, 'Come to me Gilgamesh, and be my bridegroom; grant me seed of your body, let me be your bride and you shall be my husband. I will harness for you a chariot of lapis lazuli and of gold, with wheels of gold and horns of copper; and you shall have mighty demons of the storm for draft-mules. When you enter our house in the fragrance of cedar-wood, threshold and throne will kiss your feet. Kings, rulers, and princes will bow down before you; they shall bring you tribute from the mountains and the plain. Your ewes shall drop twins and your goats triplets; your pack-ass shall outrun mules; your oxen shall have no rivals, and your chariot horses shall be famous far-off for their swiftness.'

Gilgamesh opened his mouth and answered glorious Ishtar, 'If I take you in marriage, what gifts can I give in return? What ointments and clothing for your body? I would gladly give you bread and all sorts of food fit for a god. I would give you wine to drink fit for a queen. I would pour out barley to stuff your granary; but as for making you my wife—that I will not. How would it go with me? Your lovers have found you like a brazier which smoulders in the cold, a backdoor which keeps out neither squall of wind nor storm, a castle which crushes the garrison, pitch that blackens the bearer, a water-skin that chafes the carrier, a stone which falls from the parapet, a battering-ram turned back from the enemy, a sandal that trips the wearer. Which of your lovers did you ever love for ever? What shepherd of yours has pleased you for all time? Listen to me while I tell the tale of your lovers. There was Tammuz, the lover of your youth, for him you decreed wailing, year after year. You loved the many-coloured roller, but still you struck and broke his wing; now in the grove he sits and cries, "kappi, kappi, my wing, my wing." You have loved the lion tremendous in strength: seven pits you dug for him, and seven. You have loved the stallion magnificent in battle, and for him you decreed whip and spur and a thong, to gallop seven leagues by force and to muddy the water before he drinks; and for his mother Silili lamentations. You have loved the shepherd of the flock; he made meal-cake for you day after day, he killed kids for your sake. You struck and turned him into a wolf; now his own herd-boys chase him away, his own hounds worry his flanks. And did you not love Ishullanu, the gardener of your father's palm-grove? He brought you baskets filled with dates without end; every day he loaded your table. Then you turned your eyes on him and said, "Dearest Ishullanu, come here to me, let us enjoy your manhood, come forward and take me, I am yours." Ishullanu answered, "What are you asking from me? My mother has baked and I have eaten; why should I come to such as you for food that is tainted and rotten? For when was a screen of rushes sufficient protection from frosts?" But when you had heard his answer you struck him. He was changed to a blind mole deep in the earth, one whose desire is always beyond his reach. And if you and I should be lovers, should not I be served in the same fashion as all these others whom you loved once?'

When Ishtar heard this she fell into a bitter rage, she went up to high heaven. Her tears poured down in front of her father Anu, and Antum her mother. She said, 'My father, Gilgamesh has heaped insults on me, he has told over all my abominable behaviour, my foul and hideous acts.' Anu opened his mouth and said, 'Are you a father of gods? Did not you quarrel with Gilgamesh the king, so now he has related your abominable behaviour, your foul and hideous acts?'

Ishtar opened her mouth and said again, 'My father, give me the Bull of Heaven to destroy Gilgamesh. Fill Gilgamesh, I say, with arrogance to his destruction; but if you refuse to give me the Bull of Heaven I will break in the doors of hell and smash the bolts; there will be confusion of people, those above with those from the lower depths. I shall bring up the dead to eat food like the living; and the hosts of dead will outnumber the living.' Anu said to great Ishtar, 'If I do what you desire there will be seven years of drought throughout Uruk when corn will be seedless husks. Have you saved grain enough for the people and grass for the cattle?' Ishtar replied, 'I have saved grain for the people, grass for the cattle; for seven years of seedless husks there is grain and there is grass enough.'

When Anu heard what Ishtar had said he gave her the Bull of Heaven to lead by the halter down to Uruk. When they reached the gates of Uruk the Bull went to the river; with his first snort cracks opened in the earth and a hundred young men fell down to death. With his second snort cracks opened and two hundred fell down to death. With his third snort cracks opened, Enkidu doubled over but instantly recovered, he dodged aside and leapt on the Bull and seized it by the horns. The Bull of Heaven foamed in his face, it brushed him with the thick of its tail. Enkidu cried to Gilgamesh, 'My friend, we boasted that we would leave enduring names behind us. Now thrust in your sword between the nape and the horns.' So Gilgamesh followed the Bull, he seized the thick of its tail, he thrust the sword between the nape and the horns and slew the Bull. When they had killed the Bull of Heaven they cut out its heart and gave it to Shamash, and the brothers rested.

But Ishtar rose up and mounted the great wall of Uruk; she sprang on to the tower and uttered a curse: 'Woe to Gilgamesh, for he has scorned me in killing the Bull of Heaven.' When Enkidu heard these words he tore out the Bull's right thigh and tossed it in her face saying, 'If I could lay my hands on you, it is this I should do to you, and lash the entrails to your side.' Then Ishtar called together her people, the dancing and singing girls, the prostitutes of the temple, the courtesans. Over the thigh of the Bull of Heaven she set up lamentation.

But Gilgamesh called the smiths and the armourers, all of them together. They admired the immensity of the horns. They were plated with lapis lazuli two fingers thick. They were thirty pounds each in weight, and their capacity in oil was six measures, which he gave to his guardian god, Lugulbanda. But he carried the horns into the palace and hung them on the wall. Then they washed their hands in Euphrates, they embraced each other and went away. They drove through the streets of Uruk where the heroes were gathered to see them, and Gilgamesh called to the singing girls, 'Who is most glorious of the heroes, who is most eminent among men?' 'Gilgamesh is the most glorious of heroes, Gilgamesh is most eminent among men.' And now there was feasting, and celebrations and joy in the palace, till the heroes lay down saying, 'Now we will rest for the night.'

When the daylight came Enkidu got up and cried to Gilgamesh, 'Oh my brother, such a dream I had last night. Anu, Enlil, Ea and heavenly Shamash took counsel together, and Anu said to Enlil, "Because they have killed the Bull of Heaven, and because they have killed Humbaba who guarded the Cedar Mountain one of the two must die." Then glorious Shamash answered the hero Enlil, "It was by your command they killed the Bull of Heaven, and killed Humbaba, and must Enkidu die although innocent?" Enlil flung round in rage at glorious Shamash, "You dare to say this, you who went about with them every day like one of themselves!'"

So Enkidu lay stretched out before Gilgamesh; his tears ran down in streams and he said to Gilgamesh, 'O my brother, so dear as you are to me, brother, yet they will take me from you.' Again he said, 'I must sit down on the threshold of the dead and never again will I see my dear brother with my eyes.'

While Enkidu lay alone in his sickness he cursed the gate as though it was living flesh, 'You there, wood of the gate, dull and insensible, witless, I searched for you over twenty leagues until I saw the towering cedar. There is no wood like you in our land. Seventy-two cubits high and twenty-four wide, the pivot and the ferrule and the jambs are perfect. A master craftsman from Nippur has made you; but O, if I had known the conclusion! If I had known that this was all the good that would come of it, I would have raised the axe and split you into little pieces and set up here a gate of wattle instead. Ah, if only some future king had brought you here, or some god had fashioned you. Let him obliterate my name and write his own, and the curse fall on him instead of on Enkidu.'

With the first brightening of dawn Enkidu raised his head and wept before the Sun God, in the brilliance of the sunlight his tears streamed down. 'Sun God, I beseech you, about that vile Trapper, that Trapper of nothing because of whom I was to catch less than my comrade; let him catch least; make his game scarce, make him feeble, taking the smaller of every share, let his quarry escape from his nets.'

When he had cursed the Trapper to his heart's content he turned on the harlot. He was roused to curse her also. 'As for you, woman, with a great curse I curse you! I will promise you a destiny to all eternity. My curse shall come on you soon and sudden. You shall be without a roof for your commerce, for you shall not keep house with other girls in the tavern, but do your business in places fouled by the vomit of the drunkard. Your hire will be potter's earth, your thievings will be flung into the hovel, you will sit at the cross-roads in the dust of the potter's quarter, you will make your bed on the dunghill at night, and by day take your stand in the wall's shadow. Brambles and thorns will tear your feet, the drunk and the dry will strike your cheek and your mouth will ache. Let you be stripped of your purple dyes, for I too once in the wilderness with my wife had all the treasure I wished.'

When Shamash heard the words of Enkidu he called to him from heaven: 'Enkidu, why are you cursing the woman, the mistress who taught you to eat bread fit for gods and drink wine of kings? She who put upon you a magnificent garment, did she not give you glorious Gilgamesh for your companion, and has not Gilgamesh, your own brother, made you rest on a royal bed and recline on a couch at his left hand? He has made the princes of the earth kiss your feet, and now all the people of Uruk lament and wail over you. When you are dead he will let his hair grow long for your sake, he will wear a lion's pelt and wander through the desert.'

When Enkidu heard glorious Shamash his angry heart grew quiet, he called back the curse and said, 'Woman, I promise you another destiny. The mouth which cursed you shall bless you! Kings, princes and nobles shall adore you. On your account a man though twelve miles off will clap his hand to his thigh and his hair will twitch. For you he will undo his belt and open his treasure and you shall have your desire; lapis lazuli, gold and carnelian from the heap in the treasury. A ring for your hand and a robe shall be yours. The priest will lead you into the presence of the gods. On your account a wife, a mother of seven, was forsaken.'

As Enkidu slept alone in his sickness, in bitterness of spirit he poured out his heart to his friend. 'It was I who cut down the cedar, I who levelled the forest, I who slew Humbaba and now see what has become of me. Listen, my friend, this is the dream I dreamed last night. The heavens roared, and earth rumbled back an answer; between them stood I before an awful being, the somber-faced man-bird; he had directed on me his purpose. His was a vampire face, his foot was a lion's foot, his hand was an eagle's talon. He fell on me and his claws were in my hair, he held me fast and I smothered; then he transformed me so that my arms became wings covered with feathers. He turned his stare towards me, and he led me away to the palace of Irkalla, the Queen of Darkness, to the house from which none who enters ever returns, down the road from which there is no coming back.

'There is the house whose people sit in darkness; dust is their food and clay their meat. They are clothed like birds with wings for covering, they see no light, they sit in darkness. I entered the house of dust and I saw the kings of the earth, their crowns put away for ever; rulers and princes, all those who once wore kingly crowns and ruled the world in the days of old. They who had stood in the place of the gods like Anu and Enlil, stood now like servants to fetch baked meats in the house of dust, to carry cooked meat and cold water from the water-skin. In the house of dust which I entered were high priests and acolytes, priests of the incantation and of ecstasy; there were servers of the temple, and there was Etana, that King of Kish whom the eagle carried to heaven in the days of old. I saw also Samuqan, god of cattle, and there was Ereshkigal the Queen of the Underworld; and Belit-Sheri squatted in front of her, she who is recorder of the gods and keeps the book of death. She held a tablet from which she read. She raised her head, she saw me and spoke: "Who has brought this one here?" Then I awoke like a man drained of blood who wanders alone in a waste of rushes; like one whom the bailiff has seized and his heart pounds with terror.'

Gilgamesh had peeled off his clothes, he listened to his words and wept quick tears, Gilgamesh listened and his tears flowed. He opened his mouth and spoke to Enkidu: 'Who is there in strong-walled Uruk who has wisdom like this? Strange things have been spoken, why does your heart speak strangely? The dream was marvellous but the terror was great; we must treasure the dream whatever the terror; for the dream has shown that misery comes at last to the healthy man, the end of life is sorrow.' And Gilgamesh lamented, 'Now I will pray to the great gods, for my friend had an ominous dream.'

This day on which Enkidu dreamed came to an end and he lay stricken with sickness. One whole day he lay on his bed and his suffering increased. He said to Gilgamesh, the friend on whose account he had left the wilderness, 'Once I ran for you, for the water of life, and I now have nothing.' A second day he lay on his bed and Gilgamesh watched over him but the sickness increased. A third day he lay on his bed, he called out to Gilgamesh, rousing him up. Now he was weak and his eyes were blind with weeping. Ten days he lay and his suffering increased, eleven and twelve days he lay on his bed of pain. Then he called to Gilgamesh, 'My friend, the great goddess cursed me and I must die in shame. I shall not die like a man fallen in battle; I feared to fall, but happy is the man who falls in the battle, for I must die in shame.' And Gilgamesh wept over Enkidu. . . .

He touched his heart but it did not beat, nor did he lift his eyes again. When Gilgamesh touched his heart it did not beat. So Gilgamesh laid a veil, as one veils the bride, over his friend. He began to rage like a lion, like a lioness robbed of her whelps. This way and that he paced round the bed, he tore out his hair and strewed it around. He dragged off his splendid robes and flung them down as though they were abominations.

In the first light of dawn Gilgamesh cried out, 'I made you rest on a royal bed, you reclined on a couch at my left hand, the princes of the earth kissed your feet. I will cause all the people of Uruk to weep over you and raise the dirge of the dead. The joyful people will stoop with sorrow; and when you have gone to the earth I will let my hair grow long for your sake, I will wander through the wilderness in the skin of a lion.' The next day also, in the first light, Gilgamesh lamented; seven days and seven nights he wept for Enkidu, until the worm fastened on him. Only then he gave him up to the earth, for the Anunnaki, the judges, had seized him.

Then Gilgamesh issued a proclamation through the land, he summoned them all, the coppersmiths, the goldsmiths, the stone-workers, and commanded them, 'Make a statue of my friend.' The statue was fashioned with a great weight of lapis lazuli for the breast and of gold for the body. A table of hard-wood was set out, and on it a bowl of carnelian filled with honey, and a bowl of lapis lazuli filled with butter. These he exposed and offered to the Sun; and weeping he went away.

The Story of the Flood

'You know the city Shurrupak, it stands on the banks of Euphrates? That city grew old and the gods that were in it were old. There was Anu, lord of the firmament, their father, and warrior Enlil their counsellor, Ninurta the helper, and Ennugi watcher over canals; and with them also was Ea. In those days the world teemed, the people multiplied, the world bellowed like a wild bull, and the great god was aroused by the clamour. Enlil heard the clamour and he said to the gods in council, "The uproar of mankind is intolerable and sleep is no longer possible by reason of the babel." So the gods agreed to exterminate mankind. Enlil did this, but Ea because of his oath warned me in a dream. He whispered their words to my house of reeds, "Reed-house, reed-house! Wall, O wall, hearken reed-house, wall reflect; O man of Shurrupak, son of Ubara-Tutu; tear down your house and build a boat, abandon possessions and look for life, despise worldly goods and save your soul alive. Tear down your house, I say, and build a boat. These are the measurements of the barque as you shall build her: let her beam equal her length, let her deck be roofed like the vault that covers the abyss; then take up into the boat the seed of all living creatures."

'When I had understood I said to my lord, "Behold, what you have commanded I will honour and perform, but how shall I answer the people, the city, the elders?"

Then Ea opened his mouth and said to me, his servant, "Tell them this: I have learnt that Enlil is wrathful against me, I dare no longer walk in his land nor live in his city; I will go down to the Gulf to dwell with Ea my lord. But on you he will rain down abundance, rare fish and shy wildfowl, a rich harvest-tide. In the evening the rider of the storm will bring you wheat in torrents."

'In the first light of dawn all my household gathered round me, the children brought pitch and the men whatever was necessary. On the fifth day I laid the keel and the ribs, then I made fast the planking. The ground-space was one acre, each side of the deck measured one hundred and twenty cubits, making a square. I built six decks below, seven in all, I divided them into nine sections with bulkheads between. I drove in wedges where needed, I saw to the punt-poles, and laid in supplies. The carriers brought oil in baskets, I poured pitch into the furnace and asphalt and oil; more oil was consumed in caulking, and more again the master of the board took into his stores. I slaughtered bullocks for the people and every day I killed sheep. I gave the shipwrights wine to drink as though it were river water, raw wine and red wine and oil and white wine. There was feasting then as there is at the time of the New Year's festival; I myself anointed my head. On the seventh day the boat was complete.

'Then was the launching full of difficulty; there was shifting of ballast above and below till two thirds was submerged. I loaded into her all that I had of gold and of living things, my family, my kin, the beast of the field both wild and tame, and all the craftsmen. I sent them on board, for the time that Shamash had ordained was already fulfilled when he said, "In the evening, when the rider of the storm sends down the destroying rain, enter the boat and batten her down." The time was fulfilled, the evening came, the rider of the storm sent down the rain. I looked out at the weather and it was terrible, so I too boarded the boat and battened her down. All was now complete, the battening and the caulking; so I handed the tiller to Puzur-Amurri the steersman, with the navigation and the care of the whole boat.

'With the first light of dawn a black cloud came from the horizon; it thundered within where Adad, lord of the storm was riding. In front over hill and plain Shullat and Hanish, heralds of the storm, led on. Then the gods of the abyss rose up; Nergal pulled out the dams of the nether waters, Ninurta the war-lord threw down the dykes, and the seven judges of hell, the Annunaki, raised their torches, lighting the land with their livid flame. A stupor of despair went up to heaven when the god of the storm turned daylight to darkness, when he smashed the land like a cup. One whole day the tempest raged, gathering fury as it went, it poured over the people like the tides of battle; a man could not see his brother nor the people be seen from heaven. Even the gods were terrified at the flood, they fled to the highest heaven, the firmament of Anu; they crouched against the walls, cowering like curs. Then Ishtar the sweet-voiced Queen of Heaven cried out like a woman in travail: "Alas the days of old are turned to dust because I commanded evil; why did I command this evil in the council of all the gods? I commanded wars to destroy the people, but are they not my people, for I brought them forth? Now like the spawn of fish they float in the ocean." The great gods of heaven and of hell wept, they covered their mouths.

'For six days and six nights the winds blew, torrent and tempest and flood overwhelmed the world, tempest and flood raged together like warring hosts. When the seventh day dawned the storm from the south subsided, the sea grew calm, the flood was stilled; I looked at the face of the world and there was silence, all mankind was turned to clay. The surface of the sea stretched as flat as a roof-top; I opened a hatch and the light fell on my face. Then I bowed low, I sat down and I wept, the tears streamed down my face, for on every side was the waste of water. I looked for land in vain, but fourteen leagues distant there appeared a mountain, and there the boat grounded; on the mountain of Nisir the boat held fast, she held fast and did not budge. One day she held, and a second day on the mountain of Nisir she held fast and did not budge. A third day, and a fourth day she held fast on the

mountain and did not budge; a fifth day and a sixth day she held fast on the mountain. When the seventh day dawned I loosed a dove and let her go. She flew away, but finding no resting-place she returned. Then I loosed a swallow, and she flew away but finding no resting-place she returned. I loosed a raven, she saw that the waters had retreated, she ate, she flew around, she cawed, and she did not come back. Then I threw everything open to the four winds, I made a sacrifice and poured out a libation on the mountain top. Seven and again seven cauldrons I set up on their stands, I heaped up wood and cane and cedar and myrtle. When the gods smelled the sweet savour, they gathered like flies over the sacrifice. Then, at last, Ishtar also came, she lifted her necklace with the jewels of heaven that once Anu had made to please her. "O you gods here present, by the lapis lazuli round my neck I shall remember these days as I remember the jewels of my throat; these last days I shall not forget. Let all the gods gather round the sacrifice, except Enlil. He shall not approach this offering, for without reflection he brought the flood; he consigned my people to destruction."

'When Enlil had come, when he saw the boat, he was wrath and swelled with anger at the gods, the host of heaven, "Has any of these mortals escaped? Not one was to have survived the destruction." Then the god of the wells and canals Ninurta opened his mouth and said to the warrior Enlil, "Who is there of the gods that can devise without Ea? It is Ea alone who knows all things." Then Ea opened his mouth and spoke to warrior Enlil, "Wisest of gods, hero Enlil, how could you so senselessly bring down the flood?

> Lay upon the sinner his sin,
> Lay upon the transgressor his transgression,
> Punish him a little when he breaks loose,
> Do not drive him too hard or he perishes;
> Would that a lion had ravaged mankind
> Rather than the flood,
> Would that a wolf had ravaged mankind
> Rather than the flood,
> Would that famine had wasted the world
> Rather than the flood,
> Would that pestilence had wasted mankind
> Rather than the flood.

It was not I that revealed the secret of the gods; the wise man learned it in a dream. Now take your counsel what shall be done with him."

'Then Enlil went up into the boat, he took me by the hand and my wife and made us enter the boat and kneel down on either side, he standing between us. He touched our foreheads to bless us saying, "In time past Utnapishtim was a mortal man; henceforth he and his wife shall live in the distance at the mouth of the rivers." Thus it was that the gods took me and placed me here to live in the distance, at the mouth of the rivers.'

ENHEDUANNA

The Exaltation of Inanna

Enheduanna (fl. 2330 B.C.) is history's earliest known literary figure. Princess, priestess, and poet, she left an indelible mark on her age, so that her ecclesiastical and literary exploits were celebrated for centuries afterward in Mesopotamia.

This precedent-making poet flourished during the reign of her father, Sargon (ca. 2334–2278 B.C.), an upstart-king who inaugurated Mesopotamia's Akkadian dynasty, displacing the Sumerian line when he conquered the cities of Sumer and set up his capital at Agade—the city that gave its name to his dynasty, language, and state. A legendary soldier, he forged a vast empire, stretching from Egypt to the Indus River, which he and his successors fought to control because of never-ending rebellions. To govern this unruly empire, Sargon founded garrison cities, turned enemies into allies, and began the custom of appointing royal family members to act as governors of conquered lands. He also installed Enheduanna as high priestess of the Moon-God Nanna in Ur and as priestess of An, the Heaven-God, in Uruk. His appointments were intended to align these old Sumerian cities with the new reality of Akkadian politics.

In furtherance of her father's designs, Enheduanna worked to propagandize the Sumerians and Akkadians into a harmonious union. Sargon spoke Akkadian and made this language the official language in his domains, but his daughter wrote in Sumerian, which now became a scholarly language, much as Latin was during the Middle Ages. She composed a cycle of hymns to the temples of Sumer and Akkad, thereby aiding the growth of Mesopotamian theology. These hymns also set the standard for later poets, who copied her language, poetic forms, and themes. In time, Enheduanna's life took on legendary qualities, and her name—Heduanna ("en," Sumerian for "high priestess")—became an attribute of the Moon-God, whom she had served.

Reading the Selection

The Exaltation of Inanna (Sumerian, *nin-me-sar-ra*) has definitively been linked to Enheduanna, since the text not only names her as author but also gives autobiographical details of her life. The survival of more than fifty partial or whole versions of this poem is proof of its wide prestige in later times.

In theme, this poem belongs to that branch of mythology called theogony, which usually has to do with the birth of the gods, but here it also refers to the changing status, relative to each other, of various deities within the Mesopotamian pantheon. "Exaltation" means elevation, and in this poem Inanna, the Goddess of Love, is raised from junior queen to a status "superior to An," the chief Sumerian deity. This is the first known example of its kind in this culture, though many later ones exist. The epithet "superior to An" soon became a literary cliché, used by poets to glorify a deity whose status was changing, usually for historical reasons.

On the historic level, *The Exaltation of Inanna* grew out of Sargon's victory over rebels late in his reign, a deed Enheduanna attributed to Inanna. In the uprising, the rebel Lugalanne stripped the priestess of her temple offices in Ur and Uruk, and the divine protectors of these cities, the Moon-God and the Heaven-God, respectively, refused to come to her aid. Only Inanna heeded the priestess's cries. Thus, in the poem Inanna's supremacy among the gods ("'Tis thine!") is guaranteed by her role in restoring Enheduanna to holy office, a fact made possible by Sargon's triumph over his enemies.

—⁂—

A. Exordium

(I) INANNA AND THE *ME*

Lady of all the *me*,	resplendent light,
Righteous woman clothed in radiance,	beloved of Heaven and Earth,
Hierodule of An	(you) of all the great ornaments,
Enamored of the appropriate tiara,	suitable for the high priesthood
Whose hand has attained	(all) the "seven" *me*,
Oh my lady, you are the guardian	of all the great *me*!
You have picked up the *me*,	you have hung the *me* on your hand,
You have gathered up the *me*,	you have clasped the *me* to your breast.

1

(II) INANNA AND AN

Like a dragon you have deposited venom on the land
When you roar at the earth like Thunder, no vegetation can stand up to you.

A flood descending from its mountain,
Oh foremost one, you are the Inanna of heaven and earth!

Raining the fanned fire	down upon the nation
Endowed with *me* by An,	lady mounted on a beast,
Who makes decisions	at the holy command of An.
(You) of all the great rites,	who can fathom what is yours?

10

(III) INANNA AND ENLIL

Devastatrix of the lands,	you are lent wings by the storm.
Beloved of Enlil,	you fly about in the nation.
You are at the service	of the decrees of An.
Oh my lady, at the sound of you	the lands bow down.
When mankind	comes before you
In fear and trembling	at (your) tempestuous radiance,
They receive from you	their just deserts.
Proffering a song of lamentation,	they weep before you,
They walk toward you along the path	of the house of all the great sighs.

20

(IV) INANNA AND IŠKUR

In the van of battle	everything is struck down by you.
Oh my lady, (propelled) on your own wings,	you peck away (at the land).
In the guise of a charging storm	you charge.
With a roaring storm	you roar.

With Thunder	you continually thunder.	
With all the evil winds	you snort.	30
Your feet are filled	with restlessness.	
To (the accompaniment of) the harp of sighs	you give vent to a dirge.	

(V) Inanna and the Anunna

Oh my lady, the Anunna,	the great gods,	
Fluttering like bats	fly off from before you to the clefts,	
They who dare not walk(?)	in your terrible glance,	
Who dare not proceed	before your terrible countenance.	
Who can temper	your raging heart?	
Your malevolent heart	is beyond tempering.	
Lady (who) soothes the reins,	lady (who) gladdens the heart,	
Whose rage is not tempered,	oh eldest daughter of Suen!	40
Lady supreme over the land,	who has (ever) denied (you) homage?	

(VI) Inanna and Ebih(?)

In the mountain where homage is withheld from you vegetation is accursed.
Its grand entrance   you have reduced to ashes.

Blood rises in its rivers for you, its people have nought to drink.
It leads its army captive before you of its own accord.

It disbands its regiments before you of its own accord.
It makes its able-bodied young men parade before you of their own accord.

A tempest has filled the dancing of its city.
It drives its young adults before you as captives.

50

(VII) Inanna and Uruk

Over the city which has not declared	"The land is yours,"	
Which has not declared	"It is your father's, your begettor's"	
You have spoken your holy command,	have verily turned it back from your path,	
Have verily removed your foot	from out of its byre.	
Its woman no longer speaks of love	with her husband.	
At night they no longer	have intercourse.	
She no longer reveals to him	her inmost treasures.	
Impetuous wild cow,	great daughter of Suen,	
Lady supreme over An	who has (ever) denied (you) homage?	

(VIII) Invocation of Inanna

You of the appropriate *me*,	great queen of queens,	
Issued from the holy womb,	supreme over the mother who bore you,	60
Omniscient sage,	lady of all the lands,	
Sustenance of the multitudes,	I have verily recited your sacred song!	
True goddess, fit for the *me*,	it is exalting to acclaim you.	

Merciful one, brilliantly righteous woman,   I have verily recited your *me* for you!

B. The Argument

(IX) THE BANISHMENT FROM UR

Verily I had entered   my holy *gipāru* at your behest,
I, the high priestess,   I, Enheduanna!

I carried the ritual basket,   I intoned the acclaim.
(But now) I am placed in the leper's ward,   I, even I, can no longer live with you

They approach the light of day,   the light is obscured about me,
The shadows approach the light of day,   it is covered with a (sand)storm.   70

My mellifluous mouth is cast into confusion.
My choicest features   are turned to dust.

(X) THE APPEAL TO NANNA-SUEN

What is he to me, oh Suen,   this Lugalanne!
Say thus to An: "May An release me!"

Say but to An "Now!" and An will release me.
This woman will carry off   the manhood of Lugalanne.

Mountain (and?) flood   lie at her feet.
That woman is as exalted (as he)—   she will make the city divorce him.
Surely she will assuage   her heartfelt rage for me.

Let me, Enheduanna,   recite a prayer to her.   80
Let me give free vent to my tears like sweet drink for the holy Inanna!
Let me say "Hail!" to her!

(XI) THE INDICTMENT OF LUGALANNE(?)

I cannot appease   Ashimbabbar.
(Lugalanne) has altered the lustrations of holy An and all his (other rites).

He has stripped An   of (his temple) Eanna.
He has not stood in awe   of An-lugal

That sanctuary whose attractions are irresistible, whose beauty is endless,
That sanctuary he has verily brought to destruction.

Having entered before you as a partner, he has even approached his sister-in-law.
Oh my divine impetuous wild cow, drive out this man, capture this man!   90

(XII) THE CURSE OF URUK

In the place of sustenance   what am I, even I?
(Uruk) is a malevolent rebel against your Nanna—may An make it surrender!

This city—   may it be sundered by An!
May it be cursed   by Enlil!
May its plaintive child   not be placated by his mother!

Oh lady, the (harp of) mourning   is placed on the ground.

One had verily beached your ship of mourning on a hostile shore.
At (the sound of) my sacred song   they are ready to die.

(XIII) THE INDICTMENT OF NANNA

As for me, my Nanna   takes no heed of me.
He has verily given me over to destruction   in murderous straits.   100

Ashimbabbar   has not pronounced my judgment.
Had he pronounced it: what is it to me?   Had he not pronounced it: what is it to me?

(Me) who once sat triumphant   he has driven out of the sanctuary.
Like a swallow he made me fly from the window, my life is consumed.

He made me walk   in the bramble of the mountain.
He stripped me of the crown   appropriate for the high priesthood.
He gave me dagger and sword—   "it becomes you," he said to me.

(XIV) THE APPEAL TO INANNA

Most precious lady,   beloved of An,
Your holy heart is lofty,   may it be assuaged on my behalf!

Beloved bride   of Ushumgalanna,   110
You are the senior queen   of the heavenly foundations and zenith.

The Anunna   have submitted to you.
From birth on   you were the "junior" queen.

How supreme you are over the great gods, the Anunna!
The Anunna kiss the ground with their lips (in obeisance) to you.

(But) my own sentence is not concluded,   a hostile judgment appears before my eyes as my
                                                       judgment.
(My) hands are no longer folded   on the ritual couch,
I may no longer reveal   the pronouncements of Ningal to man.

(Yet) I am the brilliant   high priestess of Nanna,
Oh my queen beloved of An,   may your heart take pity on me!   120

(XV) THE EXALTATION OF INANNA

That one has not recited as a"Known! Be it   that one has recited as a "Tis Thine!":
    known!" of Nanna,

"That you are lofty as Heaven (An)—   be it known!
That you are broad as the earth—   be it known!
That you devastate the rebellious land—   be it known!
That you roar at the land—   be it known!
That you smite the heads—   be it known!
That you devour cadavers like a dog—   be it known!
That your glance is terrible—   be it known!
That you lift your terrible glance—   be it known!
That your glance is flashing—   be it known!   130
That you are ill-disposed toward the . . . —   be it known!

That you attain victory—   be it known!"

That one has not recited (this) of Nanna,   that one has recited it as a " 'Tis Thine!"—
(That,) oh my lady, has made you great, you alone are exalted!

Oh my lady beloved of An,   I have verily recounted your fury!

C. Peroration

(XVI) THE COMPOSITION OF THE HYMN

One has heaped up the coals (in the censer), prepared the lustration
The nuptial chamber awaits you, let your heart be appeased!

With "It is enough for me, it is too much for oh exalted lady, (to this song) for you.
    me!" I have given birth
That which I recited to you at (mid)night 140
May the singer repeat it to you at noon!

(Only) on account of your captive spouse, on account of your captive child,
Your rage is increased, your heart unassuaged.

(XVII) THE RESTORATION OF ENHEDUANNA

The first lady, the reliance of the throne room,
Has accepted her offerings
Inanna's heart has been restored.

The day was favorable for her, she was she was garbed in womanly beauty.
    clothed sumptuously,
Like the light of the rising moon, how she was sumptuously attired!

When Nanna appeared in proper view,
They (all) blessed her (Inanna's) mother Ningal. 150

The (heavenly) doorsill called "Hail!"

(XVIII) DOXOLOGY

For that her (Enheduanna's) speaking to the Hierodule was exalted,
Praise be (to) the devastatrix of the lands, endowed with *me* from An,
(To) my lady wrapped in beauty, (to) Inanna!

The Dispute of a Man with His Soul

The Dispute of a Man with His Soul is probably Egypt's most philosophical work. Surviving in one manuscript found in about 1843, this complex text has aroused a great deal of curiosity and has provoked much controversy. Its text combines prose and poetry, a hybrid style of writing that also flourished in medieval Europe (see *The Consolation of Philosophy* by Boethius).

    This work dates from the Middle Kingdom (ca. 2050–1800 B.C.), a period characterized by a significant shift in the social system. The old ruling elite of high-ranking royal officials now had to make room for lower officials. Mildly "democratic," this step resulted in revised funeral customs, as nobles claimed the right to immortality enjoyed by rulers; those with sufficient wealth to afford monuments began to build private funeral chapels. *The Dispute of a Man with His Soul* provides evidence of these changes because it was found in a tomb dating from about 1850 B.C., deposited there as reading matter for the deceased in eternity.

    The Dispute is one of the outstanding achievements of the Middle Kingdom, Egypt's classical age, a period marked by an outpouring of literary works in many genres and with a complete mastery of forms. This work belongs to the Wisdom Literature genre, which began in the Old Kingdom and now reached its zenith. Wisdom Literature is didactic writing that ponders a problem of life and offers a solution. The Wisdom Literature of the Egyptians (and the Mesopotamians) contributed mightily to the subsequent flowering of this genre among the Hebrews, as in the Book of Job (see *The Holy Scriptures*).

The Wisdom Literature of the Middle Kingdom was dominated by the theme of "national distress," which portrayed the state as threatened by civil war and social upheaval, although no evidence has been unearthed to support this gloomy outlook. *The Dispute* shared the age's general pessimism, but its topic, unlike other Middle Kingdom writing, was personal and not social.

Reading the Selection

The theme of *The Dispute of a Man with His Soul* is whether death is a blessing, given the sorrows of this life. It is written in the form of a dialogue between a man ["I"] and the mysterious life force that Egyptians called the *ba* [the "soul"]. The *ba* was the inner power that guided human life, escaped from the body at death, and played a vital but ill-defined role in one's afterlife. Presented as an internal conflict without any specific references to a real person, the text is thus universally applicable to humankind. Beyond this exists very little agreement about the nature of the dispute and the positions of the two opponents.

Some well-regarded interpretations of *The Dispute* describe it as a clash between (1) the traditional belief in funerary rites (the man) and the skeptical view of those without financial means for proper burial (the *ba*); (2) a conservative, idealistic outlook (the man) and a materialistic, hedonistic view (the *ba*); (3) Osirian beliefs (the *ba*) and the solar theology of Ra (the man).

Regardless of its final meaning, the problem presented in *The Dispute of a Man with His Soul* is resolved through four poems, each marked by a repeated first line. In these poems the man laments the pain of human life and celebrates the promised joys of death and resurrection. After listening to the poems, the *ba* agrees to abide with the man—a conservative ending typical of the Wisdom Literature of the times.

—ᴍ—

. . . Then I opened my mouth to my soul, that I might answer what it had said: "This is too much for me now, that my soul does not speak with me. My soul goes forth; let it stand and wait for me!

"Behold, my soul disobeys me because I did not hearken to it, and drag myself to death ere I have come to it, to cast myself upon the fire in order to consume myself. Rather, let it be near to me on this day of misfortune, and wait on the other side!

"My soul is foolish to hold back one wretched over life and delay me from death before I have come to it. Rather, make the West pleasant for me! Is it something bad? The period of life is limited in any case: even the trees must fall! Thoth, who contents the gods, he will judge me! Khonsu, the Scribe in Truth, he will defend me! Ra, who guides the Solar Bark, he will hear my words! My distress is heavy, and he bears it for me!"

And this is what my soul said to me: "And are you not a plain man? Yet you are as concerned as if you were a possessor of wealth!"

I said: "If my soul will hearken to me, and its heart agrees with me, it will be happy. I will cause it to reach the West, like one who is in his pyramid, and at whose burial there has stood a survivor. I shall drink from the river whose water is drawn, and look down on the souls that are unsatisfied!"

Then my soul opened its mouth to me, to answer what I had said: "If you are calling burial to mind, that is a distress of the heart; it is a bringing of tears, it is making a man sorrowful. It is hauling a man from his house and throwing him upon the hill. Never shall you go up above to behold the sun. They who built in granite and fashioned pyramids—fine things of good work—when the builders have become gods, their offering tables are as empty as those of the wretches who die on the riverbank—part of their bodies held by the water and part by the heat of the sun, and the fish of the bank hold converse with them! Listen, then, to me; lo, it is good to listen to people! Follow the happy day and forget care!

"Take the case of a poor man who plows his field and then loads his harvest on to a boat, and hurries to tow the boat since his feast day approaches. He sees a flood coming on in the night, and keeps vigil when Ra goes down. He comes forth with his wife, but his children perish upon the water, dangerous with crocodiles in the night. At last he sits down, when he can regain his voice, and says: 'I do not weep for that girl; there is no coming forth into the West for her. I am troubled for her children that are broken in the egg, that behold the face of the crocodile-god before they had lived.'"

Then I opened my mouth to my soul, that I might answer what it had said:

"Behold, you make my name reek,
   lo, more than the stench of carrion
   on days in summer, when the sky is hot.

"Behold, you make my name reek
   lo, more than a fisherman
   on the day of the catch, when the sky is hot.

"Behold, you make my name reek
   lo, more than the stench of bird droppings,
   more than the hill of willows with the geese.

"Behold, you make my name reek
   lo, more than the odor of fishermen,
   more than the shores of the swamps when they have
      fished.

"Behold, you make my name reek
   lo, more than the stench of crocodiles,
   more than sitting among crocodiles.

"Behold, you make my name reek
   lo, more than that of a woman
   when lies are told about her to her man.

"Behold, you make my name reek
   lo, more than that of a lusty boy
   against whom it is said, 'He belongs to his hated one!'

"Behold, you make my name reek
   lo, more than a treacherous city,
   more than a traitor who turns his back.

"To whom shall I speak today?
   One's fellows are evil;
   the friends of today do not love.

"To whom shall I speak today?
   Men are rapacious;
   every one seizes his neighbor's goods.

"To whom shall I speak today?
   Gentleness has perished;
   insolence has access to all men.

"To whom shall I speak today?
   The evil have a contented countenance;
   good is rejected in every place.

"To whom shall I speak today?
   He who by his evil deeds should arouse wrath
   moves all men to laughter, though his iniquity is
      grievous.

"To whom shall I speak today?
   Men rob;
   Every man seizes his neighbor's goods.

"To whom shall I speak today?
   The foul man is trusted,
   but one who was a brother to him has become an
      enemy.

"To whom shall I speak today?
   No one remembers yesterday;
   no one now requites good to him who has done it.

"To whom shall I speak today?
   Brothers are evil;
   a man is treated as an enemy for his uprightness.

"To whom shall I speak today?
   Faces are not seen;
   every man's face is downcast toward his brethren.

"To whom shall I speak today?
   Hearts are greedy;
   the man on whom men rely has no heart.

"To whom shall I speak today?
   There are no righteous ones;
   the land is given over to the doers of evil.

"To whom shall I speak today?
   There is lack of a trusty friend;
   one must go to an unknown in order to complain.

"To whom shall I speak today?
   There is none that is peaceable;
   the one with whom one went no longer exists.

"To whom shall I speak today?
   I am laden with misery,
   and lack a trusted friend.

"To whom shall I speak today?
   The evil which treads the earth,
   it has no end.

"Death is in my sight today
   as when a sick man becomes whole,
   as when one goes out after an illness.

"Death is in my sight today
   as the odor of myrrh,
   as when sitting under sail on a breezy day.

"Death is in my sight today
   as the odor of lotus flowers,
   as when sitting on the riverbank getting drunk.

"Death is in my sight today
   as a well-trodden path,
   as when a man returns home to his house from war.

"Death is in my sight today
   as a clearing of the sky,
   as a man discerning what he knew not.

"Death is in my sight today
   as when a man longs to see his home again
   after he has spent many years in captivity.

"Nay, but he who is Yonder
will be as a living god,
inflicting punishment for evil upon him who does it.

"Nay, but he who is Yonder
will stand in the bark of the Sun-god
and will assign the choicest things therein to the temples.

"Nay, but he who is Yonder
will be a man of knowledge,
not hindered from petitioning Ra when he speaks."

40

This is what my soul said to me: "Set aside lamentation, you who are mine, my brother! Although offered up on the brazier, still you shall cling to life, as you say. Whether I remain here if you reject the West, or whether you reach the West and your body is joined with the earth, I will alight after you go to rest. Then we shall make an abode together!"

The Story of Sinuhe the Egyptian

Egyptian literature, although not noted for fiction, gave birth to one great work of the imagination, *The Story of Sinuhe the Egyptian,* a short narrative that ranks among the classics of world literature. Several manuscripts and many fragments of this work are extant, thus attesting to its ancient popularity. A model of style and a masterpiece of the storyteller's art, it was assigned as a "set text" for teaching Egypt's classical language to aspiring scribes. In modern times, Sinuhe's story proved its lasting appeal when it became the basis of a historical novel and a popular movie. The original tale was written in a mix of prose and poetry, the typical style of Middle Kingdom literature (see *The Dispute of a Man with His Soul*).

Like most Egyptian writing, *The Story of Sinuhe* owes its form to the cult of the dead; it is an autobiography composed for a tomb. It may be a true account, but the original tomb-text has not been discovered. Whether true or not, the work reflects an actual event: the death of Amenemhat I [Amen-em-Hat] around 1908 B.C. and the onset of the reign of his coregent, Senwosret I [Sen-Wesret] (ca. 1918–1875 B.C.).

Reading the Selection

Senwosret's abrupt change of status set in motion *The Story of Sinuhe*'s simple plot. Hearing of Amenemhat's death, Sinuhe—an attendant of Senwosret's wife—is seized by uncontrollable shaking and rushes from the scene. Why should a high official who stood to gain from the royal changes bolt and run? In his defense, Sinuhe blames his hasty retreat on anxiety over "civil strife" and fear for his safety. The words "civil strife" echo the Middle Kingdom theme of "national distress" (see *The Dispute of a Man with His Soul*), but nothing else in the tale enlarges on his fears. This opening episode appears to be simply a pretext to throw the hero into foreign lands, where, as time passes, his beloved Egypt becomes all the more precious.

The middle part of the story concerns Sinuhe's flight to and success in Palestine, where he founds a family and acquires fabled riches among the local tribes. With the patronage of a local chief, he proves his worth as a chieftain and a warrior. Most memorable is the episode in which Sinuhe conquers a boastful Syrian warrior, much as David did Goliath in the Old Testament.

Running through these adventures is the theme that contrasts the ideal order of Egyptian life with the unstructured existence of the Palestinian tribes. The story's turning point occurs in the middle of Sinuhe's rejoicing at his worldly success, when he breaks down and bemoans the futility of his life. He prays: "O whichever God ordained this flight, show mercy and return me to the Palace! Surely you will grant that I see the place where dwells my heart!" For Sinuhe, life is meaningful and lasting only within the Egyptian state, as symbolized by the king and courtly ritual.

The story concludes with the hero's homecoming and reception into Egyptian court society. Welcomed by King Senwosret, the aged Sinuhe rids himself of foreign clothing, puts on court dress, and looks forward to the day of his own burial in a "pyramid-tomb of stone," a gift from the king.

Perhaps part of the reason that this work became a classic in Egypt is that readers shared Sinuhe's disdain for foreign cultures. Sinuhe's view that the non-Egyptian world was "uncivilized" was apparently in tune with Egypt's self-image as a land of timeless values.

—⟨⟨⟨—

The Hereditary Prince and Chief, Treasurer of the King, and Unique Courtier, Administrative Dignitary of the districts and estates of the Sovereign in the lands of the Syrians, Actual Acquaintance of the King and beloved of him, the King's Retainer Sinuhe says:

I was a retainer who followed his lord, a servant of the Royal Harem and of the Princess great of praise, the wife of King Sen-Wesret and daughter of King Amen-em-Hat, namely, Neferu, Lady of Reverence.

In the year 30 of his reign, in the third month of the season of Inundation, the god ascended unto his horizon; the King of Upper and Lower Egypt, Amen-em-Hat, was taken up to heaven and united with the sun. The body of the god was united with him who made him. The city of royal residence was silent, all hearts were in grief, and the great Double Gates were sealed. The courtiers sat with heads bent down upon their laps, and the people were in mourning.

Now His Majesty had sent a great army to the land of the Lybians, with his eldest son in command of it, namely, the beautiful god Sen-Wesret. He had been sent to smite the foreign lands, to strike down the dwellers in Lybia. Indeed, even now was he returning, bringing living prisoners from among the Lybians and all kinds of cattle without limit.

The courtiers of the palace sent to the western border, advising the King's son of what had come about in the Palace. The messengers found him on the road, having reached him at the time of evening. Not a moment at all did he delay: The Falcon flew with his attendants, not letting his army know what had happened.

Now those others of the King's sons who were following him in this expedition were sought out, and one of them was called aside. And lo, I happened to be standing near by, and heard his voice as he was speaking. My heart was distraught, my arms flung apart, and trembling seized all my limbs. I sprang bounding away to seek myself a place to hide. I placed myself between two bushes to hide from the passers-by. I certainly had no intention of returning to the Residence, for I expected civil strife to break out, and I did not think I would live after the King's death.

I crossed Lake Maati near Nehet and landed at the island of Senefru. I passed the day at the edge of the fields, and at dawn the next morning I set forth again. I met a man standing on the road. He was frightened of me, and stood in awe. When it was time for supper, I reached the town of Negau. I crossed the river on a barge without a rudder, with the aid of a westerly wind. I passed eastward of the quarry, above the temple of Hathor,

Lady of the Red Hill. I gave road to my legs and went northward.

I arrived at the Walls of the Ruler, which were made to repel the Syrians and to defeat the Sand-crossers. I took up a crouching position under a bush, in fear lest the watch of the day standing on the wall would see me. At the time of late evening I journeyed on, and when the sun came forth again I reached Peten, and halted at the island of Kem-Wer. A great attack of thirst overtook me. My throat was hot and dry, and I said, "This is the taste of death."

Then I lifted up my heart and pulled my limbs together, for I heard the sound of the lowing of cattle and I spied some Syrians. A distinguished chieftain among them, who had been in Egypt, recognized me. Then he gave me water and cooked milk for me. I proceeded with him to his tribe, and they treated me well.

Land gave me to land. I went forth to Byblos, and then I turned back to Kedem. There I spent a year and a half. Then Amu-nenshi, a ruler in Palestine, fetched me. He said to me, "You will fare well with me; here you will hear the speech of Egypt." He said this since he knew my character and had heard of my capacities. The Egyptians who were there with him bore witness for me.

He said to me, "For what reason have you come to this place? What is it? Has something happened at the Residence?"

Then I said to him, "King Amen-em-Hat has proceeded to the Horizon. No one knows what can happen because of it." But I added, untruthfully:

"I was returning from an expedition to the land of the Lybians when it was reported to me. My mind became unquiet. My heart was not in my body, and it drew me to the desert roads. I had not been accused of anything, no one had spat in my face, and no wretched remarks had been heard about me. My name had not been heard in the mouth of the herald. I do not know what brought me to this land. It is like the dispensation of some god; or like a dream in which a man of the Delta might see himself in Nubia!"

Then he said to me, "What, then, will the land be without him, that excellent god, the fear of whom pervaded the foreign lands like Sekhmet in a year of pestilence?"

I spoke to him in reply, "Indeed his son has entered into the Palace and has assumed the heritance of his father.

For he is a god; there is none his equal,
    and there is none other who surpasses him.
He is a master of understanding, excellent in plans
    and beneficent of decrees;

and going and coming are according to his
    commands.
He it was who subdued the foreign lands while his
    father was within the palace;
and he reported to him that what he was ordered
    had been done.
Mighty indeed is he, achieving with his strong arm;
    a valiant one, and there is not his equal!
He slakes his wrath by smashing skulls;
    and no one can stand up about him.
He is robust of heart at the moment of attack;
    and does not let sloth rest upon his heart.
Bold of countenance is he when sees the mêlée;
    to attack the barbarian is his joy.
He girds his shield and crushes the foe;
    and does not strike twice in order to kill!
But he is lord of charm and great of sweetness;
    and through love has he conquered!
His city loves him more than itself;
    it rejoices in him more than in its god;
    men and women salute and rejoice with him
        now that he is King!
He conquered while still in the egg,
    and his face was turned to royal deeds since he
        was born.
He makes multiply those who were born with him;
    he is unique, the gift of the god.
He is one who makes wide the boundaries;
    he will seize the southern countries, and the
        northern ones with ease,
    having been created to smite the Syrians and to
        crush the Sand-crossers.
How this land rejoices now that he is come to rule!

Send to him, cause him to know your name as an inquirer far from His Majesty. He will not cease to make happy a land which will be loyal to him!"

Then he said to me, "Well, assuredly then, Egypt is happy, knowing that he flourishes. Behold, you are here, and you shall stay with me. I will treat you well."

He placed me at the head of his children, and he married me to his eldest daughter. He let me choose for myself from his land, from the choicest that he had, on his boundary adjoining another territory. It was a good land, and Yaa was its name. There were figs in it, together with grapes. It had more wine than water; great was its honey and abundant its olives. Every fruit was on its trees. There was barley there, and emmer wheat, and all kinds of cattle without limit.

And much, indeed, accrued to me as a result of the love of me. He appointed me as ruler of a tribe of the choicest of his country. Provisions were assigned for me daily, and wine for each day's needs; cooked meat and roasted fowl besides desert game. They used to snare for me and set aside game for me over and above what my hounds caught. Much wine was made for me, and milk was used in every kind of cooking.

Thus I spent many years. My children became strong men, each man in control of a tribe. The couriers who went north or south to the Palace would tarry because of me,

and I made all travelers tarry. I gave water to the thirsty; I put on the road those who had become lost, and I rescued those who were plundered.

When the Bedouin became so bold as to oppose the "Chiefs of the Foreign Lands," I advised them how to proceed. This ruler of the Syrians caused me to spend many years as commander of his army. Every foreign territory against which I went forth, I attacked and it was driven away from its pasturage and its wells. I plundered its cattle, I carried away its inhabitants, and seized their food. I slew people thereof with my strong arm, and by my movements and my excellent devices, I found favor in the ruler's heart, and he loved me. He recognized my valor, and placed me even before his children, since he saw that my arms flourished.

There came a powerful man of the Syrians to taunt me with challenges in my tent. He was a hero without peer, and he had beaten all the Syrians. He said he would fight with me. He expected to despoil me and plunder my cattle, being so counseled by his tribe.

The ruler discussed the matter with me, and I said, "I do not know him, and I certainly am not an associate of his going about in his camp. Is it that I have opened his gate, or thrown down his fence? It is envy, because he sees me carrying out your orders. Assuredly, I am like a bull who has wandered into the herd, and whom the long-horned steer of the herd attacks. Is there any man of humble origin who is loved when he becomes a superior? Well, if he wants to fight, let him speak out what he has in mind. Is a god ignorant of the fact that the nature of whatever he has ordained will eventually be known?"

During the night I strung my bow and practised my shooting. I made my dagger loose and free and polished my weapons. At dawn all Syria came, its tribes stirred up and half its peoples assembled; this fight had been planned.

Then he came toward me as I waited, and I placed myself in position near him. Every heart burned for me, and the women and even the men were murmuring. Every heart was sick for me as they said, "Is there another strong enough to fight him?"

But I escaped his missiles and made his arrows pass me by until none remained, and his shield, his ax, and his armful of spears fell down before me. Then he charged at me. I shot him; my arrow stuck in his neck. He shrieked and fell on his nose. I killed him with his own battle-ax. I gave forth my shout of victory on his back while every Syrian roared. I gave jubilant praise to Montu while his partisans mourned him.

This ruler Amu-nenshi took me in his embrace. Then I carried away my enemy's goods, and I plundered his cattle. What he had planned to do to me, this I did to him. I seized all that was in his tent, and stripped his encampment. Thus I widened my possessions and became numerous in cattle. I became great there. Thus has the god done, in being gracious unto one against whom he had been angered, and whom he had sent astray into another land. Today is his heart appeased.

A fugitive has fled in his straitened moment;
    now my good report is in the Palace.

A lingerer lingered because of hunger;
now I give bread to my neighbor.
A man left his land because of nakedness;
now I am bright of raiment and of linen.
A man ran for lack of someone to send;
now I am rich in slaves.
My house is beautiful, and broad is my abode.
The memory of me is in the Palace.

O whichever God ordained this flight, show mercy and return me to the Palace! Surely you will grant that I see the place where dwells my heart!

What is more important than that my body be buried in Egypt, the land where I was born? O come to my aid!

That which has occurred is a fortunate event—the god has shown mercy. May he do the like to bring to a good end him whom he has afflicted!

May his heart be sick for him whom he has cast out to live in a foreign land. Is it true that today he is appeased? Then let him hear the prayer of one who is afar! Let him turn his hand toward him who trod the earth, leading him back to the place whence he drew him forth!

May the King of Egypt be gracious unto me, who lives 30 in his grace! May I hail the Lady of the Land, who is in his Palace, and may I hear word of his children! Then might my limbs flourish, since old age has befallen me, and infirmity has overtaken me.

My arms are weak, and my legs have slackened. My heart is weary; I am near to departure, and they will take me away to the City of Eternity!

Might I once more serve the Lady of All! Then will she tell me that it is well with her children! May she spend eternity over me!

Now, it was told to the Majesty of the King of Upper and Lower Egypt, Kheper-Ka-Ra [Senusret I], regarding the circumstances under which I was living. And His Majesty kept sending to me bearers of gifts of the royal bounty, that he might gladden the heart of this his servant like the ruler of any foreign land. And the children of the King, who were in the Palace, let me hear word from them.

[Here Sinuhe inserts the text of the message sent by King Senusret inviting him to return to Egypt:]

Copy of the decree brought to this servant about bringing him back to Egypt:

"The Horus Living-of-Births, the Two Ladies Living- 35 of-Births, the King of Upper and Lower Egypt, Kheper-Ka-Ra, Son of Ra, Senusret, Living forever unto eternity!

"A decree of the King to the Retainer Sinuhe:

"Behold, this decree of the King is brought to you to advise you as follows: You have wandered about foreign lands—you have gone from Kedem to Tenu. Under the counsel of your own heart, land gave you to land! What have you done, that anything should be done against you? You have not blasphemed, that your words should be reproved. Your words have not been evil in the Council of the Nobles, that your utterances should be opposed. This plan of yours carried away your heart. It was not in my heart against you.

"This your 'Heaven,' who is in the Palace, today prospers and flourishes. Her head is covered with the royalty of the land. Her children are in the Residence; you shall heap up precious things of what they will give you, and you shall live by their largess.

"Do you return to Egypt, that you may see the Residence wherein you grew up. You shall kiss the earth at the Great Double Door, and you shall join the courtiers.

"For today indeed you have begun to grow old, and 40 have lost your virile powers. Be mindful of the day of burial, of passing to a revered state! A night will be assigned for you for oils and wrappings from the hands of Tayit. A funeral cortege will be made for you on the day of interment a mummy case of gold with a headpiece of lapis lazuli, and a heaven canopy above you. You will be placed upon a bier, with oxen drawing you and singers going before you, and the mortuary dances will be performed at the door of your tomb. The lists of the offering-table shall be invoked for you, sacrifices shall be made before your tomb stelae, and your tomb columns shall be built of white limestone amidst the tombs of the royal children.

"You must not die in a foreign land! The Asiatics shall not escort you to burial. You shall not be put in a sheepskin and a mound made over you!

"This is too long to tread the earth. Be mindful of illness, and come back!"

This decree reached me as I was standing in the midst of my tribe. It was recited to me; I placed myself on my belly. I touched the earth and scattered it upon my hair. I went about my camp rejoicing and saying, "How can such things be done to a servant whom his heart led astray to foreign and barbarous lands? Good indeed is the clemency which rescued me from the hand of death! Your Divine Essence will allow me to make my end with my body in the Residence!"

[Sinuhe now gives the text of his reply:]

Copy of the answer to this decree:

"The Servant of the Palace, Sinuhe, says: 45

"In very good peace! It is known to your Divine Essence, this flight made by your servant in his ignorance, O good God, Lord of the Two Lands, Beloved of Ra, Favored of Montu, Lord of Thebes!

"Amen, Lord of the Thrones of the Two Lands, Sebek, Ra, Horus, Hathor, Atum with his Ennead, Soped, Nefer-Bau, Semseru, the Eastern Horus, the Lady of Yemet—The Serpent- goddess, may she continue to enfold your head—the Council over the Nile waters, Min-Horus amidst the foreign lands, Wereret Lady of Punt, Nut, Ra-Horus the Elder, and all the Gods of Egypt and the Islands of the Sea, may they give life and strength to your nostrils, may they endow you with their bounty, may they give you eternity without bound and everlasting without limit! May the fear of you be repeated in the lowlands and the highlands, when you have subdued all that the sun encircles! This is the prayer of your servant for his Lord, who saves from the West!

"The lord of perception who perceives his people, he perceives in the Majesty of his Palace that which your servant feared to say, and which is a grave thing to repeat. O great God, likeness of Ra, make prudent one who is laboring on his own behalf! Your servant is in the hand of one who takes counsel concerning him, and verily am I placed under his guidance. Your Majesty is Horus the Conqueror; your arms are mighty over all lands.

"Lo, this flight your servant made, I did not plan it; it was not in my heart, I did not devise it. I do not know what separated me from my place. It was like some sort of dream, as when a man of the Delta marshes sees himself in Elephantine, or a man of the northern swamps in Nubia. I did not take fright, no one was pursuing me, I had heard no reviling word. My name had not been heard in the mouth of the herald.

"However, my limbs began to quiver, and my legs began to tremble. My heart led me away. The god who ordained this flight drew me, although I had not been rebellious.

"Any man who knows his land stands in awe, for Ra has set the fear of you throughout the earth, and the dread of you in every foreign land. Whether I am at the Palace or whether I am in this place, it is you, indeed, who clothes this horizon. The sun shines at your pleasure; the water in the rivers, it is drunk at your desire; the air is in the heaven, it is breathed when you so say.

"This your servant will resign the viziership which he has exercised in this place; it was a function they had requested your servant to perform. Your Majesty will act as he pleases; one lives by the breath which you bestow. Ra, Horus, and Hathor love this thy noble nose, which Montu, Lord of Thebes, desires shall live for ever!"

They came for me. I was allowed to spend a day in Yaa for transferring my possessions to my children, my eldest son having charge of my tribe—my tribe and all my property in his hands, my serfs and all my cattle, my stores of fruit and every pleasant tree of mine.

Then this servant went southward. I halted at the Roads of Horus. The commander there who was in charge of the frontier patrol sent a message to the Palace to make it known. Then His Majesty sent a capable overseer of the peasants who belonged to the Palace, followed by ships laden with gifts of the King for the Syrians who had come escorting me to the Roads of Horus. I introduced each of them by his name. Every servant was at his task when I set out and hoisted sail. They kneaded and strained before me, until I reached the vicinity of Yetchet-Tawy.

And when it dawned, very early, they came to call me, ten men coming and ten men going, to conduct me to the Palace. I touched my forehead to the ground beneath the sphinxes. The King's children were standing in the gateway to meet me. The courtiers who had been led into the Great Hall took me on the way to the royal chambers.

I found His Majesty on a great throne in a gilded niche. Then when I was stretched out on my belly, I lost consciousness before him. This god addressed me joyfully, but I was like a man overcome by dusk. My soul departed; my limbs were powerless, my heart, it was not in my body, that I should know life from death.

Then His Majesty said to one of the courtiers, "Raise him, and let him speak to me."

And His Majesty said, "Behold, you have returned! You have trodden foreign lands; you fled away. Now infirmity has seized you, and you have reached old age. It is of no little importance for your body to be buried, that you should not be interred by the Bedouin. Come, do not behave thus, not to speak when your name is pronounced!"

But I still feared punishment, and I answered with the response of one afraid, "What does my Lord say to me? I should answer, but I can do nothing. It is indeed the hand of a god. There is a terror in my belly, like that which brought about that destined flight. Behold me before you; life is yours; may Your Majesty do as he desires!"

Then they had the King's children brought in, and His Majesty said to the Queen, "Behold Sinuhe, come as a Bedouin, as if born a Syrian!"

She uttered a very great cry, and the King's children all shouted together. And they said to His Majesty, "Is it not he, in truth, O King, My Lord?"

And His Majesty said, "It is he, in truth!"

Now they had brought with them their *menit* collars and their rattles and sistra of Hathor, and they presented them before His Majesty, saying:

"Put forth your hands to these beautiful things.
    O enduring King,
    the adornments of the Lady of Heaven!
May the Golden One give life to your nostrils;
    may she join with you, the Lady of the Stars!
May the Crown-goddess of Upper Egypt sail
        northward
    and the Crown-goddess of Lower Egypt sail
        southward,
    joined and united by the utterance of Your Majesty!
The Cobra-goddess is set upon your brow,
    and you have removed your subjects from evil.
May Ra, Lord of the Two Lands, be gracious unto you;
    hail to you, as to the Lady of All!
Slacken your bow, make loose your arrow,
    give breath to him who is stifling!
Give us as good festal gift this sheik, son of the North,
    a barbarian born in Egypt!
He made flight through fear of you,
    he left the land through dread of you!
May the face of him who has seen your face not be
        afraid;
    may the eye which has looked at you not be
        terrified!"

Then said His Majesty, "Let him not fear, and let him not fall into dread. He shall be a courtier among the nobles, and he shall be placed in the midst of the courtiers. Proceed you to the Morning-chamber, and wait upon him!"

And so I went forth from the royal chambers, the King's children giving me their hands. We proceeded afterward to the Great Double Door. I was placed in the house of a son of the King, which had fine things in it;

there was a cooling room in it, and landscape decoration. There were valuables of the Treasury in it, and in every room was clothing of royal linen, and myrrh, and the best oil of the King, and of the courtiers, whom he loves. Every servingman was at his task.

The years were made to pass away from my limbs as I was shaved and my hair was combed. A load of dirt was given back to the desert, and their clothes to the sand farers. I was clothed in fine linen, and anointed with fine oil. I slept upon a bed. I gave back the sand to those who live in it, and tree oil to those who rub themselves with it.

There was given to me a house with grounds, which had belonged to a courtier. Many craftsmen restored it, and all its trees made to flourish anew. Meals from the Palace were brought to me three or four times a day besides what the King's children kept on giving me.

There was built for me a pyramid-tomb of stone, in the midst of the pyramids. The chief pyramid mason took charge of its ground, the chief draftsman designed it, the chief sculptor carved in it, and the chief builders of the necropolis concerned themselves with it. All the equipment which is placed in a tomb, those were supplied therein. Ka-priests were assigned to me. A funerary domain was made for me with fields in it, as is done for a foremost courtier. My statue was overlaid with gold, its kilt with fine gold.

By His Majesty was it caused to be done. There is no commoner for whom the like has been done. I was bestowed the favors of the King until there came the day of mooring.

IT HAS COME FROM ITS BEGINNING TO ITS END, AS WAS FOUND IN THE WRITING.

The Great Hymn to the Aten

In Egyptian culture, hymns to deities were simply part of the state religion and only incidentally expressions of literary art. Hymns functioned as a kind of metalanguage, a "language" beyond ordinary speech and writing, used by the elite to understand the universe. (The religious beliefs of the majority are virtually unknown.) Because the deities were never arranged into a logical structure, hymns (as well as rituals and figurative art) helped to shape theology, to the extent that it could be defined. Hymns offer information on ancient myths and beliefs and ritual, and over time, show the shifting "pecking order" among the deities. Recited during funerary rituals, hymns give evidence of the common belief that the divine coexists with the earthly, the eternal with the transient.

One of the most famous hymns is *The Great Hymn to the Aten,* dating from the New Kingdom (ca. 1552–1079 B.C). This hymn is well known because of its association with King Akhenaten ("the glory of Aten") (ca. 1369–1353 B.C.). This king changed his name from Amenhotep ("Amen is content") IV as part of a campaign to make the Aten—the god of the solar disk—the head of the state religion. He ordered this change to downgrade the influence of the rich priests of Amen-Re, the local deity from Thebes who rose to national prominence in the New Kingdom and became Re (the sun god).

Abandoning Thebes, Akhenaten founded a new capital called Aket-Aten ("the horizon of the Aten"), today known by its Arabic name, Tel el Amarna, or simply Amarna, from which he launched a religious and an artistic revolution. (In Amarna art, the Aten is always represented as the sun disk, emitting rays that end in tiny hands, that bless the royal family and hold the *ankh*, the symbol of eternal life.) His innovations angered the political elite and the priests of Amen-Re, who got their revenge after Akhenaten's death by restoring Amen-Re to supremacy and trying to erase the heretic's memory from history. However, knowledge of Akhenaten's reign survives in inscriptions, artworks, and *The Great Hymn to the Aten.*

Reading the Selection

The Great Hymn to the Aten, perhaps written by Akhenaten himself, was inscribed in the tomb of King Ay, a brief successor to Akhenaten who ruled before the restoration of Amen-Re. The hymn is framed within a complex literary form that includes a list of the Aten's titles and a similar list, repeated at the beginning and the end, of the titles of Akhenaten and Queen Nefertiti.

This hymn's major theme is universalism, the idea that there is one god (the Aten) who is the lord of the entire creation, as in, for example: "You [the Aten] have created the earth according to your desire, while you were alone, / With men, cattle, and wild beasts, all that is upon earth and goes upon feet, and all that soars above and flies with its wings." Paralleling a similar theme in Psalm 104 of the Old Testament, this hymn is an example of the strong influence of Egypt on Hebrew culture over the centuries.

A second theme of the hymn is the mediating role played by the king in interpreting the divine world to humankind—a theme as old as *The Story of Sinuhe*. To the elite, who composed its literature, Egypt is a cosmic stage with the king as the sole actor, performing its history through his actions. The hymn expresses this idea in these words: "[T]here is no one who knows you [the Aten] save your son [Akhenaten]."

—⚬—

Praise of the Living Ra, Horus of the Double Horizon, Rejoicing on the Horizon, in His Name of Shu Who is in the Aten, living forever unto eternity; Aten living and great, He who is in the Jubilee Festival, Lord of all that the Aten encircles, Lord of the Heavens and Lord of the Earth, Lord of the House of Aten in Akhet-Aten. The King of Upper and Lower Egypt, Living in Truth, the Lord of the Two Lands, Nefer-Kheperu-Ra Wa-en-Ra, Son of Ra, Living in Truth, Lord of Diadems, Akh-en-Aten, Great in His Duration, and the Great Wife of the King, His Beloved, the Lady of the Two Lands, Nefer-Neferu-Aten Nefert-Iti, living, healthy, and youthful forever unto eternity. He says: 1

Beautiful is your shining forth on the horizon,
  O living Aten, beginning of life!
When you arise on the eastern horizon,
  you fill every land with your beauty.
You are bright and great and gleaming,
  and are high above every land.
Your rays envelop the lands,
  as far as all you have created.
You are Ra, and you reach unto their end,   10
  and subdue them all for your beloved son.
You are afar, yet are your rays upon earth;
  you are before their face, yet one knows not their
    going!
When you go down in the western horizon,
  the earth is in darkness, as if it were dead.
They sleep in their chamber, their heads enwrapped,
  and no eye sees the other.
Though all their things were taken while under their
    heads,
  yet would they not perceive it.
Every lion comes forth from his den,   20
  and all serpents that bite.

Darkness is without and the earth is silent,
  for he who created it rests in his horizon.
When the earth brightens and you rise on the horizon,
  and shine as the Aten in the day,
When you scatter the darkness and offer your beams,
  the Two Lands are in festival,
They are awake and they stand on their feet,
  for you have raised them up.

They wash their bodies, and they take their garments,   30
  and their hands praise your arising.
  The whole land, it performs its work!

All beasts are content upon their pasture,
  and the trees and herbs are verdant.
The birds fly out of their nests,
  and their wings praise your Divine Essence.
All wild beasts prance upon their feet,
  and all that fly and alight.
  They live when you shine forth for them!
    40
The ships voyage downstream and upstream likewise,
  and every way is open, since you have arisen.
The fish in the river leap up before your face,
  and your rays are in the midst of the Great Green.

You who bring children into being in women,
  and make fluid into mankind,
Who nourishes the son in the womb of his mother,
  who soothes him so that he weeps not,
  O nurse in the womb!
Who gives breath in order to keep alive   50
  all that he has made;

When he comes forth from the womb on the day of his
    birth,
  you open his mouth in speech, and give all that he
    needs.
The chick in the egg chirps in the shell,
  for you give it breath therein to sustain its life.
You make its completion for it in the egg in order to
    break it;
It comes forth from the egg at its completion,
  and walks on its feet when it comes forth therefrom.

How manifold are the things which you have made,
  and they are hidden from before man!
  O unique god, who has no second to him!   60
You have created the earth according to your desire,
  while you were alone,
With men, cattle, and wild beasts,
  all that is upon earth and goes upon feet,
  and all that soars above and flies with its wings.

The lands of Syria and Kush,
    and the land of Egypt,
You put every man in his place,
    and supply their needs.
Each one has provision   70
    and his lifetime is reckoned.
Their tongues are diverse in speech,
    and their form likewise;
Their skins are distinguished,
    for you distinguish the peoples of foreign lands.

You make the Nile in the Other World,
    and bring it whither you wish,
In order to sustain the people,
    even as you have made them.
For you are lord of them all,   80
    who weary yourself on their behalf,
The lord of every land, who arises for them,
    O Aten of the day, great of majesty!

All strange foreign lands,
    you make that whereon they live.
You have put a Nile in the sky,
    that it may come down for them,
And make waves on the hills like the sea,
    to water their fields in their townships.
How excellently made are your designs, O Lord of
        Eternity!   90
    the Nile in heaven, you appoint it for foreign peoples,
        and all beasts of the wilderness which walk upon
        feet;
The Nile upon earth,
    it proceeds from the Other World for the Beloved
        Land.

Your rays suckle every field,
    and when you shine forth
        they live and flourish for you.

You make the seasons
    to cause to continue all you have created:
The winter to cool them,   100
    and the warmth that they may taste of you.
You have made the sky afar off to shine therein,
    in order to behold all you have made.
You are alone, shining in your forms as living Aten,
    appearing, shining, withdrawing, returning,
        you make millions of forms of yourself alone!
Cities, townships, fields, road, and river,
    all eyes behold you against them.
        O Aten of the day above the earth!

You are in my heart,   110
    and there is no one who knows you save your son,
Nefer-Kheperu-Ra Wa-en-Ra,
    whom you made understanding of your designs and
        your might.
The earth came into being by your hand,
    even as you have created them.
When you arise they live,
    and when you set they die.
But you have eternity in your members,
    and all creatures live in you.

The eyes look on your beauty until you set;   120
    all work is laid aside when you set in the west.
When you rise you make all to flourish for the King,
    you who made the foundations of the earth.
You raise them up for your son,
    he who came forth from your body,
the King of Upper and Lower Egypt, Living in Truth, the
Lord of the Two Lands, Nefer-Kheperu-Ra Wa-en-Ra, Son
of Ra, Living in Truth, Lord of Diadems, Akh-en-Aten,
Great in His Duration, and for the Great Wife of the King,
His Beloved, the Lady of the Two Lands, Nefer-Neferu-
Aten Nefert-Iti, living and youthful forever unto eternity.

2

AEGEAN CIVILIZATION
The Minoans, the Mycenaeans, and the Greeks of the Archaic Age

HOMER

Selections from the *Iliad*

The two Greek epics, the *Iliad* and the *Odyssey* (see the following selection), have never lost their appeal, though they were composed nearly three thousand years ago. Homer, with his strong grasp of the human psyche, expressed his characters' sorrow and happiness, hopes and fears, and most especially, their love of life and certainty of death. Performed as oral poetry accompanied by music, these works electrified his first audiences because they represented the basic human condition as his listeners had experienced it. In later periods, after the works were written down, readers were equally thrilled because they recognized the timeless truths contained in his words. Contributing to the epics' enduring appeal were the similes and metaphors that invoked images from Homer's world and remain memorable today as sublime expressions of poetic beauty. It is a measure of Homer's classic status that ever since his day, writers have reworked his two stories of war and travel, respectively, giving their own versions of his heroes and heroines and updating the plots to reflect their own times.

The *Iliad* focuses on the climactic year of the Greeks' nine-year siege of Ilium, or Troy (though it stops short of the fall of Troy). Composed in about the middle of the eighth century B.C., Homer's works are his own reworking of tales that previously had been circulating orally for about three hundred years. The oral tales reflected an earlier civilization, the Mycenaean (1900–1100 B.C.); thus, the Homeric heroes and the Olympian deities, who are considered the quintessence of Greek culture, are in reality Mycenaean in origin. The popularity of both the *Iliad* and the *Odyssey* resulted in their becoming moral guidebooks, offering to Greek youths models of behavior both on and off the battlefield. The works were also treated as religious scripture, providing insight into the personalities and motives of the Olympian deities.

Reading the Selections

In the selection from the *Iliad*, Book I, Homer's genius is evident in the opening line, which announces his theme: "the anger of Peleus' son Achilleus and its devastation." This theme becomes the thread

that holds the epic together, despite the convoluted plot and "cast of hundreds." The Trojan War—
the battle between the Greeks ("Achaians") and the Trojans ("Danaans")—always forms the back-
drop and sometimes the temporary foreground to the story. Further complicating the plot are the
adventures of the Olympic deities who allow nothing to happen on earth without their consent.

    The epic's climax (not included here) is the battle between Achilleus, Greece's most feared
warrior, and Hektor, Troy's champion and son of Priam, the Trojan king: Achilleus kills Hektor and
defiles his body by dragging it around the walls of Troy. The selection from Book XXIV contains the
epic's conclusion, the scene in which Priam begs Achilleus for his son's remains.

—⁓—

Book I

Sing, goddess, the anger of Peleus' son Achilleus   1
and its devastation, which put pains thousandfold upon
    the Achaians,
hurled in their multitudes to the house of Hades strong
    souls
of heroes, but gave their bodies to be the delicate feasting
of dogs, of all birds, and the will of Zeus was accomplished
since that time when first there stood in division of
    conflict
Atreus' son the lord of men and brilliant Achilleus.
  What god was it then set them together in bitter
    collision?
Zeus' son and Leto's, Apollo, who in anger at the king
    drove
the foul pestilence along the host, and the people
    perished,   10
since Atreus' son had dishonoured Chryses, priest of
    Apollo,
when he came beside the fast ships of the Achaians to
    ransom
back his daughter, carrying gifts beyond count and
    holding
in his hands wound on a staff of gold the ribbons of
    Apollo
who strikes from afar, and supplicated all the Achaians,
but above all Atreus' two sons, the marshals of the
    people:
'Sons of Atreus and you other strong-greaved Achaians,
to you may the gods grant who have their homes on
    Olympos
Priam's city to be plundered and a fair homecoming
    thereafter,
but may you give me back my own daughter and take the
    ransom,   20
giving honour to Zeus' son who strikes from afar, Apollo.'
  Then all the rest of the Achaians cried out in favour
that the priest be respected and the shining ransom be
    taken;
yet this pleased not the heart of Atreus' son Agamemnon,
but harshly he drove him away with a strong order upon
    him:
'Never let me find you again, old sir, near our hollow
ships, neither lingering now nor coming again hereafter,

for fear your staff and the god's ribbons help you no
    longer.
The girl I will not give back; sooner will old age come
    upon her
in my own house, in Argos, far from her own land, going   30
up and down by the loom and being in my bed as my
    companion.
So go now, do not make me angry; so you will be safer.'
  So he spoke, and the old man in terror obeyed him
and went silently away beside the murmuring sea beach.
Over and over the old man prayed as he walked in
    solitude
to King Apollo, whom Leto of the lovely hair bore:
    'Hear me,
lord of the silver bow who set your power about Chryse
and Killa the sacrosanct, who are lord in strength over
    Tenedos,
Smintheus, if ever it pleased your heart that I built your
    temple,
if ever it pleased you that I burned all the rich thigh pieces   40
of bulls, of goats, then bring to pass this wish I pray for:
let your arrows make the Danaans pay for my tears shed.'
  So he spoke in prayer, and Phoibos Apollo heard him,
and strode down along the pinnacles of Olympos,
    angered
in his heart, carrying across his shoulders the bow and the
    hooded
quiver; and the shafts clashed on the shoulders of the god
    walking
angrily. He came as night comes down and knelt then
apart and opposite the ships and let go an arrow.
Terrible was the clash that rose from the bow of silver.
First he went after the mules and the circling hounds, then
    let go   50
a tearing arrow against the men themselves and struck
    them.
The corpse fires burned everywhere and did not stop
    burning.
  Nine days up and down the host ranged the god's
    arrows,
but on the tenth Achilleus called the people to assembly;
a thing put into his mind by the goddess of the white
    arms, Hera,

who had pity upon the Danaans when she saw them
   dying.
Now when they were all assembled in one place together,
Achilleus of the swift feet stood up among them and
   spoke forth:
'Son of Atreus, I believe now that straggling backwards
we must make our way home if we can even escape death, 60
if fighting now must crush the Achaians and the plague
   likewise.
No, come, let us ask some holy man, some prophet,
even an interpreter of dreams, since a dream also
comes from Zeus, who can tell why Phoibus Apollo is so
   angry,
if for the sake of some vow, some hecatomb he blames us,
if given the fragrant smoke of lambs, of he goats,
   somehow
he can be made willing to beat the bane aside from us.'
   He spoke thus and sat down again, and among them
   stood up
Kalchas, Thestor's son, far the best of the bird interpreters,
who knew all things that were, the things to come and the
   things past, 70
who guided into the land of Ilion the ships of the
   Achaians
through that seercraft of his own that Phoibos Apollo gave
   him.
He in kind intention toward all stood forth and addressed
   them:
'You have bidden me, Achilleus beloved of Zeus, to
   explain to
you this anger of Apollo the lord who strikes from afar.
   Then
I will speak; yet make me a promise and swear before me
readily by word and work of your hands to defend me,
since I believe I shall make a man angry who holds great
   kingship
over the men of Argos, and all the Achaians obey him.
For a king when he is angry with a man beneath him is too
   strong, 80
and suppose even for the day itself he swallow down his
   anger,
he still keeps bitterness that remains until its fulfillment
deep in his chest. Speak forth then, tell me if you will
   protect me.'
   Then in answer again spoke Achilleus of the swift feet:
'Speak, interpreting whatever you know, and fear
   nothing.
In the name of Apollo beloved of Zeus to whom you,
   Kalchas,
make your prayers when you interpret the gods' will to
   the Danaans,
no man so long as I am alive above earth and see daylight
shall lay the weight of his hands on you beside the hollow
   ships,
not one of all the Danaans, even if you mean Agamemnon, 90
who now claims to be far the greatest of all the Achaians.'
   At this the blameless seer took courage again and spoke
   forth:
'No, it is not for the sake of some vow or hecatomb he
   blames us,

but for the sake of his priest whom Agamemnon
   dishonoured
and would not give him back his daughter nor accept the
   ransom.
Therefore the archer sent griefs against us and will send
   them
still, nor sooner thrust back the shameful plague from the
   Danaans
until we give the glancing-eyed girl back to her father
without price, without ransom, and lead also a blessed
   hecatomb
to Chryse; thus we might propitiate and persuade him.' 100
   He spoke thus and sat down again, and among them
   stood up
Atreus' son the hero wide-ruling Agamemnon
raging, the heart within filled black to the brim with
   anger
from beneath, but his two eyes showed like fire in their
   blazing.
First of all he eyed Kalchas bitterly and spoke to him:
'Seer of evil: never yet have you told me a good thing.
Always the evil things are dear to your heart to prophesy,
but nothing excellent have you said nor ever accomplished.
Now once more you make divination to the Danaans,
   argue
forth your reason why he who strikes from afar afflicts
   them, 110
because I for the sake of the girl Chryseis would not take
the shining ransom; and indeed I wish greatly to have her
in my own house; since I like her better than Klytaimnestra
my own wife, for in truth she is in no way inferior,
neither in build nor stature nor wit, not in
   accomplishment.
Still I am willing to give her back, if such is the best way.
I myself desire that my people be safe, not perish.
Find me then some prize that shall be my own, lest I only
among the Argives go without, since that were unfitting;
you are all witnesses to this thing, that my prize goes
   elsewhere.' 120
   Then in answer again spoke brilliant swift-footed
   Achilleus:
'Son of Atreus, most lordly, greediest for gain of all men,
how shall the great-hearted Achaians give you a prize
   now?
There is no great store of things lying about I know of.
But what we took from the cities by storm has been
   distributed;
it is unbecoming for the people to call back things once
   given.
No, for the present give the girl back to the god; we
   Achaians
thrice and four times over will repay you, if ever Zeus
   gives
into our hands the strong-walled citadel of Troy to be
   plundered.'
   Then in answer again spoke powerful Agamemnon: 130
'Not that way, good fighter though you be, godlike
   Achilleus,
strive to cheat, for you will not deceive, you will not
   persuade me.

What do you want? To keep your own prize and have me sit here
lacking one? Are you ordering me to give this girl back?
Either the great-hearted Achaians shall give me a new prize
chosen according to my desire to atone for the girl lost,
or else if they will not give me one I myself shall take her,
your own prize, or that of Aias, or that of Odysseus,
going myself in person; and he whom I visit will be bitter.
Still, these are things we shall deliberate again hereafter.   140
Come, now, we must haul a black ship down to the bright sea,
and assemble rowers enough for it, and put on board it
the hecatomb, and the girl herself, Chryseis of the fair cheeks,
and let there be one responsible man in charge of her,
either Aias or Idomeneus or brilliant Odysseus,
or you yourself, son of Peleus, most terrifying of all men,
to reconcile by accomplishing sacrifice the archer.'
　　Then looking darkly at him Achilleus of the swift feet spoke:
'O wrapped in shamelessness, with your mind forever on profit,
how shall any one of the Achaians readily obey you   150
either to go on a journey or to fight men strongly in battle?
I for my part did not come here for the sake of the Trojan
spearmen to fight against them, since to me they have done nothing.
Never yet have they driven away my cattle or my horses,
never in Phthia where the soil is rich and men grow great
did they
spoil my harvest, since indeed there is much that lies between us,
the shadowy mountains and the echoing sea; but for your sake,
o great shamelessness, we followed, to do you favour,
you with the dog's eyes, to win your honour and Menelaos'
from the Trojans. You forget all this or else you care nothing.   160
And now my prize you threaten in person to strip from me,
for whom I laboured much, the gift of the sons of the Achaians.
Never, when the Achaians sack some well-founded citadel
of the Trojans, do I have a prize that is equal to your prize.
Always the greater part of the painful fighting is the work of
my hands; but when the time comes to distribute the booty
yours is far the greater reward, and I with some small thing
yet dear to me go back to my ships when I am weary with fighting.
Now I am returning to Phthia, since it is much better
to go home again with my curved ships, and I am minded no longer   170
to stay here dishonoured and pile up your wealth and your luxury.'
　　Then answered him in turn the lord of men Agamemnon:

'Run away by all means if your heart drives you. I will not
entreat you to stay here for my sake. There are others with me
who will do me honour, and above all Zeus of the counsels.
To me you are the most hateful of all the kings whom the gods love.
Forever quarrelling is dear to your heart, and wars and battles;
and if you are very strong indeed, that is a god's gift.
Go home then with your own ships and your own companions,
be king over the Myrmidons. I care nothing about you.   180
I take no account of your anger. But here is my threat to you.
Even as Phoibos Apollo is taking away my Chryseis.
I shall convey her back in my own ship, with my own
followers; but I shall take the fair-cheeked Briseis,
your prize, I myself going to your shelter, that you may learn well
how much greater I am than you, and another man may shrink back
from likening himself to me and contending against me.'
　　So he spoke. And the anger came on Peleus' son, and within
his shaggy breast the heart was divided two ways, pondering
whether to draw from beside his thigh the sharp sword, driving   190
away all those who stood between and kill the son of Atreus,
or else to check the spleen within and keep down his anger.
Now as he weighed in mind and spirit these two courses
and was drawing from its scabbard the great sword, Athene descended
from the sky. For Hera the goddess of the white arms sent her,
who loved both men equally in her heart and cared for them.
The goddess standing behind Peleus' son caught him by the fair hair,
appearing to him only, for no man of the others saw her.
Achilleus in amazement turned about, and straightway
knew Pallas Athene and the terrible eyes shining.   200
He uttered winged words and addressed her: 'Why have you come now,
o child of Zeus of the aegis, once more? Is it that you may see
the outrageousness of the son of Atreus Agamemnon?
Yet will I tell you this thing, and I think it shall be accomplished.
By such acts of arrogance he may even lose his own life.'
　　Then in answer the goddess grey-eyed Athene spoke to him:
'I have come down to stay your anger—but will you obey me?—
from the sky; and the goddess of the white arms Hera sent me,
who loves both of you equally in her heart and cares for you.

Come then, do not take your sword in your hand, keep
    clear of fighting, 210
though indeed with words you may abuse him, and it will
    be that way.
And this also will I tell you and it will be a thing
    accomplished.
Some day three times over such shining gifts shall be
    given you
by reason of this outrage. Hold your hand then, and obey
    us.'
    Then in answer again spoke Achilleus of the swift feet:
'Goddess, it is necessary that I obey the word of you two,
angry though I am in my heart. So it will be better.
If any man obeys the gods, they listen to him also.'
    He spoke, and laid his heavy hand on the silver sword
    hilt
and thrust the great blade back into the scabbard nor
    disobeyed 220
the word of Athene. And she went back again to Olympos
to the house of Zeus of the aegis with the other divinities.
    But Peleus' son once again in words of derision
spoke to Atreides, and did not yet let go of his anger:
'You wine sack, with a dog's eyes, with a deer's heart.
    Never
once have you taken courage in your heart to arm with
    your people
for battle, or go into ambuscade with the best of the
    Achaians.
No, for in such things you see death. Far better to your
    mind
is it, all along the widespread host of the Achaians
to take away the gifts of any man who speaks up against
    you. 230
King who feed on your people, since you rule nonentities;
otherwise, son of Atreus, this were your last outrage.
But I will tell you this and swear a great oath upon it:
in the name of this sceptre, which never again will bear
    leaf nor
branch, now that is has left behind the cut stump in the
    mountains,
nor shall it ever blossom again, since the bronze blade
    stripped
bark and leafage, and now at last the sons of the Achaians
carry it in their hands in state when they administer
the justice of Zeus. And this shall be a great oath before you:
some day longing for Achilleus will come to the sons of
    the Achaians, 240
all of them. Then stricken at heart though you be, you will
    be able
to do nothing, when in their numbers before man-
    slaughtering Hektor
they drop and die. And then you will eat out the heart
    within you
in sorrow, that you did no honour to the best of the
    Achaians.'
    Thus spoke Peleus' son and dashed to the ground the
    sceptre
studded with golden nails, and sat down again. But
    Atreides
raged still on the other side, and between them Nestor

the fair-spoken rose up, the lucid speaker of Pylos,
from whose lips the streams of words ran sweeter than
    honey.
In his time two generations of mortal men had perished, 250
those who had grown up with him and they who had
    been born to
these in sacred Pylos, and he was king in the third age.
He in kind intention toward both stood forth and ad-
    dressed them:
'Oh, for shame. Great sorrow comes on the land of Achaia.
Now might Priam and the sons of Priam in truth be happy,
and all the rest of the Trojans be visited in their hearts with
    gladness,
were they to hear all this wherein you two are quarrelling,
you, who surpass all Danaans in council, in fighting.
Yet be persuaded. Both of you are younger than I am.
Yes, and in my time I have dealt with better men than 260
you are, and never once did they disregard me. Never
yet have I seen nor shall see again such men as these were,
men like Peirithoös, and Dryas, shepherd of the people,
Kaineus and Exadios, godlike Polyphemos,
or Theseus, Aigeus' son, in the likeness of the immortals.
These were the strongest generation of earth-born mortals,
the strongest, and they fought against the strongest, the
    beast men
living within the mountains, and terribly they destroyed
    them.
I was of the company of these men, coming from Pylos,
a long way from a distant land, since they had summoned
    me. 270
And I fought single-handed, yet against such men no one
of the mortals now alive upon earth could do battle. And
    also
these listened to the counsels I gave and heeded my
    bidding.
Do you also obey, since to be persuaded is better.
You, great man that you are, yet do not take the girl away
but let her be, a prize as the sons of the Achaians gave her
first. Nor, son of Peleus, think to match your strength with
the king, since never equal with the rest is the portion of
    honour
of the sceptred king to whom Zeus gives magnificence.
    Even
though you are the stronger man, and the mother who
    bore you was immortal, 280
yet is this man greater who is lord over more than you rule.
Son of Atreus, give up your anger; even I entreat you
to give over your bitterness against Achilleus, he who
stands as a great bulwark of battle over all the Achaians.'
    Then in answer again spoke powerful Agamemnon:
'Yes, old sir, all this you have said is fair and orderly.
Yet here is a man who wishes to be above all others,
who wishes to hold power over all, and to be lord of
all, and give them their orders, yet I think one will not
    obey him.
And if the everlasting gods have made him a spearman,
yet they have not given him the right to speak abusively.' 290
    Then looking at him darkly brilliant Achilleus answered
    him:
'So must I be called of no account and a coward

if I must carry out every order you may happen to give me.
Tell other men to do these things, but give me no more
commands, since I for my part have no intention to obey
    you.
And put away in your thoughts this other thing I tell you.
With my hands I will not fight for the girl's sake, neither
with you nor any other man, since you take her away who
    gave her.
But of all the other things that are mine beside my fast black   300
ship, you shall take nothing away against my pleasure.
Come, then, only try it, that these others may see also;

instantly your own black blood will stain my spearpoint.'
    So these two after battling in words of contention
stood up, and broke the assembly beside the ships of the
    Achaians.
Peleus' son went back to his balanced ships and his shelter
with Patroklos, Menoitios' son, and his own companions.
But the son of Atreus drew a fast ship down to the water
and allotted into it twenty rowers and put on board it
the hecatomb for the god and Chryseis of the fair cheeks   310
leading her by the hand. And in charge went crafty
    Odysseus.

—ᴡ—

Book XXIV

. . . .

So Hermes spoke, and went away to the height of
    Olympos,   1
but Priam vaulted down to the ground from behind the
    horses
and left Idaios where he was, for he stayed behind,
    holding
in hand the horses and mules. The old man made
    straight for the dwelling
where Achilleus the beloved of Zeus was sitting. He
    found him
inside, and his companions were sitting apart, as two only,
Automedon the hero and Alkimos, scion of Ares,
were busy beside him. He had just now got through
    with his dinner,
with eating and drinking, and the table still stood by.
    Tall Priam
came in unseen by the other men and stood close beside
    him   10
and caught the knees of Achilleus in his arms, and
    kissed the hands
that were dangerous and manslaughtering and had killed
    so many
of his sons. As when dense disaster closes on one who
    has murdered
a man in his own land, and he comes to the country of
    others,
to a man of substance, and wonder seizes on those who
    behold him,
so Achilleus wondered as he looked on Priam, a godlike
man, and the rest of them wondered also, and looked at
    each other.
But now Priam spoke to him in the words of a suppliant:
'Achilleus like the gods, remember your father, one who
is of years like mine, and on the door-sill of sorrowful
    old age.
And they who dwell nearby encompass him and afflict
    him,   20
nor is there any to defend him against the wrath, the
    destruction.
Yet surely he, when he hears of you and that you are
    still living,

is gladdened within his heart and all his days he is hopeful
that he will see his beloved son come home from the Troad.
But for me, my destiny was evil. I have had the noblest
of sons in Troy, but I say not one of them is left to me.
Fifty were my sons, when the sons of the Achaians came
    here.
Nineteen were born to me from the womb of a single
    mother,
and other women bore the rest in my palace; and of these   30
violent Ares broke the strength in the knees of most
    of them,
but one was left me who guarded my city and people,
    that one
you killed a few days since as he fought in defence of his
    country,
Hektor; for whose sake I come now to the ships of the
    Achaians
to win him back from you, and I bring you gifts beyond
    number.
Honour then the gods, Achilleus, and take pity upon
    me
remembering your father, yet I am still more pitiful;
I have gone through what no other mortal on earth has
    gone through;
I put my lips to the hands of the man who has killed my
    children.'
So he spoke, and stirred in the other a passion of grieving   40
for his own father. He took the old man's hand and
    pushed him
gently away, and the two remembered, as Priam sat
    huddled
at the feet of Achilleus and wept close for
    manslaughtering Hektor
and Achilleus wept now for his own father, now again
for Patroklos. The sound of their mourning moved in the
    house. Then
when great Achilleus had taken full satisfaction in
    sorrow
and the passion for it had gone from his mind and body,
    thereafter
he rose from his chair, and took the old man by the
    hand, and set him

on his feet again, in pity for the grey head and the grey
    beard,
and spoke to him and addressed him in winged words:
    'Ah, unlucky,   50
surely you have had much evil to endure in your spirit.
How could you dare to come alone to the ships of the
    Achaians
and before my eyes, when I am one who have killed in
    such numbers
such brave sons of yours? The heart in you is iron.
    Come, then,
and sit down upon this chair, and you and I will even let
our sorrows lie still in the heart for all our grieving.
    There is not
any advantage to be won from grim lamentation.
Such is the way the gods spun life for unfortunate mortals,
that we live in unhappiness, but the gods themselves
    have no sorrows.
There are two urns that stand on the door-sill of Zeus.
    They are unlike   60
for the gifts they bestow: an urn of evils, an urn of blessings.
If Zeus who delights in thunder mingles these and
    bestows them
on man, he shifts, and moves now in evil, again in good
    fortune.
But when Zeus bestows from the urn of sorrows, he
    makes a failure
of man, and the evil hunger drives him over the shining
earth, and he wanders respected neither of gods nor
    mortals.
Such were the shining gifts given by the gods to Peleus
from his birth, who outshone all men beside for his riches
and pride of possession, and was lord over the
    Myrmidons. Thereto
the gods bestowed an immortal wife on him, who was
    mortal.   70
But even on him the god piled evil also. There was not
any generation of strong sons born to him in his great
    house
but a single all-untimely child he had, and I give him
no care as he grows old, since far from the land of my
    fathers
I sit here in Troy, and bring nothing but sorrow to you
    and your children.
And you, old sir, we are told you prospered once; for as
    much
as Lesbos, Makar's hold, confines to the north above it
and Phrygia from the north confines, and enormous
    Hellespont,
of these, old sir, you were lord once in your wealth and
    your children.
But now the Uranian gods brought us, an affliction
    upon you,   80
forever there is fighting about your city, and men killed.
But bear up, nor mourn endlessly in your heart, for
    there is not
anything to be gained from grief for your son; you will
    never
bring him back; sooner you must go through yet another
    sorrow.'

    In answer to him again spoke aged Priam the godlike:
'Do not, beloved of Zeus, make me sit on a chair while
    Hektor
lies yet forlorn among the shelters; rather with all speed
give him back, so my eyes may behold him, and accept
    the ransom
we bring you, which is great. You may have joy of it,
    and go back
to the land of your own fathers, since once you have
    permitted me   90
to go on living myself and continue to look on the sunlight.'
    Then looking darkly at him spoke swift-footed
    Achilleus:
'No longer stir me up, old sir. I myself am minded
to give Hektor back to you. A messenger came to me
    from Zeus,
my mother, she who bore me, the daughter of the sea's
    ancient.
I know you, Priam, in my heart, and it does not escape me
that some god led you to the running ships of the
    Achaians.
For no mortal would dare come to our encampment, not
    even
one strong in youth. He could not get by the pickets, he
    could not
lightly unbar the bolt that secures our gateway. Therefore 100
you must not further make my spirit move in my sorrows,
for fear, old sir, I might not let you alone in my shelter,
suppliant as you are; and be guilty before the god's
    orders.'
    He spoke, and the old man was frightened and did as
    he told him.
The son of Peleus bounded to the door of the house like
    a lion,
nor went alone, but the two henchmen followed attending,
the hero Automedon and Alkimos, those whom Achilleus
honoured beyond all companions after Patroklos dead.
    These two
now set free from under the yoke the mules and the
    horses,
and led inside the herald, the old king's crier, and gave him 110
a chair to sit in, then from the smooth-polished mule
    wagon
lifted out the innumerable spoils for the head of Hektor,
but left inside it two great cloaks and a finespun tunic
to shroud the corpse in when they carried him home.
    Then Achilleus
called out to his serving-maids to wash the body and
    anoint it
all over; but take it first aside, since otherwise Priam
might see his son and in the heart's sorrow not hold in
    his anger
at the sight, and the deep heart in Achilleus be shaken
    to anger;
that he might not kill Priam and be guilty before the
    god's orders.
Then when the serving-maids had washed the corpse
    and anointed it   120
with olive oil, they threw a fair great cloak and a tunic
about him, and Achilleus himself lifted him and laid him

on a litter, and his friends helped him lift it to the
　　smooth-polished
mule wagon. He groaned then, and called by name on
　　his beloved companion:
'Be not angry with me, Patroklos, if you discover,
though you be in the house of Hades, that I gave back
　　great Hektor
to his loved father, for the ransom he gave me was not
　　unworthy.
I will give you your share of the spoils, as much as is
　　fitting.'
　　So spoke great Achilleus and went back into the shelter
and sat down on the elaborate couch from which he had
　　risen,　　　　　　　　　　　　　　　　　　　　　130
against the inward wall, and now spoke his word to Priam:
'Your son is given back to you, aged sir, as you asked it.
He lies on a bier. When dawn shows you yourself shall
　　see him
as you take him away. Now you and I must remember
　　our supper.
For even Niobe, she of the lovely tresses, remembered
to eat, whose twelve children were destroyed in her
　　palace,
six daughters, and six sons in the pride of their youth,
　　whom Apollo
killed with arrows from his silver bow, being angered
with Niobe, and shaft-showering Artemis killed the
　　daughters;
because Niobe likened herself to Leto of the fair
　　colouring　　　　　　　　　　　　　　　　　140
and said Leto had borne only two, she herself had borne
　　many;
but the two, though they were only two, destroyed all
　　those others.
Nine days long they lay in their blood, nor was there
　　anyone
to bury them, for the son of Kronos made stones out of
the people; but on the tenth day the Uranian gods
　　buried them.
But she remembered to eat when she was worn out with
　　weeping.
And now somewhere among the rocks, in the lonely
　　mountains,
in Sipylos, where they say is the resting place of the
　　goddesses
who are nymphs, and dance beside the waters of
　　Acheloios,
there, stone still, she broods on the sorrows that the
　　gods gave her.　　　　　　　　　　　　　　150
Come then, we also, aged magnificent sir, must remember
to eat, and afterwards you may take your beloved son
　　back
to Ilion, and mourn for him; and he will be much
　　lamented.'
　　So spoke fleet Achilleus and sprang to his feet and
　　slaughtered
a gleaming sheep, and his friends skinned it and
　　butchered it fairly,
and cut up the meat expertly into small pieces, and
　　spitted them,

and roasted all carefully and took off the pieces.
Automedon took the bread and set it out on the table
in fair baskets, while Achilleus served the meats. And
　　thereon
they put their hands to the good things that lay ready
　　before them.　　　　　　　　　　　　　　　160
But when they had put aside their desire for eating and
　　drinking,
Priam, son of Dardanos, gazed upon Achilleus,
　　wondering
at his size and beauty, for he seemed like an outright
　　vision
of gods. Achilleus in turn gazed on Dardanian Priam
and wondered, as he saw his brave looks and listened to
　　him talking.
But when they had taken their fill of gazing one on the
　　other,
first of the two to speak was the aged man, Priam the
　　godlike:
'Give me, beloved of Zeus, a place to sleep presently,
　　so that
we may even go to bed and take the pleasure of sweet
　　sleep.
For my eyes have not closed underneath my lids since
　　that time　　　　　　　　　　　　　　　170
when my son lost his life beneath your hands, but always
I have been grieving and brooding over my numberless
　　sorrows
and wallowed in the muck about my courtyard's enclosure.
Now I have tasted food again and have let the gleaming
wine go down my throat. Before, I had tasted nothing.'
　　He spoke, and Achilleus ordered his serving-maids and
　　companions
to make a bed in the porch's shelter and to lay upon it
fine underbedding of purple, and spread blankets above it
and fleecy robes to be an over-all covering. The
　　maid-servants
went forth from the main house, and in their hands held
　　torches,　　　　　　　　　　　　　　　　180
and set to work, and presently had two beds made.
　　Achilleus
of the swift feet now looked at Priam and said, sarcastic:
'Sleep outside, aged sir and good friend, for fear some
　　Achaian
might come in here on a matter of counsel, since they
　　keep coming
and sitting by me and making plans; as they are
　　supposed to.
But if one of these come through the fleeting black night
　　should notice you,
he would go straight and tell Agamemnon, shepherd of
　　the people,
and there would be delay in the ransoming of the body.
But come, tell me this and count off for me exactly
how many days you intend for the burial of great Hektor.　190
Tell me, so I myself shall stay still and hold back the
　　people.'
　　In answer to him again spoke aged Priam the godlike:
'If you are willing that we accomplish a complete
　　funeral

for great Hektor, this, Achilleus, is what you could do and give
me pleasure. For you know surely how we are penned in our city,
and wood is far to bring in from the hills, and the Trojans are frightened
badly. Nine days we would keep him in our palace and mourn him,
and bury him on the tenth day, and the people feast by him,
and on the eleventh day we would make the grave-barrow for him,
and on the twelfth day fight again; if so we must do.'
   Then in turn swift-footed brilliant Achilleus answered him:

'Then all this, aged Priam, shall be done as you ask it.
I will hold off our attack for as much time as you bid me.'
   So he spoke, and took the aged king by the right hand
at the wrist, so that his heart might have no fear. Then these two,
Priam and the herald who were both men of close counsel,
slept in the place outside the house, in the porch's shelter;
but Achilleus slept in the inward corner of the strong-built shelter,
and at his side lay Briseis of the fair colouring. . . . 200

HOMER

Selection from the *Odyssey*

The *Odyssey* is the story of the ten years of wandering by Odysseus, a warrior returning from the Trojan War. He is trying to return to his kingdom of Ithaca and be reunited with his faithful wife, Penelope. His odyssey is in fact a divine punishment for offending the Olympic deities by cleverly planning the fall of Troy through trickery with the Trojan Horse. Pretending to abandon their siege of Troy, the Greeks hid themselves inside a huge wooden horse that they artfully placed outside the city's gates, knowing the curious Trojans would find this "Greek gift" irresistible. The ruse worked, for the Trojans took the horse into Troy. By night, the Greeks crept from their hiding place and proceeded to utterly destroy the city, after which the Greek warriors sailed their separate ways back to their homeland.

Reading the Selection

This excerpt from Book XII of the *Odyssey* contains the first flashback in Western literature. In it, Odysseus tells his story (only three of his escapades are included here) from the time he left Troy until he arrived in the land of the Phaeacians, where he is welcomed by King Alcinous. This selection from the *Odyssey* emphasizes Odysseus's adventures and close brushes with death.

In the first part of Book XII (omitted here), Circe, a goddess, warns Odysseus of the dangers facing him and his crew once they leave her island. The excerpt opens with Odysseus returning to his ship after receiving Circe's advice. He prepares his men to withstand the alluring sounds of the Sirens but decides that he wants to listen to their enchanting songs. To make sure that he will not be tempted to land on the Sirens' island, he orders his crew to lash him to the mast and not release him no matter how much he pleads. Two further adventures await him and his men before they are out of danger. First, they have to sail their ship between Skylla, the beast who snatches men from their boats, and Charybdis, the swirling force that sucks ships into a whirlpool. Second, having maneuvered successfully through these dangers, they land on the island of Hyperion, the sun god. Going against Odysseus's warnings, his soldiers kill one of the sun god's oxen, thus laying a curse on themselves. Upon leaving the island, their ship is lost in a storm. Odysseus, the sole survivor, is washed ashore in the land of the Phaeacians and brought to King Alcinous's court. Here, at the end of Book XII, he finishes the tale of his adventures.

Homer writes more than an adventure story. He makes Odysseus, for all his faults, into a hero blessed with *arete,* or leadership qualities, including physical bravery, a keen wit, and a high regard for his servants. Above all, he has a deep resolve, come what may, to return to his devoted wife. Among the world's literary classics, the *Odyssey* is one of the few that celebrate the love of a husband and wife.

—m—

Book XII

. . . .

[']Then, going back on board my ship, I told my companions   1
also to go aboard, and to cast off the stern cables,
and quickly they went aboard the ship and sat to the oarlocks,
and sitting well in order dashed the oars in the gray sea;
but fair-haired Circe, the dread goddess who talks with mortals,
sent us an excellent companion, a following wind, filling
the sails, to carry from astern the ship with the dark prow.
We ourselves, over all the ship making fast the running gear,
sat there, and let the wind and the steersman hold her steady.
Then, sorrowful as I was, I spoke and told my companions: 10
"Friends, since it is not right for one or two of us only
to know the divinations that Circe, bright among goddesses,
gave me, so I will tell you, and knowing all we may either
die, or turn aside from death and escape destruction.
First of all she tells us to keep away from the magical
Sirens and their singing and their flowery meadow, but only
I, she said, was to listen to them, but you must tie me
hard in hurtful bonds, to hold me fast in position
upright against the mast, with the ropes' ends fastened around it;
but if I supplicate you and implore you to set me   20
free, then you must tie me fast with even more lashings."
    'So as I was telling all the details to my companions,
meanwhile the well-made ship was coming rapidly closer
to the Sirens' isle, for the harmless wind was driving her onward;
but immediately then the breeze dropped, and a windless
calm fell there, and some divinity stilled the tossing
waters. My companions stood up, and took the sails down,
and stowed them away in the hollow hull, and took their places
for rowing, and with their planed oarblades whitened the water.
Then I, taking a great wheel of wax, with the sharp bronze   30
cut a little piece off, and rubbed it together in my heavy
hands, and soon the wax grew softer, under the powerful
stress of the sun, and the heat and light of Hyperion's lordling.
One after another, I stopped the ears of all my companions,
and they then bound me hand and foot in the fast ship, standing

upright against the mast with the ropes' ends lashed around it,
and sitting then to row they dashed their oars in the gray sea.
But when we were as far from the land as a voice shouting
carries, lightly plying, the swift ship as it drew nearer
was seen by the Sirens, and they directed their sweet song toward us: 40
"Come this way, honored Odysseus, great glory of the Achaians,
and stay your ship, so that you can listen here to our singing;
for no one else has ever sailed past this place in his black ship
until he has listened to the honey-sweet voice that issues
from our lips; then goes on, well pleased, knowing more than ever
he did; for we know everything that the Argives and Trojans
did and suffered in wide Troy through the gods' despite.
Over all the generous earth we know everything that happens."
    'So they sang, in sweet utterance, and the heart within me
desired to listen, and I signaled my companions to set me   50
free, nodding with my brows, but they leaned on and rowed hard,
and Perimedes and Eurylochos, rising up, straightway
fastened me with even more lashings and squeezed me tighter.
But when they had rowed on past the Sirens, and we could no longer
hear their voices and lost the sound of their singing, presently
my eager companions took away from their ears the beeswax
with which I had stopped them. Then they set me free from my lashings.
    'But after we had left the island behind, the next thing
we saw was smoke, and a heavy surf, and we heard it thundering.
The men were terrified, and they let the oars fall out of   60
their hands, and these banged all about in the wash. The ship stopped
still, with the men no longer rowing to keep way on her.
Then I going up and down the ship urged on my companions,
standing beside each man and speaking to him in kind words:
    "Dear friends, surely we are not unlearned in evils.
This is no greater evil now than it was when the Cyclops

had us cooped in his hollow cave by force and violence,
but even there, by my courage and counsel and my
    intelligence,
we escaped away. I think that all this will be remembered
some day too. Then do as I say, let us all be won over.   70
Sit well, all of you, to your oarlocks, and dash your oars
    deep
into the breaking surf of the water, so in that way Zeus
might grant that we get clear of this danger and flee
    away from it.
For you, steersman, I have this order; so store it deeply
in your mind, as you control the steering oar of this
    hollow
ship; you must keep her clear from where the smoke
    and the breakers
are, and make hard for the sea rock lest, without your
    knowing,
she might drift that way, and you bring all of us into
    disaster."
    'So I spoke, and they quickly obeyed my words. I had not
spoken yet of Skylla, a plague that could not be dealt
    with,   80
for fear my companions might be terrified and give over
their rowing, and take cover inside the ship. For my part,
I let go from my mind the difficult instruction that Circe
had given me, for she told me not to be armed for
    combat;
but I put on my glorious armor and, taking up two long
spears in my hands, I stood bestriding the vessel's
    foredeck
at the prow, for I expected Skylla of the rocks to appear
    first
from that direction, she who brought pain to my
    companions.
I could not make her out anywhere, and my eyes grew
    weary
from looking everywhere on the misty face of the sea
    rock.   90
    'So we sailed up the narrow strait lamenting. On one
    side
was Skylla, and on the other side was shining Charybdis,
who made her terrible ebb and flow of the sea's water.
When she vomited it up, like a caldron over a strong fire,
the whole sea would boil up in turbulence, and the foam
    flying
spattered the pinnacles of the rocks in either direction;
but when in turn again she sucked down the sea's salt
    water,
the turbulence showed all the inner sea, and the rock
    around it
groaned terribly, and the ground showed at the sea's
    bottom,
black with sand; and green fear seized upon my
    companions.   100
We in fear of destruction kept our eyes on Charybdis,
but meanwhile Skylla out of the hollow vessel snatched six
of my companions, the best of them for strength and
    hands' work,
and when I turned to look at the ship, with my other
    companions,

I saw their feet and hands from below, already lifted
high above me, and they cried out to me and called me
by name, the last time they ever did it, in heart's sorrow.
And as a fisherman with a very long rod, on a jutting
rock, will cast his treacherous bait for the little fishes,
and sinks the horn of a field-ranging ox into the water,   110
then hauls them up and throws them on the dry land,
    gasping
and struggling, so they gasped and struggled as they
    were hoisted
up the cliff. Right in her doorway she ate them up. They
    were screaming
and reaching out their hands to me in this horrid
    encounter.
That was the most pitiful scene that these eyes have
    looked on
in my sufferings as I explored the routes over the water.
    'Now when we had fled away from the rocks and
    dreaded Charybdis
and Skylla, next we made our way to the excellent island
of the god, where ranged the handsome wide-browed
    oxen, and many
fat flocks of sheep, belonging to the Sun God, Hyperion.   120
While I was on the black ship, still out on the open
    water,
I heard the lowing of the cattle as they were driven
home, and the bleating of sheep, and my mind was
    struck by the saying
of the blind prophet, Teiresias the Theban, and also
Aiaian Circe. Both had told me many times over
to avoid the island of Helios who brings joy to mortals.
Then sorrowful as I was I spoke and told my companions:
"Listen to what I say, my companions, though you are
    suffering
evils, while I tell you the prophecies of Teiresias
and Aiaian Circe. Both have told me many times over   130
to avoid the island of Helios who brings joy to mortals,
for there they spoke of the most dreadful disaster that
    waited
for us. So drive the black ship onward, and pass the island."
    'So I spoke, and the inward heart in them was broken.
At once Eurylochos answered me with a bitter saying:
"You are a hard man, Odysseus. Your force is greater,
your limbs never wear out. You must be made all of iron,
when you will not let your companions, worn with hard
    work and wanting
sleep, set foot on this land, where if we did, on the seagirt
island we could once more make ready a greedy dinner;   140
but you force us to blunder along just as we are through
    the running
night, driven from the island over the misty face of the
    water.
In the nights the hard stormwinds arise, and they bring
    damage
to ships. How could any of us escape sheer destruction,
if suddenly there rises the blast of a storm from the bitter
blowing of the South Wind or the West Wind, who
    beyond others
hammer a ship apart, in despite of the gods, our masters?
But now let us give way to black night's persuasion; let us

make ready our evening meal, remaining close by our
    fast ship,
and at dawn we will go aboard and put forth onto the
    wide sea." 150
    'So spoke Eurylochos, and my other companions
    assented.
I saw then what evil the divinity had in mind for us,
and so I spoke aloud to him and addressed him in
    winged words:
"Eurylochos, I am only one man. You force me to it.
But come then all of you, swear a strong oath to me, that if
we come upon some herd of cattle or on some great flock
of sheep, no one of you in evil and reckless action
will slaughter any ox or sheep. No, rather than this, eat
at your pleasure of the food immortal Circe provided."
    'So I spoke, and they all swore me the oath that I
    asked them. 160
But after they had sworn me the oath and made an end
    of it,
we beached the well-made ship inside of the hollow
    harbor,
close to sweet water, and my companions disembarked
    also
from the ship, and expertly made the evening meal
    ready.
But when they had put away their desire for eating and
    drinking,
they remembered and they cried for their beloved
    companions
whom Skylla had caught out of the hollow ship and
    eaten,
and on their crying a quiet sleep descended; but after
the third part of the night had come, and the star changes,
Zeus the cloud gatherer let loose on us a gale that
    blustered 170
in a supernatural storm, and huddled under the cloud
    scuds
land alike and the great water. Night sprang from heaven.
But when the young Dawn showed again with her rosy
    fingers,
we berthed our ship, dragging her into a hollow sea
    cave
where the nymphs had their beautiful dancing places
    and sessions.
Then I held an assembly and spoke my opinion before
    them:
"Friends, since there is food and drink stored in the fast
    ship,
let us then keep our hands off the cattle, for fear that
    something
may befall us. These are the cattle and fat sheep of a
    dreaded
god, Helios, who sees all things and listens to all things." 180
    'So I spoke, and the proud heart in them was persuaded.
But the South Wind blew for a whole month long, nor
    did any other
wind befall after that, but only the South and the East
    Wind.
As long as they still had food to eat and red wine, the
    men kept

their hands off the cattle, striving as they were for
    sustenance. Then, when
all the provisions that had been in the ship had given
out, they turned to hunting, forced to it, and went
    ranging
after fish and birds, anything that they could lay hands on,
and with curved hooks, for the hunger was exhausting
    their stomachs.
Then I went away along the island in order 190
to pray to the gods, if any of them might show me some
    course
to sail on, but when, crossing the isle, I had left my
    companions
behind, I washed my hands, where there was a place
    sheltered
from the wind, and prayed to all the gods whose hold is
    Olympos;
but what they did was to shed a sweet sleep on my
    eyelids,
and Eurylochos put an evil counsel before his
    companions:
"Listen to what I say, my companions, though you are
    suffering
evils. All deaths are detestable for wretched mortals,
but hunger is the sorriest way to die and encounter
fate. Come then, let us cut out the best of Helios' cattle, 200
and sacrifice them to the immortals who hold wide
    heaven,
and if we ever come back to Ithaka, land of our fathers,
presently we will build a rich temple to the Sun God
    Helios
Hyperion, and store it with dedications, many
and good. But if, in anger over his high-horned cattle,
he wishes to wreck our ship, and the rest of the gods
    stand by him,
I would far rather gulp the waves and lose my life in
    them
once for all, than be pinched to death on this desolate
    island."
    'So spoke Eurylochos, and the other companions
    assented.
At once, cutting out from near at hand the best of Helios' 210
cattle; for the handsome broad-faced horn-curved oxen
were pasturing there, not far from the dark-prowed ship;
    driving
these, they stationed themselves around them, and made
    their prayers
to the gods, pulling tender leaves from a deep-leaved oak
    tree;
for they had no white barley left on the strong-benched
    vessel.
When they had made their prayer and slaughtered the
    oxen and skinned them,
they cut away the meat from the thighs and wrapped
    them in fat,
making a double fold, and laid shreds of flesh upon
    them;
and since they had no wine to pour on the burning
    offerings,
they made a libation of water, and roasted all of the entrails; 220

but when they had burned the thigh pieces and tasted
the vitals,
they cut all the remainder into pieces and spitted them.
'At that time the quiet sleep was lost from my eyelids,
and I went back down to my fast ship and the sand of
the seashore,
but on my way, as I was close to the oar-swept vessel,
the pleasant savor of cooking meat came drifting around
me,
and I cried out my grief aloud to the gods immortal:
"Father Zeus, and you other everlasting and blessed
gods, with a pitiless sleep you lulled me, to my confusion,
and my companions staying here dared a deed that was
monstrous."   230
'Lampetia of the light robes ran swift with the message
to Hyperion the Sun God, that we had killed his cattle,
and angered at the heart he spoke forth among the
immortals:
"Father Zeus, and you other everlasting and blessed
gods, punish the companions of Odysseus, son of Laertes;
for they outrageously killed my cattle, in whom I always
delighted, on my way up into the starry heaven,
or when I turned back again from heaven toward earth.
Unless
these are made to give me just recompense for my cattle,
I will go down to Hades and give my light to the dead
men."   240
'Then in turn Zeus who gathers the clouds answered
him:
"Helios, shine on as you do, among the immortals
and mortal men, all over the grain-giving earth. For my
part
I will strike these men's fast ship midway on the open
wine-blue sea with a shining bolt and dash it to pieces."
'All this I heard afterward from fair-haired Kalypso,
and she told me she herself had heard it from the guide,
Hermes.
'But when I came back again to the ship and the seashore,
they all stood about and blamed each other, but we were
not able
to find any remedy, for the oxen were already dead. The
next thing   250
was that the gods began to show forth portents before us.
The skins crawled, and the meat that was stuck on the
spits bellowed,
both roast and raw, and the noise was like the lowing of
cattle.
'Six days thereafter my own eager companions feasted
on the cattle of Helios the Sun God, cutting the best ones
out; but when Zeus the son of Kronos established the
seventh
day, then at last the wind ceased from its stormy blowing,
and presently we went aboard and put forth on the
wide sea,
and set the mast upright and hoisted the white sails on it.
'But after we had left the island and there was no more   260
land in sight, but only the sky and the sea, then Kronian
Zeus drew on a blue-black cloud, and settled it over
the hollow ship, and the open sea was darkened beneath it;
and she ran on, but not for a very long time, as suddenly

a screaming West Wind came upon us, stormily blowing,
and the blast of the stormwind snapped both the
forestays that were holding
the mast, and the mast went over backwards, and all the
running gear
collapsed in the wash; and at the stern of the ship the
mast pole
crashed down on the steersman's head and pounded to
pieces
all the bones of his head, so that he like a diver   270
dropped from the high deck, and the proud life left his
bones there.
Zeus with thunder and lightning together crashed on our
vessel,
and, struck by the thunderbolt of Zeus, she spun in a
circle,
and all was full of brimstone. My men were thrown in
the water,
and bobbing like sea crows they were washed away on
the running
waves all around the black ship, and the god took away
their homecoming.
'But I went on my way through the vessel, to where
the high seas
had worked the keel free out of the hull, and the bare
keel floated
on the swell, which had broken the mast off at the keel; yet
still there was a backstay made out of oxhide fastened   280
to it. With this I lashed together both keel and mast, then
rode the two of them, while the deadly stormwinds
carried me.
'After this the West Wind ceased from its stormy
blowing,
and the South Wind came swiftly on, bringing to my
spirit
grief that I must measure the whole way back to Charybdis.
All that night I was carried along, and with the sun rising
I came to the sea rock of Skylla, and dreaded Charybdis.
At this time Charybdis sucked down the sea's salt water,
but I reached high in the air above me, to where the tall
fig tree
grew, and caught hold of it and clung like a bat; there
was no   290
place where I could firmly brace my feet, or climb up it,
for the roots of it were far from me, and the branches
hung out
far, big and long branches that overshadowed Charybdis.
Inexorably I hung on, waiting for her to vomit
the keel and mast back up again. I longed for them, and
they came
late; at the time when a man leaves the law court, for
dinner,
after judging the many disputes brought him by litigious
young men;
that was the time it took the timbers to appear from
Charybdis.
Then I let go my hold with hands and feet, and dropped
off,
and came crashing down between and missing the two
long timbers,   300

but I mounted these, and with both hands I paddled my
  way out.
But the Father of Gods and men did not let Skylla see me
again, or I could not have escaped from sheer destruction.
    'From there I was carried along nine days, and on the
      tenth night
the gods brought me to the island Ogygia, home of Kalypso

with the lovely hair, a dreaded goddess who talks with
  mortals.
She befriended me and took care of me. Why tell the
  rest of
this story again, since yesterday in your house I told it
to you and your majestic wife? It is hateful to me
to tell a story over again, when it has been well told.'   310

HESIOD

Selection from *Works and Days*

The epic poet Hesiod (sometime between 750 and 650 B.C.) spent his entire life in Boeotia, a thinly populated agricultural area on the Greek mainland north of Athens. In eighth-century Boeotia, poets followed in Homer's footsteps, using the epic form with its formulaic meter and rhythm, but shunning the Homeric focus on a spellbinding tale. Instead, they wrote verses with loosely connected themes, such as mythological handbooks and catalogues of names and legends of male and female mortals and divinities, though they usually managed to introduce an individualistic note by commenting on religion and politics. Hesiod belonged to the Boeotian school, and nothing could be more different from his poetic world than that of Homer. Homer spoke for the Greek aristocracy of Asia Minor; Hesiod was basically a Boeotian peasant. In Classical times, the Greeks looked down on the Boeotians as uncultured and consequently honored Homer more than Hesiod. Nonetheless, Hesiod's books—*Theogony* and *Works and Days*—are masterworks of epic poetry that offer valuable insight into religion and everyday life at the dawn of Greek civilization.

Homer, of course, was the first theologian of Greece, though he did not invent the system of Olympic deities. The Greeks had been worshiping these gods and goddesses for at least four hundred years before he appeared on the scene. Hesiod clarified Homer's theology by focusing on the deities' origins and relationships. In the *Theogony*, Hesiod traces the evolution of the deities, beginning with the first family of gods and goddesses, continuing through fights between successive dynasties, and culminating with Zeus and his generation who reign from Mount Olympus in northern Greece. He also spells out the proper respect toward immortals, warning his readers against weakness, especially the sin of excessive pride, or hubris.

In *Works and Days*, Hesiod turns to secular matters, although he still offers moral advice. This advice takes the form of proverbs and fables, similar to the Wisdom Literature of Mesopotamia, Egypt, and the Old Testament. Similarly, he plays prophet and speaks for Zeus, predicting that evildoers, particularly those in high places, who abuse the less fortunate will be punished. Hesiod also gives useful advice: on planting, plowing, and harvesting in tune with his own farmer's calendar; on sailing the seas in order to sell one's crops; and on choosing a wife. Throughout *Works and Days*, Hesiod's unique voice is heard admonishing his worthless brother, Perses, on the need to work hard and be honest and self-reliant—the first proclamation in the West of what is called the gospel of labor.

Reading the Selection

Work and Days begins with a hymn in praise of Zeus. Next, Hesiod contrasts two kinds of strife, one to stir up evil and the other to inspire dynamic struggle, and then offers two myths to illustrate the two. The first myth, illustrative of strife that stirs up evil, involves Prometheus, who steals fire from heaven and gives it to mortals. Prometheus's theft brings civilization but also prompts Zeus's revenge, which becomes the second myth. Zeus's revenge, exemplary of strife that inspires dynamic struggle, results in the creation of Pandora (the Gift of All), the first woman. Ignoring a divine command, Pandora opens a forbidden jar and releases misery and disease on humankind, thereby forcing all mortals to work to avoid sickness and despair. In the end, Zeus's will prevails, although work is both a curse and a blessing.

In the "Five Ages of Man" passage, Hesiod's teaching is clear: human morals have declined over time. This decline may be compared to the way metals are valued, ranging from gold to iron. The poet, much to his dismay, lives in the Age of Iron, when mortals must work by day and be subject to anguish at night. In this bleak age, he sees only pain and suffering: people quarrel continuously, children dishonor their parents, and the wicked prosper and injure the good.

—⁑—

And now with art and skill I'll summarize 1
Another tale, which you should take to heart,
Of how both gods and men began the same.
The gods, who live on Mount Olympus, first
Fashioned a golden race of mortal men;
These lived in the reign of Kronos, king of heaven,
And like the gods they lived with happy hearts
Untouched by work or sorrow. Vile old age
Never appeared, but always lively-limbed,
Far from all ills, they feasted happily. 10
Death came to them as sleep, and all good things
Were theirs; ungrudgingly, the fertile land
Gave up her fruits unasked. Happy to be
At peace, they lived with every want supplied,
[Rich in their flocks, dear to the blessed gods.]

And then this race was hidden in the ground.
But still they live as spirits of the earth,
Holy and good, guardians who keep off harm,
Givers of wealth: this kingly right is theirs.
The gods, who live on Mount Olympus, next 20
Fashioned a lesser, silver race of men:
Unlike the gold in stature or in mind.
A child was raised at home a hundred years
And played, huge baby, by his mother's side.
When they were grown and reached their prime, they
     lived
Brief, anguished lives, from foolishness, for they
Could not control themselves, but recklessly
Injured each other and forsook the gods;
They did not sacrifice, as all tribes must, but left
The holy altars bare. And, angry, Zeus 30
The son of Kronos, hid this race away,
For they dishonoured the Olympian gods.

The earth then hid this second race, and they
Are called the spirits of the underworld,
Inferior to the gold, but honoured, too.
And Zeus the father made a race of bronze,
Sprung from the ash tree, worse than the silver race,
But strange and full of power. And they loved
The groans and violence of war; they ate
No bread; their hearts were flinty-hard; they were 40
Terrible men; their strength was great, their arms
And shoulders and their limbs invincible.
Their weapons were of bronze, their houses bronze;
Their tools were bronze: black iron was not known.
They died by their own hands, and nameless, went
To Hades' chilly house. Although they were

Great soldiers, they were captured by black Death,
And left the shining brightness of the sun.

But when this race was covered by the earth,
The son of Kronos made another, fourth, 50
Upon the fruitful land, more just and good,
A godlike race of heroes, who are called
The demi-gods—the race before our own.
Foul wars and dreadful battles ruined some;
Some sought the flocks of Oedipus, and died
In Cadmus' land, at seven-gated Thebes;
And some, who crossed the open sea in ships,
For fair-haired Helen's sake, were killed at Troy.
These men were covered up in death, but Zeus
The son of Kronos gave the others life 60
And homes apart from mortals, at Earth's edge.
And there they live a carefree life, beside
The whirling Ocean, on the Blessed Isles.
Three times a year the blooming, fertile earth
Bears honeyed fruits for them, the happy ones.
[And Kronos is their king, far from the gods,
For Zeus released him from his bonds, and these,
The race of heroes, well deserve their fame.

Far-seeing Zeus then made another race,
The fifth, who live now on the fertile earth.] 70
I wish I were not of this race, that I
Had died before, or had not yet been born.
This is the race of iron. Now, by day,
Men work and grieve unceasingly; by night,
They waste away and die. The gods will give
Harsh burdens, but will mingle in some good;
Zeus will destroy this race of mortal men,
When babies shall be born with greying hair.
Father will have no common bond with son,
Neither will guest with host, nor friend with friend; 80
The brother-love of past days will be gone.
Men will dishonour parents, who grow old
Too quickly, and will blame and criticize
With cruel words. Wretched and godless, they
Refusing to repay their bringing up,
Will cheat their aged parents of their due.
Men will destroy the towns of other men.
The just, the good, the man who keeps his word
Will be despised, but men will praise the bad
And insolent. Might will be Right, and shame 90
Will cease to be. Men will do injury
To better men by speaking crooked words
And adding lying oaths; and everywhere

Harsh-voiced and sullen-faced and loving harm,
Envy will walk along with wretched men.
Last, to Olympus from the broad-pathed Earth,
Hiding their loveliness in robes of white,

To join the gods, abandoning mankind,
Will go the spirits Righteousness and Shame.
And only grievous troubles will be left
For men, and no defence against our wrongs.

100

SAPPHO

Poems

Sappho is unquestionably Greece's finest composer of lyric poetry, which originally meant verses sung to the music of a lyre (a stringed instrument) but later was applied to poetry characterized by musical qualities, subjectivism, and sensual words. Ancient writers, including Plato (see *The Republic* and *Phaedo*), hailed her as the master of lyric poetry; modern critics tend to do the same. Unlike epic poetry, in which the author speaks for an entire community (see Homer's *Iliad* and *Odyssey,* and Vergil's *Aeneid*), lyric poetry focuses on the speaker's personal, private thoughts. Sappho's autobiographical works helped to make lyric verse popular in her day, and this genre has dominated Western poetry ever since (see Theocritus's *Idylls,* Catullus's poems, Horace's *Odes,* Ovid's *Metamorphoses,* and Petrarch's *Canzoniere*).

Lyric poetry flowered during Greece's Archaic Age (800–480 B.C.), a tumultuous period of change on many fronts. Coming after three centuries of cultural breakdown, the Archaic Age was a time of rebirth; it was marked by the growth of trade and the spread of Greek peoples around the shores of the Mediterranean and Black seas. The old hereditary kingships gave way to independent city-states ruled by landed aristocrats. In the city-states, the invention of money permitted the rise of a monied class, a group of savers and lenders who both challenged the power of the aristocrats and enslaved poorer debtors. These events embittered social relations and sparked class warfare, which led to new types of regimes, such as tyranny, and expansion of voting rights to ordinary male citizens. The shift from epic to lyric poetry in the sixth century B.C. coincided with these changes in the city-states, where the rising democratic spirit encouraged a variety of voices to be heard.

The meager facts of Sappho's life (ca. 600 B.C.) reflect this turbulent age. Her home was the island of Lesbos in the Aegean, an Archaic cultural center that produced two well-known lyric poets before her birth. An aristocrat, she experienced exile twice—the penalty for being related to the landed elite who were overthrown by a coalition of merchants and poor citizens. Eventually, she opened a school on Lesbos for aristocratic young women, to whom she taught poetry, music, and dancing.

Reading the Selections

These poems (actually sections taken from extant works, which are fragmented in the extreme and number only about 600 lines), show that love was never far from Sappho's thoughts. Addressed to her circle, this poetry is private, filled with intimate expression. The first two fragments offer burning descriptions of erotic feelings and thus give a glimpse into this world. In the first, the speaker laments young Anactoria, "far from us here": "The vivid movement of her face—I'd rather see [than any other sight on earth]." In the second, the speaker feels paralyzed by the actions of an unnamed woman friend who flirts with a youth: "My voice when I see you suddenly near / Refuses to come . . . I see not a thing / With my eyes, . . ."

In "Let's Not Pretend," she speaks of love and old age. Gray and wrinkled, she likens herself to Tithonos, the mythic hero whom the gods gave eternal life but not eternal youth; just as Tithonos, ever older and feebler, makes love to the goddess Dawn each day, so does Sappho, grown old herself, continue to seek beauty and light.

Sappho's poetic legacy lives on in today's confessional verses and most especially in popular love songs.

—⚯—

To a Soldier's Wife in Sardis: Anactoria

A cavalry corps, a column of men,   1
A flotilla in line, is the finest thing
In this rich world to see—for some . . . but for me
   It's the person you love.
There's nothing more easy than this to prove:
Helen whose beauty far outshone
The rest of man's chose to desert
   The best of men:

Willingly sailed away to Troy;
Thought nothing of child and nothing of
      fond   10
Parents, but was herself led astray
   By a love faraway;

(For woman is always easy to bend
The moment she's bent on her heart's desire.)
Now Anactoria's in my mind,
   Far from us here.

The way she walks, her lovable style,
The vivid movement of her face—
I'd rather see than Lydian horse
   And glitter of mail.   20

We cannot, alas, I know, have the best,
Yet to wish for a part of the past
Once shared is better for man at least
   Than that we forget.

—⚯—

I More Than Envy Him

He is a god in my eyes, that man,   1
Given to sit in front of you
And close to himself sweetly to hear
   The sound of you speaking.

Your magical laughter—this I swear—
Batters my heart—my breast astir—
My voice when I see you suddenly near
   Refuses to come.

My tongue breaks up and a delicate fire
Runs through my flesh; I see not a thing
With my eyes, and all that I hear   10
   In my ears is a hum.

The sweat runs down, a shuddering takes
Me in every part and pale as the drying
Grasses, then, I think I am near
   The moment of dying

—⚯—

Let's Not Pretend

No, Children, do not delude me.   1
You mock the good gifts of the Muses
When you say: "Dear Sappho we'll crown you,
Resonant player,
First on the clear sweet lyre. . . ."
Do you not see how I alter:
My skin with its aging,
My black hair gone white,
My legs scarcely carrying
Me, who went dancing   10
More neatly than fawns once
(Neatest of creatures)?

No, no one can cure it; keep beauty from going,
And *I* cannot help it.
God himself cannot do what cannot be done.
So age follows after and catches
Everything living.
Even rosy-armed Eos, the Dawn,
Who ushers in morning to the ends of the earth,
Could not save from the grasp of old age   20
Her lover immortal Tithonus.
And I too, I know, must waste away.
Yet for me—listen well—
My delight is the exquisite.
Yes, for me,
Glitter and sunlight and love
Are one society.
So I shall not go creeping away
To die in the dark:
I shall go on living with you,   30
Loving and loved.

3

CLASSICAL GREEK CIVILIZATION
The Hellenic Age

ARISTOPHANES

Selection from *Lysistrata*

Lysistrata is a hilarious work by Aristophanes (ca. 445–388 B.C.), the founder of comedy. Still fresh after twenty-three centuries, *Lysistrata* belongs to the first phase of Greek comedy called Old Comedy, which originated in fertility rites honoring the god Dionysus. Comedy became official in the early fifth century B.C. (ca. 480–470), when civic leaders added it to Athens' Great Dionysia, the premier festival of the wine god.

It is Aristophanes who defines Old Comedy, because no other plays except for his eleven (out of the forty-four total he was purported to have written) survive this period. These first comedies featured a comic hero driven by a madcap idea, typically of a political nature; a chorus tried to foil the hero's plan and also represented the playwright's views. The style of these plays was seemingly spontaneous and in tune with life's passing parade—similar to that of their modern descendant, *Saturday Night Live.* There were no sacred cows. All was grist for the dramatist's mill: venal politicians, social upstarts, sexual misfits, heads-in-the-clouds thinkers, even the deities. Old Comedy often used burlesque and obscenity, signs of its Dionysiac roots. Comic devices included slapstick, pratfalls, naughty words and situations, animal sounds, and actors costumed grotesquely with padded bellies or rumps. Unlike tragedy with its idealism, comedy was down-to-earth and as realistic as possible.

Greek comedy was born in Athens during Greece's Hellenic Age (479–323 B.C.), a golden age marked by cultural explosion and bloody warfare among rival city-states. Athens, to its citizens, became "the model for Greece" (the words of the Athenian leader Pericles from his Funeral Oration), as Athenian writers and artists created or brought to perfection a variety of creative forms and amassed a legacy of masterpieces that later generations judged as classics—the best. In literature, besides comedy, this age produced tragedy (see Sophocles' *Oedipus the King*), history (see Thucydides' *History of the Peloponnesian War*), and reflective philosophy (see Plato's *Republic* and *Phaedo,* and Aristotle's *Poetics*). In these new genres, the history of Athens asserted itself.

Lysistrata was first staged during the Peloponnesian War (431–404 B.C.), the prolonged struggle between Athens and Sparta, which slowly tore the Greek world apart. The year was 411 B.C., a time in Athens of military loss and impending revolt of aristocrats against the ruling democracy. Uneasy about the drift of events, Aristophanes used this play to mock war and the men who wage it.

Reading the Selection

Seemingly disillusioned with his own gender, Aristophanes in *Lysistrata* sides with women, claiming that only they can save Greece from war's stupidity and bloodshed. The play's heroine, Lysistrata ("Dissolver of Armies"), is a matron who convinces the women of Greece to refrain from sexual activity with their mates until the men agree to peace. Much of the play consists of sexual innuendoes and dirty jokes, made at the expense of the forlorn males who miss contact with their mates. Sexual harmony and civic peace are finally restored to Greece, but only after Lysistrata reminds the men of their shared kinship, history, and religion. Not a feminist, the aristocratic Aristophanes in this play speaks for Athenian conservatives, who were anti-empire and pro-peace.

It is enlightening to compare Greek ideas of sexuality in *Lysistrata* with those of early Christians, since both are part of the ancient world's legacy to the West. Early Christians tied sexuality to original sin (see St. Augustine's *Confessions*), making sex an emblem of human wickedness. In contrast, Greeks saw sexuality as joyous, even healthy; sex was a common ground—the source of joy and laughter.

—ᴍ—

. . . .

MAGISTRATE.   Foremost and first I would wish to inquire of them,   1
  what is this silly disturbance about?
Why have ye ventured to seize the Acropolis,
  locking the gates and barring us out?
LYSISTRATA.   Keeping the silver securely in custody,
  lest for its sake ye continue the war.
MAGISTRATE.   What, is the war for the sake of the silver, then?
LYSISTRATA.   Yes; and all other disputes that there are.
Why is Peisander for ever embroiling us,
  why do the rest of our officers feel   10
Always a pleasure in strife and disturbances?
  Simply to gain an occasion to steal.
Act as they please for the future, the treasury
  never a penny shall yield them, I vow.
MAGISTRATE.   How, may I ask, will you hinder their getting it?
LYSISTRATA.   We will ourselves be the Treasurers now.
MAGISTRATE.   You, woman, you be the treasurers?
LYSISTRATA.   Certainly.
  Ah, you esteem us unable, perchance!
Are we not skilled in domestic economy,   20
  do we not manage the household finance?
MAGISTRATE.   O, that is different.
LYSISTRATA.   Why is it different?
MAGISTRATE.   This is required for the fighting, my dear.
LYSISTRATA.   Well, but the fighting itself isn't requisite.
MAGISTRATE.   Only, without it, we're ruined, I fear.
LYSISTRATA.   *We* will deliver you.
MAGISTRATE.   You will deliver us!
LYSISTRATA.   Truly we will.
MAGISTRATE.   What a capital notion!   30
LYSISTRATA.   Whether you like it or not, we'll deliver you.
MAGISTRATE.   Impudent hussy!

LYSISTRATA.   You seem in commotion.
  Nevertheless we will do as we promise you.
MAGISTRATE.   That were a terrible shame, by Demeter.
LYSISTRATA.   Friend, we must save you.
MAGISTRATE.   But how if I wish it not?
LYSISTRATA.   That will but make our resolve the completer.
MAGISTRATE.   Fools! what on earth can possess you to meddle with
  matters of war, and matters of peace?   40
LYSISTRATA.   Well, I will tell you the reason.
MAGISTRATE.   And speedily,
  else you will rue it.
LYSISTRATA.   Then listen, and cease
  Clutching and clenching your fingers so angrily;
  keep yourself peaceable.
MAGISTRATE.   Hanged if I can;
  Such is the rage that I feel at your impudence.
STRATYLLIS.   Then it is *you* that will rue it, my man.
MAGISTRATE.   Croak your own fate, you ill-omened antiquity.   50

(*To* LYSISTRATA.) *You* be the spokeswoman, lady.

LYSISTRATA.   I will.
  Think of our old moderation and gentleness,
  think how we bore with your pranks, and were still,
All through the days of your former pugnacity,
  all through the war that is over and spent:
Not that (be sure) we approved of your policy;
  never our griefs you allowed us to vent.
Well we perceived your mistakes and mismanagement.
  Often at home on our housekeeping cares,   60
Often we heard of some foolish proposal you
  made for conducting the public affairs.
Then would we question you mildly and pleasantly,
  inwardly grieving, but outwardly gay;
Husband, how goes it abroad? we would ask of him;
  what have ye done in Assembly to-day?

What would ye write on the side of the Treaty stone?
   Husband says angrily, What's that to you?
You, hold your tongue! And I held it accordingly.
STRATYLLIS.   That is a thing which I *never* would do!   70
MAGISTRATE.   Ma'am, if you hadn't, you'd soon have
   repented it.
LYSISTRATA.   Therefore I held it, and spake not a word.
   Soon of another tremendous absurdity,
      wilder and worse than the former we heard.
   Husband, I say, with a tender solicitude,
      Why have ye passed such a foolish decree?
   Vicious, moodily, glaring askance at me,
      Stick to your spinning, my mistress, says he,
   Else you will speedily find it the worse for you,
      War is the care and the business of men!   80
MAGISTRATE.   Zeus! 'twas a worthy reply, and an
   excellent!
LYSISTRATA.   What! you unfortunate, shall we not then,
   Then, when we see you perplexed and incompetent,
      shall we not tender advice to the State?
   So when aloud in the streets and the thoroughfares
      sadly we heard you bewailing of late,
   Is there a Man to defend and deliver us?
      No, says another, *there's none in the land;*
   Then by the Women assembled in conference
      jointly a great Revolution was planned,   90
   Hellas to save from her grief and perplexity.
      Where is the use of a longer delay?
   Shift for the future our parts and our characters;
      you, as the women, in silence obey;
   We, as the men, will harangue and provide for you;
      then shall the State be triumphant again,
   Then shall we do what is best for the citizens.
MAGISTRATE.   Women to do what is best for the men!
   That were a shameful reproach and unbearable!
LYSISTRATA.   Silence, old gentleman.   100
MAGISTRATE.   Silence for *you?*
   Stop for a wench with a wimple enfolding her?
      No, by the Powers, may I *die* if I do!
LYSISTRATA.   Do not, my pretty one, do not, I pray,
   Suffer my wimple to stand in the way.

Here, take it, and wear it, and gracefully tie it,
   Enfolding it over your head, and be quiet.
      Now to your task.
CALONICE.   Here is an excellent spindle to pull.
MYRRHINA.   Here is a basket for carding the wool.   110
LYSISTRATA.   Now, to your task.
   Haricots chawing up, petticoats drawing up,
   Off to your carding, your combing, your trimming,
   War is the care and the business of women.

(During the foregoing lines the WOMEN *have been arraying
the* MAGISTRATE *in the garb and with the apparatus of a
spinning-woman: just as below, they bedeck him in the
habiliments of a corpse.)*

CHORUS OF WOMEN.   Up, up, and leave the pitchers
      there,
      and on, resolved and eager,
   Our own allotted part to bear
      in this illustrious leaguer.

   I will dance with resolute, tireless feet all day;
   My limbs shall never grow faint, my strength
      give way;   120
   I will march all lengths with the noble hearts and the
      true,
   For theirs is the ready wit and the patriot hand,
   And womanly grace, and courage to dare and do,
      And Love of our own bright land.

   Children of stiff and intractable grandmothers,
      heirs of the stinging viragoes that bore you,
   On, with an eager, unyielding tenacity,
      wind in your sails, and the haven before you.
LYSISTRATA.   Only let Love, the entrancing, the fanciful,
      only let Queen Aphrodite to-day   130
   Breathe on our persons a charm and a tenderness,
      lend us their own irresistible sway,
   Drawing the men to admire us and long for us;
      then shall the war everlastingly cease,
   Then shall the people revere us and honour us,
      givers of Joy, and givers of Peace.

SOPHOCLES

Oedipus the King

Sophocles' *Oedipus the King* is the most famous tragedy of antiquity. When first staged (about 430 B.C.) in Athens, it was awarded first prize—the civic honor voted by judges for reasons as political and social as they were aesthetic. In the fourth century B.C. it was used by Aristotle as the ground for his analysis of tragedy in the *Poetics*, the West's earliest book of literary criticism. In modern times, it has come to mean the perfect tragedy.

Tragedy (Greek, "goat song") developed from the choral odes sung to the rural god Dionysus. In sixth-century B.C. Athens, a tyrant introduced this god's cult to the city and made the staging of tragedies part of the Great Dionysia. The coming of democracy to Athens (after 508 B.C.) made these plays even more popular, as people of all classes formed the audience (though it is uncertain if women were present). The Hellenic Age—with Persia in retreat and Athens as the center of Greece—saw the flowering of this genre in the works of three native Athenians: Aeschylus (ca. 525–456 B.C.), Sophocles (ca. 496–406 B.C.), and Euripides (ca. 480–406 B.C.).

Tragedy was basically political in that it addressed the city-state, or its metaphorical equivalent in the audience at the Great Dionysia. Tragedians wrote for this community, speaking as citizens to citizens. A city leader chose three dramatists to present four plays each, and other officials appointed wealthy citizens to pay production costs. The spectators were seated according to tribes, thus mapping the city's political structure. A panel of ten judges was chosen, one from each tribe. Before the plays, the city scored propaganda points by parading orphans of soldiers killed in service and welcoming foreign emissaries. In sum, the drama was the centerpiece of a rite devoted to reinforcing community cohesion.

At first, tragedy (like comedy) had two distinct elements, the actors and the chorus, symbolic of opposing forces in the city-state. In political terms, the actors symbolized individualism (a democratic idea), and the chorus stood for community values (an aristocratic idea). As tragedy evolved, the chorus waned in importance until it disappeared in the fourth century B.C., leaving the actors supreme. This event paralleled the decline of both the city-state and tragic drama.

Reading the Selection

Oedipus the King is typical of what became known as Sophoclean tragedy in that it has two themes: the relation between humans and gods, and the hero's moral dilemmas. These themes converge in the character Oedipus, a king destroyed by the gods as he tries to act morally. Highly ironic, the plot shows Oedipus unleashing new catastrophes despite good intentions. Warned by an oracle that he will kill his father and marry his mother, the well-meaning Oedipus flees from Corinth to Thebes, only to learn that his efforts to escape his dread fate have been in vain. Oedipus's downfall is the result of good motives, for he discovers his true identity after ordering an investigation into the old king's murder, so that a plague may be driven from the city.

Above all else, this tragedy is about the unbridgeable gulf between gods and humans. Oedipus repeatedly shows arrogance in his desire to credit himself and deny the truth of oracles ("the world knows my fame"; "I count myself the son of Chance"). Struck down, he finally recognizes that humans, even kings, are fated to suffer. The chorus makes this harsh vision the moral of the tragedy: "[L]ook on Oedipus. . . . [C]ount no man happy till he dies, free of pain at last."

—m—

Characters

OEDIPUS *king of Thebes*

A PRIEST *of Zeus*

CREON *brother of Jocasta*

A CHORUS *of Theban citizens and their* LEADER

TIRESIAS *a blind prophet*

JOCASTA *the queen, wife of Oedipus*

A MESSENGER *from Corinth*

A SHEPHERD

A MESSENGER *from inside the palace*

ANTIGONE, ISMENE *daughters of Oedipus and Jocasta*

Guards and attendants

Priests of Thebes

TIME AND SCENE: *The royal house of Thebes. Double doors dominate the façade; a stone altar stands at the center of the stage.*

Many years have passed since OEDIPUS *solved the riddle of the Sphinx and ascended the throne of Thebes, and now a plague has struck the city. A procession of priests enters; suppliants, broken and despondent, they carry branches wound in wool and lay them on the altar.*

The doors open. Guards assemble. OEDIPUS *comes forward, majestic but for a telltale limp, and slowly views the condition of his people.*

OEDIPUS:

Oh my children, the new blood of ancient Thebes,
why are you here? Huddling at my altar,
praying before me, your branches wound in wool.

1

Our city reeks with the smoke of burning incense,
rings with cries for the Healer and wailing for the dead.
I thought it wrong, my children, to hear the truth
from others, messengers. Here I am myself—
you all know me, the world knows my fame:
I am Oedipus.

Helping a Priest to his feet.

Speak up, old man. Your years,   10
your dignity—you should speak for the others.
Why here and kneeling, what preys upon you so?
Some sudden fear? some strong desire?
You can trust me. I am ready to help,
I'll do anything. I would be blind to misery
not to pity my people kneeling at my feet.

PRIEST:

Oh Oedipus, king of the land, our greatest power!
You see us before you now, men of all ages
clinging to your altars. Here are boys,
still too weak to fly from the nest,   20
and here the old, bowed down with the years,
the holy ones—a priest of Zeus myself—and here
the picked, unmarried men, the young hope of Thebes.
And all the rest, your great family gathers now,
branches wreathed, massing in the squares,
kneeling before the two temples of queen Athena
or the river-shrine where the embers glow and die
and Apollo sees the future in the ashes.

Our city—
look around you, see with your own eyes—   30
our ship pitches wildly, cannot lift her head
from the depths, the red waves of death . . .
Thebes is dying. A blight on the fresh crops
and the rich pastures, cattle sicken and die,
and the women die in labor, children stillborn,
and the plague, the fiery god of fever hurls down
on the city, his lightning slashing through us—
raging plague in all its vengeance, devastating
the house of Cadmus! And black Death luxuriates
in the raw, wailing miseries of Thebes.   40

Now we pray to you. You cannot equal the gods,
your children know that, bending at your altar.
But we do rate you first of men,
both in the common crises of our lives
and face-to-face encounters with the gods.
You freed us from the Sphinx, you came to Thebes
and cut us loose from the bloody tribute we had paid
that harsh, brutal singer. We taught you nothing,
no skill, no extra knowledge, still you triumphed.

A god was with you, so they say, and we believe it—   50
you lifted up our lives.
So now again,
Oedipus, king, we bend to you, your power—
we implore you, all of us on our knees:
find us strength, rescue! Perhaps you've heard
the voice of a god or something from other men,
Oedipus . . . what do you know?
The man of experience—you see it every day—
his plans will work in a crisis, his first of all.

Act now—we beg you, best of men, raise up our city!   60
Act, defend yourself, your former glory!
Your country calls you savior now
for your zeal, your action years ago.
Never let us remember of your reign:
you helped us stand, only to fall once more.
Oh raise up our city, set us on our feet.
The omens were good that day you brought us joy—
be the same man today!
Rule our land, you know you have the power,
but rule a land of the living, not a wasteland.   70
Ship and towered city are nothing, stripped of men
alive within it, living all as one.

OEDIPUS:

My children,
I pity you. I see—how could I fail to see
what longings bring you here? Well I know
you are sick to death, all of you,
but sick as you are, not one is sick as I.
Your pain strikes each of you alone, each
in the confines of himself, no other. But my spirit
grieves for the city, for myself and all of you.   80
I wasn't asleep, dreaming. You haven't wakened me—
I have wept through the nights, you must know that,
groping, laboring over many paths of thought.
After a painful search I found one cure:
I acted at once. I sent Creon,
my wife's own brother, to Delphi—
Apollo the Prophet's oracle—to learn
what I might do or say to save our city.

Today's the day. When I count the days gone by
it torments me . . . what is he doing?   90
Strange, he's late, he's gone too long.
But once he returns, then, then I'll be a traitor
if I do not do all the god makes clear.

PRIEST:

Timely words. The men over there
are signaling—Creon's just arriving.

OEDIPUS:

Sighting CREON, *then turning to the altar.*

Lord Apollo,
let him come with a lucky word of rescue,
shining like his eyes!

PRIEST:

Welcome news, I think—he's crowned, look,
and the laurel wreath is bright with berries.   100

OEDIPUS:

We'll soon see. He's close enough to hear—

Enter CREON *from the side; his face is shaded with a wreath.*

Creon, prince, my kinsman, what do you bring us?
What message from the god?

CREON:

                              Good news.
I tell you even the hardest things to bear,
if they should turn out well, all would be well.

OEDIPUS:

Of course, but what were the god's *words?* There's no
      hope
and nothing to fear in what you've said so far.

CREON:

If you want my report in the presence of these people . . .
Pointing to the priests while drawing OEDIPUS *toward the
palace.*

I'm ready now, or we might go inside.   110

OEDIPUS:

                                   Speak out,
speak to us all. I grieve for these, my people,
far more than I fear for my own life.

CREON:

                                   Very well,
I will tell you what I heard from the god.
Apollo commands us—he was quite clear—
"Drive the corruption from the land,
don't harbor it any longer, past all cure,
don't nurse it in your soil—root it out!"

OEDIPUS:

How can we cleanse ourselves—what rites?   120
What's the source of the trouble?

CREON:

Banish the man, or pay back blood with blood.
Murder sets the plague-storm on the city.

OEDIPUS:

                              Whose murder?
Whose fate does Apollo bring to light?

CREON:

                              Our leader,
my lord, was once a man named Laius,
before you came and put us straight on course.

OEDIPUS:

                                   I know—
or so I've heard. I never saw the man myself.   130

CREON:

Well, he was killed, and Apollo commands us now—
he could not be more clear,
"Pay the killers back—whoever is responsible."

OEDIPUS:

Where on earth are they? Where to find it now,
the trail of the ancient guilt so hard to trace?

CREON:

"Here in Thebes," he said.
Whatever is sought for can be caught, you know,
whatever is neglected slips away.

OEDIPUS:

                              But where,
in the palace, the fields or foreign soil,   140
where did Laius meet his bloody death?

CREON:

He went to consult an oracle, Apollo said,
and he set out and never came home again.

OEDIPUS:

No messenger, no fellow-traveler saw what happened?
Someone to cross-examine?

CREON:

                              No,
they were all killed but one. He escaped,
terrified, he could tell us nothing clearly,
nothing of what he saw—just one thing.

OEDIPUS:

                              What's that?   150
One thing could hold the key to it all,
a small beginning give us grounds for hope.

CREON:

He said thieves attacked them—a whole band,
not single-handed, cut King Laius down.

OEDIPUS:

                              A thief,
so daring, so wild, he'd kill a king? Impossible,
unless conspirators paid him off in Thebes.

CREON:

We suspected as much. But with Laius dead
no leader appeared to help us in our troubles.

OEDIPUS:

Trouble? Your *king* was murdered—royal blood!   160
What stopped you from tracking down the killer
then and there?

CREON:

The singing, riddling Sphinx.
She . . . persuaded us to let the mystery go
and concentrate on what lay at our feet.

OEDIPUS:

                              No,
I'll start again—I'll bring it all to light myself!
Apollo is right, and so are you, Creon,

to turn our attention back to the murdered man.
Now you have *me* to fight for you, you'll see: 170
I am the land's avenger by all rights,
and Apollo's champion too.
But not to assist some distant kinsman, no,
for my own sake I'll rid us of this corruption.
Whoever killed the king may decide to kill me too,
with the same violent hand—by avenging Laius
I defend myself.

To the priests.

                    Quickly, my children.
Up from the steps, take up your branches now.

To the guards.

One of you summon the city here before us,   180
tell them I'll do everything. God help us,
we will see our triumph—or our fall.

OEDIPUS *and* CREON *enter the palace, followed by the guards.*

PRIEST:

Rise, my sons. The kindness we came for
Oedipus volunteers himself.
Apollo has sent his word, his oracle—
Come down, Apollo, save us, stop the plague.

The priests rise, remove their branches and exit to the side.

Enter a CHORUS, *the citizens of Thebes, who have not heard
the news that* CREON *brings. They march around the altar,
chanting.*

CHORUS:

                              Zeus!
Great welcome voice of Zeus, what do you bring?
What word from the gold vaults of Delphi
comes to brilliant Thebes? Racked with terror—   190
                    terror shakes my heart
and I cry your wild cries, Apollo, Healer of Delos
I worship you in dread . . . what now, what is your price?
some new sacrifice? some ancient rite from the past
come round again each spring?—
          what will you bring to birth?
Tell me, child of golden Hope
     warm voice that never dies!

You are the first I call, daughter of Zeus
deathless Athena—I call your sister Artemis,   200
heart of the market place enthroned in glory,
               guardian of our earth—
I call Apollo, Archer astride the thunderheads of heaven—
O triple shield against death, shine before me now!
If ever, once in the past, you stopped some ruin
launched against our walls
          you hurled the flame of pain
far, far from Thebes—you gods
     come now, come down once more!
                    No, no   210
the miseries numberless, grief on grief, no end—
too much to bear, we are all dying
O my people . . .
     Thebes like a great army dying

and there is no sword of thought to save us, no
and the fruits of our famous earth, they will not ripen
no and the women cannot scream their pangs to birth—
screams for the Healer, children dead in the womb
          and life on life goes down
                    you can watch them go   220
     like seabirds winging west, outracing the day's fire
down the horizon, irresistibly
          streaking on to the shores of Evening
                                        Death
so many deaths, numberless deaths on deaths, no end—
Thebes is dying, look, her children
stripped of pity . . .
     generations strewn on the ground
unburied, unwept, the dead spreading death
and the young wives and gray-haired mothers with them   230
cling to the altars, trailing in from all over the city—
Thebes, city of death, one long cortege
          and the suffering rises
                    wails for mercy rise
     and the wild hymn for the Healer blazes out
clashing with our sobs our cries of mourning—
     O golden daughter of god, send rescue
     radiant as the kindness in your eyes!

Drive him back!—the fever, the god of death
               that raging god of war   240
not armored in bronze, not shielded now, he burns me,
battle cries in the onslaught burning on—
O rout him from our borders!
Sail him, blast him out to the Sea-queen's chamber
                         the black Atlantic gulfs
or the northern harbor, death to all
where the Thracian surf comes crashing.
Now what the night spares he comes by day and kills—
the god of death.

               O lord of the stormcloud,   250
you who twirl the lightning, Zeus, Father,
thunder Death to nothing!

Apollo, lord of the light, I beg you—
     whip your longbow's golden cord
showering arrows on our enemies—shafts of power
champions strong before us rushing on!

Artemis, Huntress,
torches flaring over the eastern ridges—
               ride Death down in pain!

God of the headdress gleaming gold, I cry to you—   260
your name and ours are one, Dionysus—
     come with your face aflame with wine
               your raving women's cries
          your army on the march! Come with the lightning
come with torches blazing, eyes ablaze with glory!
Burn that god of death that all gods hate!

OEDIPUS *enters from the palace to address the* CHORUS, *as if
addressing the entire city of Thebes.*

OEDIPUS:

You pray to the gods? Let me grant your prayers.
Come, listen to me—do what the plague demands:
you'll find relief and lift your head from the depths.

I will speak out now as a stranger to the story,   270
a stranger to the crime. If I'd been present then,
there would have been no mystery, no long hunt
without a clue in hand. So now, counted
a native Theban years after the murder,
to all of Thebes I make this proclamation:
if any one of you knows who murdered Laius,
the son of Labdacus, I order him to reveal
the whole truth to me. Nothing to fear,
even if he must denounce himself,
let him speak up   280
and so escape the brunt of the charge—
he will suffer no unbearable punishment,
nothing worse than exile, totally unharmed.

OEDIPUS *pauses, waiting for a reply.*

                                                    Next,
if anyone knows the murderer is a stranger,
a man from alien soil, come, speak up.
I will give him a handsome reward, and lay up
gratitude in my heart for him besides.

Silence again, no reply.

But if you keep silent, if anyone panicking,
trying to shield himself or friend or kin,   290
rejects my offer, then hear what I will do.
I order you, every citizen of the state
where I hold throne and power: banish this man—
whoever he may be—never shelter him, never
speak a word to him, never make him partner
to your prayers, your victims burned to the gods.
Never let the holy water touch his hands.
Drive him out, each of you, from every home.
He is the plague, the heart of our corruption,
as Apollo's oracle has just revealed to me.   300
So I honor my obligations:
I fight for the god and for the murdered man.

Now my curse on the murderer. Whoever he is,
a lone man unknown in his crime
or one among many, let that man drag out
his life in agony, step by painful step—
I curse myself as well . . . if by any chance
he proves to be an intimate of our house,
here at my hearth, with my full knowledge,
may the curse I just called down on him strike me!   310

These are your orders: perform them to the last.
I command you, for my sake, for Apollo's, for this country
blasted root and branch by the angry heavens.
Even if god had never urged you on to act,
how could you leave the crime uncleansed so long?
A man so noble—your king, brought down in blood—
you should have searched. But I am the king now,
I hold the throne that he held then, possess his bed
and a wife who shares our seed . . . why, our seed

might be the same, children born of the same mother   320
might have created blood-bonds between us
if his hope of offspring had not met disaster—
but fate swooped at his head and cut him short.
So I will fight for him as if he were my father,
stop at nothing, search the world
to lay my hands on the man who shed his blood,
the son of Labdacus descended of Polydorus,
Cadmus of old and Agenor, founder of the line:
their power and mine are one.

                                        Oh dear gods,   330
my curse on those who disobey these orders!
Let no crops grow out of the earth for them—
shrivel their women, kill their sons,
burn them to nothing in this plague
that hits us now, or something even worse.
But you, loyal men of Thebes who approve my actions,
may our champion, Justice, may all the gods
be with us, fight beside us to the end!

LEADER:

In the grip of your curse, my king, I swear
I'm not the murderer, I cannot point him out.   340
As for the search, Apollo pressed it on us—
he should name the killer.

OEDIPUS:

                                        Quite right,
but to force the gods to act against their will—
no man has the power.

LEADER:

                                Then if I might mention
the next best thing . . .

OEDIPUS:

                                The third best too—
don't hold back, say it.

LEADER:

                                I still believe . . .   350
Lord Tiresias sees with the eyes of Lord Apollo.
Anyone searching for the truth, my king,
might learn it from the prophet, clear as day.

OEDIPUS:

I've not been slow with that. On Creon's cue
I sent the escorts, twice, within the hour.
I'm surprised he isn't here.

LEADER:

                                We need him—
without him we have nothing but old, useless rumors.

OEDIPUS:

Which rumors? I'll search out every word.

LEADER:

Laius was killed, they say, by certain travelers.   360

OEDIPUS:

I know—but no one can find the murderer.

LEADER:

If the man has a trace of fear in him
he won't stay silent long,
not with your curses ringing in his ears.

OEDIPUS:

He didn't flinch at murder,
he'll never flinch at words.

Enter TIRESIAS, *the blind prophet, led by a boy with escorts in attendance. He remains at a distance.*

LEADER:

Here is the one who will convict him, look,
they bring him on at last, the seer, the man of god.
The truth lives inside him, him alone.

OEDIPUS:

                                        O Tiresias,   370
master of all the mysteries of our life,
all you teach and all you dare not tell,
signs in the heavens, signs that walk the earth!
Blind as you are, you can feel all the more
what sickness haunts our city. You, my lord,
are the one shield, the one savior we can find.

We asked Apollo—perhaps the messengers
haven't told you—he sent his answer back:
"Relief from the plague can only come one way.
Uncover the murderers of Laius,   380
put them to death or drive them into exile."
So I beg you, grudge us nothing now, no voice,
no message plucked from the birds, the embers
or the other mantic ways within your grasp.
Rescue yourself, your city, rescue me—
rescue everything infected by the dead.
We are in your hands. For a man to help others
with all his gifts and native strength:
that is the noblest work.

TIRESIAS:

                                        How terrible—to see the truth   390
when the truth is only pain to him who sees!
I knew it well, but I put it from my mind,
else I never would have come.

OEDIPUS:

What's this? Why so grim, so dire?

TIRESIAS:

Just send me home. You bear your burdens,
I'll bear mine. It's better that way,
please believe me.

OEDIPUS:

                                        Strange response . . . unlawful,
unfriendly too to the state that bred and reared you—
you withhold the word of god.   400

TIRESIAS:

                                        I fail to see
that your own words are so well-timed.
I'd rather not have the same thing said of me . . .

OEDIPUS:

For the love of god, don't turn away,
not if you know something. We beg you,
all of us on our knees.

TIRESIAS:

                                        None of you knows—
and I will never reveal my dreadful secrets,
not to say your own.

OEDIPUS:

What? You know and you won't tell?   410
You're bent on betraying us, destroying Thebes?

TIRESIAS:

I'd rather not cause pain for you or me.
So why this . . . useless interrogation?
You'll get nothing from me.

OEDIPUS:

                                        Nothing! You,
you scum of the earth, you'd enrage a heart of stone!
You won't talk? Nothing moves you?
Out with it, once and for all!

TIRESIAS:

You criticize my temper . . . unaware
of the one *you* live with, you revile me.   420

OEDIPUS:

Who could restrain his anger hearing you?
What outrage—you spurn the city!

TIRESIAS:

What will come will come.
Even if I shroud it all in silence.

OEDIPUS:

What will come? You're bound to *tell* me that.

TIRESIAS:

I will say no more. Do as you like, build your anger
to whatever pitch you please, rage your worst—

OEDIPUS:

Oh I'll let loose, I have such fury in me—
now I see it all. You helped hatch the plot,
you did the work, yes, short of killing him
with your own hands—and given eyes I'd say
you did the killing single-handed!

TIRESIAS:

                            Is that so!
I charge you, then, submit to that decree
you just laid down: from this day onward
speak to no one, not these citizens, not myself.
You are the curse, the corruption of the land!

OEDIPUS:

You, shameless—
aren't you appalled to start up such a story?
You think you can get away with this?

TIRESIAS:

                          I have already.
The truth with all its power lives inside me.

OEDIPUS:

Who primed you for this? Not your prophet's trade.

TIRESIAS:

You did, you forced me, twisted it out of me.

OEDIPUS:

What? Say it again—I'll understand it better.

TIRESIAS:

Didn't you understand, just now?
Or are you tempting me to talk?

OEDIPUS:

No, I can't say I grasped your meaning.
Out with it, again!

TIRESIAS:

I say you are the murderer you hunt.

OEDIPUS:

That obscenity, twice—by god, you'll pay.

TIRESIAS:

Shall I say more, so you can really rage?

OEDIPUS:

Much as you want. Your words are nothing—
futile.

TIRESIAS:

      You cannot imagine . . . I tell you,
you and your loved ones live together in infamy,
you cannot see how far you've gone in guilt.

OEDIPUS:

You think you can keep this up and never suffer?

TIRESIAS:

Indeed, if the truth has any power.

OEDIPUS:

                        It does
but not for you, old man. You've lost your power,
stone-blind, stone-deaf—senses, eyes blind as stone!

TIRESIAS:

I pity you, flinging at me the very insults
each man here will fling at you so soon.

OEDIPUS:

                         Blind,
lost in the night, endless night that nursed you!
You can't hurt me or anyone else who sees the light—
you can never touch me.

TIRESIAS:

                   True, it is not your fate
to fall at my hands. Apollo is quite enough,
and he will take some pains to work this out.

OEDIPUS:

Creon! Is this conspiracy his or yours?

TIRESIAS:

Creon is not your downfall, no, you are your own.

OEDIPUS:

                       O power—
wealth and empire, skill outstripping skill
in the heady rivalries of life,
what envy lurks inside you! Just for this,
the crown the city gave me—I never sought it,
they laid it in my hands—for this alone, Creon,
the soul of trust, my loyal friend from the start
steals against me . . . so hungry to overthrow me
he sets this wizard on me, this scheming quack,
this fortune-teller peddling lies, eyes peeled
for his own profit—seer blind in his craft!

Come here, you pious fraud. Tell me,
when did you ever prove yourself a prophet?
When the Sphinx, that chanting Fury kept her
deathwatch here,
why silent then, not a word to set our people free?
There was a riddle, not for some passer-by to solve—
it cried out for a prophet. Where were you?
Did you rise to the crisis? Not a word,
you and your birds, your gods—nothing.
No, but I came by, Oedipus the ignorant,
I stopped the Sphinx! With no help from the birds,
the flight of my own intelligence hit the mark.

And this is the man you'd try to overthrow?
You think you'll stand by Creon when he's king?
You and the great mastermind—
you'll pay in tears, I promise you, for this,   500
this witch-hunt. If you didn't look so senile
the lash would teach you what your scheming means!

LEADER:

I would suggest his words were spoken in anger,
Oedipus . . . yours too, and it isn't what we need.
The best solution to the oracle, the riddle
posed by god—we should look for that.

TIRESIAS:

You are the king no doubt, but in one respect,
at least, I am your equal: the right to reply.
I claim that privilege too.
I am not your slave. I serve Apollo.   510
I don't need Creon to speak for me in public.
                                        So,
you mock my blindness? Let me tell you this.
You with your precious eyes,
you're blind to the corruption of your life,
to the house you live in, those you live with—
who *are* your parents? Do you know? All unknowing
you are the scourge of your own flesh and blood,
the dead below the earth and the living here above,
and the double lash of your mother and your father's
      curse   520
will whip you from this land one day, their footfall
treading you down in terror, darkness shrouding
your eyes that now can see the light!
                              Soon, soon
you'll scream aloud—what haven won't reverberate?
What rock of Cithaeron won't scream back in echo?
That day you learn the truth about your marriage,
the wedding-march that sang you into your halls,
the lusty voyage home to the fatal harbor!
And a crowd of other horrors you'd never dream   530
will level you with yourself and all your children.
There. Now smear us with insults—Creon, myself
and every word I've said. No man will ever
be rooted from the earth as brutally as you.

OEDIPUS:

Enough! Such filth from him? Insufferable—
what, still alive? Get out—
faster, back where you came from—vanish!

TIRESIAS:

I would never have come if you hadn't called me here.

OEDIPUS:

If I thought you would blurt out such absurdities,
you'd have died waiting before I'd had you summoned.   540

TIRESIAS:

Absurd, am I! To you, not to your parents:
the ones who bore you found me sane enough.

OEDIPUS:

Parents—who? Wait . . . who is my father?

TIRESIAS:

This day will bring your birth and your destruction.

OEDIPUS:

Riddles—all you can say are riddles, murk and darkness.

TIRESIAS:

Ah, but aren't you the best man alive at solving riddles?

OEDIPUS:

Mock me for that, go on, and you'll reveal my greatness.

TIRESIAS:

Your great fortune, true, it was your ruin.

OEDIPUS:

Not if I saved the city—what do I care?

TIRESIAS:

Well then, I'll be going.   550
To his attendant.
                              Take me home, boy.

OEDIPUS:

Yes, take him away. You're a nuisance here.
Out of the way, the irritation's gone.
Turning his back on TIRESIAS, *moving toward the palace.*

TIRESIAS:

                              I will go,
once I have said what I came here to say.
I will never shrink from the anger in your eyes—
you can't destroy me. Listen to me closely:
the man you've sought so long, proclaiming,
cursing up and down, the murderer of Laius—
he is here. A stranger,   560
you may think, who lives among you,
he soon will be revealed a native Theban
but he will take no joy in the revelation.
Blind who now has eyes, beggar who now is rich,
he will grope his way toward a foreign soil,
a stick tapping before him step by step.
OEDIPUS *enters the palace.*

Revealed at last, brother and father both
to the children he embraces, to his mother
son and husband both—he sowed the loins
his father sowed, he spilled his father's blood!   570

Go in and reflect on that, solve that.
And if you find I've lied
from this day onward call the prophet blind.
TIRESIAS *and the boy exit to the side.*

CHORUS:

Who—

who is the man the voice of god denounces
resounding out of the rocky gorge of Delphi?
    The horror too dark to tell,
whose ruthless bloody hands have done the work?
His time has come to fly
        to outrace the stallions of the storm   580
                    his feet a streak of speed—
Cased in armor, Apollo son of the Father
lunges on him, lightning-bolts afire!
And the grim unerring Furies
            closing for the kill.

Look,

the word of god has just come blazing
flashing off Parnassus' snowy heights!
    That man who left no trace—
after him, hunt him down with all our strength!   590
Now under bristling timber
    up through rocks and caves he stalks
                like the wild mountain bull—
cut off from men, each step an agony, frenzied, racing
        blind
but he cannot outrace the dread voices of Delphi
ringing out of the heart of Earth,
        the dark wings beating around him shrieking doom
                    the doom that never dies, the terror—
The skilled prophet scans the birds and shatters me
        with terror!
I can't accept him, can't deny him, don't know what to say,   600
I'm lost, and the wings of dark foreboding beating—
I cannot see what's come, what's still to come . . .
and what could breed a blood feud between
        Laius' house and the son of Polybus?
I know of nothing, not in the past and not now,
no charge to bring against our king, no cause
to attack his fame that rings throughout Thebes—
    not without proof—not for the ghost of Laius,
    not to avenge a murder gone without a trace.
Zeus and Apollo know, they know, the great masters   610
        of all the dark and depth of human life.
But whether a mere man can know the truth,
whether a seer can fathom more than I—
there is no test, no certain proof
    though matching skill for skill
a man can outstrip a rival. No, not till I see
these charges proved will I side with his accusers.
We saw him then, when the she-hawk swept against
        him,
saw with our own eyes his skill, his brilliant triumph—
    there was the test—he was the joy of Thebes!   620
    Never will I convict my king, never in my heart.

Enter CREON *from the side.*

CREON:

My fellow-citizens, I hear King Oedipus
levels terrible charges at me. I had to come.
I resent it deeply. If, in the present crisis,
he thinks he suffers any abuse from me,

anything I've done or said that offers him
the slightest injury, why, I've no desire
to linger out this life, my reputation in ruins.
The damage I'd face from such an accusation   630
is nothing simple. No, there's nothing worse:
branded a traitor in the city, a traitor
to all of you and my good friends.

LEADER:

True,

but a slur might have been forced out of him,
by anger perhaps, not any firm conviction.

CREON:

The charge was made in public, wasn't it?
I put the prophet up to spreading lies?

LEADER:

Such things were said . . .
I don't know with what intent, if any.

CREON:

Was his glance steady, his mind right   640
when the charge was brought against me?

LEADER:

I really couldn't say. I never look
to judge the ones in power.

The doors open. OEDIPUS *enters.*

Wait,

here's Oedipus now.

OEDIPUS:

You—here? You have the gall
to show your face before the palace gates?
You, plotting to kill me, kill the king—
I see it all, the marauding thief himself
scheming to steal my crown and power!   650

Tell me,

in god's name, what did you take me for,
coward or fool, when you spun out your plot?
Your treachery—you think I'd never detect it
creeping against me in the dark? Or sensing it,
not defend myself? Aren't you the fool,
you and your high adventure. Lacking numbers,
powerful friends, out for the big game of empire—
you need riches, armies to bring that quarry down!

CREON:

Are you quite finished? It's your turn to listen   660
for just as long as you've . . . instructed me.
Hear me out, then judge me on the facts.

OEDIPUS:

You've a wicked way with words, Creon,
but I'll be slow to learn—from you.
I find you a menace, a great burden to me.

CREON:

Just one thing, hear me out in this.

OEDIPUS:

Just one thing,
don't tell *me* you're not the enemy, the traitor.

CREON:

Look, if you think crude, mindless stubbornness
such a gift, you've lost your sense of balance.   670

OEDIPUS:

If you think you can abuse a kinsman,
then escape the penalty, you're insane.

CREON:

Fair enough, I grant you. But this injury
you say I've done you, what is it?

OEDIPUS:

Did you induce me, yes or no,
to send for that sanctimonious prophet?

CREON:

I did. And I'd do the same again.

OEDIPUS:

All right then, tell me, how long is it now
since Laius . . .

CREON:

Laius—what did *he* do?   680

OEDIPUS:

Vanished,
swept from sight, murdered in his tracks.

CREON:

The count of the years would run you far back . . .

OEDIPUS:

And that far back, was the prophet at his trade?

CREON:

Skilled as he is today, and just as honored.

OEDIPUS:

Did he ever refer to me then, at that time?

CREON:

No,
never, at least, when I was in his presence.

OEDIPUS:

But you did investigate the murder, didn't you?

CREON:

We did our best, of course, discovered nothing.   690

OEDIPUS:

But the great seer never accused me then—why not?

CREON:

I don't know. And when I don't, *I* keep quiet.

OEDIPUS:

You do know this, you'd tell it too—
if you had a shred of decency.

CREON:

What?
If I know, I won't hold back.

OEDIPUS:

Simply this:
if the two of you had never put heads together,
we would never have heard about *my* killing Laius.

CREON:

If that's what he says . . . well, you know best.   700
But now I have a right to learn from you
as you just learned from me.

OEDIPUS:

Learn your fill,
you never will convict me of the murder.

CREON:

Tell me, you're married to my sister, aren't you?

OEDIPUS:

A genuine discovery—there's no denying that.

CREON:

And you rule the land with her, with equal power?

OEDIPUS:

She receives from me whatever she desires.

CREON:

And I am the third, all of us are equals?

OEDIPUS:

Yes, and it's there you show your stripes—   710
you betray a kinsman.

CREON:

Not at all.
Not if you see things calmly, rationally,
as I do. Look at it this way first:
who in his right mind would rather rule
and live in anxiety than sleep in peace?

Particularly if he enjoys the same authority.
Not I, I'm not the man to yearn for kingship,
not with a king's power in my hands. Who would?
No one with any sense of self-control.   720
Now, as it is, you offer me all I need,
not a fear in the world. But if I wore the crown . . .
there'd be many painful duties to perform,
hardly to my taste.
                        How could kingship
please me more than influence, power
without a qualm? I'm not that deluded yet,
to reach for anything but privilege outright,
profit free and clear.
Now all men sing my praises, all salute me,
now all who request your favors curry mine.   730
I am their best hope: success rests in me.
Why give up that, I ask you, and borrow trouble?
A man of sense, someone who sees things clearly
would never resort to treason.
No, I have no lust for conspiracy in me,
nor could I ever suffer one who does.

Do you want proof? Go to Delphi yourself,
examine the oracle and see if I've reported
the message word-for-word. This too: 740
if you detect that I and the clairvoyant
have plotted anything in common, arrest me,
execute me. Not on the strength of one vote,
two in this case, mine as well as yours.
But don't convict me on sheer unverified surmise.
How wrong it is to take the good for bad,
purely at random, or take the bad for good.
But reject a friend, a kinsman? I would as soon
tear out the life within us, priceless life itself.
You'll learn this well, without fail, in time.   750
Time alone can bring the just man to light—
the criminal you can spot in one short day.

LEADER:
                                    Good advice,
my lord, for anyone who wants to avoid disaster.
Those who jump to conclusions may go wrong.

OEDIPUS:

When my enemy moves against me quickly,
plots in secret, I move quickly too, I must,
I plot and pay him back. Relax my guard a moment,
waiting his next move—he wins his objective,   760
I lose mine.

CREON:
            What do you want?
You want me banished?

OEDIPUS:
                    No, I want you dead.

CREON:

Just to show how ugly a grudge can . . .

OEDIPUS:
                So,
still stubborn? You don't think I'm serious?

CREON:

I think you're insane.

OEDIPUS:
                    Quite sane—in my behalf.

CREON:

Not just as much in mine?

OEDIPUS:
                        You—my mortal enemy?   770

CREON:

What if you're wholly wrong?

OEDIPUS:
                        No matter—I must rule.

CREON:

Not if you rule unjustly.

OEDIPUS:
                    Hear him, Thebes, my city!

CREON:

My city too, not yours alone!

LEADER:

Please, my lords.
Enter JOCASTA *from the palace.*
                    Look, Jocasta's coming,
and just in time too. With her help
you must put this fighting of yours to rest.

JOCASTA:

Have you no sense? Poor misguided men,   780
such shouting—why this public outburst?
Aren't you ashamed, with the land so sick,
to stir up private quarrels?
To OEDIPUS.

Into the palace now. And Creon, you go home.
Why make such a furor over nothing?

CREON:

My sister, it's dreadful . . . Oedipus, your husband,
he's bent on a choice of punishments for me,
banishment from the fatherland or death.

OEDIPUS:

Precisely. I caught him in the act, Jocasta,
plotting, about to stab me in the back.   790

CREON:
Never—curse me, let me die and be damned
if I've done you any wrong you charge me with.

JOCASTA:
Oh god, believe it, Oedipus,
honor the solemn oath he swears to heaven.
Do it for me, for the sake of all your people.

The CHORUS *begins to chant.*
CHORUS:
Believe it, be sensible
    give way, my king, I beg you!

OEDIPUS:
What do you want from me, concessions?

CHORUS:
Respect him—he's been no fool in the past
and now he's strong with the oath he swears to god.   800

OEDIPUS:
You know what you're asking?

CHORUS:
                          I do.

OEDIPUS:
                              Then out with it!

CHORUS:
The man's your friend, your kin, he's under oath—
don't cast him out, disgraced
branded with guilt on the strength of hearsay only.

OEDIPUS:
Know full well, if that is what you want
you want me dead or banished from the land.

CHORUS:
                                    Never—
no, by the blazing Sun, first god of the heavens!   810
    Stripped of the gods, stripped of loved ones,
let me die by inches if that ever crossed my mind.
But the heart inside me sickens, dies as the land
    dies
and now on top of the old griefs you pile this,
your fury—both of you!

OEDIPUS:
                    Then let him go,
even if it does lead to my ruin, my death
or my disgrace, driven from Thebes for life.
It's you, not him I pity—your words move me.
He, wherever he goes, my hate goes with him.   820

CREON:
Look at you, sullen in yielding, brutal in your rage—
you will go too far. It's perfect justice:
natures like yours are hardest on themselves.

OEDIPUS:
Then leave me alone—get out!

CREON:
                          I'm going.
You're wrong, so wrong. These men know I'm right.
Exit to the side. The CHORUS *turns to* JOCASTA.

CHORUS:
Why do you hesitate, my lady
    why not help him in?

JOCASTA:
Tell me what's happened first.

CHORUS:
Loose, ignorant talk started dark suspicions   830
and a sense of injustice cut deeply too.

JOCASTA:
On both sides?

CHORUS:
              Oh yes.

JOCASTA:
              What did they say?

CHORUS:
Enough, please, enough! The land's so racked already
or so it seems to me . . .
End the trouble here, just where they left it.

OEDIPUS:
You see what comes of your good intentions now?
And all because you tried to blunt my anger.

CHORUS:
                              My king,   840
I've said it once, I'll say it time and again—
    I'd be insane, you know it,
senseless, ever to turn my back on you.
You who set our beloved land—storm-tossed,
    shattered—
straight on course. Now again, good helmsman,
steer us through the storm!

The chorus draws away, leaving OEDIPUS *and* JOCASTA *side
by side.*

JOCASTA:

For the love of god,
Oedipus, tell me too, what is it?
Why this rage? You're so unbending.

OEDIPUS:

I will tell you. I respect you, Jocasta,   850
much more than these men here . . .

Glancing at the CHORUS.

Creon's to blame, Creon schemes against me.

JOCASTA:

Tell me clearly, how did the quarrel start?

OEDIPUS:

He says *I* murdered Laius—I am guilty.

JOCASTA:

How does he know? Some secret knowledge
or simple hearsay?

OEDIPUS:

Oh, he sent his prophet in
to do his dirty work. You know Creon,
Creon keeps his own lips clean.

JOCASTA:

A prophet?   860
Well then, free yourself of every charge!
Listen to me and learn some peace of mind:
no skill in the world,
nothing human can penetrate the future.
Here is proof, quick and to the point.

An oracle came to Laius one fine day
(I won't say from Apollo himself
but his underlings, his priests) and it declared
that doom would strike him down at the hands of a son,
our son, to be born of our own flesh and blood. But Laius,   870
so the report goes at least, was killed by strangers,
thieves, at a place where three roads meet . . . my son—
he wasn't three days old and the boy's father
fastened his ankles, had a henchman fling him away
on a barren, trackless mountain.
There, you see?
Apollo brought neither thing to pass. My baby
no more murdered his father than Laius suffered—
his wildest fear—death at his own son's hands.
That's how the seers and all their revelations   880
mapped out the future. Brush them from your mind.
Whatever the god needs and seeks
he'll bring to light himself, with ease.

OEDIPUS:

Strange,
hearing you just now . . . my mind wandered,
my thoughts racing back and forth.

JOCASTA:

What do you mean? Why so anxious, startled?

OEDIPUS:

I thought I heard you say that Laius
was cut down at a place where three roads meet.

JOCASTA:

That was the story. It hasn't died out yet.   890

OEDIPUS:

Where did this thing happen? Be precise.

JOCASTA:

A place called Phocis, where two branching roads,
one from Daulia, one from Delphi,
come together—a crossroads.

OEDIPUS:

When? How long ago?

JOCASTA:

The heralds no sooner reported Laius dead
than you appeared and they hailed you king of Thebes.

OEDIPUS:

My god, my god—what have you planned to do to me?

JOCASTA:

What, Oedipus? What haunts you so?

OEDIPUS:

Not yet.   900
Laius—how did he look? Describe him.
Had he reached his prime?

JOCASTA:

He was swarthy,
and the gray had just begun to streak his temples,
and his build . . . wasn't far from yours.

OEDIPUS:

Oh no no,
I think I've just called down a dreadful curse
upon myself—I simply didn't know!

JOCASTA:

What are you saying? I shudder to look at you.

OEDIPUS:

I have a terrible fear the blind seer can see.   910
I'll know in a moment. One thing more—

JOCASTA:

Anything,
afraid as I am—ask, I'll answer, all I can.

OEDIPUS:

Did he go with a light or heavy escort,
several men-at-arms, like a lord, a king?

JOCASTA:

There were five in the party, a herald among them,
and a single wagon carrying Laius.

OEDIPUS:

Ai—
now I can see it all, clear as day.
Who told you all this at the time, Jocasta?   920

JOCASTA:

A servant who reached home, the lone survivor.

OEDIPUS:

So, could he still be in the palace—even now?

JOCASTA:

No indeed. Soon as he returned from the scene
and saw you on the throne with Laius dead and gone,
he knelt and clutched my hand, pleading with me
to send him into the hinterlands, to pasture,
far as possible, out of sight of Thebes.
I sent him away. Slave though he was,
he'd earned that favor—and much more.

OEDIPUS:

Can we bring him back, quickly?   930

JOCASTA:

Easily. Why do you want him so?

OEDIPUS:

I am afraid,
Jocasta, I have said too much already.
That man—I've got to see him.

JOCASTA:

Then he'll come.
But even I have a right, I'd like to think,
to know what's torturing you, my lord.

OEDIPUS:

And so you shall—I can hold nothing back from you,
now I've reached this pitch of dark foreboding.
Who means more to me than you? Tell me,   940
whom would I turn toward but you
as I go through all this?

My father was Polybus, king of Corinth.
My mother, a Dorian, Merope. And I was held
the prince of the realm among the people there,
till something struck me out of nowhere,
something strange . . . worth remarking perhaps,
hardly worth the anxiety I gave it.

Some man at a banquet who had drunk too much
shouted out—he was far gone, mind you—   950
that I am not my father's son. Fighting words!
I barely restrained myself that day
but early the next I went to mother and father,
questioned them closely, and they were enraged
at the accusation and the fool who let it fly.
So as for my parents I was satisfied,
but still this thing kept gnawing at me,
the slander spread—I had to make my move.
And so,
unknown to mother and father I set out for Delphi,   960
and the god Apollo spurned me, sent me away
denied the facts I came for,
but first he flashed before my eyes a future
great with pain, terror, disaster—I can hear him cry,
"You are fated to couple with your mother, you will bring
a breed of children into the light no man can bear to see—
you will kill your father, the one who gave you life!"
I heard all that and ran. I abandoned Corinth,
from that day on I gauged its landfall only
by the stars, running, always running   970
toward some place where I would never see
the shame of all those oracles come true.
And as I fled I reached that very spot
where the great king, you say, met his death.

Now, Jocasta, I will tell you all.
Making my way toward this triple crossroad
I began to see a herald, then a brace of colts
drawing a wagon, and mounted on the bench . . . a man,
just as you've described him, coming face-to-face,
and the one in the lead and the old man himself   980
were about to thrust me off the road—brute force—
and the one shouldering me aside, the driver,
I strike him in anger!—and the old man, watching me
coming up along his wheels—he brings down
his prod, two prongs straight at my head!
I paid him back with interest!
Short work, by god—with one blow of the staff
in this right hand I knock him out of his high seat,
roll him out of the wagon, sprawling headlong—
I killed them all—every mother's son!   990

Oh, but if there is any blood-tie
between Laius and this stranger . . .
what man alive more miserable than I?
More hated by the gods? I am the man
no alien, no citizen welcomes to his house,
law forbids it—not a word to me in public,
driven out of every hearth and home.
And all these curses I—no one but I
brought down these piling curses on myself!
And you, his wife, I've touched your body with these,   1000
the hands that killed your husband cover you with blood.

Wasn't I born for torment? Look me in the eyes!
I am abomination—heart and soul!
I must be exiled, and even in exile
never see my parents, never set foot

on native ground again. Else I am doomed
to couple with my mother and cut my father down . . .
Polybus who reared me, gave me life.
                                        But why, why?
Wouldn't a man of judgment say—and wouldn't he be
    right—   1010
some savage power has brought this down upon my
    head?

Oh no, not that, you pure and awesome gods,
never let me see that day! Let me slip
from a world of men, vanish without a trace
before I see myself stained with such corruption,
stained to the heart.

LEADER:

My lord, you fill our hearts with fear.
But at least until you question the witness,
do take hope.

OEDIPUS:

                    Exactly. He is my last hope—   1020
I am waiting for the shepherd. He is crucial.

JOCASTA:

And once he appears, what then? Why so urgent?

OEDIPUS:

I will tell you. If it turns out that his story
matches yours, I've escaped the worst.

JOCASTA:

What did I say? What struck you so?

OEDIPUS:

                    You said *thieves*—
he told you a whole band of them murdered Laius.
So, if he still holds to the same number,
I cannot be the killer. One can't equal many.
But if he refers to one man, one alone,   1030
clearly the scales come down on me:
I am guilty.

JOCASTA:

            Impossible. Trust me,
I told you precisely what he said,
and he can't retract it now;
the whole city heard it, not just I.
And even if he should vary his first report
by one man more or less, still, my lord,
he could never make the murder of Laius
truly fit the prophecy. Apollo was explicit: 1040
my son was doomed to kill my husband . . . my son,
poor defenseless thing, he never had a chance
to kill his father. They destroyed him first.

So much for prophecy. It's neither here nor there.
From this day on, I wouldn't look right or left.

OEDIPUS:

True, true. Still, that shepherd,
someone fetch him—now!

JOCASTA:

I'll send at once. But do let's go inside.
I'd never displease you, least of all in this.

OEDIPUS *and* JOCASTA *enter the palace.*

CHORUS:

Destiny guide me always   1050
Destiny find me filled with reverence
    pure in word and deed.
Great laws tower above us, reared on high
born for the brilliant value of heaven—
    Olympian Sky their only father,
nothing mortal, no man gave them birth,
their memory deathless, never lost in sleep:
within them lives a mighty god, the god does not
    grow old.

Pride breeds the tyrant
violent pride, gorging, crammed to bursting   1060
    with all that is overripe and rich with ruin—
clawing up to the heights, headlong pride
crashes down the abyss—sheer doom!
    No footing helps, all foothold lost and gone.
But the healthy strife that makes the city strong—
I pray that god will never end that wrestling:
god, my champion, I will never let you go.

But if any man comes striding, high and mighty
    in all he says and does,
no fear of justice, no reverence   1070
for the temples of the gods—
    let a rough doom tear him down,
repay his pride, breakneck, ruinous pride!
If he cannot reap his profits fairly
    cannot restrain himself from outrage—
mad, laying hands on the holy things untouchable!

    Can such a man, so desperate, still boast
    he can save his life from the flashing bolts of god?
        If all such violence goes with honor now
            why join the sacred dance?   1080

Never again will I go reverent to Delphi,
    the inviolate heart of Earth
or Apollo's ancient oracle at Abae
or Olympia of the fires—
    unless these prophecies all come true
for all mankind to point toward in wonder.
King of kings, if you deserve your titles
    Zeus, remember, never forget!
You and your deathless, everlasting reign.

        They are dying, the old oracles sent to Laius,   1090
        now our masters strike them off the rolls.

Nowhere Apollo's golden glory now—
the gods, the gods go down.

Enter JOCASTA *from the palace, carrying a suppliant's branch wound in wool.*

JOCASTA:

Lords of the realm, it occurred to me,
just now, to visit the temples of the gods,
so I have a branch in hand and incense too.

Oedipus is beside himself. Racked with anguish,
no longer a man of sense, he won't admit
the latest prophecies are hollow as the old—
he's at the mercy of every passing voice   1100
if the voice tells of terror.
I urge him gently, nothing seems to help,
so I turn to you, Apollo, you are nearest.

Placing her branch on the altar, while an old herdsman enters from the side, not the one just summoned by the King but an unexpected MESSENGER *from Corinth.*

I come with prayers and offerings . . . I beg you,
cleanse us, set us free of defilement!
Look at us, passengers in the grip of fear,
watching the pilot of the vessel go to pieces.

MESSENGER:

Approaching JOCASTA *and the* CHORUS.

Strangers, please, I wonder if you could lead us
to the palace of the king . . . I think it's Oedipus.
Better, the man himself—you know where he is?   1110

LEADER:

This is his palace, stranger. He's inside.
But here is his queen, his wife and mother
of his children.

MESSENGER:

                  Blessings on you, noble queen,
queen of Oedipus crowned with all your family—
blessings on you always!

JOCASTA:

And the same to you, stranger, you deserve it . . .
such a greeting. But what have you come for?
Have you brought us news?

MESSENGER:

                  Wonderful news—   1120
for the house, my lady, for your husband too.

JOCASTA:

Really, what? Who sent you?

MESSENGER:

                  Corinth.
I'll give you the message in a moment.

You'll be glad of it—how could you help it?—
though it costs a little sorrow in the bargain.

JOCASTA:

What can it be, with such a double edge?

MESSENGER:

The people there, they want to make your Oedipus
king of Corinth, so they're saying now.

JOCASTA:

Why? Isn't old Polybus still in power?   1130

MESSENGER:

No more. Death has got him in the tomb.

JOCASTA:

What are you saying? Polybus, dead?—dead?

MESSENGER:

                                      If not,
if I'm not telling the truth, strike me dead too.

JOCASTA:

To a servant.

Quickly, go to your master, tell him this!

You prophecies of the gods, where are you now?
This is the man that Oedipus feared for years,
he fled him, not to kill him—and now he's dead,
quite by chance, a normal, natural death,
not murdered by his son.   1140

OEDIPUS:

Emerging from the palace.

                  Dearest,
what now? Why call me from the palace?

JOCASTA:

Bringing the MESSENGER *closer.*

Listen to *him*, see for yourself what all
those awful prophecies of god have come to.

OEDIPUS:

And who is he? What can he have for me?

JOCASTA:

He's from Corinth, he's come to tell you
your father is no more—Polybus—he's dead!

OEDIPUS:

Wheeling on the MESSENGER.

What? Let me have it from your lips.

MESSENGER:
Well,
if that's what you want first, then here it is: 1150
make no mistake, Polybus is dead and gone.

OEDIPUS:
How—murder? sickness?—what? what killed him?

MESSENGER:
A light tip of the scales can put old bones to rest.

OEDIPUS:
Sickness then—poor man, it wore him down.

MESSENGER:
That,
and the long count of years he'd measured out.

OEDIPUS:
So!
Jocasta, why, why look to the Prophet's hearth,
the fires of the future? Why scan the birds
that scream above our heads? They winged me on 1160
to the murder of my father, did they? That was my doom?
Well look, he's dead and buried, hidden under the earth,
and here I am in Thebes, I never put hand to sword—
unless some longing for me wasted him away,
then in a sense you'd say I caused his death.
But now, all those prophecies I feared—Polybus
packs them off to sleep with him in hell!
They're nothing, worthless.

JOCASTA:
There.
Didn't I tell you from the start? 1170

OEDIPUS:
So you did. I was lost in fear.

JOCASTA:
No more, sweep it from your mind forever.

OEDIPUS:
But my mother's bed, surely I must fear—

JOCASTA:
Fear?
What should a man fear? It's all chance,
chance rules our lives. Not a man on earth
can see a day ahead, groping through the dark.
Better to live at random, best we can.
And as for this marriage with your mother—
have no fear. Many a man before you,
in his dreams, has shared his mother's bed. 1180
Take such things for shadows, nothing at all—
Live, Oedipus,
as if there's no tomorrow!

OEDIPUS:
Brave words,
and you'd persuade me if mother weren't alive.
But mother lives, so for all your reassurances
I live in fear, I must.

JOCASTA:
But your father's death,
that, at least, is a great blessing, joy to the eyes! 1190

OEDIPUS:
Great, I know . . . but I fear *her*—she's still alive.

MESSENGER:
Wait, who is this woman, makes you so afraid?

OEDIPUS:
Merope, old man. The wife of Polybus.

MESSENGER:
The queen? What's there to fear in her?

OEDIPUS:
A dreadful prophecy, stranger, sent by the gods.

MESSENGER:
Tell me, could you? Unless it's forbidden
other ears to hear.

OEDIPUS:
Not at all.
Apollo told me once—it is my fate—
I must make love with my own mother, 1200
shed my father's blood with my own hands.
So for years I've given Corinth a wide berth,
and it's been my good fortune too. But still,
to see one's parents and look into their eyes
is the greatest joy I know.

MESSENGER:
You're afraid of that?
That kept you out of Corinth?

OEDIPUS:
My *father*, old man—
so I wouldn't kill my father.

MESSENGER:
So that's it. 1210
Well then, seeing I came with such good will, my king,
why don't I rid you of that old worry now?

OEDIPUS:
What a rich reward you'd have for that!

MESSENGER:

What do you think I came for, majesty?
So you'd come home and I'd be better off.

OEDIPUS:

Never, I will never go near my parents.

MESSENGER:

My boy, it's clear, you don't know what you're doing.

OEDIPUS:

What do you mean, old man? For god's sake, explain.

MESSENGER:

If you ran from *them*, always dodging home . . .

OEDIPUS:

Always, terrified Apollo's oracle might come true—   1220

MESSENGER:

And you'd be covered with guilt, from both your parents.

OEDIPUS:

That's right, old man, that fear is always with me.

MESSENGER:

Don't you know? You've really nothing to fear.

OEDIPUS:

But why? If I'm their son—Merope, Polybus?

MESSENGER:

Polybus was nothing to you, that's why, not in blood.

OEDIPUS:

What are you saying—Polybus was not my father?

MESSENGER:

No more than I am. He and I are equals.

OEDIPUS:

                              My father—
how can my father equal nothing? You're nothing to me!

MESSENGER:

Neither was he, no more your father than I am.   1230

OEDIPUS:

Then why did he call me his son?

MESSENGER:

                              You were a gift,
years ago—know for a fact he took you
from my hands.

OEDIPUS:

                    No, from another's hands?
Then how could he love me so? He loved me, deeply . . .

MESSENGER:

True, and his early years without a child
made him love you all the more.

OEDIPUS:

                              And you, did you . . .
buy me? find me by accident?   1240

MESSENGER:

                              I stumbled on you,
down the woody flanks of Mount Cithaeron.

OEDIPUS:

                              So close,
what were you doing here, just passing through?

MESSENGER:

Watching over my flocks, grazing them on the slopes.

OEDIPUS:

A herdsman, were you? A vagabond, scraping for wages?

MESSENGER:

Your savior too, my son, in your worst hour.

OEDIPUS:

                              Oh—
when you picked me up, was I in pain? What exactly?

MESSENGER:

Your ankles . . . they tell the story. Look at them.   1250

OEDIPUS:

Why remind me of that, that old affliction?

MESSENGER:

Your ankles were pinned together. I set you free.

OEDIPUS:

That dreadful mark—I've had it from the cradle.

MESSENGER:

And you got your name from that misfortune too,
the name's still with you.

OEDIPUS:

                              Dear god, who did it?—
mother? father? Tell me.

MESSENGER:

                              I don't know.
The one who gave you to me, he'd know more.

OEDIPUS:

What? You took me from someone else?   1260
You didn't find me yourself?

MESSENGER:

No sir,
another shepherd passed you on to me.

OEDIPUS:

Who? Do you know? Describe him.

MESSENGER:

He called himself a servant of . . .
if I remember rightly—Laius.
JOCASTA *turns sharply.*

OEDIPUS:

The king of the land who ruled here long ago?

MESSENGER:

That's the one. That herdsman was *his* man.

OEDIPUS:

Is he still alive? Can I see him?

MESSENGER:

They'd know best, the people of these parts.   1270
OEDIPUS *and the* MESSENGER *turn to the* CHORUS.

OEDIPUS:

Does anyone know that herdsman,
the one he mentioned? Anyone seen him
in the fields, here in the city? Out with it!
The time has come to reveal this once for all.

LEADER:

I think he's the very shepherd you wanted to see,
a moment ago. But the queen, Jocasta,
she's the one to say.

OEDIPUS:

Jocasta,
you remember the man we just sent for?
Is *that* the one he means?   1280

JOCASTA:

That man . . .
why ask? Old shepherd, talk, empty nonsense,
don't give it another thought, don't even think—

OEDIPUS:

What—give up now, with a clue like this?
Fail to solve the mystery of my birth?
Not for all the world!

JOCASTA:

Stop—in the name of god,
if you love your own life, call off this search!
My suffering is enough.

OEDIPUS:

Courage!   1290
Even if my mother turns out to be a slave,
and I a slave, three generations back,
you would not seem common.

JOCASTA:

Oh no,
listen to me, I beg you, don't do this.

OEDIPUS:

Listen to you? No more. I must know it all,
must see the truth at last.

JOCASTA:

No, please—
for your sake—I want the best for you!

OEDIPUS:

Your best is more than I can bear.   1300

JOCASTA:

You're doomed—
may you never fathom who you are!

OEDIPUS:

To a servant.

Hurry, fetch me the herdsman, now!
Leave her to glory in her royal birth.

JOCASTA:

Aieeeeee—
man of agony—
that is the only name I have for you,
that, no other—ever, ever, ever!
Flinging through the palace doors. A long, tense silence follows.

LEADER:

Where's she gone, Oedipus?
Rushing off, such wild grief . . .   1310
I'm afraid that from this silence
something monstrous may come bursting forth.

OEDIPUS:

Let it burst! Whatever will, whatever must!
I must know my birth, no matter how common
it may be—I must see my origins face-to-face.
She perhaps, she with her woman's pride
may well be mortified by my birth,
but I, I count myself the son of Chance,
the great goddess, giver of all good things—
I'll never see myself disgraced. She is my mother!   1320
And the moons have marked me out, my blood-brothers,
one moon on the wane, the next moon great with power.
That is my blood, my nature—I will never betray it,
never fail to search and learn my birth!

CHORUS:

Yes—if I am a true prophet
    if I can grasp the truth,
  by the boundless skies of Olympus,
at the full moon of tomorrow, Mount Cithaeron
you will know how Oedipus glories in you—
you, his birthplace, nurse, his mountain-mother!   1330
And we will sing you, dancing out your praise—
you lift our monarch's heart!
    Apollo, Apollo, god of the wild cry
        may our dancing please you!
                Oedipus—
        son, dear child, who bore you?
Who of the nymphs who seem to live forever
mated with Pan, the mountain-striding Father?
Who was your mother? who, some bride of Apollo
the god who loves the pastures spreading toward the sun?   1340
    Or was it Hermes, king of the lightning ridges?
Or Dionysus, lord of frenzy, lord of the barren peaks—
did he seize you in his hands, dearest of all his lucky
    finds?—
    found by the nymphs, their warm eyes dancing, gift
to the lord who loves them dancing out his joy!

OEDIPUS *strains to see a figure coming from the distance.*
Attended by palace guards, an old SHEPHERD *enters slowly,*
reluctant to approach the king.

OEDIPUS:

I never met the man, my friends . . . still,
if I had to guess, I'd say that's the shepherd,
the very one we've looked for all along.
Brothers in old age, two of a kind,
he and our guest here. At any rate   1350
the ones who bring him in are my own men,
I recognize them.
Turning to the LEADER.

            But you know more than I,
you should, you've seen the man before.

LEADER:

I know him, definitely. One of Laius' men,
a trusty shepherd, if there ever was one.

OEDIPUS:

You, I ask you first, stranger,
you from Corinth—is this the one you mean?

MESSENGER:

You're looking at him. He's your man.

OEDIPUS:

To the SHEPHERD.

You, old man, come over here—   1360
look at me. Answer all my questions.
Did you ever serve King Laius?

SHEPHERD:

                So I did . . .
a slave, not bought on the block though,
born and reared in the palace.

OEDIPUS:

Your duties, your kind of work?

SHEPHERD:

Herding the flocks, the better part of my life.

OEDIPUS:

Where, mostly? Where did you do your grazing?

SHEPHERD:

                        Well,
Cithaeron sometimes, or the foothills round about.   1370

OEDIPUS:

This man—you know him? ever see him there?

SHEPHERD:

Confused, glancing from the MESSENGER *to the King.*

Doing what?—what man do you mean?

OEDIPUS:

Pointing to the MESSENGER.

This one here—ever have dealings with him?

SHEPHERD:

Not so I could say, but give me a chance,
my memory's bad . . .

MESSENGER:

No wonder he doesn't know me, master.
But let me refresh his memory for him.
I'm sure he recalls old times we had
on the slopes of Mount Cithaeron;
he and I, grazing our flocks, he with two   1380
and I with one—we both struck up together,
three whole seasons, six months at a stretch
from spring to the rising of Arcturus in the fall,
then with winter coming on I'd drive my herds
to my own pens, and back he'd go with his
to Laius' folds.
To the SHEPHERD.

            Now that's how it was,
wasn't it—yes or no?

SHEPHERD:

                Yes, I suppose . . .
it's all so long ago.   1390

MESSENGER:

Come, tell me,
you gave me a child back then, a boy, remember?
A little fellow to rear, my very own.

SHEPHERD:

What? Why rake up that again?

MESSENGER:

Look, here he is, my fine old friend—
the same man who was just a baby then.

SHEPHERD:

Damn you, shut your mouth—quiet!

OEDIPUS:

Don't lash out at him, old man—
you need lashing more than he does.

SHEPHERD:

Why,   1400
master, majesty—what have I done wrong?

OEDIPUS:

You won't answer his question about the boy.

SHEPHERD:

He's talking nonsense, wasting his breath.

OEDIPUS:

So, you won't talk willingly—
then you'll talk with pain.
The guards seize the SHEPHERD.

SHEPHERD:

No, dear god, don't torture an old man!

OEDIPUS:

Twist his arms back, quickly!

SHEPHERD:

God help us, why?—
what more do you need to know?

OEDIPUS:

Did you give him that child? He's asking.   1410

SHEPHERD:

I did . . . I wish to god I'd died that day.

OEDIPUS:

You've got your wish if you don't tell the truth.

SHEPHERD:

The more I tell, the worse the death I'll die.

OEDIPUS:

Our friend here wants to stretch things out, does he?
Motioning to his men for torture.

SHEPHERD:

No, no, I gave it to him—I just said so.

OEDIPUS:

Where did you get it? Your house? Someone else's?

SHEPHERD:

It wasn't mine, no, I got it from . . . someone.

OEDIPUS:

Which one of them?
Looking at the citizens.
Whose house?

SHEPHERD:

No—   1420
god's sake, master, no more questions!

OEDIPUS:

You're a dead man if I have to ask again.

SHEPHERD:

Then—the child came from the house . . .
of Laius.

OEDIPUS:

A slave? or born of his own blood?

SHEPHERD:

Oh no,
I'm right at the edge, the horrible truth—I've got to say it!

OEDIPUS:

And I'm at the edge of hearing horrors, yes, but I must
hear!

SHEPHERD:

All right! His son, they said it was—his son!
But the one inside, your wife,   1430
she'd tell it best.

OEDIPUS:

My wife—
she gave it to you?

SHEPHERD:

Yes, yes, my king.

OEDIPUS:

Why, what for?

SHEPHERD:

To kill it.

OEDIPUS:

Her own child,
how could she?

SHEPHERD:

She was afraid—
frightening prophecies.   1440

OEDIPUS:

What?

SHEPHERD:

    They said—
he'd kill his parents.

OEDIPUS:

But you gave him to this old man—why?

SHEPHERD:

I pitied the little baby, master,
hoped he'd take him off to his own country,
far away, but he saved him for this, this fate.
If you are the man he says you are, believe me,
you were born for pain.

OEDIPUS:

           O god—   1450
all come true, all burst to light!
O light—now let me look my last on you!
I stand revealed at last—
cursed in my birth, cursed in marriage,
cursed in the lives I cut down with these hands!

*Rushing through the doors with a great cry. The
Corinthian* MESSENGER, *the* SHEPHERD *and
attendants exit slowly to the side.*

CHORUS:

  O the generations of men
the dying generations—adding the total
of all your lives I find they come to nothing . . .
      does there exist, is there a man on earth
who seizes more joy than just a dream, a vision?   1460
And the vision no sooner dawns than dies
blazing into oblivion.

You are my great example, you, your life
your destiny, Oedipus, man of misery—
I count no man blest.

      You outranged all men!
  Bending your bow to the breaking-point
you captured priceless glory, O dear god,
and the Sphinx came crashing down,
      the virgin, claws hooked   1470

like a bird of omen singing, shrieking death—
like a fortress reared in the face of death
you rose and saved our land.

From that day on we called you king
we crowned you with honors, Oedipus, towering over all—
mighty king of the seven gates of Thebes.
But now to hear your story—is there a man more
      agonized?
More wed to pain and frenzy? Not a man on earth,
the joy of your life ground down to nothing
O Oedipus, name for the ages—   1480
    one and the same wide harbor served you
                son and father both
son and father came to rest in the same bridal chamber.
How, how could the furrows your father plowed
bear you, your agony, harrowing on
in silence O so long?

           But now for all your power
Time, all-seeing Time has dragged you to the light,
judged your marriage monstrous from the start—
the son and the father tangling, both one—   1490
O child of Laius, would to god
  I'd never seen you, never never!
    Now I weep like a man who wails the dead
and the dirge comes pouring forth with all my heart!
I tell you the truth, you gave me life
my breath leapt up in you
and now you bring down night upon my eyes.

Enter a MESSENGER *from the palace.*

MESSENGER:

Men of Thebes, always first in honor,
what horrors you will hear, what you will see,
what a heavy weight of sorrow you will shoulder . . .   1500
if you are true to your birth, if you still have
some feeling for the royal house of Thebes.
I tell you neither the waters of the Danube
nor the Nile can wash this palace clean.
Such things it hides, it soon will bring to light—
terrible things, and none done blindly now,
all done with a will. The pains
we inflict upon ourselves hurt most of all.

LEADER:

God knows we have pains enough already.
What can you add to them?   1510

MESSENGER:

The queen is dead.

LEADER:

        Poor lady—how?

MESSENGER:

By her own hand. But you are spared the worst,
you never had to watch . . . I saw it all,

and with all the memory that's in me
you will learn what that poor woman suffered.

Once she'd broken in through the gates
dashing past us, frantic, whipped to fury,
ripping her hair out with both hands—
straight to her rooms she rushed, flinging herself   1520
across the bridal-bed, doors slamming behind her—
once inside, she wailed for Laius, dead so long,
remembering how she bore his child long ago,
the life that rose up to destroy him, leaving
its mother to mother living creatures
with the very son she'd borne.
Oh how she wept, mourning the marriage-bed
where she let loose that double brood—monsters—
husband by her husband, children by her child.

                                    And then—   1530
but how she died is more than I can say. Suddenly
Oedipus burst in, screaming, he stunned us so
we couldn't watch her agony to the end,
our eyes were fixed on him. Circling
like a maddened beast, stalking, here, there,
crying out to us—
                    Give him a sword! His wife,
no wife, his mother, where can he find the mother earth
that cropped two crops at once, himself and all his
        children?
He was raging—one of the dark powers pointing the
        way,   1540
none of us mortals crowding around him, no,
with a great shattering cry—someone, something
        leading
him on—
he hurled at the twin doors and bending the bolts
        back
out of their sockets, crashed through the chamber.
And there we saw the woman hanging by the neck,
cradled high in the woven noose, spinning,
swinging back and forth. And when he saw her,
giving a low, wrenching sob that broke our hearts,
slipping the halter from her throat, he eased her down,   1550
in a slow embrace he laid her down, poor thing . . .
then, what came next, what horror we beheld!

He rips off her brooches, the long gold pins
holding her robes—and lifting them high,
looking straight up into the points,
he digs them down the sockets of his eyes, crying,
        "You,
you'll see no more the pain I suffered, all the pain I
        caused!
Too long you looked on the bones you never should
        have seen,
blind to the ones you longed to see, to know! Blind
from this hour on! Blind in the darkness—blind!"   1560
His voice like a dirge, rising, over and over
raising the pins, raking them down his eyes.
And at each stroke blood spurts from the roots,
splashing his beard, a swirl of it, nerves and clots—
black hail of blood pulsing, gushing down.

These are the griefs that burst upon them both,
coupling man and woman. The joy they had so lately,
the fortune of their old ancestral house
was deep joy indeed. Now, in this one day,
wailing, madness and doom, death, disgrace,   1570
all the griefs in the world that you can name,
all are theirs forever.

LEADER:

                            Oh poor man, the misery—
has he any rest from pain now?

A voice within, in torment.

MESSENGER:

                            He's shouting,
"Loose the bolts, someone, show me to all of Thebes!
My father's murderer, my mother's—"
No, I can't repeat it, it's unholy.
Now he'll tear himself from his native earth,
not linger, curse the house with his own curse.   1580
But he needs strength, and a guide to lead him on.
This is sickness more than he can bear.

The palace doors open.

                            Look,
he'll show you himself. The great doors are opening—
you are about to see a sight, a horror
even his mortal enemy would pity.

Enter OEDIPUS, *blinded, led by a boy. He stands at the palace
steps, as if surveying his people once again.*

CHORUS:

                            O the terror—
the suffering, for all the world to see,
the worst terror that ever met my eyes.
What madness swept over you? What god,   1590
what dark power leapt beyond all bounds,
beyond belief, to crush your wretched life?—
godforsaken, cursed by the gods!
I pity you but I can't bear to look.
I've much to ask, so much to learn,
so much fascinates my eyes,
but you . . . I shudder at the sight.

OEDIPUS:

                            Oh, Ohh—
the agony! I am agony—
where am I going? where on earth?   1600
    where does all this agony hurl me?
where's my voice—
    winging, swept away on a dark tide—
My destiny, my dark power, what a leap you made!

CHORUS:

To the depths of terror, too dark to hear, to see.

OEDIPUS:

Dark, horror of darkness
my darkness, drowning, swirling around me
crashing wave on wave—unspeakable, irresistible
    headwind, fatal harbor! Oh again,
the misery, all at once, over and over   1610
the stabbing daggers, stab of memory
raking me insane.

CHORUS:

                    No wonder you suffer
twice over, the pain of your wounds,
the lasting grief of pain.

OEDIPUS:

                    Dear friend, still here?
Standing by me, still with a care for me,
the blind man? Such compassion,
    loyal to the last. Oh it's you,
I know you're here, dark as it is   1620
I'd know you anywhere, your voice—
it's yours, clearly yours.

CHORUS:

                    Dreadful, what you've done . . .
how could you bear it, gouging out your eyes?
What superhuman power drove you on?

OEDIPUS:

    Apollo, friends, Apollo—
he ordained my agonies—these, my pains on pains!
But the hand that struck my eyes was mine,
mine alone—no one else—
        I did it all myself!   1630
What good were eyes to me?
Nothing I could see could bring me joy.

CHORUS:

No, no, exactly as you say.

OEDIPUS:

                    What can I ever see?
    What love, what call of the heart
can touch my ears with joy? Nothing, friends.
    Take me away, far, far from Thebes,
    quickly, cast me away, my friends—
this great murderous ruin, this man cursed to heaven,
    the man the deathless gods hate most of all!   1640

CHORUS:

Pitiful, you suffer so, you understand so much . . .
I wish you had never known.

OEDIPUS:

                    Die, die—
whoever he was that day in the wilds
who cut my ankles free of the ruthless pins,

he pulled me clear of death, he saved my life
for this, this kindness—
                    Curse him, kill him!
If I'd died then, I'd never have dragged myself,
my loved ones through such hell.   1650

CHORUS:

Oh if only . . . would to god.

OEDIPUS:

                            I'd never have come to this,
    my father's murderer—never been branded
mother's husband, all men see me now! Now,
    loathed by the gods, son of the mother I defiled
    coupling in my father's bed, spawning lives in the
        loins
that spawned my wretched life. What grief can crown
    this grief?
    It's mine alone, my destiny—I am Oedipus!

CHORUS:

How can I say you've chosen for the best?
Better to die than be alive and blind.   1660

OEDIPUS:

What I did was best—don't lecture me,
no more advice. I, with *my* eyes,
how could I look my father in the eyes
when I go down to death? Or mother, so abused . . .
I have done such things to the two of them,
crimes too huge for hanging.
                    Worse yet,
the sight of my children, born as they were born,
how could I long to look into their eyes?
No, not with these eyes of mine, never.   1670
Not this city either, her high towers,
the sacred glittering images of her gods—
I am misery! I, her best son, reared
as no other son of Thebes was ever reared,
I've stripped myself, I gave the command myself.
All men must cast away the great blasphemer,
the curse now brought to light by the gods,
the son of Laius—I, my father's son!

Now I've exposed my guilt, horrendous guilt,
could I train a level glance on you, my countrymen?   1680
Impossible! No, if I could just block off my ears,
the springs of hearing, I would stop at nothing—
I'd wall up my loathsome body like a prison,
blind to the sound of life, not just the sight.
Oblivion—what a blessing . . .
for the mind to dwell a world away from pain.

O Cithaeron, why did you give me shelter?
Why didn't you take me, crush my life out on the spot?
I'd never have revealed my birth to all mankind.

O Polybus, Corinth, the old house of my fathers,   1690
so I believed—what a handsome prince you raised—

under the skin, what sickness to the core.
Look at me! Born of outrage, outrage to the core.
O triple roads—it all comes back, the secret,
dark ravine, and the oaks closing in
where the three roads join . . .
You drank my father's blood, my own blood
spilled by my own hands—you still remember me?
What things you saw me do? Then I came here
and did them all once more!   1700
                              Marriages! O marriage,
you gave me birth, and once you brought me into the
     world
you brought my sperm rising back, springing to light
fathers, brothers, sons—one murderous breed—
brides, wives, mothers. The blackest things
a man can do, I have done them all!
                              No more—
it's wrong to name what's wrong to do. Quickly,
for the love of god, hide me somewhere,
kill me, hurl me into the sea   1710
where you can never look on me again.

Beckoning to the CHORUS *as they shrink away.*
                              Closer,
it's all right. Touch the man of grief.
Do. Don't be afraid. My troubles are mine
and I am the only man alive who can sustain them.

Enter CREON *from the palace, attended by palace guards.*

LEADER:

Put your requests to Creon. Here he is,
just when we need him. He'll have a plan, he'll act.
Now that he's the sole defense of the country
in your place.

OEDIPUS:

                              Oh no, what can I say to him?   1720
How can I ever hope to win his trust?
I wronged him so, just now, in every way.
You must see that—I was so wrong, so wrong.

CREON:

I haven't come to mock you, Oedipus,
or to criticize your former failings.
Turning to the guards.
                              You there,
have you lost all respect for human feelings?
At least revere the Sun, the holy fire
that keeps us all alive. Never expose a thing
of guilt and holy dread so great it appalls   1730
the earth, the rain from heaven, the light of day!
Get him into the halls—quickly as you can.
Piety demands no less. Kindred alone
should see a kinsman's shame. This is obscene.

OEDIPUS:

Please, in god's name . . . you wipe my fears away,
coming so generously to me, the worst of men.
Do one thing more, for your sake, not mine.

CREON:

What do you want? Why so insistent?

OEDIPUS:

Drive me out of the land at once, far from sight,
where I can never hear a human voice.   1740

CREON:

I'd have done that already, I promise you.
First I wanted the god to clarify my duties.

OEDIPUS:

The god? His command was clear, every word:
death for the father-killer, the curse—
he said destroy me!

CREON:

So he did. Still in such a crisis
it's better to ask precisely what to do.

OEDIPUS:

                              So miserable—
you would consult the god about a man like me?

CREON:

By all means. And this time, I assume,   1750
even you will obey the god's decrees.

OEDIPUS:

                              I will,
I will. And you, I command you—I beg you . . .
the woman inside, bury her as you see fit.
It's the only decent thing,
to give your own the last rites. As for me,
never condemn the city of my fathers
to house my body, not while I'm alive, no,
let me live on the mountains, on Cithaeron,
my favorite haunt, I have made it famous.   1760
Mother and father marked out that rock
to be my everlasting tomb—buried alive.
Let me die there, where they tried to kill me.

Oh but this I know: no sickness can destroy me,
nothing can. I would never have been saved
from death—I have been saved
for something great and terrible, something strange.
Well let my destiny come and take me on its way!
About my children, Creon, the boys at least,
don't burden yourself. They're men,   1770
wherever they go, they'll find the means to live.
But my two daughters, my poor helpless girls,
clustering at our table, never without me
hovering near them . . . whatever I touched,
they always had their share. Take care of them,
I beg you. Wait, better—permit me, would you?
Just to touch them with my hands and take

our fill of tears. Please . . . my king.
Grant it, with all your noble heart.
If I could hold them, just once, I'd think   1780
I had them with me, like the early days
when I could see their eyes.

ANTIGONE *and* ISMENE, *two small children, are led in from*
the palace by a nurse.

What's that?
O god! Do I really hear you sobbing?—
my two children. Creon, you've pitied me?
Sent me my darling girls, my own flesh and blood!
Am I right?

CREON:

Yes, it's my doing.
I know the joy they gave you all these years,
the joy you must feel now.   1790

OEDIPUS:

Bless you, Creon!
May god watch over you for this kindness,
better than he ever guarded me.
Children, where are you?
Here, come quickly—

Groping for ANTIGONE *and* ISMENE, *who approach their*
father cautiously, then embrace him.

Come to these hands of mine,
your brother's hands, your own father's hands
that served his once bright eyes so well—
that made them blind. Seeing nothing, children,
knowing nothing. I became your father,   1800
I fathered you in the soil that gave me life.

How I weep for you—I cannot see you now . . .
just thinking of all your days to come, the bitterness,
the life that rough mankind will thrust upon you.
Where are the public gatherings you can join,
the banquets of the clans? Home you'll come,
in tears, cut off from the sight of it all,
the brilliant rites unfinished.
And when you reach perfection, ripe for marriage,
who will he be, my dear ones? Risking all   1810
to shoulder the curse that weighs down my parents,
yes and you too—that wounds us all together.
What more misery could you want?
Your father killed his father, sowed his mother,
one, one and the selfsame womb sprang you—
he cropped the very roots of his existence.

Such disgrace, and you must bear it all!
Who will marry you then? Not a man on earth.
Your doom is clear: you'll wither away to nothing,
single, without a child.   1820

Turning to CREON.

Oh Creon,
you are the only father they have now . . .

we who brought them into the world
are gone, both gone at a stroke—
Don't let them go begging, abandoned,
women without men. Your own flesh and blood!
Never bring them down to the level of my pains.
Pity them. Look at them, so young, so vulnerable,
shorn of everything—you're their only hope.
Promise me, noble Creon, touch my hand!   1830

Reaching toward CREON, *who draws back.*

You, little ones, if you were old enough
to understand, there is much I'd tell you.
Now, as it is, I'd have you say a prayer.
Pray for life, my children,
live where you are free to grow and season.
Pray god you find a better life than mine,
the father who begot you.

CREON:

Enough.
You've wept enough. Into the palace now.

OEDIPUS:

I must, but I find it very hard.   1840

CREON:

Time is the great healer, you will see.

OEDIPUS:

I am going—you know on what condition?

CREON:

Tell me. I'm listening.

OEDIPUS:

Drive me out of Thebes, in exile.

CREON:

Not I. Only the gods can give you that.

OEDIPUS:

Surely the gods hate me so much—

CREON:

You'll get your wish at once.

OEDIPUS:

You consent?

CREON:

I try to say what I mean; it's my habit.

OEDIPUS:

Then take me away. It's time.   1850

CREON:

Come along, let go of the children.

OEDIPUS:

No—

don't take them away from me, not now! No no no!

Clutching his daughters as the guards wrench them loose and take them through the palace doors.

CREON:

Still the king, the master of all things?
No more: here your power ends.
None of your power follows you through life.

Exit OEDIPUS *and* CREON *to the palace. The* CHORUS *comes forward to address the audience directly.*

CHORUS:

People of Thebes, my countrymen, look on Oedipus.
He solved the famous riddle with his brilliance,
he rose to power, a man beyond all power.
Who could behold his greatness without envy?   1860
Now what a black sea of terror has overwhelmed him.
Now as we keep our watch and wait the final day,
count no man happy till he dies, free of pain at last.

Exit in procession.

THUCYDIDES

Selection from *History of the Peloponnesian War*

In about 450 B.C. Athens was at the height of its political and cultural accomplishments; however, its towering position came at a high cost to other Greek city-states and, ultimately, to itself. Its decades of greatness were bracketed by two costly wars—the first against the Persians, which Athens won, at the beginning of the century; and the second against a coalition of other Greek city-states, which Athens lost, at the century's end.

In the second war—known as the Peloponnesian War—Athens, with a group of like-minded allies, attempted to impose its will on neighboring city-states. Alarmed at Athenian imperialism, these city-states turned to Sparta, who, responding to their pleas, formed a military alliance that overran Athens in 404 B.C. The events of this struggle were recorded by Thucydides, an Athenian general who fought in the war until he was forced into exile for his inability to raise a siege during the war.

In his history, Thucydides set standards of scholarship that have seldom been equaled. He interviewed eyewitnesses, read the sources, and attempted to verify findings with the goal of being as accurate as possible. Although he left the work unfinished, stopping in about 410 B.C., he detailed events so vividly that the narrative still holds the attention of today's readers. He displayed a dramatic flair by inserting speeches that were attributed to generals and politicians whose decisions affected the war's outcome. Of special note is his distinction as the first writer to interpret war in purely human terms, rather than searching for divine causes. He also presented his history as "philosophy teaching by example"; that is, he used the events of the war as fodder for his speculations about human nature and behavior.

Reading the Selection

Pericles, the Athenian general, delivered this funeral oration during the first year of the war (430 B.C.) to honor the young men who had died in battle. (Pericles himself was carried off by the plague in the next year.) In a brief introduction, Thucydides sets the scene before Pericles gives his memorial speech to the mourners.

Pericles' speech has two themes: praise for Athens and the Athenian way of life, and the traditional argument that the soldiers have not died in vain. He envisions Athens as a model for the Greek world to follow, a place where the individual is honored in a free and open society. There, tolerance and respect for others in their private lives is matched by respect for the law on the part of those engaged in public affairs. He praises Athenian education because it emphasizes natural rather than "state-induced" courage—a dig at Sparta. Thus, the city-state produced brave and loyal citizens eager to defend their open way of life. He even has praise for the Athenian business community, pointing out that it, like other segments of society, is committed to the general welfare. In sum, Athens is "an education to Greece."

While such fulsome praise of Athens may have comforted the grieving and stirred the hearts of the audience, it is also clear that these same words could be interpreted as signs of arrogance and a hint at imperialistic designs. This was, of course, Thucydides' intention; in later chapters of his history, he shows the gradual unmasking of Athenian imperialism as events move to an inevitable climax.

—⁂—

Book II
Pericles' Funeral Oration

. . .

'Many of those who have spoken here in the past have praised the institution of this speech at the close of our ceremony. It seemed to them a mark of honour to our soldiers who have fallen in war that a speech should be made over them. I do not agree. These men have shown themselves valiant in action, and it would be enough, I think, for their glories to be proclaimed in action, as you have just seen it done at this funeral organized by the state. Our belief in the courage and manliness of so many should not be hazarded on the goodness or badness of one man's speech. Then it is not easy to speak with a proper sense of balance, when a man's listeners find it difficult to believe in the truth of what one is saying. The man who knows the facts and loves the dead may well think that an oration tells less than what he knows and what he would like to hear: others who do not know so much may feel envy for the dead, and think the orator over-praises them, when he speaks of exploits that are beyond their own capacities. Praise of other people is tolerable only up to a certain point, the point where one still believes that one could do oneself some of the things one is hearing about. Once you get beyond this point, you will find people becoming jealous and incredulous. However, the fact is that this institution was set up and approved by our forefathers, and it is my duty to follow the tradition and do my best to meet the wishes and the expectations of every one of you.

'I shall begin by speaking about our ancestors, since it is only right and proper on such an occasion to pay them the honour of recalling what they did. In this land of ours there have always been the same people living from generation to generation up till now, and they, by their courage and their virtues, have handed it on to us, a free country. They certainly deserve our praise. Even more so do our fathers deserve it. For to the inheritance they had received they added all the empire we have now, and it was not without blood and toil that they handed it down to us of the present generation. And then we ourselves, assembled here today, who are mostly in the prime of life, have, in most directions, added to the power of our empire and have organized our State in such a way that it is perfectly well able to look after itself both in peace and in war.

'I have no wish to make a long speech on subjects familiar to you all: so I shall say nothing about the warlike deeds by which we acquired our power or the battles in which we or our fathers gallantly resisted our enemies, Greek or foreign. What I want to do is, in the first place, to discuss the spirit in which we faced our trials and also our constitution and the way of life which has made us great. After that I shall speak in praise of the dead, believing that this kind of speech is not inappropriate to the present occasion, and that this whole assembly, of citizens and foreigners, may listen to it with advantage.

'Let me say that our system of government does not copy the institutions of our neighbours. It is more the case of our being a model to others, than of our imitating anyone else. Our constitution is called a democracy because power is in the hands not of a minority but of the whole people. When it is a question of settling private disputes, everyone is equal before the law; when it is a question of putting one person before another in positions of public responsibility, what counts is not membership of a particular class, but the actual ability which the man possesses. No one, so long as he has it in him to be of service to the state, is kept in political obscurity because of poverty. And, just as our political life is free and open, so is our day-to-day life in our relations with each other. We do not get into a state with our next-door neighbour if he enjoys himself in his own way, nor do we give him the kind of black looks which, though they do no real harm, still do hurt people's feelings. We are free and tolerant in our private lives; but in public affairs we keep to the law. This is because it commands our deep respect.

'We give our obedience to those whom we put in positions of authority, and we obey the laws themselves, especially those which are for the protection of the oppressed, and those unwritten laws which it is an acknowledged shame to break.

'And here is another point. When our work is over, we are in a position to enjoy all kinds of recreation for our spirits. There are various kinds of contests and sacrifices regularly throughout the year; in our own homes we find a beauty and a good taste which delight us every day and which drive away our cares. Then the greatness of our city brings it about that all the good things from all over the world flow in to us, so that to us it seems just as natural to enjoy foreign goods as our own local products.

'Then there is a great difference between us and our opponents, in our attitude towards military security. Here are some examples: Our city is open to the world, and we have no periodical deportations in order to prevent people observing or finding out secrets which might be of military advantage to the enemy. This is because we rely, not on secret weapons, but on our own real courage and loyalty. There is a difference, too, in our educational systems. The Spartans, from their earliest boyhood, are submitted to the most laborious training in courage; we pass our lives without all these restrictions, and yet are just as ready to face the same dangers as they are. Here is a proof of this: When the Spartans invade our land, they do not come by themselves, but bring all their allies with them; whereas we, when we launch an attack abroad, do the job by ourselves, and, though fighting on foreign soil, do not often fail to defeat opponents who are fighting for their own hearths and homes. As a matter of fact none of our enemies has ever yet been confronted with our total strength, because we have to divide our attention between our navy and the many missions on which our troops are sent on land. Yet, if our enemies engage a detachment of our forces and defeat it, they give themselves credit for having thrown back our entire army; or, if they lose, they claim that they were beaten by us in full strength. There are certain advantages, I think, in our way of meeting danger voluntarily, with an easy mind, instead of with a laborious training, with natural rather than with state-induced courage. We do not have to spend our time practising to meet sufferings which are still in the future; and when they are actually upon us we show ourselves just as brave as these others who are always in strict training. This is one point in which, I think, our city deserves to be admired. There are also others:

'Our love of what is beautiful does not lead to extravagance; our love of the things of the mind does not make us soft. We regard wealth as something to be properly used, rather than as something to boast about. As for poverty, no one need be ashamed to admit it: the real shame is in not taking practical measures to escape from it. Here each individual is interested not only in his own affairs but in the affairs of the state as well: even those who are mostly occupied with their own business are extremely well informed on general politics—this is a peculiarity of ours: we do not say that a man who takes no interest in politics is a man who minds his own business; we say that he has no business here at all. We Athenians, in our own persons, make our decisions on policy or submit them to proper discussions: for we do not think that there is an incompatibility between words and deeds; the worst thing is to rush into action before the consequences have been properly debated. And this is another point where we differ from other people. We are capable at the same time of taking risks and of estimating them beforehand. Others are brave out of ignorance; and, when they stop to think, they begin to fear. But the man who can most truly be accounted brave is he who best knows the meaning of what is sweet in life and of what is terrible, and then goes out undeterred to meet what is to come.

'Again, in questions of general good feeling there is a great contrast between us and most other people. We make friends by doing good to others, not by receiving good from them. This makes our friendship all the more reliable, since we want to keep alive the gratitude of those who are in our debt by showing continued goodwill to them: whereas the feelings of one who owes us something lack the same enthusiasm, since he knows that, when he repays our kindness, it will be more like paying back a debt than giving something spontaneously. We are unique in this. When we do kindnesses to others, we do not do them out of any calculations of profit or loss: we do them without afterthought, relying on our free liberality. Taking everything together then, I declare that our city is an education to Greece, and I declare that in my opinion each single one of our citizens, in all the manifold aspects of life, is able to show himself the rightful lord and owner of his own person, and do this, moreover, with exceptional grace and exceptional versatility. And to show that this is no empty boasting for the present occasion, but real tangible fact, you have only to consider the power which our city possesses and which has been won by those very qualities which I have mentioned. Athens, alone of the states we know, comes to her testing time in a greatness that surpasses what was imagined of her. In her case, and in her case alone, no invading enemy is ashamed at being defeated, and no subject can complain of being governed by people unfit for their responsibilities. Mighty indeed are the marks and monuments of our empire which we have left. Future ages will wonder at us, as the present age wonders at us now. We do not need the praises of a Homer, or of anyone else whose words may delight us for the moment, but whose estimation of facts will fall short of what is really true. For our adventurous spirit has forced an entry into every sea and into every land; and everywhere we have left behind us everlasting memorials of good done to our friends or suffering inflicted on our enemies.

'This, then, is the kind of city for which these men, who could not bear the thought of losing her, nobly fought and nobly died. It is only natural that every one of us who survive them should be willing to undergo hardships in her service. And it was for this reason that I have spoken at such length about our city, because I wanted to make it clear that for us there is more at stake than there is for others who lack our advantages; also I wanted my words of praise for the dead to be set in the bright light of evidence. And now the most important of these words has been spoken. I have sung the praises of our city; but it was the courage and gallantry of these men, and of people like them, which made her splendid. Nor would you find it true in the case of many of the Greeks, as it is true of them, that no words can do more than justice to their deeds.

'To me it seems that the consummation which has overtaken these men shows us the meaning of manliness in its first revelation and in its final proof. Some of them, no doubt, had their faults; but what we ought to remember first is their gallant conduct against the enemy in defence of their native land. They have blotted out evil with good, and done more service to the commonwealth than they ever did harm in their private lives. No one of these men weakened because he wanted to go on enjoying his wealth: no one put off the awful day in the hope that he might live to escape his poverty and grow rich. More to be desired than such things, they chose to check the enemy's pride. This, to them, was a risk most glorious, and they accepted it, willing to strike down the enemy and relinquish everything else. As for success or failure, they left that in the doubtful hands of Hope, and when the reality of battle was before their faces, they put their trust in their own selves. In the fighting, they thought it more honourable to stand their ground and suffer death than to give in and save their lives. So they fled from the reproaches of men, abiding with life and limb the brunt of battle; and, in a small moment of time, the climax of their lives, a culmination of glory, not of fear, were swept away from us.

'So and such they were, these men—worthy of their city. We who remain behind may hope to be spared their fate, but must resolve to keep the same daring spirit against the foe. It is not simply a question of estimating the advantages in theory. I could tell you a long story (and you know it as well as I do) about what is to be gained by beating the enemy back. What I would prefer is that you should fix your eyes every day on the greatness of Athens as she really is, and should fall in love with her. When you realize her greatness, then reflect that what made her great was men with a spirit of adventure, men who knew their duty, men who were ashamed to fall below a certain standard. If they ever failed in an enterprise, they made up

their minds that at any rate the city should not find their courage lacking to her, and they gave to her the best contribution that they could. They gave her their lives, to her and to all of us, and for their own selves they won praises that never grow old, the most splendid of sepulchres—not the sepulchre in which their bodies are laid, but where their glory remains eternal in men's minds, always there on the right occasion to stir others to speech or to action. For famous men have the whole earth as their memorial: it is not only the inscriptions on their graves in their own country that mark them out; no, in foreign lands also, not in any visible form but in people's hearts, their memory abides and grows. It is for you to try to be like them. Make up your minds that happiness depends on being free, and freedom depends on being courageous. Let there be no relaxation in face of the perils of the war. The people who have most excuse for despising death are not the wretched and unfortunate, who have no hope of doing well for themselves, but those who run the risk of a complete reversal in their lives, and who would feel the difference most intensely, if things went wrong for them. Any intelligent man would find a humiliation caused by his own slackness more painful to bear than death, when death comes to him unperceived, in battle, and in the confidence of his patriotism.'

PLATO

Selections from *The Republic*

Plato (ca. 427–347 B.C.), who was Socrates' (ca. 470–399 B.C.) best-known student, dedicated his life to explaining his master's methods of learning and his ideas. According to Plato, whose writings constitute the most authentic source for Socrates' life, the older philosopher saw himself as a "gadfly" whose mission was to annoy others by questioning their knowledge. Rather than being concerned with such issues as the nature of matter or the structure of the universe, the only topics being studied by philosophers at the time, Socrates caused an intellectual revolution by turning to more human interests such as Justice, Beauty, Love, and Wisdom. By recording in dialogue form the discussions between Socrates and others (sometimes a pupil, sometimes a critic), Plato illustrated Socrates' method of discourse, which reflected the belief that admitting one's ignorance is the first step toward wisdom. The Socratic method has three steps: First, Socrates encouraged his students to express opinions on a topic; second, he analyzed these opinions, pointing out faulty premises (things taken for granted) and weak arguments; third, through a series of questions, he led them not to a new truth but to a recognition of the rational steps needed to attain enlightenment. The Socratic method became a standard mode of inquiry that is still practiced today, formally in classroom settings and informally in personal discussions.

When Plato was not writing about Socrates, he taught in the Academy, the school he founded in Athens after 400 B.C. for the instruction of would-be political leaders. Its curriculum was mathematics and philosophy, ideal subjects for philosophers and kings—a reflection of Plato's antidemocratic beliefs. In his classes he put into practice his and Socrates' learning ideal—to lead students to ever higher levels of abstract thought, concluding with the ultimate truth. This intellectual journey required total concentration, in isolation from everyday life. Plato's students, upon graduation, spread the tenets of Platonism, as his philosophy is called, across the ancient world. Platonism helped shape

Hellenistic (see Epicurus's *Letter to Menoeceus*), Roman (see Cicero's *On the Republic*), and early Christian (see St. Augustine's *Confessions*) thought. Athens became the intellectual center of the Classical world, and Plato's Academy taught generations of thinkers until the Christians closed it in the sixth century A.D.

Reading the Selections

Plato was perhaps the first feminist in Western culture. Women as well as men were taught in his school, the Academy, thus contradicting the basic norm of Greek life—to keep women fully separate from men in public. In *The Republic*, the West's first text in political theory, Plato made the case for equality between the sexes to be achieved through equal educational opportunity. His complete rationale for female equality is set forth in *The Republic*, Book V, part of which is excerpted in the selection.

"The Allegory of the Cave," taken from Book VII, is the most famous episode in *The Republic*. An allegory is a parable meant to clarify an idea too complex to understand on its own. In this selection, Socrates uses an allegory to explain his method of learning, introduced earlier in the book. For Socrates, the learning process is of prime concern, because he believed that only when rulers ("philosopher-kings") are well versed in the meaning of Justice can a state be said to be well regulated. Defining Justice and determining how it can be taught to future leaders is thus *The Republic*'s purpose, constituting, in effect, a textbook to be studied in the Academy.

Socrates' words about the nature of the learning process leave his audience puzzled, so he offers "The Allegory of the Cave" by way of explanation. In the allegory, set within a cave lit only by flickering shadows cast from an unseen fire, an exemplary individual releases himself from bondage; this person then moves, step by step, out of the darkness, upward through a passage, and into the natural world to stare at the sun. The allegorical journey symbolizes the intellectual journey that Socrates thought all students must undergo if they were to reach the ultimate truth.

—⚏—

Book V

. . .

The men have fully played their part on our stage and made their exit; and now perhaps it would be right to call in the women, especially since you invite me to do it.

"For people then, born and educated as we explained, the only right way, in my opinion, for them to get and use children and women is the way we started them to go. You remember we tried in our discourse to establish the men as it were guardians of a herd."

"Yes."

"Then let us follow up by giving the women birth and training like theirs, and see if it is proper for us or not."

"How?" he asked.

"Thus; do we think that the females of the guardian dogs ought to share in the guard which the males keep? Ought they to join in the hunt and whatever else they do? Or should the females keep kennel indoors, as being unable because of the birth and training of pups, and should the males do the hard work and have all the care of the flocks?"

"They ought to do everything together," he said, "except that we treat the males as stronger and the females as weaker."

"But is it possible," I said, "to use animals for the same things, if you do not give them the same training and education?"

"Impossible."

"Then if we are to use the women for the same things as the men, we must teach them the same things."

"Yes."

"Now music and gymnastic were taught to the men."

"Yes."

"So we must teach the women those same two arts, and matters of war too, and use them in the same way."

"That seems fair from what you say," he replied.

"Well then," said I, "perhaps much in our present proposals would appear funny in contrast with usual custom, if they were done in the way we say."

"Likely enough," he said.

"And what will be the biggest joke of all?" I asked. "Surely to see naked women in the wrestling schools exercising with the men—not only the young women, but even the older ones too? Like old men in the gymnasium, all over wrinkles and not pleasant to look at, who still fancy the game!"

"You are right, upon my word!" said he; "it would seem funny as things are now!"

"Very well," said I, "since we have set out to speak, let us not fear the jests of refined people. Let them talk how they like and say what they like of such an upheaval, about gymnastic and music, and not least about wearing armour and riding on horseback."

"Quite right," said he.

"But since we have begun let us march on to the rough part of our law. We will entreat these wits to leave their usual business and be serious for once; we will remind them that it is not so very long since Hellenes thought it ugly and funny, as most barbarians do still, to see men naked; and when the Cretans began naked athletics, and the Lacedaimonians followed, the clever people then were able to make fun of the thing. Don't you agree?"

"Yes, I do."

"But we found by experience that it was better to strip than to hide all such things; and soon the seeming funny to the eyes melted away before that which was revealed in the light of reason to be the best. It showed also that he is a vain fool who thinks anything ridiculous but what is evil; and he is a fool who tries to raise laughter against any sight, as being that of something funny, other than the sight of folly and evil; or in earnest sets up any other mark to aim at than what is honourable and good."

"By all manner of means," he said.

"Then surely we must decide first whether this is possible or not. Next, we must open the debate to all, whether a man chooses to argue in jest or in earnest; and let them discuss whether the female nature in mankind allows women to share the same work with men in everything, or in nothing, or only in some things, and if in some, to which class war belongs. Would not this be the best beginning which would lead most likely to the best end?"

"Much the best," he said.

"Are you willing, then," said I, "that we should defend the others against ourselves, and not take the fort of the counterargument undefended?"

"There's nothing to hinder that," he replied.

"Then let us say on their behalf, 'You need no others to dispute with you, Socrates and Glaucon; you yourselves at the first foundation of your city admitted that each single person must do his own one business according to nature.' 'We admitted it, I think; of course.' 'Is there not all the difference in the world between man and woman according to nature?' 'There is a difference, certainly.' 'Then further, is it not proper to appoint work for each according to the nature of each?' 'What then?' 'Then you are mistaken surely, and contradict yourselves, when you say now that men and women must do the same things, although their natures are very different!' Come on now, answer me that and I will thank you!"

"What! all of a sudden!" he said. "That's not altogether easy; but I beg and pray you to interpret our argument for us, whatever that may be."

"That is what I expected, my dear Glaucon," said I, "and there are many other such objections, which I foresaw long ago; that is why I feared and shrank to touch the law about getting and training women and children."

"No, by heaven, it does not look like an easy thing," said he.

"And it is not," said I, "but it's like this: If anyone tumbles into a small swimming pool, or if into the middle of the broad sea, he has to swim all the same."

"Certainly."

"Then we must swim too, and try to save ourselves out of the argument; we may hope for some dolphin to take us on his back, or some other desperate salvation."

"So it seems," he said.

"Come along then," said I, "see if we can find the way out anywhere. We agreed, you know, that a different nature ought to practise a different work, and that man and woman have different natures; now we say that these different natures must do the same work. Is that the accusation against us?"

"Exactly."

"How noble is the power, my dear Glaucon," said I, "of the art of word controversy!"

"How so?" he said.

"Because," I said, "so many seem unable to help falling into it; they think they are arguing, when they are only striving quarrelsomely. The reason is that they don't know how to split up a given utterance into its different divisions, but pursue simply a verbal opposition to what is uttered. They bandy words with each other, instead of using reasoned discussion."

"That certainly does happen," he said, "in many cases; but surely it does not apply to us in this case?"

"It does, by all manner of means," I said; "at any rate we appear to have got into a word controversy without meaning to."

"How?"

"That *different* natures ought not to engage in the *same* practices; we have been chasing the words about with plenty of courage and eristic wrangling, and never thought of enquiring in any way what was the sense of 'different nature' and what was the sense of 'same nature,' and what we were aiming at in our definition when we allotted to a different nature different practices, and to the same nature the same."

"True, we did not," said he.

"It seems we might just as well ask ourselves," I said, "whether the natures of bald men and hairy men are the same or opposite; and in case we agree that they are opposite, we might forbid long-haired men to make shoes if bald men do, and forbid bald men if long-haired men do."

"That would be ridiculous," he said.

"Yes, ridiculous," I said, "but only because we did not then mean the words 'different' and 'same nature' absolutely; we were thinking only of that kind of sameness or difference which had to do with their actual callings. Thus we meant that a man and a woman who have a physician's mind have the same nature, didn't we?"

"Yes."

"But a man physician and a man carpenter different natures?"

"Yes, I suppose so."

"Now," said I, "take the male and the female sex; if either is found to be better as regards any art or other practice, we shall say that this ought to be assigned to it. But if we find that they differ only in one thing, that the male begets and the female bears the child, we shall not take that difference as having proved any more clearly that a woman differs from a man for what we are speaking of; but we shall still believe that our guardians and their wives should practise the same things."

"And rightly so," he said.

. . .

My friend, no practice or calling in the life of the city belongs to woman as woman, or to man as man, but the various natures are dispersed among both sexes alike; by nature the woman has a share in all practices, and so has man, but in all, woman is rather weaker than man."

"Certainly."

"Then shall we assign all to man and none to woman?"

"Why, how can we?" 60

"No, for as I believe, we shall say one woman is musical by nature, one not, one is medical by nature, one not."

"Of course."

"But are we not to add—one woman is athletic or warlike, and another is unwarlike and unathletic?"

"Indeed we are."

"Shall we not say the same of philosophy and misosophy, one loves wisdom and one hates it? One has high spirit, one no spirit?"

"That is so also." 65

"Then there may be a woman fit to be a guardian, although another is not; for such was the nature we chose for our guardian men also?"

"Yes, it was."

"Then both woman and man may have the same nature fit for guarding the city, only one is weaker and one stronger."

"So it seems." 70

"Such women, then, must be chosen for such men, to live with them and to guard with them, since they are fit for it and akin to them by nature."

"Certainly."

"Practice and calling must be assigned to both sexes, the same for the same natures?"

"Just the same."

"So we have come round to where we began, and we agree that it is not against nature to assign music and gymnastic to the wives of the guardians."

"By all means." 75

"Then our law was not impossible, not only like a pious dream; the law we laid down was natural. But rather, it seems, what happens now, the other way of doing things, is unnatural."

"So it seems."

"Our question then was: Is our proposal possible, and is it best?"

"Yes, that was it."

"It is possible, we are both agreed, aren't we?" 80

"Yes."

"Then the next thing is to agree if it is best."

"Clearly."

"Well, for a woman to become fit to be a guardian, we shall not need one education to make men fit and a different one to make women fit, especially as it will be dealing with the same nature in both?"

"No; the same education." 85

"Then what is your opinion about the following?"

"What?"

"About the notion in your mind that one man is better, another is worse. Or do you think all men are alike?"

"Not by any means."

"In the city that we were founding, then, which do you 90 think we formed into better men, the guardians educated as we described, or the cobblers educated in cobbling?"

"A ridiculous question," said he.

"I understand," said I, "but tell me—are not the guardians the best of all the citizens?"

"Much the best."

"Very well, will not these women be the best of the women?"

"Again the very best," he said. 95

"And is there anything better for a city than that both women and men in it should be as good as they can be?"

"There is not."

"But this will be brought about by the aid of music and gymnastic, as we have described?"

"Of course."

"Then the plan we proposed is not only possible, but 100 best for the city?"

"Just so."

"So the women of the guardians must strip, since naked they will be clothed in virtue for gowns; they must share in war and in all the guarding of the city, and that shall be their only work. But in these same things lighter parts will be given to women than men because of the weakness of their sex. And the man who laughs at naked women, exercising for the greatest good, plucks an unripe fruit of wisdom from his laughter; he apparently does not know what he laughs at or what he is doing. For it is and will be the best thing ever said, that the useful is beautiful and the harmful is ugly."

"Assuredly so."

—〜—

Book VII
The Allegory of the Cave

"Next, then," I said, "take the following parable of educa- 1 tion and ignorance as a picture of the condition of our nature. Imagine mankind as dwelling in an underground cave with a long entrance open to the light across the whole width of the cave; in this they have been from child- hood, with necks and legs fettered, so they have to stay where they are. They cannot move their heads round because of the fetters, and they can only look forward, but light comes to them from fire burning behind them higher up at a distance. Between the fire and the prisoners is a road above their level, and along it imagine a low wall has been built, as puppet showmen have screens in front of their people over which they work their puppets."

"I see," he said.

"See, then, bearers carrying along this wall all sorts of articles which they hold projecting above the wall, statues of men and other living things, made of stone or wood and all kinds of stuff, some of the bearers speaking and some silent, as you might expect."

"What a remarkable image," he said, "and what re-markable prisoners!"

"Just like ourselves," I said. "For, first of all, tell me 5 this: What do you think such people would have seen of themselves and each other except their shadows, which the fire cast on the opposite wall of the cave?"

"I don't see how they could see anything else," said he, "if they were compelled to keep their heads unmoving all their lives!"

"Very well, what of the things being carried along? Would not this be the same?"

"Of course it would."

"Suppose the prisoners were able to talk together, don't you think that when they named the shadows which they saw passing they would believe they were naming things?"

"Necessarily." 10

"Then if their prison had an echo from the opposite wall, whenever one of the passing bearers uttered a sound, would they not suppose that the passing shadow must be making the sound? Don't you think so?"

"Indeed I do," he said.

"If so," said I, "such persons would certainly believe that there were no realities except those shadows of hand-made things."

"So it must be," said he.

"Now consider," said I, "what their release would be 15 like, and their cure from these fetters and their folly; let us imagine whether it might naturally be something like this. One might be released, and compelled suddenly to stand up and turn his neck round, and to walk and look towards the firelight; all this would hurt him, and he would be too much dazzled to see distinctly those things whose shad-ows he had seen before. What do you think he would say, if someone told him that what he saw before was foolery, but now he saw more rightly, being a bit nearer reality and turned towards what was a little more real? What if he were shown each of the passing things, and compelled by questions to answer what each one was? Don't you think he would be puzzled, and believe what he saw before was more true than what was shown to him now?"

"Far more," he said.

"Then suppose he were compelled to look towards the real light, it would hurt his eyes, and he would escape by turning them away to the things which he was able to look at, and these he would believe to be clearer than what was being shown to him."

"Just so," said he.

"Suppose, now," said I, "that someone should drag him thence by force, up the rough ascent, the steep way

up, and never stop until he could drag him out into the light of the sun, would he not be distressed and furious at being dragged; and when he came into the light, the bril-liance would fill his eyes and he would not be able to see even one of the things now called real?"

"That he would not," said he, "all of a sudden." 20

"He would have to get used to it, surely, I think, if he is to see the things above. First he would most easily look at shadows, after that images of mankind and the rest in water, lastly the things themselves. After this he would find it easier to survey by night the heavens them-selves and all that is in them, gazing at the light of the stars and moon, rather than by day the sun and the sun's light."

"Of course."

"Last of all, I suppose, the sun; he could look on the sun itself by itself in its own place, and see what it is like, not reflections of it in water or as it appears in some alien setting."

"Necessarily," said he.

"And only after all this he might reason about it, how 25 this is he who provides seasons and years, and is set over all there is in the visible region, and he is in a manner the cause of all things which they saw."

"Yes, it is clear," said he, "that after all that, he would come to this last."

"Very good. Let him be reminded of his first habita-tion, and what was wisdom in that place, and of his fellow-prisoners there; don't you think he would bless himself for the change, and pity them?"

"Yes, indeed."

"And if there were honours and praises among them and prizes for the one who saw the passing things most sharply and remembered best which of them used to come before and which after and which together, and from these was best able to prophesy accordingly what was going to come—do you believe he would set his desire on that, and envy those who were honoured men or potentates among them? Would he not feel as Homer says, and heartily de-sire rather to be serf of some landless man on earth and to endure anything in the world, rather than to opine as they did and to live in that way?"

"Yes, indeed," said he, "he would rather accept any- 30 thing than live like that."

"Then again," I said, "just consider; if such a one should go down again and sit on his old seat, would he not get his eyes full of darkness coming in suddenly out of the sun?"

"Very much so," said he.

"And if he should have to compete with those who had been always prisoners, by laying down the law about those shadows while he was blinking before his eyes were settled down—and it would take a good long time to get used to things—wouldn't they all laugh at him and say he had spoiled his eyesight by going up there, and it was not worth-while so much as to try to go up? And would they not kill anyone who tried to release them and take them up, if they could somehow lay hands on him and kill him?"

"That they would!" said he.

"Then we must apply this image, my dear Glaucon," said I, "to all we have been saying. The world of our sight is like the habitation in prison, the firelight there to the sunlight here, the ascent and the view of the upper world is the rising of the soul into the world of mind; put it so and you will not be far from my own surmise, since that is what you want to hear; but God knows if it is really true. At least, what appears to me is, that in the world of the known, last of all, is the idea of the good, and with what toil to be seen! And seen, this must be inferred to be the cause of all right and beautiful things for all, which gives birth to light and the king of light in the world of sight, and, in the world of mind, herself the queen produces truth and reason; and she must be seen by one who is to act with reason publicly or privately."

PLATO

Selection from *Phaedo*

Reading the Selection

Plato's dialogue entitled *Phaedo* lovingly recounts the last hours of Socrates: Having been convicted of impiety against the gods and corrupting Athenian youth, Socrates awaits execution. During these hours, he is shown talking with family and friends, drinking hemlock, as required by law, and quietly dying—an exemplary death. This setting enabled Plato to discourse on life's meaning, death's role in shaping life, and his belief in the soul's immortality.

Since Plato was not present, he made Phaedo, who was there, the narrator of these events. Phaedo first names those present and then describes their anguished reactions to Socrates' impending death, thus setting the stage for a discussion on immortality. The center of attention, Socrates keeps the discussion moving by various means to illustrate his views. For example, early on, he takes the position that the true philosopher (from Greek, "lover of wisdom") does not fear death, for in a sense he is always seeking death. Elaborating this idea, he points out that the soul is imprisoned inside the body by the need for drink, sex, and sleep, with the result that it is kept from its true aim, the gaining of knowledge. Thus, when death releases the soul from its prison, it is free to roam among the ideas that it dimly perceived while alive.

Not merely a philosophical discussion, the *Phaedo* resembles a stage drama, through such dramatically realistic details as the jailer's comings and goings and Socrates' friends referring to the passage of time. These details, while heightening the tension in the dialogue, also build toward one of the most poignant and memorable death scenes ever written in Western literature.

[Socrates is speaking.] "Now then, I want to give the proof at once, to you as my judges, why I think it likely that one who has spent his life in philosophy should be confident when he is going to die, and have good hopes that he will win the greatest blessings in the next world when he has ended: so Simmias and Cebes my judges, I will try to show how this could be true.

"The fact is, those who tackle philosophy aright are simply and solely practising dying, practising death, all the time, but nobody sees it. If this is true, then it would surely be unreasonable that they should earnestly do this and nothing else all their lives, yet when death comes they should object to what they had been so long earnestly practising."

Simmias laughed at this, and said, "I don't feel like laughing just now, Socrates, but you have made me laugh. I think the many if they heard that would say, 'That's a good one for the philosophers!' And other people in my city would heartily agree that philosophers are really suffering from a wish to die, and now they have found them out, that they richly deserve it!"

"That would be true, Simmias," said Socrates, "except the words 'found out.' For they have not found out in what sense the real philosophers wish to die and deserve to die, and what kind of death it is. Let us say good-bye to them," he went on, "and ask ourselves: Do we think there is such a thing as death?"

"Certainly," Simmias put in.

"Is it anything more than the separation of the soul from the body?" said Socrates. "Death is, that the body separates from the soul, and remains by itself apart from the soul, and the soul, separated from the body, exists by itself apart from the body. Is death anything but that?"

"No," he said, "that is what death is."

"Then consider, my good friend, if you agree with me here, for I think this is the best way to understand the question we are examining. Do you think it the part of a philosopher to be earnestly concerned with what are called pleasures, such as these—eating and drinking, for example?"

"Not at all," said Simmias.

"The pleasures of love, then?"   10

"Oh no."

"Well, do you suppose a man like that regards the other bodily indulgences as precious? Getting fine clothes and shoes and other bodily adornments—ought he to price them high or low, beyond whatever share of them it is absolutely necessary to have?"

"Low, I think," he said, "if he is a true philosopher."

"Then in general," he said, "do you think that such a man's concern is not for the body, but as far as he can he stands aloof from that and turns towards the soul?"

"I do."   15

"Then firstly, is it not clear that in such things the philosopher as much as possible sets free the soul from communion with the body, more than other men?"

"So it appears."

"And I suppose, Simmias, it must seem to most men that he who has no pleasure in such things and takes no share in them does not deserve to live, but he is getting pretty close to death if he does not care about pleasures which he has by means of the body."

"Quite true, indeed."

"Well then, what about the actual getting of wisdom?   20
Is the body in the way or not, if a man takes it with him as companion in the search? I mean, for example, is there any truth for men in their sight and hearing? Or as poets are forever dinning into our ears, do we hear nothing and see nothing exactly? Yet if these of our bodily senses are not exact and clear, the others will hardly be, for they are all inferior to these, don't you think so?"

"Certainly," he said.

"Then," said he, "when does the soul get hold of the truth? For whenever the soul tries to examine anything in company with the body, it is plain that it is deceived by it."

"Quite true."

"Then is it not clear that in reasoning, if anywhere, something of the realities becomes visible to it?"

"Yes."   25

"And I suppose it reasons best when none of these senses disturbs it, hearing or sight, or pain, or pleasure indeed, but when it is completely by itself and says good-bye to the body, and so far as possible has no dealings with it, when it reaches out and grasps that which really is."

"That is true."

"And is it not then that the philosopher's soul chiefly holds the body cheap and escapes from it, while it seeks to be by itself?"

"So it seems."

"Let us pass on, Simmias. Do we say there is such a   30
thing as justice by itself, or not?"

"We do say so, certainly!"

"Such a thing as the good and beautiful?"

"Of course!"

"And did you ever see one of them with your eyes?"

"Never," said he.   35

"By any other sense of those the body has did you ever grasp them? I mean all such things, greatness, health, strength, in short everything that really is the nature of things whatever they are: Is it through the body that the real truth is perceived? Or is this better—whoever of us prepares himself most completely and most exactly to comprehend each thing which he examines would come nearest to knowing each one?"

"Certainly."

"And would he do that most purely who should approach each with his intelligence alone, not adding sight to intelligence, or dragging in any other sense along with reasoning, but using the intelligence uncontaminated alone by itself, while he tries to hunt out each essence uncontaminated, keeping clear of eyes and ears and, one might say, of the whole body, because he thinks the body disturbs him and hinders the soul from getting possession of truth and wisdom when body and soul are companions—is not this the man, Simmias, if anyone, who will hit reality?"

"Nothing could be more true, Socrates," said Simmias.

"Then from all this," said Socrates, "genuine philoso-   40
phers must come to some such opinion as follows, so as to make to one another statements such as these: 'A sort of direct path, so to speak, seems to take us to the conclusion that so long as we have the body with us in our enquiry, and our soul is mixed up with so great an evil, we shall never attain sufficiently what we desire, and that, we say, is the truth. For the body provides thousands of busy distractions because of its necessary food; besides, if diseases fall upon us, they hinder us from the pursuit of the real. With loves and desires and fears and all kinds of fancies and much rubbish, it infects us, and really and truly makes us, as they say, unable to think one little bit about anything at any time. Indeed, wars and factions and battles all come from the body and its desires, and from nothing else. For the desire of getting wealth causes all wars, and we are compelled to desire wealth by the body, being slaves to its culture; therefore we have no leisure for philosophy, from all these reasons. Chief of all is that if we do have some leisure, and turn away from the body to speculate on something, in our searches it is everywhere interfering, it causes confusion and disturbance, and dazzles us so that it will not let us see the truth; so in fact we see that if we are ever to know anything purely we must get rid of it, and examine the real things by the soul alone; and then, it seems, after we are dead, as the reasoning shows, not while we live, we shall possess that which we desire, lovers of which we say we are, namely wisdom. For if it is impossible in company with the body to know anything purely, one thing of two follows: either knowledge is possible nowhere, or only after death; for then alone the soul will be quite by itself apart from the body, but not before.

And while we are alive, we shall be nearest to knowing, as it seems, if as far as possible we have no commerce or communion with the body which is not absolutely necessary, and if we are not infected with its nature, but keep ourselves pure from it, until God himself shall set us free. And so, pure and rid of the body's foolishness, we shall probably be in the company of those like ourselves, and shall know through our own selves complete incontamination, and that is perhaps the truth. But for the impure to grasp the pure is not, it seems, allowed.' So we must think, Simmias, and so we must say to one another, all who are rightly lovers of learning; don't you agree?"

"Assuredly, Socrates."

"Then," said Socrates, "if this is true, my comrade, there is great hope that when I arrive where I am travelling, there if anywhere I shall sufficiently possess that for which all our study has been pursued in this past life. So the journey which has been commanded for me is made with good hope, and the same for any other man who believes he has got his mind purified, as I may call it."

"Certainly," replied Simmias.

"And is not purification really that which has been mentioned so often in our discussion, to separate as far as possible the soul from the body, and to accustom it to collect itself together out of the body in every part, and to dwell alone by itself as far as it can, both at this present and in the future, being freed from the body as if from a prison?"

"By all means," said he.

"Then is not this called death—a freeing and separation of soul from body?"

"Not a doubt of that," said he.

"But to set it free, as we say, is the chief endeavour of those who rightly love wisdom, nay of those alone, and the very care and practice of the philosophers is nothing but the freeing and separation of soul from body, don't you think so?"

"It appears to be so."

"Then, as I said at first, it would be absurd for a man preparing himself in his life to be as near as possible to death, so to live, and then when death came, to object?"

"Of course."

"Then in fact, Simmias," he said, "those who rightly love wisdom are practising dying, and death to them is the least terrible thing in the world. Look at it in this way: If they are everywhere at enmity with the body, and desire the soul to be alone by itself, and if, when this very thing happens, they shall fear and object—would not that be wholly unreasonable? Should they not willingly go to a place where there is good hope of finding what they were in love with all through life (and they loved wisdom), and of ridding themselves of the companion which they hated? When human favourites and wives and sons have died, many have been willing to go down to the grave, drawn by the hope of seeing there those they used to desire, and of being with them; but one who is really in love with wisdom and holds firm to this same hope, that he will find it in the grave, and nowhere else worth speaking of—will he then fret at dying and not go thither rejoicing? We must surely think, my comrade, that he will go rejoicing, if he is really a philosopher; he will surely believe that he will find wisdom in its purity there and there alone. If this is true, would it not be most unreasonable, as I said just now, if such a one feared death?"

"Unreasonable, I do declare," said he. . . .

With these words, he got up and retired into another room for the bath, and Criton went after him, telling us to wait. So we waited discussing and talking together about what had been said, or sometimes speaking of the great misfortune which had befallen us, for we felt really as if we had lost a father and had to spend the rest of our lives as orphans. When he had bathed, and his children had been brought to see him—for he had two little sons, and one big—and when the women of his family had come, he talked to them before Criton and gave what instructions he wished. Then he asked the women and children to go, and came back to us. It was now near sunset, for he had spent a long time within. He came and sat down after his bath, and he had not talked long after this when the servant of the Eleven came in, and standing by him said, "O Socrates! I have not to complain of you as I do of others, that they are angry with me, and curse me, because I bring them word to drink their potion, which my officers make me do! But I have always found you in this time most generous and gentle, and the best man who ever came here. And now too, I know well you are not angry with me, for you know who are responsible, and you keep it for them. Now you know what I came to tell you, so farewell, and try to bear as well as you can what can't be helped."

Then he turned and was going out, with tears running down his cheeks. And Socrates looked up at him and said, "Farewell to you also, I will do so." Then, at the same time turning to us, "What a nice fellow!" he said. "All the time he has been coming and talking to me, a real good sort, and now how generously he sheds tears for me! Come along, Criton, let's obey him. Someone bring the potion, if the stuff has been ground; if not, let the fellow grind it."

Then Criton said, "But Socrates, I think the sun is still over the hills, it has not set yet. Yes, and I know of others who, having been told to drink the poison, have done it very late; they had dinner first and a good one, and some enjoyed the company of any they wanted. Please don't be in a hurry, there is time to spare."

But Socrates said, "Those you speak of have very good reason for doing that, for they think they will gain by doing it; and I have good reasons why I won't do it. For I think I shall gain nothing by drinking a little later, only that I shall think myself a fool for clinging to life and sparing when the cask's empty. Come along," he said, "do what I tell you, if you please."

And Criton, hearing this, nodded to the boy who stood near. The boy went out, and after spending a long time, came in with the man who was to give the poison carrying it ground ready in a cup. Socrates caught sight of the man and said, "Here, my good man, you know about these things; what must I do?"

"Just drink it," he said, "and walk about till your legs get heavy, then lie down. In that way the drug will act of itself."

At the same time, he held out the cup to Socrates, and he took it quite cheerfully, Echecrates, not a tremble, not a change in colour or looks; but looking full at the man under his brows, as he used to do, he asked him, "What do you say about this drink? What of a libation to someone? Is that allowed, or not?"

He said, "We only grind so much as we think enough for a moderate potion."

"I understand," he said, "but at least, I suppose, it is allowed to offer a prayer to the gods and that must be done, for good luck in the migration from here to there. Then that is my prayer, and so may it be!"

With these words he put the cup to his lips and, quite easy and contented, drank it up. So far most of us had been able to hold back our tears pretty well; but when we saw him begin drinking and end drinking, we could no longer. I burst into a flood of tears for all I could do, so I wrapped up my face and cried myself out; not for him indeed, but for my own misfortune in losing such a man and such a comrade. Criton had got up and gone out even before I did, for he could not hold the tears in. Apollodoros had never ceased weeping all this time, and now he burst out into loud sobs, and by his weeping and lamentations completely broke down every man there except Socrates himself. He only said, "What a scene! You amaze me. That's just why I sent the women away, to keep them from making a scene like this. I've heard that one

ought to make an end in decent silence. Quiet yourselves and endure."

When we heard him we felt ashamed and restrained our tears. He walked about, and when he said that his legs were feeling heavy, he lay down on his back, as the man told him to do; at the same time the one who gave him the potion felt him, and after a while examined his feet and legs; then pinching a foot hard, he asked if he felt anything; he said no. After this, again, he pressed the shins; and, moving up like this, he showed us that he was growing cold and stiff. Again he felt him, and told us that when it came to his heart, he would be gone. Already the cold had come nearly as far as the abdomen, when Socrates threw off the covering from his face—for he had covered it over—and said, the last words he uttered, "Criton," he said, "we owe a cock to Asclepios; pay it without fail."

"That indeed shall be done," said Criton. "Have you anything more to say?" 65

When Criton had asked this, Socrates gave no further answer, but after a little time, he stirred, and the man uncovered him, and his eyes were still. Criton, seeing this, closed the mouth and eyelids.

This was the end of our comrade, Echecrates, a man, as we would say, of all then living we had ever met, the noblest and the wisest and most just.

ARISTOTLE

Selections from *Poetics*

In many ways Aristotle (384–322 B.C.) has had a more far-reaching effect on Western thought than Plato (see *The Republic, Phaedo*). Aristotle, for example, wrote on many topics that Plato never addressed, notably in the natural and physical sciences; thus, Aristotle was considered the greater authority. Western thinkers have also tended to favor Aristotle's empirical approach, with its reliance on the senses, rather than Plato's deductive method based on abstract reasoning and mathematics. Most of all, Westerners have preferred Aristotle's focus on what exists to Plato's imaginings about an ideal world, beyond the here and now.

Reading the Selections

In the *Poetics*—the first work of literary criticism that we know of and thus the one that established this genre—Aristotle addressed the topic of "poetry." At the time, poetry included tragedy, comedy, and the epic. Over the centuries Aristotle's section on comedy disappeared, and the part discussing the epic grew so mutilated that it is generally ignored today. The result is that the portion dealing with tragedy is all that effectively survives from Aristotle's original essay.

The section on tragedy shows Aristotle's empirical method in action, as he tries to define the rules to guide an author working in this genre. Typical of his method, he gathered scripts of existing tragedies on which to base his theory. In particular, he relied on Sophocles' *Oedipus the King*, which he claimed as the most perfect drama ever written. From his studies of playscripts, he isolated the six cardinal features of tragedy—plot, character, diction, thought, spectacle, and song—gave definitions of each, and showed the part each played in making tragedy work. Aristotle's terms and definitions are still used by modern literary critics. This treatise itself has had tremendous influence on Western literature as a whole and in particular on seventeenth-century French classical drama (see Racine's *Phaedra*).

Aristotle was at his most original when he claimed that tragedy was cathartic ("purgative"). He proposed that tragedy's function was to arouse fear and pity in the spectators, thereby purging them of negative feelings and restoring them to psychic wholeness. Though under fire from today's critics, who believe that violence breeds violence, Aristotle's claim for tragedy as catharsis has had tremendous significance for Western drama.

—m—

The Rise of Comedy. Epic Compared with Tragedy

As I have remarked, comedy represents the worse types of men; worse, however, not in the sense that it embraces any and every kind of badness, but in the sense that the ridiculous is a species of ugliness or badness. For the ridiculous consists in some form of error or ugliness that is not painful or injurious; the comic mask, for example, is distorted and ugly, but causes no pain.

Now we know something of the successive stages by which tragedy developed, and of those who were responsible for them; the early history of comedy, however, is obscure, because it was not taken seriously. It was a long time before the archon granted a chorus to comedies; until then the performers were volunteers.[1] Comedy had already acquired certain clear-cut forms before there is any mention of those who are named as its poets. Nor is it known who introduced masks, or prologues, or a plurality of actors, and other things of that kind. Properly worked out plots originated in Sicily with Epicharmus and Phormis; of Athenian poets Crates was the first to discard the lampoon pattern and to adopt stories and plots of a more general nature.

Epic poetry agrees with tragedy to the extent that it is a representation, in dignified verse, of serious actions. They differ, however, in that epic keeps to a single metre and is in narrative form. Another point of difference is their length: tragedy tries as far as possible to keep within a single revolution of the sun, or only slightly to exceed it, whereas the epic observes no limits in its time of action—although at first the practice in this respect was the same in tragedies as in epics. Of the constituent parts, some are common to both kinds, and some are peculiar to tragedy. Thus anyone who can discriminate between what is good and what is bad in tragedy can do the same with epic; for all the elements of epic are found in tragedy, though not everything that belongs to tragedy is to be found in epic.

—m—

A Description of Tragedy

. . .

Tragedy, then, is a representation of an action that is worth serious attention, complete in itself, and of some amplitude; in language enriched by a variety of artistic devices appropriate to the several parts of the play; presented in the form of action, not narration; by means of pity and fear bringing about the purgation of such emotions. By language that is enriched I refer to language possessing rhythm, and music or song; and by artistic devices appropriate to the several parts I mean that some are produced by the medium of verse alone, and others again with the help of song.

Now since the representation is carried out by men performing the actions, it follows, in the first place, that spectacle is an essential part of tragedy, and secondly that there must be song and diction, these being the medium of representation. By diction I mean here the arrangement of the verses; song is a term whose sense is obvious to everyone.

In tragedy it is action that is imitated, and this action is brought about by agents who necessarily display certain distinctive qualities both of character and of thought, according to which we also define the nature of the actions. Thought and character are, then, the two natural causes of actions, and it is on them that all men depend for success or failure. The representation of the action is the plot of the

[1] The Greek dramatist submitted his play to the archon, or magistrate, in charge of the religious festival at which he hoped to have it performed. If the play was chosen for performance, the archon 'granted it a chorus'; that is, he provided a choregus, a wealthy citizen who, as a form of public service, paid the expenses of the production. The earlier 'volunteers' presumably paid their own expenses.

tragedy; for the ordered arrangement of the incidents is what I mean by plot. Character, on the other hand, is that which enables us to define the nature of the participants, and thought comes out in what they say when they are proving a point or expressing an opinion.

Necessarily, then, every tragedy has six constituents, which will determine its quality. They are plot, character, diction, thought, spectacle, and song. Of these, two represent the media in which the action is represented, one involves the manner of representation, and three are connected with the objects of the representation; beyond them nothing further is required. These, it may be said, are the dramatic elements that have been used by practically all playwrights; for all plays alike possess spectacle, character, plot, diction, song, and thought.

Of these elements the most important is the plot, the ordering of the incidents; for tragedy is a representation, not of men, but of action and life, of happiness and unhappiness—and happiness and unhappiness are bound up with action. The purpose of living is an end which is a kind of activity, not a quality; it is their characters, indeed, that make men what they are, but it is by reason of their actions that they are happy or the reverse. Tragedies are not performed, therefore, in order to represent character, although character is involved for the sake of the action. Thus the incidents and the plot are the end aimed at in tragedy, and as always, the end is everything. Furthermore, there could not be a tragedy without action, but there could be without character; indeed the tragedies of most of our recent playwrights fail to present character, and the same might be said of many playwrights of other periods. A similar contrast could be drawn between Zeuxis and Polygnotus as painters, for Polygnotus represents character well, whereas Zeuxis is not concerned with it in his painting. Again, if someone writes a series of speeches expressive of character, and well composed as far as thought and diction are concerned, he will still not achieve the proper effect of tragedy; this will be done much better by a tragedy which is less successful in its use of these elements, but which has a plot giving an ordered combination of incidents. Another point to note is that the two most important means by which tragedy plays on our feelings, that is, 'reversals' and 'recognitions', are both constituents of the plot. A further proof is that beginners can achieve accuracy in diction and the portrayal of character before they can construct a plot out of the incidents, and this could be said of almost all the earliest dramatic poets.

The plot, then, is the first essential of tragedy, its lifeblood, so to speak, and character takes the second place. It is much the same in painting; for if an artist were to daub his canvas with the most beautiful colours laid on at random, he would not give the same pleasure as he would by drawing a recognizable portrait in black and white. Tragedy is the representation of an action, and it is chiefly on account of the action that it is also a representation of persons.

The third property of tragedy is thought. This is the ability to say what is possible and appropriate in any given circumstances; it is what, in the speeches in the play, is related to the arts of politics and rhetoric. The older dramatic poets made their characters talk like statesmen, whereas those of today make them talk like rhetoricians. Character is that which reveals personal choice, the kinds of thing a man chooses or rejects when that is not obvious. Thus there is no revelation of character in speeches in which the speaker shows no preferences or aversions whatever. Thought, on the other hand, is present in speeches where something is being shown to be true or untrue, or where some general opinion is being expressed.

Fourth comes the diction of the speeches. By diction I mean, as I have already explained, the expressive use of words, and this has the same force in verse and in prose.

Of the remaining elements, the music is the most important of the pleasurable additions to the play. Spectacle, or stage-effect, is an attraction, of course, but it has the least to do with the playwright's craft or with the art of poetry. For the power of tragedy is independent both of performance and of actors, and besides, the production of spectacular effects is more the province of the property-man than of the playwright.

—⁊⁊—

Reversal, Discovery, and Calamity

As has already been noted, a reversal is a change from one state of affairs to its opposite, one which conforms, as I have said, to probability or necessity. In *Oedipus,* for example, the Messenger who came to cheer Oedipus and relieve him of his fear about his mother did the very opposite by revealing to him who he was. In the *Lynceus,* again, Lynceus is being led off to execution, followed by Danaus who is to kill him, when, as a result of events that occurred earlier, it comes about that he is saved and it is Danaus who is put to death.

As the word itself indicates, a discovery is a change from ignorance to knowledge, and it leads either to love or to hatred between persons destined for good or ill fortune. The most effective form of discovery is that which is accompanied by reversals, like the one in *Oedipus.* There are of course other forms of discovery, for what I have described may happen in relation to inanimate and trifling objects, and moreover it is possible to discover whether a person has done something or not. But the form of discovery most essentially related to the plot and action of the play is the one described above, for a discovery of this kind in combination with a reversal will carry with it either pity or fear, and it is such actions as these that, according to my definition, tragedy represents; and further, such a combination is likely to lead to a happy or an unhappy ending.

As it is persons who are involved in the discovery, it may be that only one person's identity is revealed to another, that of the second being already known. Sometimes, however, a natural recognition of two parties is necessary, as for example, when the identity of Iphigenia was made known to Orestes by the sending of the letter, and a second discovery was required to make him known to Iphigenia.

Two elements of plot, then, reversal and discovery, turn upon such incidents as these. A third is suffering, or calamity. Of these three, reversal and discovery have already been defined. A calamity is an action of a destructive or painful nature, such as death openly represented, excessive suffering, wounding, and the like. . . .

Tragic Action

Following upon the points I have already made, I must go on to say what is to be aimed at and what guarded against in the construction of plots, and what are the sources of the tragic effect.

We saw that the structure of tragedy at its best should be complex, not simple, and that it should represent actions capable of awakening fear and pity—for this is a characteristic function of representations of this type. It follows in the first place that good men should not be shown passing from prosperity to misery, for this does not inspire fear or pity, it merely disgusts us. Nor should evil men be shown progressing from misery to prosperity. This is the most untragic of all plots, for it has none of the requisites of tragedy; it does not appeal to our humanity, or awaken pity or fear in us. Nor again should an utterly worthless man be seen falling from prosperity into misery. Such a course might indeed play upon our humane feelings, but it would not arouse either pity or fear; for our pity is awakened by undeserved misfortune, and our fear by that of someone just like ourselves—pity for the undeserving sufferer and fear for the man like ourselves—so that the situation in question would have nothing in it either pitiful or fearful.

There remains a mean between these extremes. This is the sort of man who is not conspicuous for virtue and justice, and whose fall into misery is not due to vice and depravity, but rather to some error, a man who enjoys prosperity and a high reputation, like Oedipus and Thyestes and other famous members of families like theirs.

Inevitably, then, the well-conceived plot will have a single interest, and not, as some say, a double. The change in fortune will be, not from misery to prosperity, but the reverse, from prosperity to misery, and it will be due, not to depravity, but to some great error either in such a man as I have described or in one better than this, but not worse. This is borne out by existing practice. For at first the poets treated any stories that came to hand, but nowadays the best tragedies are written about a handful of families, those of Alcmaeon, for example, and Oedipus and Orestes and Meleager and Thyestes and Telephus, and others whom it has befallen to suffer or inflict terrible experiences.

The best tragedies in the technical sense are constructed in this way. Those critics are on the wrong tack, therefore, who criticize Euripides for following such a procedure in his tragedies, and complain that many of them end in misfortune; for, as I have said, this is the right ending. The strongest evidence of this is that on the stage and in the dramatic competitions plays of this kind, when properly worked out, are the most tragic of all, and Euripides, faulty as is his management of other points, is nevertheless regarded as the most tragic of our dramatic poets.

The next best type of structure, ranked first by some critics, is that which, like the *Odyssey*, has a double thread of plot, and ends in opposite ways for the good and the bad characters. It is considered the best only because of the feeble judgement of the audience, for the poets pander to the taste of the spectators. But this is not the pleasure that is proper to tragedy. It belongs rather to comedy, where those who have been the bitterest of enemies in the original story, Orestes and Aegisthus, for example, go off at the end as friends, and nobody is killed by anybody.

Fear and Pity

Fear and pity may be excited by means of spectacle; but they can also take their rise from the very structure of the action, which is the preferable method and the mark of a better dramatic poet. For the plot should be so ordered that even without seeing it performed anyone merely hearing what is afoot will shudder with fear and pity as a result of what is happening—as indeed would be the experience of anyone hearing the story of Oedipus. To produce this effect by means of stage-spectacle is less artistic, and requires the cooperation of the producer. Those who employ spectacle to produce an effect, not of fear, but of something merely monstrous, have nothing to do with tragedy, for not every kind of pleasure should be demanded of tragedy, but only that which is proper to it; and since the dramatic poet has by means of his representation to produce the tragic pleasure that is associated with pity and fear, it is obvious that this effect is bound up with the events of the plot.

Let us now consider what kinds of incident are to be regarded as fearful or pitiable. Deeds that fit this description must of course involve people who are either friends to one another, or enemies, or neither. Now if a man injures his enemy, there is nothing pitiable either in his act or in his intention, except in so far as suffering is inflicted; nor is there if they are indifferent to each other. But when the sufferings involve those who are near and dear to one another, when for example brother kills brother, son father, mother son, or son mother, or if such a deed is contemplated, or something else of the kind is actually done, then we have a situation of the kind to be aimed at. Thus it will not do to tamper with the traditional stories, the murder of Clytemnestra by Orestes, for instance, and that of Eriphyle by Alcmaeon; on the other hand, the poet must use his imagination and handle the traditional material effectively.

I must explain more clearly what I mean by 'effectively.' The deed may be done by characters acting consciously and in full knowledge of the facts, as was the way of the early dramatic poets, when for instance Euripides made Medea kill her children. Or they may do it without realizing the horror of the deed until later, when they discover the truth; this is what Sophocles did with Oedipus. Here indeed the relevant incident occurs outside the action of the play; but it may be a part of the tragedy, as with Alcmaeon in Astydamas's play, or Telegonus in *The Wounded Odysseus*. A third alternative is for someone who is about to do a terrible deed in ignorance of the relationship to discover the truth before he does it. These are the only possibilities, for the deed must either be done or not done, and by someone either with or without knowledge of the facts.

The least acceptable of these alternatives is when someone in possession of the facts is on the point of acting but fails to do so, for this merely shocks us, and, since no suffering is involved, it is not tragic. Hence nobody is allowed to behave like this, or only seldom, as when Haemon fails to kill Creon in the *Antigone*. Next in order of effectiveness is when the deed is actually done, and here it is better that the character should act in ignorance and only learn the truth afterwards, for there is nothing in this to outrage our feelings, and the revelation comes as a surprise. However, the best method is the last, when, for example, in the *Cresphontes* Merope intends to kill her son, but recognizes him and does not do so; or when the same thing happens with brother and sister in *Iphigenia in Tauris*; or when, in the *Helle*, the son recognizes his mother when he is just about to betray her.

This then is the reason why, as I said before, our tragedies keep to a few families. For in their search for dramatic material it was by chance rather than by technical knowledge that the poets discovered how to gain tragic effects in their plots. And they are still obliged to have recourse to those families in which sufferings of the kind I have described have been experienced.

I have said enough now about the arrangement of the incidents in a tragedy and the type of plot it ought to have.

The Characters of Tragedy

In characterization there are four things to aim at. First and foremost, the characters should be good. Now character will be displayed, as I have pointed out, if some preference is revealed in speech or action, and if it is a preference for what is good the character will be good. There can be goodness in every class of person; for instance, a woman or a slave may be good, though the one is possibly an inferior being and the other in general an insignificant one.

In the second place the portrayal should be appropriate. For example, a character may possess manly qualities, but it is not appropriate that a female character should be given manliness or cleverness.

Thirdly, the characters should be lifelike. This is not the same thing as making them good, or appropriate in the sense in which I have used the word.

And fourthly, they should be consistent. Even if the person who is being represented is inconsistent, and this trait is the basis of his character, he must nevertheless be portrayed as consistently inconsistent.

As an example of unnecessary badness of character, there is Menelaus in the *Orestes*. The character who behaves in an unsuitable and inappropriate way is exemplified in Odysseus' lament in the *Scylla*, and in Melanippe's speech. An inconsistent character is shown in *Iphigenia at Aulis*, for Iphigenia as a suppliant is quite unlike what she is later.

As in the arrangement of the incidents, so too in characterization one must always bear in mind what will be either necessary or probable; in other words, it should be necessary or probable that such and such a person should say or do such and such a thing, and similarly that this particular incident should follow on that.

Furthermore, it is obvious that the unravelling of the plot should arise from the circumstances of the plot itself, and not be brought about *ex machina*, as is done in the *Medea* and in the episode of the embarkation in the *Iliad*. The *deus ex machina* should be used only for matters outside the play proper, either for things that happened before it and that cannot be known by the human characters, or for things that are yet to come and that require to be foretold prophetically—for we allow to the gods the power to see all things. However, there should be nothing inexplicable about what happens, or if there must be, it should be kept outside the tragedy, as is done in Sophocles's *Oedipus*.

Since tragedy is a representation of people who are better than average, we must copy the good portrait-painters. These, while reproducing the distinctive appearance of their sitters and making likenesses, paint them better-looking than they are. In the same way the poet, in portraying men who are hot-tempered, or phlegmatic, or who have other defects of character, must bring out these qualities in them, and at the same time show them as decent people, as Agathon and Homer have portrayed Achilles.

These points must be carefully watched, as too must those means used to appeal to the eye, which are necessarily dependent on the poet's art; for here too it is often possible to make mistakes. However, enough has been said about these matters in my published works.

CLASSICAL GREEK CIVILIZATION
The Hellenistic Age

MENANDER

Selection from *The Woman of Samos*

Menander's *The Woman of Samos* typifies New Comedy, the final phase of Greek comedy and also a potent force in Western comedy. Menander's works became the basis of Roman comedy, which passed the spirit of his work into the dramas of the Italian Renaissance and from there into the comedies of Shakespeare and Molière. Menander's spirit lives today in romantic comedies and situation comedies.

Of Menander (ca. 342–293 B.C.) very little was known directly until this century. His 108 plays, like the rest of New Comedy, disappeared with the fall of Rome, leaving only traces—lines from his plays quoted by other authors, and Latin versions of his works (by Terence and Plautus, the founders of Roman comedy). Then, a series of dramatic finds helped to partly restore Menander's legacy. *The Woman of Samos* is one such discovery: A nearly complete text was found in the 1920s in an Egyptian tomb.

New Comedy flourished in the Hellenistic Age (323–146 B.C.), a period of rapid change between the death of Alexander the Great and the triumph of Rome. A new political order now engulfed Greece as self-governing city-states were eclipsed by large kingdoms ruled by men claiming to be gods. Beyond the concept of kingdoms loomed the dream of a world-state, an ideal behind many of this period's wars. Society was also in turmoil, with old aristocrats and their traditional pursuits giving way to "new money" and constant pleasure-seeking. In cultural terms, the trend was toward eclecticism (selecting the best from various sources), as Greek ideals spread into non-Greek lands, mingling there with other traditions. This age's enormous cities, such as Alexandria with one million people, bred feelings of alienation and fears of anonymity.

Faced with this troubled world, Menander's New Comedy moved away from its Old Comedy (see Aristophanes' *Lysistrata*) roots. His plays were intended for pleasure-loving audiences in the cities, and not simply for Athenian festivals. Steering clear of politics and topical satire, the plays offered sentimental stories with happy endings. Plots featured thwarted lovers, kept apart by an older male, who were finally united following a scene of recognition in which the persons were correctly identified. Most of all, Menander insisted on civility and courtesy, an ideal meant to balance the loss of personal control in a world gone mad.

Reading the Selection

The Woman of Samos, with its complex plot, stock characters, and a would-be foundling, is a superb example of Menander's style. Chrysis, a freeborn woman from Samos, who gives the play its title, is the mistress of a wealthy Athenian, Demeas. Demeas has a son, Moschion, who is involved with Plangon (Dolly), the daughter of a neighbor. Plangon bears a child, which Chrysis, out of kindness toward the girl, claims as her own, pretending it is a foundling. Demeas, returning from an absence, discovers that Moschion is the baby's father. Convinced that Chrysis has seduced his son, Demeas drives her from the house. Typical of Menander's comedies, all ends happily after the misunderstandings are sorted out: Father and son are reconciled, and Moschion and Plangon are wed in a torchlight ceremony. A discordant note for modern readers, however, is the treatment of Chrysis, who virtually disappears from the plot once the relationship between Demeas and Moschion is resolved. Chrysis is blameless and suffers more than anyone else, but Menander has little interest in her fate, reflecting perhaps his limited concern for this non-Athenian character.

The characters are stereotypes who were part of Hellenistic society and who are now a legacy to world drama: the stern father (Demeas), the young lover (Moschion), the innocent young woman (Plangon), the understanding mistress (Chrysis), and most especially the slave—a sly fellow who outwits his master and pulls the plot strings while remembering where his own advantage lies. This slave and characters like him inspired Molière's servants twenty centuries later (see *The Misanthrope*).

—m—

Act III

[Demeas is preparing for his son Moschion's wedding. Moschion is marrying the woman he impregnated, who gave birth while Demeas was traveling. Fearing parental wrath at his premarital indiscretions, Moschion has concocted a scheme with Chrysis (Demeas's consort) to convince Demeas that the baby is really his, by Chrysis. However, the plot thickens when Demeas overhears a conversation, as he relates here.—Ed.]

(Demeas comes out of his house with an elaborate show of being casual, and walks downstage. Suddenly shedding his casual air, he addresses the audience in great perturbation. His opening words have been lost.)

DEMEAS   ... the hurricane that suddenly comes out of the blue during a calm voyage—you're sailing along under clear skies, and it smashes right into you and over you go. Sometimes like that is what I'm going through right now. I'm the one who's holding the wedding, who's appeasing all the gods, who just a while ago was having things go exactly the way I wanted—my god, right now I'm not sure any longer whether I can see straight! I'm here before you with a sudden aching hurt in my heart. *(Shaking his head in bewilderment)* It's incredible! Look here. Am I in my right mind? Or am I crazy and, because I jumped to all the wrong conclusions a moment ago, heading for disaster for no good reason?

(Visibly getting hold of himself, in calmer tones) As soon as I went inside, since I was very anxious to get on with the wedding, I simply announced to the servants what was going to happen and ordered them to make all the necessary preparations—clean up, do the baking, get everything set for the ceremony. Things were getting done, all right, but naturally, there was some confusion because of the rush. The baby had been sort of left on a couch out of the way and was screaming its head off. And everybody was hollering at the same time: *(imitating the voices)* "Bring some flour. Bring some water. Bring some oil. Bring some charcoal." I pitched in myself and helped hand things out. That's how I happened to go into the pantry and, since I was busy there picking out extra supplies and looking things over, I didn't come right out. Well, while I was in there, one of the women came down from the second floor into the room in front of the pantry. We do our weaving there, and you have to go through it either to get to the staircase or the pantry. It was an old woman who used to be Moschion's nanny; she was one of my slaves until I freed her. She saw the baby screaming away because nobody was minding it and, having no idea that I was inside and that she ought to watch out what she was saying, she goes up to it and starts to talk to it the way they do *(imitating her)*: "Sweet little baby," and "My precious, where's your mommy?" And she kissed it and rocked it and, when it stopped crying, she says to herself, "Dear me! It seems just yesterday that I was petting and nursing Moschion when he was no bigger than this, and now he's got a baby of his own." [Two or three lines are lost here.]

While she was prattling on, one of the serving girls came running in, and the old one shouts at her: "Here you! Give this baby a bath! What is this? His own father's getting married, and you're not giving his little one the least bit of attention!" Right away the other one whispers to her *(dropping his voice and imitating her)*, "What are you talking so loud for, you poor fool? He's in there." "No! Where?" "In the pantry!" And then, speaking in her natural voice, she says *(raising his voice)*, "Nurse, Chrysis is calling for you" and "Hurry, run along," and then *(lowering it again)*, "We're in luck, he hasn't heard anything." So the old one

1

scuttled off somewhere mumbling to herself (*mimicking her*), "Dear me, this big mouth of mine!"

Then I came out, very calmly, just as you saw me come out a moment ago, acting as if I hadn't heard or didn't know a thing. And, right outside, what do I see? Chrysis herself with the baby, nursing it. So one thing we know for certain: it's her baby. But who the father is, I or—no, gentlemen, I'm not going to say it to you, I'm not even going to suspect it. I'm reporting the facts, what I heard with my own ears. I'm not angry with anybody—not yet. (*As the calm he has been struggling to maintain starts to desert him, em-*

phatically) Good god, I know that boy of mine; he's always been thoroughly decent, always been as considerate toward me as any son could be. (*Shakes his head worriedly*) Yet, when I consider that it was his old nanny who said it and that it was something I wasn't supposed to hear, and when I look back at the way that woman of mine fondled the child and forced me to let her keep it against my will—I can go out of my mind! (*Looks toward the wings, stage left, and sees someone approaching*) Good—here comes Parmeno back from the market just in time. But first I've got to let him take in the help he's brought back with him. . . .

THEOCRITUS

Selections from the *Idylls*

During the Hellenistic Age, original creative literature hardly existed; most writers either imitated the forms and styles of their Hellenic predecessors or, following the lead of Aristotle, turned to literary criticism. These authors, often working from manuscripts on deposit at the library in Egypt's port city of Alexandria, perfected a literary style known as Alexandrianism. What distinguished these writers were their wide knowledge of details of Greek myths and history, their understanding of exotic literary figures and references, and their masterful command of the Greek language. They polished the Greek styles until their own works only faintly echoed the robustness of the originals. The Alexandrians owed their success, in part, to Egypt's Ptolemaic rulers, who were great patrons of culture, building the great library in Alexandria, stocking it with ancient manuscripts either through purchase or as spoils of war, and providing financial subsidies for scholars. Alexandrianism eventually spread across the Hellenistic world, affecting local literary styles and later influencing Roman culture.

In the cosmopolitan Hellenistic world, educated readers turned to scientific essays or to biographies; the writers based in Alexandria tended to serve the mass market, who demanded updated copies of Greek works. Among the popular but mediocre writers who catered to this market, only one or two, such as Theocritus, were able to establish reputations beyond their lifetime.

Theocritus (ca. 310–250 B.C.) was more original than his contemporaries for he pioneered two literary forms: the pastoral and the idyll. The pastoral focuses on the lives of shepherds in the wilds; it became a popular genre in this period because it had special appeal to those who had moved from the countryside to newly founded Hellenistic cities. Theocritus's sensitive descriptions of unspoiled nature, lowing cattle, and lovesick shepherds resulted in charming, though artificial, poems. However, Theocritus's reputation rests on his idylls—small portraits or vignettes of Hellenistic life. These poems evoked a simpler past or addressed themselves to familiar human traits such as love and jealousy.

Reading the Selections

These poems from the *Idylls* explore two topics close to all poets: unrequited love and unappreciated poets. In "The Cyclops," Theocritus transforms the ugly creature of Homer's *Odyssey* into a "simple countryman." The Cyclops, or Polyphemus, is madly in love with Galatea, a sea nymph who cares nothing for him. The burden of the poem is that there is no cure for love except through obeying the Muses—the nine goddesses who preside over the arts. Thus, Polyphemus must sing to the cruel Galatea, lamenting her cold heart and his cruel fate. Only in this way, according to Theocritus, is the Cyclops able to endure.

In "The Graces," the author argues that unlike in the good old days (meaning earlier Greece), humans no longer appreciate poets. Today's rich and famous, he complains, just hoard their wealth and refuse to pay those who praise them. Yet, if one is to be remembered, it must be through a poet's verses, as King Priam of Troy lives on in the works of Homer, the "blind Ionian." In this idyll, Theocritus is openly begging for money from Hiero II, tyrant of Syracuse, though he does write prettily about the Muses, who will be dejected if the poet comes home empty-handed.

—⁓—

The Cyclops

I have learnt that there can be no remedy for love,   1
No special herb or ointment to soothe the heart
Except the Muses. It is light and quick, their drug,
And works for all, but is very hard to find.
I think you know this, Nicias, without my saying,
Since you are doctor and poet, a child of the Nine.
My simple countryman, Polyphemus the Cyclops,
Discovered this long ago when he loved Galatea
And down spread over his cheeks and round his mouth.
His was no game of love-locks and little gifts   10
But a pure madness that shut out all other thoughts.
His flock would come home to the cave unshepherded
From the green pasture, while he would be off by himself
All day, singing up the dawn on the weedstrewn shore
And pining for Galatea as he nursed the wound
Which the dart from Cypris had cut into his bowels.
Gazing seaward from the high rock where he sat
He found and applied the one remedy.
                                                    This was his song:

· ·

Galatea, why do you treat your lover harshly?   20
You are whiter than ricotta, gentler than a lamb,
Livelier than a calf, firmer than an unripe grape.
You wait until sleep takes hold of me to come here
And when sleep lets me go, then you slip away
As if you were a sheep and I the great grey wolf.
I fell in love with you, girl, on your first visit.
You came with my mother, wanting to gather orchids
In the hill-meadows. It was I who showed the way.
To you it meant nothing at all. But to me the moment
When I set eyes on you lasts from that day to this.   30
You slip away from me, girl, unreachably graceful.
No need to say the reason: this shaggy eyebrow
Which stretches from ear to ear across my forehead;
This single eye and flattened nose, these lips.
But fine looks could not buy me the flock I graze,
A thousand strong, nor the milk I draw and drink
Nor the cheese which lasts through summer into autumn
And loads the racks down even to winter's end.
No other Cyclops plays the pipe as I can,
Singing far into the night, my silver pippin,   40
Of you and me. For your amusement I rear
Four bear-cubs and eleven fawns with dappled coats.

Come to me then. You will never wish yourself back.
Let the green sea waste its anger on the shore:
Night spent in the cave beside me is far more sweet.
Baytrees and slender cypresses grow there, ivy
With its dark leaves and vines with sugary grapes.
Fresh water flows there, which forest-sided Etna
Sends down for me, cold fruit of her white snow.
Who could refuse such things for the cheerless sea?   50
And if I seem shaggy, I keep in my heart's cave
A fire of oaklogs glowing beneath the cinders.
Let it blaze: I shall not mind how it sears my life
Or shrivels this treasure of treasures, my single eye.
If Mother had only borne me with fish's gills!
I might have dived and found you and kissed your hand
(If you would not give your lips); I might have brought you
Delicate poppies with broad red petals, or snowdrops;
A posy for summer or winter, each in its time.
I could not bring you their white and scarlet together.   60
I must learn to swim at once; but perhaps if I wait
Some kindly stranger will come in a ship to teach me.
Then I may fathom what pleasure lives in the depths.
Come up from the sea, Galatea. Forget to go home.
I will teach you by my example, sitting her late.
Follow the flocks with me and help me to milk them,
Help me to set the cheese with a dribble of rennet.
Mother is to blame. Though she might have won you
By speaking for me, she said not a single word.
Doesn't she see me grow thinner day by day?   70
I will tell her my head and feet ache fit to burst,
To make her sicken with worry and suffer like me.
O Cyclops, Cyclops, have you gone out of your mind?
You should be gathering browse to feed your lambs
Or plaiting baskets for cheese; that would show more
      sense.
Milk the beast you can catch; let the others range.
You will find a new Galatea with lovelier looks.
The girls call after me, "Shall I see you tonight?"
And laugh in a huddle as soon as I turn my head.
On land, I clearly have something to show for myself.   80

· ·

So Polyphemus shepherded his love by singing
And found more relief than if he had paid out gold.

—·*w*·—

The Graces

The proper task of Zeus's daughters and of poets   1
Is to celebrate the gods and great men's lives.
The Muses are heavenly beings; they sing of heaven.
We are earthbound creatures; we too should sing our own.

Where does he live, beneath what glittering sky,
The man who will open his house to receive our Graces,
Not turn them away unrecognized, unrewarded?
They come home sulky, trailing their bare feet
And blame me for sending them on a wasted journey;
Then they crouch at the bottom of a wooden coffer,   10
Their heads on their cold knees, their confidence gone.
Where can they turn, when every door is closed?
Show me the man with a proper sense of glory,
Who knows the praiser's worth. Can he still be found?
Now the cry is, "Give me the money, keep the praise",
And each man cradles silver under his shirt,
Jealous even of its tarnish, with greed in his eyes
And a smug rebuff on his lips: "It's all in Homer";
"The gods will look after the poets—that's their job";
"Charity begins at home"—and goes no further;   20
"The poet I like is the one who costs me nothing".

But, gentlemen, how does it help you to lock away
Your wealth? A wise man, putting his money to use,
Takes care of himself, but does not forget the poet.
A crowd of dependents and family count on his help;
He provides the altars with offerings for the gods;
He welcomes guests to his table, a generous host,
And sends them away cheered when they choose to leave;
But the Muses' servants receive his special care.
That way you shall be rewarded when death hides you,   30
Not loiter by cold Acheron, shorn of your fame,
No better than a poor labourer with callused hands
Who swings a mattock and hoards a birthright of tears.
In the halls of Antiochus and kingly Aleuas
An army of bondsmen gathered for a monthly dole;
At nightfall the pens of the Scopadae were crowded
With wide-horned cattle lowing to meet their young;
The shepherds who served the hospitable Creondae
Ranged Crannon's open ground with numberless flocks:
All joy of possession vanished when once their souls   40
Were emptied into the sour old ferryman's barge
And they went down into darkness with the common
   ghosts,
Severed from their fortunes; they would be clean
   forgotten
If the subtle music and bright-emblazoning voice
Of the Cean poet had not named and made them known
In times to come. We remember even their horses,
Honoured creatures who brought them prizes from the
   games.
What would they mean to us, Cycnus with womanly skin
Or the Lycian chiefs or Priam's long-haired sons,
If poetry did not ring with their ancient war-cries?   50

Or Odysseus? For ten years he wandered the wide
   world;
He came alive to Hades, he entered the cave
Of the deadly Cyclops and lived to tell the tale,
While Eumaeus watched the pigs and Philoetius the cows
And noble Laertes tended his patch of ground:
Great names, but they would have vanished all alike
If the blind Ionian had not come to their rescue.

Though living men make free with a dead man's goods,
The Muses' gift of fame can never be taken.
But to sit and count the waves which wind and sea   60
Drive shoreward in grey succession, or fetch clear water
To wash a mudbrick clean, is the game of a fool;
And you will as soon heal a miser's damaged heart.
Goodbye to the miser! Let him keep his silver;
With all his useless wealth, let him pine for more.
I think goodwill and honour are truer possessions
Than the mules and horses in a rich man's stable.
I look for a patron eager to take me in,
And the Muses with me. The roads are not safe for
   poets
Unless wise Zeus's daughters are there to guide them.   70
Untiringly heaven brings the months and years;
The horses stir, and day's bright wheel lifts high:
I will find the Achilles, the Ajax of our age,
And celebrate exploits great as those performed
Where Simois runs by the tomb of Phrygian Ilus.
Now the Phoenicians, dwellers on the hot shore
Of Africa, shiver with fear; their sun sinks low.
The men of Syracuse grip their spears for battle,
They shoulder their heavy wicker shields; among them
Hiero stands, armed and ready, a pattern of valour,   80
His gleaming helmet shadowed by a horsehair crest.

I beg you, Father Zeus and Lady Athena,
And you who watch over Syracuse, the great city
By the Lake of Lysimeleia, you and your mother:
Let violence clear our enemies from this island,
Allowing a handful only to sail back home
To bring their women and children news of slaughter.
May the old inhabitants repossess their cities,
Build on ruins and restore what has been spoiled.
May the fields be worked and bring forth crops once
   more   90
While bleating flocks, too many to count, grow fat
On the grassy plains. May the passer-by at nightfall
Quicken his steps as the cattle are driven home.
Let fallows be ploughed for sowing while the cicada,
The shepherd's sentinel, high among branches, rasps
The midday silence. Let the armoury be shrouded
In cobwebs, the war-cry become a forgotten sound.
Let poetry carry Hiero's fame through the world
From Scythian waters to where the asphalt rampart
Raised by Semiramis guards her ancient kingdom.   100

I am one among many poets, each with a claim
On the Muses, each ready to celebrate Arethusa,
Her brave Sicilians and Hiero, lord of the spear.
O Gracious Goddesses, worshipped by Eteocles,
Who love Orchomenus, Thebes's once loathed rival,

I will not jostle for notice but, if summoned,
Will answer gratefully, gladly—I and my Muses.
You too must accompany me. There is no delight
When once the Graces have gone. Let me not betray
   them.

EPICURUS

"Letter to Menoeceus"

The Greek philosopher Epicurus (ca. 342–270 B.C.) is the founder of a type of hedonism that identifies the good with pleasure and the bad with pain—epicureanism. Born on the island of Samos, he moved to Athens, where he founded a school. Most of his writings have been lost; only scattered fragments survive. His disciples, including the Roman thinker Lucretius, wrote extensively on his teachings, preserving their basic ideas. Consequently, Epicurus's personal letter to Menoeceus is a treasured document because it records both the philosopher's observations, in his own words, on what is needed to gain happiness and his view of the "good life."

Epicurus apparently practiced what he preached, living a simple and frugal, almost monastic, existence in the company of his pupils. Among them, he expounded his simple rules for becoming happy and avoiding fear and pain. He cautioned them against seeking wealth and power, which he thought were likely to bring suffering and pain. He also pointed out that death should not be feared, since dying has little meaning to a person who understands the workings of nature. Building on the ideas of the Greek thinker Democritus (ca. 460 B.C.–?), the founder of the Atomic theory, Epicurus argued that death is simply the loss of a few atoms from the body. He believed that everything, including soul and body, is composed of atoms, or particles of matter. That being the case, humans should shut their ears to priests who try to put fear of death into their hearts. Instead, the best way to live is serenely, in the face of one's own death. Many educated people in his day, and later in Roman times, found satisfaction in this teaching about calmness in the face of death; thus, Epicurus came to be known as a "savior of souls."

Reading the Selection

In this letter, Epicurus advises Menoeceus on how to become happy, the final goal of most philosophies and religions. For Epicurus, the beginning of happiness lies in accepting that the gods exist but, at the same time, rejecting the common notion that the deities have any interest in mortals. It also involves realizing that death should not be feared, since it is nothing more than depriving the body of its senses.

Having offered these preconditions of happiness, Epicurus next explains the meaning of the good life. He maintains that the human ability to differentiate between "natural" and "unnecessary" desires will help bring us happiness. A healthy body and a sound mind, which are the twin goals of "happy living," will aid the individual in gaining pleasure and avoiding pain. Epicurus further asserts that a simple but wholesome diet combined with a life of moderation and sober thinking will free the individual from pain. In his final observations, Epicurus turns to a question that is central to many philosophies and religions, that of free will versus predestination. He acknowledges that some events are predetermined, but he thinks that others occur by chance, thus allowing individuals to exercise free will and take advantage of opportunities to do good or evil.

No one should postpone the study of philosophy when he is young, nor should he weary of it when he becomes mature, because the search for mental health is never untimely or out of season. To say that the time to study philosophy has not yet arrived or that it is past is like saying that the time for happiness is not yet at hand or is no longer present. Thus both the young and the mature should pursue philosophy, the latter in order to be rejuvenated as they age by the blessings that accrue from pleasurable past experience, and the youthful in order to become mature immediately through having no fear of the future. Hence we should make a practice of the things that make for happiness, for assuredly when we have this, we have everything, and we do everything we can to get it when we don't have it.

The Preconditions of Happiness

[1. You should do and practice all the things I constantly recommended to you, with the knowledge that they are the fundamentals of the good life. First of all, you should think of deity as imperishable and blessed being (as delineated in the universal conception of it common to all men), and you should not attribute to it anything foreign to its immortality or inconsistent with its blessedness. On the contrary, you should hold every doctrine that is capable of safeguarding its blessedness in common with its imperishability. The gods do indeed exist, since our knowledge of them is a matter of clear and distinct perception; but they are not like what the masses suppose them to be, because most people do not maintain the pure conception of the gods. The irreligious man is not the person who destroys the gods of the masses but the person who imposes the ideas of the masses on the gods. The opinions held by most people about the gods are not true conceptions of them but fallacious notions, according to which awful penalties are meted out to the evil and the greatest of blessings to the good. The masses, by assimilating the gods in every respect to their own moral qualities, accept deities similar to themselves and regard anything not of this sort as alien.

Second, you should accustom yourself to believing that death means nothing to us, since every good and every evil lies in sensation; but death is the privation of sensation. Hence a correct comprehension of the fact that death means nothing to us makes the mortal aspect of life pleasurable, not by conferring on us a boundless period of time but by removing the yearning for deathlessness. There is nothing fearful in living for the person who has really laid hold of the fact that there is nothing fearful in not living. So it is silly for a person to say that he dreads death—not because it will be painful when it arrives but because it pains him now as a future certainty; for that which makes no trouble for us when it arrives is a meaningless pain when we await it. This, the most horrifying of evils, means nothing to us, then, because so long as we are

existent death is not present and whenever it is present we are nonexistent. Thus it is of no concern either to the living or to those who have completed their lives. For the former it is nonexistent, and the latter are themselves nonexistent.

Most people, however, recoil from death as though it were the greatest of evils; at other times they welcome it as the end-all of life's ills. The sophisticated person, on the other hand, neither begs off from living nor dreads not living. Life is not a stumbling block to him, nor does he regard not being alive as any sort of evil. As in the case of food he prefers the most savory dish to merely the larger portion, so in the case of time, he garners to himself the most agreeable moments rather than the longest span.

Anyone who urges the youth to lead a good life but counsels the older man to end his life in good style is silly, not merely because of the welcome character of life but because of the fact that living well and dying well are one and the same discipline. Much worse off, however, is the person who says it were well not to have been born "but once born to pass Hades' portals as swiftly as may be." Now if he says such a thing from inner persuasion why does he not withdraw from life? Everything is in readiness for him once he has firmly resolved on this course. But if he speaks facetiously he is a trifler standing in the midst of men who do not welcome him.

It should be borne in mind, then, that the time to come is neither ours nor altogether not ours. In this way we shall neither expect the future outright as something destined to be, nor despair of it as something absolutely not destined to be.

The Good Life

[2. It should be recognized that within the category of desire certain desires are natural, certain others unnecessary and trivial; that in the case of the natural desires certain ones are necessary, certain others merely natural; and that in the case of necessary desires certain ones are necessary for happiness, others to promote freedom from bodily discomfort, others for the maintenance of life itself. A steady view of these matters shows us how to refer all moral choice and aversion to bodily health and imperturbability of mind, these being the twin goals of happy living. It is on this account that we do everything we do—to achieve freedom from pain and freedom from fear. When once we come to this, the tumult in the soul is calmed and the human being does not have to go about looking for something that is lacking or to search for something additional with which to supplement the welfare of soul and body. Accordingly we have need of pleasure only when we feel pain because of the absence of pleasure, but whenever we do not feel pain we no longer stand in need of pleasure. And so we speak of pleasure as the starting point and the goal of the happy life because we realize that it is our primary native good, because every act of choice and aversion originates with it, and because we come back to it when we judge every good by using the pleasure feeling as our criterion.

Because of the very fact that pleasure is our primary and congenital good we do not select every pleasure; there are times when we forego certain pleasures, particularly when they are followed by too much unpleasantness. Furthermore, we regard certain states of pain as preferable to pleasures, particularly when greater satisfaction results from our having submitted to discomforts for a long period of time. Thus every pleasure is a good by reason of its having a nature akin to our own, but not every pleasure is desirable. In like manner every state of pain is an evil, but not all pains are uniformly to be rejected. At any rate, it is our duty to judge all such cases by measuring pleasures against pains, with a view to their respective assets and liabilities, inasmuch as we do experience the good as being bad at times and, contrariwise, the bad as being good.

In addition, we consider limitation of the appetites a major good, and we recommend this practice not for the purpose of enjoying just a few things and no more but rather for the purpose of enjoying those few in case we do not have much. We are firmly convinced that those who need expensive fare least are the ones who relish it most keenly and that a natural way of life is easily procured, while trivialities are hard to come by. Plain foods afford pleasure equivalent to that of a sumptuous diet, provided that the pains of penury are wholly eliminated. Barley bread and water yield the peak of pleasure whenever a person who needs them sets them in front of himself. Hence becoming habituated to a simple rather than a lavish way of life provides us with the full complement of health; it makes a person ready for the necessary business of life; it puts us in a position of advantage when we happen upon sumptuous fare at intervals and prepares us to be fearless in facing fortune.

Thus when I say that pleasure is the goal of living I do not mean the pleasures of libertines or the pleasures inherent in positive enjoyment, as is supposed by certain persons who are ignorant of our doctrine or who are not in agreement with it or who interpret it perversely. I mean, on the contrary, the pleasure that consists in freedom from bodily pain and mental agitation. The pleasant life is not the product of one drinking party after another or of sexual intercourse with women and boys or of the sea food and other delicacies afforded by a luxurious table. On the contrary, it is the result of sober thinking—namely, investigation of the reasons for every act of choice and aversion and elimination of those false ideas about the gods and death which are the chief source of mental disturbances.

The starting point of this whole scheme and the most important of its values is good judgment, which consequently is more highly esteemed even than philosophy. All the other virtues stem from sound judgment, which shows us that it is impossible to live the pleasant Epicurean life without also living sensibly, nobly, and justly and, vice versa, that it is impossible to live sensibly, nobly, and justly without living pleasantly. The traditional virtues grow up together with the pleasant life; they are indivisible. Can you think of anyone more moral than the person who has devout beliefs about the gods, who is consistently without fears about death, and who has pondered man's natural end? Or who realizes that the goal of the good life is easily gained and achieved and that the term of evil is brief, both in extent of time and duration of pain? Or the man who laughs at the "decrees of Fate," a deity whom some people have set up as sovereign of all?

The good Epicurean believes that certain events occur deterministically, that others are chance events, and that still others are in our own hands. He sees also that necessity cannot be held morally responsible and that chance is an unpredictable thing, but that what is in our own hands, since it has no master, is naturally associated with blameworthiness and the opposite. (Actually it would be better to subscribe to the popular mythology than to become a slave by accepting the determinism of the natural philosophers, because popular religion underwrites the hope of supplicating the gods by offerings but determinism contains an element of necessity, which is inexorable.) As for chance, the Epicurean does not assume that it is a deity (as in popular belief) because a god does nothing irregular; nor does he regard it as an unpredictable cause of all events. It is his belief that good and evil are not the chance contributions of a deity, donated to mankind for the happy life, but rather that the initial circumstances for great good and evil are sometimes provided by chance. He thinks it preferable to have bad luck rationally than good luck irrationally. In other words, in human action it is better for a rational choice to be unsuccessful than for an irrational choice to succeed through the agency of chance.

Think about these and related matters day and night, by yourself and in company with someone like yourself. If you do, you will never experience anxiety, waking or sleeping, but you will live like a god among men. For a human being who lives in the midst of immortal blessings is in no way like mortal man!

ROMAN CIVILIZATION
The Pre-Christian Centuries

CICERO

Selection from *On the Republic*

For more than two thousand years Cicero (106–43 B.C.) has been one of the West's guiding spirits. The impact of his writings first on Rome and later on Europe cannot be overestimated. Within his vast works, the most famous passage is perhaps "The Dream of Scipio" from *On the Republic,* a study of the ideal polity. Its popularity stems largely from its lofty theme: The joys of heaven are greater than the glories of earth. Romans heard in this theme an echo of Plato; later, Christians thought it signaled that Cicero was one of them, even if he did live before Christ. Today's readers can still appreciate "The Dream" as a noble vision by one of Rome's leading thinkers.

Cicero was both a man of action and a man of letters. When in power, he worked to heal the social ills of late republican Rome (133–31 B.C.), a period wracked by civil wars. When in eclipse, he wrote prodigiously and quickly, advocating constitutionalism and opposing autocracy. In the end he failed as a statesman and, though not a conspirator, was killed in the fallout from the plot to murder Julius Caesar. Mark Antony, Caesar's friend and self-proclaimed heir, distrusted Cicero and ordered his death.

Cicero wrote from the vantage point of an eclectic thinker, one who knew philosophy but was not a true philosopher. He was open to criticism and claimed the right to change his mind. In his letters he describes his method of reaching a decision—by debating both sides of a problem. For his treatises, such as *On the Republic,* he favored the dialogue form because its "give-and-take" format enabled readers to make up their minds based on opposing viewpoints.

Two traits characterized Cicero's world: It was civilized and tolerant. To express this ideal, he coined the term *humanitas* (humanity), meaning devotion to books, language, and art. He gave *humanitas* a social face in his dialogues, setting them in a courteous society free of rudeness. He himself lived this ideal, being well read in Greek and Roman letters, philosophy, history, and law. His learning, though highly valued, still could not compete with his love of politics. When called to office, he welcomed the chance to be a "man of the world." Hence, the claim in "The Dream" that contemplation is superior to action must be doubted, reflecting instead Cicero's exile from politics when he wrote it.

Reading the Selection

"The Dream of Scipio" offers a cosmic perspective on human affairs. Not original in outlook, it is a Romanized synthesis of Greek thought on the soul and the afterlife; it is drawn largely from sixth-century thinker Pythagoras, whose ideas were passed on to Plato (*Phaedo*). Expressive of *humanitas* and his love of Rome, Cicero's "The Dream" claims that there is a life beyond the grave for deserving politicians and philosophers.

Cicero's choice of Publius Cornelius Scipio (the younger) (ca. 184–129 B.C.) as his mouthpiece reflects Cicero's patriotism and Hellenism (love of Greek culture), the bedrock of his ideals. Deeply aware of his status as a "new man" (the first in his family to achieve the consulship), Cicero adopted as spiritual ancestors the younger Scipio and his friends. The grandson of Scipio Africanus (the elder) (237–183 B.C.), Rome's savior during the Second Punic War, Scipio the younger was, in his own right, a great statesman and the leader of a highly educated literary circle. It was this circle that introduced to Rome the Stoic ideas that Cicero quoted in "The Dream," such as the stress on virtue and duty.

—〰—

The Dream of Scipio

As you know, I was military tribune in the Fourth Legion in Africa under the command of the consul Manius Manilius. When I arrived there I was particularly eager to meet King Masinissa, who for good reason was a close friend of my family. When I came into his presence the old man embraced me and wept. Then, after a moment, he lifted his eyes to heaven and uttered these words.

'Most glorious Sun and other heavenly beings, I offer you my thanks! For before I depart from this life, I am now seeing with my own eyes, within this kingdom of mine and beneath my roof, Publius Cornelius Scipio. The very sound of his name revives my strength. For never a moment has the recollection of his glorious, invincible forbear faded from my memory.'

Then I began asking him questions about his kingdom, and he in turn interrogated me about Rome; and so we spent the whole day in conversation. Afterwards, he entertained me in regal splendour, and we continued our discussion far into the night, as the aged king wanted nothing better than to talk of Africanus. He had not forgotten a single deed the great man had ever done, or a single word he had ever uttered.

When we finally parted and retired to bed, my journey and the lateness of the hour had made me tired, and I fell into a deeper sleep than usual. As I slept I had a dream, prompted no doubt by what we had been talking about. For it frequently happens that the subjects of our meditations and discussions reappear in our dreams. This happened for example to the poet Ennius; he writes of his dream about Homer, who was naturally the constant subject of his thoughts and conversations when he was awake. And so I dreamt that Africanus was with me; his appearance recalled his portrait busts rather than his actual living self.

. . .

I recognized him—and trembled with fear. But he spoke to me; and this is what he said.

'Calm yourself, Scipio. Do not be afraid. But remember carefully the things I am about to tell you. Do you see that city there? It was I who made its people submit to Rome. But now they are starting up the old conflicts once again; they refuse to remain at peace!' And from where he stood amid the bright illumination of radiant stars, he pointed down at Carthage, and began speaking once more. 'This,' he declared, is the city you have come to attack. At present you are not much more than an ordinary soldier. But within the space of two years you will have been elected consul, and then you will overthrow the place utterly. Thereafter the surname, which you now bear as an inheritance from myself, will be yours by your own right. Later on, after you have destroyed Carthage and celebrated a Triumph, after you have held the office of censor and undertaken missions to Egypt, Syria, Asia and Greece, you will be elected to the consulship for the second time, while you are absent, and you will win a very great war and raze Numantia to the ground. But at the time when you yourself are proceeding in Triumph to the Capitol, you will find the government in a state of confusion: for which the machinations of my grandson will be responsible.

'After that, Africanus, it will be your duty to devote to your people the full splendid benefit of all your integrity, talent and wisdom. But at that juncture I see two divergent paths of destiny opening up before you. For when your life has completed seven times eight circuitous revolutions of the sun, and when these two numbers, each of which for a different reason is regarded as possessing some quality of perfection, have in their natural course brought you to your supreme moment of destiny, that is the time when the entire Roman State will turn to you and all that you stand for: the Senate, every right-minded citizen, our subject allies, the entire Latin people. The fate of the whole country, at that juncture, will depend on you and you alone. In other words, it will be your duty to assume the role of dictator, and restore order to our commonwealth—

provided only that death does not overtake you at the criminal hands of your own kinsmen!'

At this, Laelius cried out aloud, and a deep groan was heard from all. But the younger Scipio smiled serenely, and went on: 'Hush! Do not, I beg you, awaken me from my sleep. Listen a little longer, and take heed of what my ancestor went on to say next.'

For then he continued speaking. 'But consider this, Africanus,' he said, 'and the thought will make your determination to defend your homeland even greater than it is already. Every man who has preserved or helped his country, or has made its greatness even greater, is reserved a special place in heaven, where he may enjoy an eternal life of happiness. For all things that are done on earth nothing is more acceptable to the Supreme God, who rules the whole universe, than those gatherings and assemblages of men who are bound together by law, the communities which are known as states. Indeed, it is from here in heaven that the rulers and preservers of those states once came; and it is to here that they eventually return.'

By now I was thoroughly alarmed. It was not the idea 10 of death that frightened me so much, but the thought of treachery inside my own family. Nevertheless, I managed to ask Africanus a question. Was he, was my father Paullus, were the other men we think of as having died, really dead? Or were they still alive?

'To be sure they are still living,' he replied, 'seeing that they have escaped from the prison-house of their bodies— that is to say from "life", as you call it, which is, in fact, death. Look: do you not see your father Paullus coming towards you?'

Indeed I now saw him approaching; and I burst into a flood of tears. But my father put his arms round me and kissed me, and told me not to weep. So when I had suppressed my tears and felt able to speak, I cried out, 'Since this, most revered and best of fathers, is true life, as I hear Africanus declare, why must I stay any longer upon earth? Why should I not come and join you, with the utmost possible speed?'

'That must not be,' replied Paullus. 'For unless God, whose sacred domain is all that you see around you here, has freed you from your confinement in the body, you cannot be admitted to this place. For men were brought into existence in order that they should inhabit the globe known as the earth, which you see here at the centre of this holy space. They have been endowed with souls made out of the everlasting fires called stars and constellations, consisting of globular, spherical bodies which are animated by the divine mind and move with marvellous speed, each in its own orbit and cycle. Therefore it is destined that you, Publius, and all other righteous men, shall suffer your souls to stay in the custody of the body. You must not abandon human life except at the command of him who gave it to you. For otherwise you would have failed in the duty which you, like the rest of humanity, have to fulfil.

'Instead, then, Scipio, do upon earth as your grandfather has done. Do as I have done, who begot you. Cherish justice and devotion. These qualities in abundance are owed to parents and kinsmen; and most of all they are owed to one's country.

'That is the life which leads to heaven, and to the com- 15 pany of those who, having completed their lives in the world, are now released from their bodies and dwell in that region you see over there, which the Greeks have taught you people on earth to call the Milky Way.' And he pointed to a circle of light, blazing brilliantly among all other fires.

As I gazed out from where I stood, first in one direction and then another, the whole prospect looked marvellously beautiful. There were stars we never see from the earth, and they were larger than we could possibly have imagined. The smallest was the luminary which is farthest away from heaven and nearest to the earth, and shines with reflected light. These starry spheres were much larger than the earth. Indeed the earth now seemed to me so small that I began to think less of this empire of ours, which only amounts to a pinpoint on its surface.

. . .

While I looked more and more intently down at the earth Africanus checked me. 'How long,' he asked, 'do you propose to keep your eyes fastened down there upon that world of yours? Look up, instead, and look round at the sacred region into which you have now entered.

'The universe is held together by nine concentric spheres. The outermost sphere is heaven itself, and it includes and embraces all the rest. For it is the Supreme God in person, enclosing and comprehending everything that exists, that is to say all the stars which are fixed in the sky yet rotate upon their eternal courses. Within this outermost sphere are eight others. Seven of them contain the planets—a single one in each sphere, all moving in the contrary direction to the great movement of heaven itself. The next sphere to the outermost is occupied by the orb which people on earth name after Saturn. Below Saturn shines the brilliant light of Jupiter, which is benign and healthful to mankind. Then comes the star we call Mars, red and terrible to men upon earth.

'Next, almost midway between heaven and earth, blazes the Sun. He is the prince, lord and ruler of all the other worlds, the mind and guiding principle of the entire universe, so gigantic in size that everything, everywhere, is pervaded and drenched by his light. In attendance upon the Sun are Venus and Mercury, each in its own orbit; and the lowest sphere of all contains the Moon, which takes its light, as it revolves, from the rays of the sun. Above the Moon there is nothing which is not eternal, but beneath that level everything is moral and transient (except only for the souls in human beings, which are a gift to mankind from the gods). For there below the Moon is the earth, the ninth and lowest of the spheres, lying at the centre of the universe. The earth remains fixed and without motion; all things are drawn to it, because the natural force of gravity pulls them down.'

I surveyed the scene in a stupor. But finally I recov- 20 ered enough to ask: 'What is this sound, so strong and so sweet, which fills my ears?'

'That,' he replied, 'is the music of the spheres. They create it by their own motion as they rush upon their way.

The intervals between them, although differing in length, are all measured according to a fixed scheme of proportions; and this arrangement produces a melodious blend of high and low notes, from which emerges a varied harmony. For it cannot be that these vast movements should take place in silence, and nature has ordained that the spheres utter music, those at the summit giving forth high sounds, whereas the sounds of those beneath are low and deep. That is to say, the spheres containing the uppermost stars, comprising those regions of the sky where the movements are speediest, give out a high and piercing sound, whereas the Moon, which lies beneath all the others, sends forth the lowest note.

'The ninth of the spheres, the earth, fixed at the centre of the universe, is motionless and silent. But the other eight spheres produce seven different sounds on the scale—not eight, since two of these orbs move at identical speeds, but seven, a number which is the key to almost all things that exist. Clever men, by imitating these musical effects with their stringed instruments and voices, have given themselves the possibility of eventually returning to this place; and the same chance exists for others too, who during their earthly lives have devoted their outstanding talents to heavenly activities.

'The ears of mankind are filled with this music all the time. But they have become completely deaf to its melody; no other human faculty has become so atrophied as this. The same thing happens where the Nile rushes down from high mountains to the place known as Catadupa. For the sound there is so loud that the people who live nearby have entirely lost their sense of hearing. And that, too, is why the mighty music of the spheres, created by the immeasurably fast rotations of the whole universe, cannot be apprehended by the human ears—any more than you can look at the light of the Sun, which is so intense it blots out your power of vision altogether.'

The scene filled me with awe and delight. And yet all the time I still could not help riveting my eyes upon our own world there below. Africanus noticed this, and spoke again. 'I see,' he said, 'that your gaze is still fastened, even now, upon the places where mortals dwell upon the earth. But can you not understand that the earth is totally insignificant? Contemplate these heavenly regions instead! Scorn what is mortal!

'For the lips of mankind can give you no fame or glory worth the seeking. Note how few and minute are the inhabited portions of the earth, and look upon the vast deserts that divide each one of these patches from the next. See, the inhabitants of the world are so cut off from one another that their different centres cannot even communicate with each other. The place where you yourself dwell, for example, is far removed from certain of the other populated areas, both in latitude and longitude; and some people live in regions that are at the very opposite end of the world from yours. Surely you cannot expect *them* to honour your name.

'Furthermore, you will observe that the surface of the earth is girdled and encompassed by a number of different zones; and that the two which are most widely separated from one another, and lie beneath opposite poles of the heavens, are rigid with icy cold, while the central, broadest zone is burnt up with the heat of the sun. Two others, situated between the hot zones and the cold, are habitable. The zone which lies towards the south has no connexion with yours at all; it represents your antipodes. As to its northern counterpart, where you yourselves live, you will realize, if you look, what a diminutive section of this region can really be regarded as your property. For the territory you occupy is nothing more than a small island, narrow from north to south, somewhat less narrow from east to west, and surrounded by the sea which is known on earth as the Atlantic, or the Great Sea, or the Ocean. In spite of the grand name this stretch of water bears, you can tell from here how tiny it really is.

'And I must disabuse you of any idea that your own fame, or the fame of any one of us, could ever be great enough to extend beyond these known and settled lands. It could never scale the Caucasus mountains (you see them down there); it could never swim the river Ganges. Not one of the inhabitants of all those eastern tracts, or the remote west either, or the far off north and south, will ever so much as hear the sound of your name! And once you leave all these hosts of people out of account, you will have to conclude that the area over which your glory is so eager to extend itself is really of the most trifling dimensions.

'And now about the people who *do* know and speak about us. The point is, how long will this go on? Assume, if you like, that future generations, having inherited our praises from their fathers, will indeed retain the desire to hand them down to their children as well. Even so the deluges and conflagrations which inevitably descend upon the earth at fixed intervals will make it impossible for any glory we may gain in this way to be eternal—or even to last for any length of time. But in any case why do you regard it as so important to be talked about by people who have not yet been born? After all, you were never spoken of by all the multitudes who lived before you—and they were every bit as numerous, and were better men.

'It is also necessary to remind ourselves that even the people who may in fact hear our names mentioned will not retain the recollection even for as much as the space of one year. I am not referring to the year as it is commonly understood, which is measured according to the revolution of the sun, that is to say according to the movements of one single star. But when *all* the stars return to the places where they started from, so that after an immense interval has elapsed the entire heavens finally resume their original configuration, then that great period of rotation can truly be called a year—but how many generations of human life it comprises, I should not venture to say.

'Long ago, when the spirit of Romulus ascended into these sacred expanses, it seemed to those living at the time that a shadow suddenly passed over the sun, and its light was blotted out. When, once again, the sun shall go into eclipse in the very same position and at the very same hour, that will signify that all the constellations and stars have returned to their original positions: and then you will know that the Year has been completed. But you must understand that, up to now, not one twentieth part of its course has been run.

. . .

'As for yourself, do not abandon hope of coming back here one day. For this is the place which offers great and eminent men their authentic reward—and, after all, such fame as you are able to win among mere human beings can evidently be disregarded, seeing that it is scarcely capable of enduring even for a small part of one single year. Look upwards, then! Contemplate this place which is a habitation for all eternity! Then you will not need any longer to be at the mercy of what the multitude says about you: then you will not have to put your trust in whatever human rewards your achievements may earn.

'Instead let Virtue herself, by her own unaided allurements, summon you to a glory that is genuine and real. Feel no concern about what other people may say about you. They will say it in any case. Besides, whatever words they may choose to utter will not pass beyond the narrow limits you now see below you. No utterance of man about his fellowmen has ever been lasting. When a person dies his words die with him. Posterity forgets them; and they pass into annihilation.'

He stopped speaking, and I cried out my assent. 'Even when I was only a boy, Africanus,' I declared, 'I was already exerting myself to the utmost to follow in your footsteps, and in those of my father. I longed to be not unworthy of your fame! And if there is really a path leading right to the entrance of heaven for those who have served their country well, the knowledge of this great goal before me will inspire me to redouble my endeavours.'

'Strive on,' he replied. 'And rest assured that it is only your body that is mortal; your true self is nothing of the kind. For the man you outwardly appear to be is not yourself at all. Your real self is not that corporeal, palpable shape, but the spirit inside. *Understand that you are god.* You have a god's capacity of aliveness and sensation and memory and foresight; a god's power to rule and govern and direct the body that is your servant, in the same way as God himself, who reigns over us, directs the entire universe. And this rule exercised by eternal God is mirrored in the dominance of your frail body by your immortal soul.

. . .

'That which is always in motion is eternal; yet that which 35 communicates motion to something else, but is itself moved by another force, must necessarily cease to live when the transmission of this motion to it has ceased. Consequently the only thing that never ceases to move is something which has the power of starting up motion all *on its own*—it can go on moving because its power to achieve motion depends on itself and itself alone. This, therefore, it must be concluded, is the source and first principle of motion for all things that move.

'Being the first principle, it never had a beginning: since the first principle is what everything else has originated from, it cannot possibly have originated from anything else. For if it owed its origin to something else, it could not be described as the first principle.

'And since it never had a beginning it will never have an end. For if the first principle were destroyed it could never be reborn from any other source and would no longer be able to create things on its own account—which is obviously what the first principle has to do.

'The beginning of all movement, then, comes from that which has set itself in motion: which can neither be born nor die. For if that were not so, one would have to envisage the entire heavens and all things that have ever been created crashing down and coming to an end—for that is what would happen if the force generating their motion were taken away from them.

'Since, therefore, it is plain that the self-moving principle is eternal, the same must evidently apply to the human soul. For unlike lifeless objects which can only be set in motion from outside, the soul, by its very essence and nature, is a living thing such as can only derive its life and motion from within itself. And since, uniquely, it possesses this characteristic of self-impulsion, surely it has no beginning, and lives for ever.

. . .

'Use this eternal force, therefore, for the most splendid 40 deeds it is in you to achieve! And the very best deeds are those which serve your country. A soul devoted to such pursuits will find it easiest of all to soar upwards to this place, which is its proper habitation and home. And its flight will be all the more rapid if already during the period of its confinement within the body it has ranged freely abroad, and, by contemplating what lies outside itself, has contrived to detach itself from the body to the greatest possible degree.

'When, on the other hand, a man has failed to do this, and has abandoned himself instead to bodily indulgence and become its slave, letting the passions which serve pleasure impel him to flout the laws both of gods and of men, his soul, after departing from his body, hovers about close to the earth. Nor does it return to this place until many ages of torment have been undergone.'

Then Africanus vanished; and I awoke from my sleep.

CATULLUS

Poems

Born into a wealthy and distinguished Italian family, Catullus (ca. 84–57 B.C.) enjoyed a short, bittersweet life during the turbulent last years of the Roman Republic. Indeed, his life seemed to mirror the unsettled times of political intrigue and the scramble for power as he suffered through torrid love affairs, experienced fickle friendships, and endured life's capriciousness.

Often rebuffed by his manipulative mistress, Clodia, the wife of a Roman consul, whom he immortalized in his love poetry as "Lesbia" (named for Sappho; see the selection of her extant poetry), Catullus chose to spend much of his time in travel. While away from Rome, he was intent on trying to heal his wounded heart and restore his fortune. During one long voyage to the eastern Mediterranean, he wrote a series of poems setting forth his adventures, as he tried to put his life in perspective. This poetry survived his own short life to leave a personal testament; it transcends the times and reminds readers that sometimes the best way to survive calamity is to turn inward and commune with one's soul.

Catullus's poems, closely linked with the Alexandrian style (see Theocritus's *Idylls*), fall into three categories: the "small" or short epic, epigrams or elegies, and love poetry. In his short epics, he exhibits his vast knowledge of Greek myth. His epigrams, short and diverse, range across the spectrum of human life—from mourning a friend's death to attacking Julius Caesar. His love poems—his best-known works—express his innermost feelings, from raw lust to calculated betrayals and total rejection that break the heart.

Reading the Selections

Four of the five poems included here treat of Catullus's love for his beloved Lesbia, though in contradictory ways. In the first poem, the earliest of the four, he is besotted, relishing her kisses and declaring the eternity of their love. The three later poems show him sadder but no wiser; he accuses Lesbia of unfaithfulness yet still confesses his love for her.

The other poem included here reveals Catullus's sharp insight into the human condition. In the opening stanzas he notes that Suffenus, a fellow poet, publishes his works in finely crafted scrolls (bookbinding had not yet been invented). These scrolls were similar, perhaps, to handsome and lavishly illustrated twentieth-century "coffee table" books in which content is second to appearance. Catullus charges that Suffenus, who dines out on his glossy products, composes very mediocre poetry. Turning the tables on the reader, Catullus, in his concluding comments, asks if we are not all like Suffenus, self-deluded about our own talents and our place in the world—a conclusion that echoes the folk wisdom of the Greek storyteller Aesop. What Catullus wrote regarding the human tendency to self-delusion still rings true after more than two thousand years.

—⁓—

5

Lesbia   1
  live with me
& love me so
we'll laugh at all
the sour-faced strict-
ures of the wise.
This sun once set
will rise again,
when our sun sets
follows night &   10
an endless sleep.
Kiss me now a
thousand times &
now a hundred
more & then a

hundred & a
thousand more again
till with so many
hundred thousand
kisses you & I   20
shall both lose count
nor any can
from envy of
so much of kissing
put his finger
on the number
of sweet kisses
you of me &
I of you,
darling, have had.   30

—⁓—

22

I must, Varus, tell you: 1
  Suffenus, known to us both as
a man of elegance, wit
  & sophistication
is also a poet
  who turns out verse by the yard.
No palimpsest copies
  but new books with new ivories
inscribed on Augustan Royal,
  the lines lead-ruled,   10
red tabs & red wrappers,
  the ends shaved with pumice.
But unwind the scroll
  & Suffenus
the well-known diner-out
  disappears.
A goatherd
  a country bumpkin

looks at us—
  strangely transmogrified.   20
What should one think?
  The envy of wits
becomes
  at the touch of the Muses
a bundle of gaucheries. . . .
  and he likes nothing better
fancies himself
  in the role of a poet. . . .
Yet who,
  in his own way,   30
is not a Suffenus?
  Each has his blind spot.
The mote & the beam.
  As Aesop says,
the pack on our own back
  that we don't see.

51

Godlike the man who   1
sits at her side, who
watches and catches
    that laughter
which (softly) tears me
to tatters: nothing is
left of me, each time
    I see her,
. . . tongue numbed; arms, legs
melting, on fire; drum   10
drumming in ears; head-
    lights gone black.

Coda

Her ease is your sloth, Catullus
you itch & roll in her ease:

former kings and cities
lost in the valley of her arm.

72

There was a time, Lesbia, when   1
you confessed only to Catullus in love:
you would set me above Jupiter himself.
I loved you then
    not as men love their women
but as a father his children—his family.
Today I know you too well
    and desire burns deeper in me

and you are more coarse
    more frivolous in my thought.   10
"How," you may ask, "can this be?"
Such actions as yours excite
    increased violence of love,
Lesbia, but with friendless intention.

75

Reason blinded by sin, Lesbia,   1
a mind drowned in its own devotion:
come clothed in your excellences—

I cannot think tenderly of you,
sink to what acts you dare—
I can never cut this love.

VERGIL

Selection from the *Aeneid*

Vergil (70–19 B.C.), from a modest rural family of northern Italy, studied, as part of his education, the Greek and Alexandrian poets and writers. Homer, his chief inspiration, would guide him through much of his literary career. Returning to his family farm upon completing his education, Vergil worked the land and began to compose poetry. By a series of chance circumstances, he met Octavian, the future Caesar Augustus (31 B.C.–A.D. 14), to whom he dedicated his first collection of poems. Vergil, upon moving to Rome, was introduced to the wealthy and powerful who became his patrons. His two books of poems, *Eclogues* and *Georgics,* reminded the Romans of the simple rural values that had made them masters of the Mediterranean and the envy of all nations; these poems established Vergil as the leading voice of the Golden Age of Roman literature. Vergil drew on his earlier years as a farmer to argue that the plain life of the early Romans had prepared them for their mission and responsibility as world leaders, but he warned his readers to return to the good old days and to reject the temptation to amass wealth and live in cities.

As Vergil's fame grew, he decided to write an epic that would portray Rome's glorious past down to the triumph of Augustus. His tale was to be a sweeping story of symbolic events built around the adventures of Aeneas, the Trojan prince, who escaped from Troy at the time of its fall with his son, father, and loyal band of soldiers. Driven by fate and his own sense of duty, Aeneas overcame one obstacle after another to fulfill his destiny to found Rome. In laying the foundation of this great nation, Aeneas was foreshadowing Augustus; under his wise and just leadership, Rome was prepared to play a dominant role in history. By today's standards, Vergil's praise for Augustus flatters his hero too much; for the Romans, however, the *Aeneid* inspired generations of young men to take their place among those who served Rome.

Reading the Selection

Book VI of the *Aeneid* records Aeneas's journey through the underworld with the aid of a Sibyl (a female prophet). Along the way, they encounter many of Aeneas's friends and a few enemies. On several occasions, Aeneas and a former companion recall shared adventures. One of the most poignant scenes in the underworld has Aeneas meeting Dido, the queen of Carthage, who killed herself when he rejected her love and pleadings to remain with him in northern Africa.

As Aeneas and the Sibyl pass from one hideous scene in the underworld to the next, she explains to him why the dead souls behave as they do. They eventually locate Anchises, Aeneas's father, who rejoices in this reunion with his son. Telling his father how much he values his moral teaching about obedience to duty, Aeneas asks for his father's blessing and tries to embrace him, only to discover that he is a ghostly shade.

In this particular book of the *Aeneid,* Vergil is heavily indebted to Homer, his literary hero; indeed, he modeled his epic's first six books on the *Odyssey* and imitated the *Iliad* in the last six books. Although Vergil's style and method (using invocations, digressions, and similes) recall Homer's, Vergil is a more "civilized" poet, a more self-conscious artist who has an intense feeling for and sense of the past.

Book VI

· · ·

You gods who rule the world of the spirits, you silent shades, and Chaos, and Phlegethon, you dark and silent wastes, let it be right for me to tell what I have been told, let it be with your divine blessing that I reveal what is hidden deep in the mists beneath the earth.

They walked in the darkness of that lonely night with shadows all about them, through the empty halls of Dis and his desolate kingdom, as men walk in a wood by the sinister light of a fitful moon when Jupiter has buried the sky in shade and black night has robbed all things of their colour. Before the entrance hall of Orcus, in the very throat of hell, Grief and Revenge have made their beds and Old Age lives there in despair, with white faced Diseases and Fear and Hunger, corrupter of men, and squalid Poverty, things dreadful to look upon, and Death and Drudgery besides. Then there are Sleep, Death's sister, perverted Pleasures, murderous War astride the threshold, the iron chambers of the Furies and raving Discord with blood-soaked ribbons binding her viperous hair. In the middle a huge dark elm spreads out its ancient arms, the resting-place, so they say, of flocks of idle dreams, one clinging under every leaf. Here too are all manner of monstrous beasts, Centaurs stabling inside the gate, Scyllas—half dogs, half women—Briareus with his hundred heads, the Hydra of Lerna hissing fiercely, the Chimaera armed in fire, Gorgons and Harpies and the triple phantom of Geryon. Now Aeneas drew his sword in sudden alarm to meet them with naked steel as they came at him, and if his wise companion had not warned him that this was the fluttering of disembodied spirits, a mere semblance of living substance, he would have rushed upon them and parted empty shadows with steel.

Here begins the road that leads to the rolling waters of Acheron, the river of Tartarus. Here is a vast quagmire of boiling whirlpools which belches sand and slime into Cocytus, and these are the rivers and waters guarded by the terrible Charon in his filthy rags. On his chin there grows a thick grey beard, never trimmed. His glaring eyes are lit with fire and a foul cloak hangs from a knot at his shoulder. With his own hands he plies the pole and sees to the sails as he ferries the dead in a boat the colour of burnt iron. He is no longer young but, being a god, enjoys rude strength and a green old age. The whole throng of the dead was rushing to this part of the bank, mothers, men, great-hearted heroes whose lives were ended, boys, unmarried girls and young men laid on the pyre before the faces of their parents, as many as are the leaves that fall in the forest at the first chill of autumn, as many as the birds that flock to land from deep ocean when the cold season of the year drives them over the sea to lands bathed in sun. There they stood begging to be allowed to be the first to cross and stretching out their arms in longing for the further shore. But the grim boatman takes some here and some there, and others he pushes away far back from the sandy shore.

Aeneas, amazed and distressed by all this tumult, cried out: 'Tell me, virgin priestess, what is the meaning of this crowding to the river? What do the spirits want? Why are some pushed away from the bank while others sweep the livid water with their oars?' The aged Sibyl made this brief reply: 'Son of Anchises, beyond all doubt the offspring of the gods, what you are seeing is the deep pools of the Cocytus and the swamp of the Styx, by whose divine power the gods are afraid to swear and lie. The throng you see on this side are the helpless souls of the unburied. The ferryman there is Charon. Those sailing the waters of the Styx have all been buried. No man may be ferried from fearful bank to fearful bank of this roaring current until his bones are laid to rest. Instead they wander for a hundred years, fluttering round these shores until they are at last allowed to return to the pools they have so longed for.' The

son of Anchises checked his stride and stood stock still with many thoughts coursing through his mind as he pitied their cruel fate, when there among the sufferers, lacking all honour in death, he caught sight of Leucaspis, and Orontes, the captain of the Lycian fleet, men who had started with him from Troy, sailed the wind-torn seas and been overwhelmed by gales from the south that rolled them in the ocean, ships and crews. . . .

And so they carried on to the end of the road on which they had started, and at last came near the river. When the boatman, now in mid-stream, looked ashore from the waves of the Styx and saw them coming through the silent wood towards the bank, he called out to them and challenged them: 'You there, whoever you are, making for our river with a sword by your side, come tell us why you are here. Speak to us from where you stand. Take not another step. This place belongs to the shades, to Sleep and to Night, the bringer of Sleep. Living bodies may not be carried on the boat that plies the Styx. It gave me little enough pleasure to take even Hercules aboard when he came, or Theseus, or Pirithous, although they said they were born of gods and their strength was irresistible. It was Hercules whose hand put chains on the watchdog of Tartarus and dragged him shivering from the very throne of our king. The others had taken it upon themselves to steal the queen, my mistress, from the chamber of Dis.' The answer of the Amphrysian Sibyl was brief: 'Here there are no such designs. You have no need for alarm. These weapons of his bring no violence. The monstrous keeper of the gate can bark in his cave and frighten the bloodless shades till the end of time and Proserpina can stay chaste behind her uncle's doors. Trojan Aeneas, famous for his devotion and his feats of arms, is going down to his father in the darkest depths of Erebus. If the sight of such devotion does not move you, then look at this branch,' she said, showing the branch that had been hidden in her robes, 'and realize what it is.' At this the swelling anger subsided in his heart. No more words were needed. Seeing it again after a long age, and marvelling at the fateful branch, the holy offering, he turned his dark boat and steered towards the bank. He then drove off the souls who were on board with him sitting all along the cross benches, and cleared the gangways. In the same moment he took the huge Aeneas into the hull of his little boat. Being only sewn together, it groaned under his weight, shipping great volumes of stagnant water through the seams, but in the end it carried priestess and hero safely over and landed them on the foul slime among the grey-green reeds.

The kingdom on this side resounded with barking from the three throats of the huge monster Cerberus lying in a cave in front of them. When the priestess was close enough to see the snakes writhing on his neck, she threw him a honey cake steeped in soporific drugs. He opened his three jaws, each of them rabid with hunger, and snapped it up where it fell. The massive back relaxed and he sprawled full length on the ground, filling his cave. The sentry now sunk in sleep, Aeneas leapt to take command of the entrance and was soon free of the bank of that river which no man may recross.

In that instant they heard voices, a great weeping and wailing of the souls of infants who had lost their share of the sweetness of life on its very threshold, torn from the breast on some black day and drowned in the bitterness of death. Next to them were those who had been condemned to death on false charges, but they did not receive their places without the casting of lots and the appointment of juries. Minos, the president of the court, shakes the lots in the urn, summoning the silent dead to act as jurymen, and holds inquiry into the lives of the accused and the charges against them. Next to them were those unhappy people who had raised their innocent hands against themselves, who had so loathed the light that they had thrown away their own lives. But now how they would wish to be under high heaven, enduring poverty and drudgery, however hard! That cannot be, for they are bound in the coils of the hateful swamp of the waters of death, trapped in the ninefold windings of the river Styx. Not far from here could be seen what they call the Mourning Plains, stretching away in every direction. Here are the victims of unhappy love, consumed by that cruel wasting sickness, hidden in the lonely byways of an encircling wood of myrtle trees, and their suffering does not leave them even in death. Here Aeneas saw Phaedra, and Procris, and Eriphyle in tears as she displayed the wounds her cruel son had given her. Here he saw Evadne and Pasiphae with Laodamia walking by their side, and Caeneus, once a young man, but now a woman restored by destiny to her former shape.

Wandering among them in that great wood was Phoenician Dido with her wound still fresh. When the Trojan hero stopped beside her, recognizing her dim form in the darkness, like a man who sees or thinks he has seen the new moon rising through the clouds at the beginning of the month, in that instant he wept and spoke sweet words of love to her: 'So the news they brought me was true, unhappy Dido? They told me you were dead and had ended your life with the sword. Alas! Alas! Was I the cause of your dying? I swear by the stars, by the gods above, by whatever there is to swear by in the depths of the earth, it was against my will, O queen, that I left your shore. It was the stern authority of the commands of the gods that drove me on, as it drives me now through the shades of this dark night in this foul and mouldering place. I could not have believed that my leaving would cause you such sorrow. Do not move away. Do not leave my sight. Who are you running from? Fate has decreed that I shall not speak to you again.' With these words Aeneas, shedding tears, tried to comfort that burning spirit, but grim-faced she kept her eyes upon the ground and did not look at him. Her features moved no more when he began to speak than if she had been a block of flint or Parian marble quarried on Mount Marpessus. Then at last she rushed away, hating him, into the shadows of the wood where Sychaeus, who had been her husband, answered her grief with grief and her love with love. Aeneas was no less stricken by the injustice of her fate and long did he gaze after her, pitying her as she went.

From here they continued on their appointed road and they were soon on the most distant of these fields, the place set apart for brave warriors. Here Tydeus came to meet him, and Parthenopaeus, famous for his feats of arms, and the pale phantom of Adrastus. Here he saw and groaned to see standing in their long ranks all the sons of Dardanus who had fallen in battle and been bitterly lamented in the upper world, Glaucus, Medon and Thersilochus, the three sons of Antenor, and Polyboetes, the consecrated priest of Ceres, and Idaeus still keeping hold of Priam's chariot, still keeping hold of his armour. The shades crowded round him on the right and on the left and it was not enough just to see him, they wished to delay him, to walk with him, to learn the reasons for his coming. But when the Greek leaders and the soldiers of Agamemnon in their phalanxes saw the hero and his armour gleaming through the shadows, a wild panic seized them. Some turned and ran as they had run once before to get back to their ships, while others lifted up their voices and raised a tiny cry, which started as a shout from mouth wide open, but no shout came.

Here too he saw Deiphobus, son of Priam, his whole body mutilated and his face cruelly torn. The face and both hands were in shreds. The ears had been ripped from the head. He was noseless and hideous. Aeneas, barely recognizing him as he tried frantically to hide the fearsome punishment he had received, went up to him and spoke in the voice he knew so well: 'Deiphobus, mighty warrior, descended from the noble blood of Teucer, who could have wished to inflict such a punishment upon you? And who was able to do this? I was told that on that last night you wore yourself out killing the enemy and fell on a huge pile of Greek and Trojan dead. At that time I did all I could do, raising an empty tomb for you on the shore of Cape Rhoeteum and lifting up my voice to call three times upon your shade. Your name and your arms mark the place but you I could not find, my friend, to bury your body in our native land as I was leaving it.'

To this the son of Priam answered: 'You, my friend, have left nothing undone. You have paid all that is owed to Deiphobus and to his dead shade. It is my own destiny and the crimes of the murderess from Sparta that have brought me to this. These are reminders of Helen. You know how we spent that last night in false joy. It is our lot to remember it only too well. When the horse that was the instrument of Fate, heavy with the brood of armed men in its belly, leapt over the high walls of Pergamum, Helen was pretending to be worshipping Bacchus, leading the women of Phrygia around the city, dancing and shrieking their ritual cries. There she was in the middle of them with a huge torch, signalling to the Greeks from the top of the citadel, and all the time I was sleeping soundly in our accursed bed, worn out by all I had suffered and sunk in a sleep that was sweet and deep and like the peace of death. Meanwhile this excellent wife of mine, after moving all my armour out of the house and taking the good sword from under my head, called in Menelaus and threw open the doors, hoping no doubt that her loving husband would take this as a great favour to wipe out the memory of her past sins. You can guess the rest. They burst into the room, taking with them the man who had incited them to their crimes, their comrade Ulixes—they say he is descended from Aeolus. You gods, if the punishment I ask is just, grant that a fate like mine should strike again and strike Greeks. But come, it is now time for you to tell me what chance has brought you here alive. Is it your sea wanderings that have taken you here? Are you under the instructions of the gods? What fortune is dogging you, that you should come here to our sad and sunless homes in this troubled place?'

While they were speaking to one another, Dawn's rosy chariot had already run its heavenly course past the midpoint of the vault of the sky, and they might have spent all the allotted time in talking but for Aeneas' companion. The Sibyl gave her warning in few words: 'Night is running quickly by, Aeneas, and we waste the hours in weeping. This is where the way divides. On the right it leads up to the walls of great Dis. This is the road we take for Elysium. On the left is the road of punishment for evildoers, leading to Tartarus, the place of the damned.' 'There is no need for anger, great priestess,' replied Deiphobus. 'I shall go to take my place among the dead and return to darkness. Go, Aeneas, go, great glory of our Troy, and enjoy a better fate than mine.' These were his only words, and as he spoke he turned on his heel and strode away.

Aeneas looked back suddenly and saw under a cliff on his left a broad city encircled by a triple wall and washed all round by Phlegethon, one of the rivers of Tartarus, a torrent of fire and flame, rolling and grinding great boulders in its current. There before him stood a huge gate with columns of solid adamant so strong that neither the violence of men nor of the heavenly gods themselves could ever uproot them in war, and an iron tower rose into the air where Tisiphone sat with her blood-soaked dress girt up, guarding the entrance and never sleeping, night or day. They could hear the groans from the city, the cruel crack of the lash, the dragging and clanking of iron chains. Aeneas stood in terror, listening to the noise. 'What kinds of criminal are here? Tell me, virgin priestess, what punishments are inflicted on them? What is this wild lamentation in the air?' The Sibyl replied: 'Great leader of the Trojans, the chaste may not set foot upon the threshold of that evil place, but when Hecate put me in charge of the groves of Avernus, she herself explained the punishments the gods had imposed and showed me them all. Here Rhadamanthus, king of Cnossus, holds sway with his unbending laws, chastising men, hearing all the frauds they have practised and forcing them to confess the undiscovered crimes they have gloated over in the upper world—foolishly, for they have only delayed the day of atonement till after death. Immediately the avenging Tisiphone leaps upon the guilty and flogs them till they writhe, waving fearful serpents over them in her left hand and calling up the cohorts of her savage sisters, the Furies. Then at last the gates sacred to the gods below shriek in their sockets and open wide. You see what a watch she keeps, sitting in the entrance? What a sight she is guarding the threshold? Inside, more savage still, the huge, black-throated, fifty-headed Hydra has its lair. And then there is Tartarus itself, stretching sheer down into its dark chasm twice as far as we look up to the ethereal Olympus in the sky. Here, rolling in the bottom of the abyss, is the ancient brood of Earth, the army of Titans, hurled down by the thunderbolt. Here too I saw the huge bodies of the twin sons of Aloeus who laid violent

hands on the immeasurable sky to wrench it from its place and tear down Jupiter from his heavenly kingdom. I saw too Salmoneus suffering cruel punishment, still miming the flames of Jupiter and the rumblings of Olympus. He it was who, riding his four-horse chariot and brandishing a torch, used to go in glory through the peoples of Greece and the city of Olympia in the heart of Elis, laying claim to divine honours for himself—fool that he was to copy the storm and the inimitable thunderbolt with the rattle of the horn of his horses' hooves on bronze. Through the thick clouds the All-powerful Father hurled his lightning—no smoky light from pitchy torches for him—and sent him spinning deep into the abyss. Tityos too I could see, the nurseling of Earth, mother of all, his body sprawling over nine whole acres while a huge vulture with hooked beak cropped his immortal liver and the flesh that was such a rich supplier of punishment. Deep in his breast it roosts and forages for its dinners, while the filaments of his liver know no rest but are restored as soon as they are consumed. I do not need to speak of the Lapiths, of Ixion or Pirithous, over whose heads the boulder of black flint is always slipping, always seeming to be falling. The gold gleams on the high supports of festal couches and a feast is laid in regal splendour before the eyes of the guilty, but the greatest of the Furies is reclining at table and allows no hand to touch the food, but leaps up brandishing a torch and shouting with a voice of thunder. Immured in this place and waiting for punishment are those who in life hated their brothers, beat their fathers, defrauded their dependants, found wealth and brooded over it alone without setting aside a share for their kinsmen—these are most numerous of all—men caught and killed in adultery, men who took up arms against their own people and did not shrink from abusing their masters' trust. Do not ask to know what their punishments are, what form of pain or what misfortune has engulfed them. Some are rolling huge rocks, or hang spreadeagled on the spokes of wheels. Theseus is sitting there dejected, and there he will sit until the end of time, while Phlegyas, most wretched of them all, shouts this lesson for all men at the top of his voice in the darkness: "Learn to be just and not to slight the gods. You have been warned." Here is the man who has sold his native land for gold, and set a tyrant over it, putting up tablets with new laws for a price and for a price removing them. Here is the man who forced his way into his daughter's bed and a forbidden union. They have all dared to attempt some monstrous crime against the gods and have succeeded in their attempt. If I had a hundred tongues, a hundred mouths and a voice of iron, I could not encompass all their different crimes or speak the names of all their different punishments.'

When the aged priestess of Apollo had finished her answer, she added these words: 'But come now, you must take the road and complete the task you have begun. Let us hasten. I can see the high walls forged in the furnaces of the Cyclopes and the gates there in front of us in the arch. This is where we have been told to lay the gift that is required of us.' After these words they walked the dark road together, soon covering the distance and coming close to the doors. There Aeneas leapt on the threshold, sprinkled his body with fresh water and fixed the bough full in the doorway.

When this rite was at last performed and his duty to the goddess was done, they entered the land of joy, the lovely glades of the fortunate woods and the home of the blest. Here a broader sky clothes the plains in glowing light, and the spirits have their own sun and their own stars. Some take exercise on grassy wrestling-grounds and hold athletic contests and wrestling bouts on the golden sand. Others pound the earth with dancing feet and sing their songs while Orpheus, the priest of Thrace, accompanies their measures on his seven-stringed lyre, plucking the notes sometimes with his fingers, sometimes with his ivory plectrum. Here was the ancient line of Teucer, the fairest of all families, great-hearted heroes born in a better time, Ilus, Assaracus and Dardanus, the founder of Troy. Aeneas admired from a distance their armour and empty chariots. Their swords were planted in the ground and their horses wandered free on the plain cropping the grass. Reposing there below the earth, they took the same joy in their chariots and their armour as when alive, and the same care to feed their sleek horses. Then suddenly he saw others on both sides of him feasting on the grass, singing in a joyful choir their paean to Apollo all through a grove of fragrant laurels where the mighty river Eridanus rolls through the forest to the upper world. Here were armies of men bearing wounds received while fighting for their native land, priests who had been chaste unto death and true prophets whose words were worthy of Apollo; then those who have raised human life to new heights by the skills they have discovered and those whom men remember for what they have done for men. All these with sacred ribbons of white round their foreheads gathered round Aeneas and the Sibyl, and she addressed these words to them, especially to Musaeus, for the whole great throng looked up to him as he stood there in the middle, head and shoulders above them all: 'Tell me, blessed spirits, and you, best of poets, which part of this world holds Anchises? Where is he to be found? It is because of Anchises that we have come here and crossed the great rivers of Erebus.' The hero returned a short answer: 'None of us has a fixed home. We live in these densely wooded groves and rest on the soft couches of the river bank and in the fresh water-meadows. But if that is the desire of your hearts, come climb this ridge and I shall soon set you on an easy path.' So saying, he walked on in front of them to a place from where they could see the plains below them bathed in light, and from that point Aeneas and the Sibyl came down from the mountain tops.

Father Anchises was deep in a green valley, walking among the souls who were enclosed there and eagerly surveying them as they waited to rise into the upper light. It so happened that at that moment he was counting the number of his people, reviewing his dear descendants, their fates and their fortunes, their characters and their courage in war. When he saw Aeneas coming towards him over the grass, he stretched out both hands in eager welcome, with the tears streaming down his cheeks, and these were the words that broke from his mouth: 'You have

come at last,' he cried. 'I knew your devotion would prevail over all the rigour of the journey and bring you to your father. Am I to be allowed to look upon your face, my son, to hear the voice I know so well and answer it with my own? I never doubted it. I counted the hours, knowing you would come, and my love has not deceived me. I understand how many lands you have travelled and how many seas you have sailed to come to me here. I know the dangers that have beset you. I so feared the kingdom of Libya would do you harm.' 'It was my vision of you,' replied Aeneas, 'always before my eyes and always stricken with sorrow, that drove me to the threshold of this place. The fleet is moored in the Tyrrhenian sea on the shores of Italy. Give me your right hand, father. Give it me. Do not avoid my embrace.' As he spoke these words his cheeks were washed with tears and three times he tried to put his arms around his father's neck. Three times the phantom melted in his hands, as weightless as the wind, as light as the flight of sleep.

And now Aeneas saw in a side valley a secluded grove with copses of rustling trees where the river Lethe glided along past peaceful dwelling houses. Around it fluttered numberless races and tribes of men, like bees in a meadow on a clear summer day, settling on all the many-coloured flowers and crowding round the gleaming white lilies while the whole plain is loud with their buzzing. Not understanding what he saw, Aeneas shuddered at the sudden sight of them and asked why this was, what was that river in the distance and who were all those companies of men crowding its banks. 'These are the souls to whom Fate owes a second body,' replied Anchises. 'They come to the waves of the river Lethe and drink the waters of serenity and draughts of long oblivion. I have long been eager to tell you who they are, to show them to you face to face and count the generations of my people to you so that you could rejoice the more with me at the finding of Italy.' 'But are we to believe,' replied Aeneas to his dear father, 'that there are some souls who rise from here to go back under the sky and return to sluggish bodies? Why do the poor wretches have this terrible longing for the light?' 'I shall tell you, my son, and leave you no longer in doubt,' replied Anchises, and he began to explain all things in due order.

'In the beginning Spirit fed all things from within, the sky and the earth, the level waters, the shining globe of the moon and the Titan's star, the sun. It was Mind that set all this matter in motion. Infused through all the limbs, it mingled with that great body, and from the union there sprang the families of men and of animals, the living things of the air and the strange creatures born beneath the marble surface of the sea. The living force within them is of fire and its seeds have their source in heaven, but their guilt-ridden bodies make them slow and they are dulled by earthly limbs and dying flesh. It is this that gives them their fears and desires, their griefs and joys. Closed in the blind darkness of this prison they do not see out to the winds of air. Even when life leaves them on their last day of light, they are not wholly freed from all the many ills and miseries of the body which must harden in them over the long years and become ingrained in ways we cannot understand. And so they are put to punishment, to pay the penalty for all their ancient sins. Some are stretched and hung out empty to dry in the winds. Some have the stain of evil washed out of them under a vast tide of water or scorched out by fire. Each of us suffers his own fate in the after-life. From here we are sent over the broad plains of Elysium and some few of us possess these fields of joy until the circle of time is completed and the length of days has removed ingrained corruption and left us pure ethereal sense, the fire of elemental air. All these others whom you see, when they have rolled the wheel for a thousand years, are called out by God to come in great columns to the river of Lethe, so that they may duly go back and see the vault of heaven again remembering nothing, and begin to be willing to return to bodies.' . . .

HORACE

Selections from *Odes* and *Satires*

Horace's *Odes* (Books I–III, 23 B.C.; Book IV, ca. 13 B.C.) were a milestone in ancient literature. They signal the beginning of Latin lyric poetry and are also its zenith. They confirmed Horace's literary reputation and brought him favor from Augustus, Rome's first emperor. Ignored in medieval Europe, Horace's works came into their own during the Renaissance (see Petrarch's *Canzoniere*) and enjoyed their finest hour in the classical revival of the seventeenth and eighteenth centuries. The poems' tact and good taste are traits of the Augustan Age (31 B.C.–A.D. 14), which gave them birth.

Horace (65–8 B.C.) and the Greek poet Pindar (522–442 B.C.) are usually credited with begetting the ode, a lyric poem expressing lofty feelings and ideas in a stately tone. Pindar's odes were written for public occasions, such as honoring victors in the games. In contrast, Horace's odes were private and personal, speaking of love and wine, religion and the state, life and death, and praise for his patron, Maecenas. Their variety reflects Horace's love of Greek literature and his experiences as a man of both city and countryside.

In the *Odes,* Horace adapted Greek verse forms, borrowing largely from Sappho ("To Anactoria," etc.) and Alcaeus (flourished about 611–580 B.C.). Following them, he grew into a master of poetic subtlety and tightly compressed lyrics. He delighted in finding the exact word to convey a precise shade of meaning: "If a clever combination makes a familiar word new, that is distinguished writing." One feature, however, made his odes distinctive—unlike Alcaeus's and Sappho's lyrics, his odes were not composed for musical performance.

The *Odes* are normally called his greatest work, but Horace also wrote poetic epistles, epodes ("refrains"), and satires (see Juvenal's *Satire III*), the latter of which he pioneered. He also wrote the *Art of Poetry,* a book of literary advice whose focus on decorum undergirded the classicism of seventeenth- and eighteenth-century literature.

A sketch of Horace's life shows Rome's social diversity. Horace was the son of an ex-slave. Partly because of the paradox that freedmen were second-class citizens yet their sons had full rights, he had a keen eye for social slights. Even at the height of his fame, he detected traces of resentment. Nevertheless, he experienced the best of his world. Paternal wealth enabled him to study at an aristocratic school in Rome and at the Academy in Athens; and his literary works won the esteem of the imperial court.

Reading the Selections

Horace's theme in Ode II.16 is peace of mind and how to achieve it. Addressed to a rich man named Grosphus, the ode gently chides as it gives advice. The advice the speaker offers is epicurean: Avoid politics, live modestly, and cultivate poetry. The reference to "a little farm" is Horace's Sabine farm, a gift from Maecenas.

Ode III.6 is a public ode, reflecting Horace's critique of Rome written before Augustus's reign. Paying no heed to the gods has brought tragedy to Rome: military defeat, civil war, adultery. The ode concludes with a chilling forecast. A highlight of this lyric is that, near the end, it conveys the poet's love of nature.

An amused, though gently critical, spectator of his fellow Romans, Horace wrote two books of satires (issued 34 B.C. and 30 B.C.) in which he dissected the foibles and vices of the capital city. "The Bore" is typical of the satire genre he pioneered, in that it depicts a social type, allowing the subject to speak in an almost colloquial voice. In this selection, an ever polite speaker ("I") is tormented by a talkative bore, who monopolizes the conversation and refuses to go away despite the speaker's evasive maneuvers. In real life, Horace turned his back on Rome, rejecting its "smoke and wealth and noise" in favor of a quiet country existence.

—∿—

Ode II.16
Otium divos

Peace, Grosphus, is what the man on the open
Aegean requires of the Gods when black cloud
obscures the moon and no fixed star can
    flash for the sailors.

Peace for the Thracians enraged with war,
peace for the Medes with their stylish quivers,
is not to be bought with gems or gold
    or gleaming fabrics.

Neither Persian treasure nor the consul's
lictor can disperse the wretched mob   10
of the mind or the cares that flit about
    your coffered ceilings.

He lives well on a little whose family
salt-cellar shines amid a modest
table, whose gentle sleep is not dispelled
    by fear or base greed.

Why do we aim so high, so bravely,
so briefly? Why hanker for countries scorched
by an alien sun? What exile from home
    can avoid himself?   20

Care clambers aboard the armoured ships,   1
keeps pace with the cavalry squadrons, comes
swift as East-Wind-driven rain, comes
    swift as any stag.

The soul content with the present
is not concerned with the future and tempers
dismay with an easy laugh. No
    blessing is unmixed.

An early death snatched bright Achilles;
long senility reduced Tithonus: 30
this hour will offer to me, maybe, the good
    it denies to you.

For you a hundred herds of Sicilian
cattle moo; for you are bred
neighing mares apt for the chariot;
    you dress in twice-dyed

Tyrian purple wool: to me honest Fate
has given a little farm, the delicate breath
of the Grecian Muse, and disdain
    for the jealous mob.   40

—∿—

Ode III.6
Delicta maiorum

Though innocent you shall atone for the crimes   1
of your fathers, Roman, until you have restored
the temples and crumbling shrines of the Gods
and their statues grimy with smoke.

Acknowledge the rule of the Gods—and rule:
hence all things begin, to this ascribe the outcome.
Contemned, the Gods have visited many
evils on grieving Hesperia.

Already twice Monaeses and Pacorus' band
have crushed our ill-starred offensive   10
and preen themselves on having added
Roman spoils to their paltry gauds.

Our city busied with sedition has almost
suffered destruction by Egypt allied to Dacia,
the former renowned for her fleet, the latter
rather for hurtling arrows.

Teeming with sin, the times have sullied
first marriage, our children, our homes:
sprung from that source disaster has whelmed
our fatherland and our people.   20

The grown girl loves to be taught to be
artful and dance oriental dances,
obsessed to her dainty fingernails
with illicit amours.

She sniffs out young philand'rers at her
husband's feast, nor is she nice to choose
to whom she (hurriedly) grants her favours
when the lamps are removed,

but brazenly stands when called—with her
husband's assent—though some travelling   30
salesman or Spanish ship's captain
may be the agent of Shame.

The generation that dyed the Punic
sea with blood and laid low Pyrrhus,
Antiochus and Hannibal was not born
of parents such as these,

but of manly comrades, yeoman soldiers
taught to turn the soil with Sabine hoes
and carry cut firewood at a strict
mother's bidding when the Sun   40

advanced the shadows of the hills
and lifted the yokes from weary steers,
his departing chariot leading in
the hours of comfort.

What does corrupting time not diminish?
Our grandparents brought forth feebler heirs;
we are further degen'rate; and soon will beget
progeny yet more wicked.

—m—

Satire I.9
The Bore

Ibam forte via Sacra, sicut meus est mos

I was walking down the Sacred Way, my usual route,   1
Turning over some lines in my head, completely
          absorbed.
A man I knew only by name ran up, seized my hand:
"How *are* you, my dear old fellow?" "Just fine," I
          answered,
"The way things are going. I hope *you* are getting on
          nicely."
When he kept up with me, I thought I'd forestall him by
          asking
"There's nothing I can do for you, is there?" "Oh, YES!" he
          shot back,
"Get to know me. I'm quite avant-garde." "Oh, good," I
          replied,
"I like you for that." Trying awfully hard to shake him,
I went on faster, then stopped in my tracks and whispered   10
Something in my slave's ear while sweat streamed down
          to my ankles.
"Bolanus," I thought to myself, "I envy the way
You blow your top. That would fix this fellow," who
          meanwhile
Kept yammering on, ga-ga with the big city sights.
When I failed to respond, he piped up, "I see how
          impatient
You are to be off. It's no use. I'm sticking with you—
I'll just tag along—where are you headed?" "Oh, NO,
Don't put yourself out! I'm going to see a sick friend,

Someone you don't know, way over in Trastevere
Near the Villa Aurelia." "Oh, well, I've got nothing to do,   20
And I'm not afraid of the walk, so I'll go along with you."
          My ears drooped down as a donkey's will do when
          he knows
He's loaded beyond his strength. Then he started in,
"If I know myself, you'll find me as good a friend
As Varius or Viscus. What author writes *more*, for
          example,
Or *faster* than I do? What dancer is more suggestive?
And sing? Why, Hermogenes [he meant Tigellius H.,
The singer, not the dessert] would envy my voice."
This was my chance to cut in, "And your poor old
          mother,
The relatives who care for you, won't they be worried
          if . . . ?"   30
"I haven't a soul in the world! I've buried them all."
"Lucky people," I sighed. "I seem to be all that's left.
Finish me off! For the hour is come the old gypsy
Foretold in my youth, as she shook the lots in an urn:

          'This lad shall not be killed by malignant poison
          Nor by the enemy's sword, neither by pleurisy
          Nor pneumonia, nor gout that goes slow. But
                    someday someone
          Will simply talk him to death. When he comes of
                    age,

If he's smart let him keep his distance from Talkative
  Persons.'"

By now it was nine o'clock, and we had arrived   40
At the temple of Vesta. My companion, it seemed, was due
In court at nine, or would forfeit his case. "Won't you
  please
Stay around and lend me support?" he asked. "Hell, no!"
I answered. "I can't stand around, and I'm no good at law.
You know where I'm hurrying off to." "I just don't know
What to do," he mused, "leave you, or my case." "ME,
  please."
"I couldn't do that," he concluded, and started on ahead.
And I—well, you can't beat a winner—so I followed after
  him.
  "How are things with you and Maecenas?" he asked. I
  answered,
"He's a man of much sense and few friends." But he kept
  boring in,   50
"You've drawn good cards and played your hand right,
  you have.
Now if you wanted to do something more, you'd bring in
  myself,
The fellow who's talking to you. I'd be a help,
And I'm willing to play second fiddle. Damn it all, man,
You'd make them all knuckle under." "We don't carry on
Quite the way you think," I said icily; "there's no place so
  free
From intrigue as Maecenas', no place so thoroughly
  honest.
It just doesn't matter to them whether someone is richer
Or smarter than somebody else. Everyone gets along."
"A TALL one," he said, "hard to believe." "But it's true!"   60
"Well, it just makes me hotter than ever to be admitted."
"Keep wishing. Your talent is such that you'll storm his
  defenses.

He's a man one can conquer—for this is surely the reason
He makes the approaches so hard." "I bet I don't fail.
I'll bribe all his servants. I'll keep coming back, pick my
  times,
Meet him walking in town, join his escort. Nothing
In life comes to men without labor."
                                    While we were talking
Along comes my dear friend Aristius Fuscus, who knew,
Perfectly well, the man I was with. We stopped.   70
"Where are you coming from, where are you going?" got
  asked
And answered. I started pulling his sleeve and tugging
At his unfeeling arm. No response! I nodded, and winked
Fiercely at him to save me. No response but a laugh from
  the wag,
Who pretended to misunderstand. I was livid and
  spluttered
"Oh, Fuscus, you said you had something to say to me
  privately."
"Yes, I know, but let's save it for some other time. Today
Is the Thirtieth Sabbath. You wouldn't want to offend
The circumcised Jews, now would you?" "Oh, I'm not
  religious."
I said. "Well, *I* am," he said, "it's a weakness I share   80
With most people. You forgive me? Some other time
I'll tell you what I had in mind to say." How black
Can things look? That best of all blackguards, Aristius
  Fuscus,
Ran off and left the knife at my throat.
                                    Just then
The plaintiff chanced to come by and see his opponent.
"You scoundrel, where are you off to?" he yelled. "Would
  you
[Turning to me] be a witness to this arrest?"
WOULD I! He dragged him to court, both of them shouting.
A crowd had formed. And thus I was saved by Apollo.   90

OVID

Selection from *Metamorphoses*

Ovid (43 B.C.–A.D. 17), like Horace (see *Odes*), was a great Latin writer who was not a native Roman.
From Sulmo (central Italy) Ovid came to Rome to study in an aristocratic school. Trained for politics, he
turned to poetry and became the epitome of the worldly set that dominated Roman fashion in his day.
    Ovid's *Metamorphoses* has delighted readers since it first circulated (A.D. 8) in Rome's Augustan
Age; few works from any period have had such a lasting impact on later culture. Since the Middle
Ages, poets and artists have mined it for subjects and plots. In it they found a collection of Roman and
mainly Greek myths and legends—the intellectual stock-in-trade of Ovid's day. The *Metamorphoses*
mediated these myths to the whole of Europe.
    A long poem, the *Metamorphoses* consists of more than two hundred stories divided into
fifteen "books" and organized around a simple theme: All are tales of shape-shifting, or magical
changes of form. They are about people, usually legendary, changed into stone, trees, animals, birds,
and stars. The poet's tone toward these shape-shiftings is lighthearted, even tongue-in-cheek.
    The poem's subject touched on a growing trend in Rome: the worship of rulers as gods—an inher-
itance from the Middle East as new peoples joined the empire. Ovid welcomed this trend, for he made

the poem's climax (Book XV) the transformation of Julius Caesar into a blazing comet, with the added prediction that Augustus too would "make his way to heaven. . . ." Here Ovid showed his patriotism, because the Senate had voted Caesar divine status and plans were afoot to do the same for Augustus.

The *Metamorphoses* is ironical in that Ovid's praise for Augustus did not save him from the emperor's wrath. As the poet was finishing this work, Augustus banished him to a remote frontier-post of the empire, Tomis (Constanta in Rumania). He was never granted permission to return. Why Ovid was banished is not clear. Perhaps it was the flippant *Art of Love*, a handbook on seduction, which offended propriety and thus damaged Augustus's efforts to reform Roman morals. Perhaps he knew too much about a sex scandal involving the emperor's granddaughter Julia. Whatever the reason, Ovid saw his exile as a spiritual death. He nevertheless continued to write, sustained by the thought that his poetry would make him immortal. "I shall live to all eternity, immortalized by fame."

Reading the Selection

The story of Daphne and Apollo (Book I of the *Metamorphoses*) is Ovid's account of the star-crossed love of the god Apollo (called Phoebus) for the nymph Daphne. Its premise is that the gods have absolute power but lack moral scruples. Apollo, pierced by Cupid's arrow, is overcome with lust, so that his prophetic powers are useless. To win Daphne, he first tries to woo her; when that fails, he decides on rape. Apollo is depicted as the slave of his passions. Daphne ultimately escapes rape by being changed into a laurel tree. True "happy endings" are rare in this poem.

Ovid's lighthearted style sugarcoats his basic cynicism. He wrote to entertain, not to improve. Not religious in any ordinary sense, Ovid did not shrink from depicting the gods in indecent roles, as in Apollo's rape attempt. Ovid's world was conspicuously amoral, where divine caprice ran riot. As with humans, the gods were victims of their emotions and liable to be swept away by fate.

—⁓—

Book I
Daphne and Apollo

. . .

Daphne, the daughter of Peneus, was Phoebus' first love, and it was not blind chance which brought this about, but Cupid's savage spite. Not long before, the Delian god, still exultant over his slaying of the serpent, had seen Cupid bending his taut bow, and had said: 'You naughty boy, what have you to do with a warrior's arms? Weapons such as these are suited to my shoulders: for I can aim my shafts unerringly, to wound wild beast or human foe, as I lately slew the bloated Python with my countless arrows, though it covered so many acres with its pestilential coils. You be content with your torch to excite love, whatever that may be, and do not aspire to praises that are my prerogative.' But Venus' son replied: 'Your bow may pierce everything else, Phoebus, but mine will pierce *you*: and as all animals are inferior to the gods, your glory is to that extent less than mine.'

With these words he swiftly winged his way through the air, till he alighted on the shady summit of Parnassus. From his quiver, full of arrows, he drew two darts, with different properties. The one puts love to flight, the other kindles it. That which kindles love is golden, and shining, sharp-tipped; but that which puts it to flight is blunt, its shaft tipped with lead. With this arrow the god pierced the nymph, Peneus' daughter, but Apollo he wounded with the other, shooting it into the marrow of his bones. Immediately the one fell in love; the other, fleeing the very word 'lover', took her delight in woodland haunts and in the spoils of captured beasts, emulating Diana, the maiden goddess, with her hair carelessly caught back by a single ribbon.

Many a suitor wooed her but, turning away from their entreaties, she roamed the pathless woods, knowing nothing of men, and caring nothing for them, heedless of what marriage or love or wedded life might be. Again and again her father said: 'It is your duty to marry and give me a son-in-law, my child.' Often he repeated: 'My child, it is your duty to give me grandchildren.' But she blushed, hating the thought of marriage as if it were some crime. The modest colour crimsoned her fair face and, throwing her arms round her father's neck, she cried imploringly: 'My dear, dear father, let me enjoy this state of maiden bliss for ever! Diana's father granted her such a boon in days gone by!' Her father did, indeed, yield to her request, but her very loveliness prevented her from being what she desired, and her beauty defeated her own wishes.

As soon as Phoebus saw Daphne, he fell in love with her, and wanted to marry her. His own prophetic powers deceived him and he hoped to achieve his desire. As the light stubble blazes up in a harvested field, or as the hedge is set alight, if a traveller chance to kindle a fire too close, or leaves one smouldering when he goes off at daybreak, so the god was all on fire, his whole heart was aflame, and he nourished his fruitless love on hope. He eyed her hair as it hung carelessly about her neck, and sighed: 'What if it were properly arranged!' He looked at her eyes, sparkling bright as stars, he looked at her lips, and wanted to do more than look at them. He praised her fingers, her hands and arms, bare almost to the shoulder. Her hidden charms he imagined lovelier still.

But Daphne ran off, swifter than the wind's breath, and did not stop to hear his words, though he called her back: 'I implore you, nymph, daughter of Peneus, do not run away! Though I pursue you, I am no enemy. Stay, sweet nymph! You flee as a lamb flees the wolf, or the deer the lion, as doves on fluttering wings fly from an eagle, as all creatures flee their natural foes! But it is love that drives me to follow you. Alas, how I fear lest you trip and fall, lest briars scratch your innocent legs, and I be the cause of your hurting yourself. These are rough places through which you are running—go less swiftly, I beg of you, slow your flight, and I in turn shall pursue less swiftly!

'Yet stay to inquire whose heart you have charmed. I am no peasant, living in a mountain hut, nor am I a shepherd or boorish herdsman who tends his flocks and cattle in these regions. Silly girl, you do not know from whom you are fleeing: indeed, you do not, or else you would not flee. I am lord of Delphi, Claros, and Tenedos, and of the realms of Patara too. I am the son of Jupiter. By my skill, the past, the present, and the future are revealed; thanks to me, the lyre strings thrill with music. My arrow is sure, though there is one surer still, which has wounded my carefree heart. The art of medicine is my invention, and men the world over give me the name of healer. All the properties of herbs are known to me: but alas, there are no herbs to cure love, and the skill which helps others cannot help its master.'

He would have said more, but the frightened maiden fled from him, leaving him with his words unfinished; even then, she was graceful to see, as the wind bared her limbs and its gusts stirred her garments, blowing them out behind her. Her hair streamed in the light breeze, and her beauty was enhanced by her flight. But the youthful god could not endure to waste his time on further blandishments and, as love itself prompted, sped swiftly after her. Even so, when a Gallic hound spies a hare in some open

meadow he tries by his swiftness to secure his prey, while the hare, by her swiftness, seeks safety: the dog, seeming just about to fasten on his quarry, hopes at every moment that he has her, and grazes her hind quarters with outstretched muzzle, but the hare, uncertain whether she has not already been caught, snatches herself out of his very jaws, and escapes the teeth which almost touch her.

Thus the god and the nymph sped on, one made swift by hope and one by fear; but he who pursued was swifter, for he was assisted by love's wings. He gave the fleeing maiden no respite, but followed close on her heels, and his breath touched the locks that lay scattered on her neck, till Daphne's strength was spent, and she grew pale and weary with the effort of her swift flight. Then she saw the waters of the Peneus: 'O father,' she cried, 'help me! If you rivers really have divine powers, work some transformation, and destroy this beauty which makes me please all too well!' Her prayer was scarcely ended when a deep languor took hold on her limbs, her soft breast was enclosed in thin bark, her hair grew into leaves, her arms into branches, and her feet that were lately so swift were held fast by sluggish roots, while her face became the treetop. Nothing of her was left, except her shining loveliness.

Even as a tree, Phoebus loved her. He placed his hand against the trunk, and felt her heart still beating under the new bark. Embracing the branches as if they were limbs he kissed the wood: but, even as a tree, she shrank from his kisses. Then the god said: 'Since you cannot be my bride, surely you will at least be my tree. My hair, my lyre, my quivers will always display the laurel. You will accompany the generals of Rome, when the Capitol beholds their long triumphal processions, when joyful voices raise the song of victory. You will stand by Augustus' gateposts too, faithfully guarding his doors, and keeping watch from either side over the wreath of oak leaves that will hang there. Further, as my head is ever young, my tresses never shorn, so do you also, at all times, wear the crowning glory of never-fading foliage.' Paean, the healer, had done: the laurel tree inclined her newmade branches, and seemed to nod her leafy top, as if it were a head, in consent. . . .

JUVENAL

Satire III

Much of Juvenal's life (ca. A.D. 60–140) remains a mystery. He is seldom mentioned by his contemporaries, and his satires contain very little autobiographical material. Some events can be dated in his satires, which aid scholars in determining when and where Juvenal wrote. Evidence indicates that he was the son of a fairly prosperous Spanish freedman and that he served in the Roman army. Upon returning from a campaign in Britain, he became mayor of his hometown but failed to launch a political career. Meanwhile, Juvenal started to write satirical works. He soon displeased the Emperor Domitian, who exiled him to Egypt and stripped him of his property and civil rights. Emperor Nerva,

Domitian's successor, permitted Juvenal to return to Rome; however, being poor and without patrons, he was forced to live the life of a hanger-on, one who survived only by flattering those in power. This experience led him to write many embittered and vindictive poems. Only in his later years, when he received patronage from influential Romans, including the Emperor Hadrian, did his satires lose their coarse tone and become nostalgic. When he died, he was not well known, and for two hundred years Juvenal was a forgotten poet. In about A.D. 400, he was rediscovered, and his reputation has remained high ever since.

Many of Juvenal's satires reflected his contempt for his age. He was highly critical of its literature, which seemed to be written by second-rate authors and read by an uncultured public. He specifically singled out the Greeks, whom he denounced for undermining Roman values. Looking at the Rome of his day, he saw only the decline of those values that he believed still survived in small villages among simple folk who appreciated the old ways.

Reading the Selection

Satire III contains most of Juvenal's major complaints and popular targets against contemporary Rome. In the opening lines he confesses his admiration for an old friend, Umbricius, who was leaving Rome for good to live in a provincial town. As they walked from one familiar site to another and observed the changes—all for the worse—Umbricius blamed his own lowered standard of living on the corrupt engineers and flattering hypocrites who dominated society. He deplored this "Greek-struck Rome," which had brought on degeneration, drunkenness, and sexual perversity. He thought that the worth of an individual was determined by what he owned—the number of slaves, the amount of land, or his dinner service. He saw no hope for the poor, who were victims of inflation and civil injustice. Wherever he looked, he saw urban blight and inhuman existence, as manifested in slipshod construction and apartment fires. He was convinced that no one could live amid the constant noise and endless moving of carts and humans; to walk in the street was to subject oneself to bodily harm from flying objects or from drunken bullies looking for a fight. He saved his richest invective for the Jews and Greeks, who seemed to have overrun Rome. As a result of this deterioration, the city was under siege and its inhabitants afraid to leave their homes. In closing, Umbricius bade final farewell, asking Juvenal to visit him when he tired of the city.

The poet's description of street life and the "terrors" in this urban nightmare has to strike a modern note for many readers. Rome, in Juvenal's eyes, had become the symbol of all that was evil in his day; the parallels to urban areas of today are inescapable.

—m—

Despite the wrench of parting, I applaud my old friend's   1
Decision to make his home in lonely Cumae—the poor
Sibyl will get at least *one* fellow-citizen now!
It's a charming coastal retreat, and just across the point
From our smartest watering-spot. Myself, I would value
A barren offshore island more than Rome's urban heart:
Squalor and isolation are minor evils compared
To this endless nightmare of fires and collapsing houses,
The cruel city's myriad perils—and poets reciting
Their work in *August!*   10
           While his goods were being loaded
On one small waggon, my old friend lingered a while
By the ancient dripping arches of the Capuan Gate, where once
King Numa had nightly meetings with his mistress. (But today

Egeria's grove and shrine and sacred spring are rented
To Jewish squatters, their sole possession a Sabbath
    haybox.
Each tree must show a profit, the Muses have been
    evicted,
The wood's aswarm with beggars.)
                From here we strolled down
To the nymph's new, modernized grotto. (What a gain in
    sanctity   20
And atmosphere there would be if grassy banks
Surrounded the pool, if no flash marble affronted
Our native limestone!) Here Umbricius stood, and
Opened his heart to me.
                'There's no room in this city,'
He said, 'for the decent professions: they don't show any
    profit.

My resources have shrunk since yesterday, and tomorrow
Will eat away more of what's left. So I am going
Where Daedalus put off his weary wings, while as yet
I'm in vigorous middle age, while active years are left me,   30
While my white hairs are still few, and I need no stick
To guide my tottering feet. So farewell Rome, I leave you
To sanitary engineers and municipal architects, men
Who by swearing black is white land all the juicy contracts
Just like that—a new temple, swamp-drainage,
    harbour-works,
River-clearance, undertaking, the lot—then pocket the
    cash
And fraudulently file their petition in bankruptcy.
Once these fellows were horn-players, stumping the
    provinces
In road-shows, their puffed-out cheeks a familiar sight
To every country village. But now they stage shows
    themselves,   40
Of the gladiatorial sort, and at the mob's thumbs-down
Will butcher a loser for popularity's sake, and
Pass on from that to erecting public privies. Why not?
These are such men as Fortune, by way of a joke,
Will sometimes raise from the gutter and make Top
    People.
What can I do in Rome? I never learnt how
To lie. If a book is bad, I cannot puff it, or bother
To ask around for a copy; astrological clap-trap
Is not in my stars. I cannot and will not promise
To encompass any man's death by way of obliging his son.   50
I have never meddled with frogs' guts; the task of
    carrying
Letters and presents between adulterous lovers
I resign to those who know it. I refuse to become
An accomplice in theft—which means that no governor
Will accept me on his staff. It's like being a cripple
With a paralysed right hand. Yet who today is favoured
Above the conspirator, his head externally seething
With confidential matters, never to be revealed?
Harmless secrets carry no obligations, and he
Who shares them with you feels no great call thereafter   60
To keep you sweet. But if Verres promotes a man
You can safely assume that man has the screws on Verres
And could turn him in tomorrow. Not all the gold
Washed seaward with the silt of tree-lined Tagus
Is worth the price you pay, racked by insomnia, seeing
Your high-placed friends all cringe at your approach—
    and
For what? Too-transient prizes, unwillingly resigned.
    'Now let me turn to that race which goes down so well
With our millionaires, but remains *my* special pet
    aversion,
And not mince my words. I cannot, citizens, stomach   70
A Greek-struck Rome. Yet what fraction of these
    sweepings
Derives, in fact, from Greece? For years now Syrian
Orontes has poured its sewerage into our native Tiber—
Its lingo and manners, its flutes, its outlandish harps
With their transverse strings, its native tambourines,
And the whores who hang out round the race-course.
    (That's where to go

If you fancy a foreign piece in one of those saucy toques.)
Our beloved Founder should see how his homespun
    rustics
Behave today, with their dinner-pumps—*trechedipna*
They call them—not to mention their *niceteria*   80
(Decorations to you) hung round their *ceromatic* (that's
Well-greased) wrestlers' necks. Here's one from Sicyon,
Another from Macedonia, two from Aegean islands—
Andros, say, or Samos—two more from Caria,
All of them lighting out for the City's classiest districts
And burrowing into great houses, with a long-term plan
For taking them over. Quick wit, unlimited nerve, a gift
Of the gab that outsmarts a professional public speaker—
These are their characteristics. What do you take
That fellow's profession to be? He has brought a whole
    bundle   90
Of personalities with him—schoolmaster, rhetorician,
Surveyor, artist, masseur, diviner, tightrope-walker,
Magician or quack, your versatile hungry Greekling
Is all by turns. Tell him to fly—he's airborne.
The inventor of wings was no Moor or Slav, remember,
Or Thracian, but born in the very heart of Athens.
    'When such men as these wear the purple, when some
    creature
Blown into Rome along with the figs and damsons
Precedes me at dinner-parties, or for the witnessing
Of manumissions and wills—*me*, who drew my first
    breath   100
On these Roman hills, and was nourished on Sabine
    olives!—
Things have reached a pretty pass. What's more, their
    talent
For flattery is unmatched. They praise the conversation
Of their dimmest friends; the ugly they call handsome,
So that your scrag-necked weakling finds himself
    compared
To Hercules holding the giant Antaeus aloft
Way off the earth. They go into ecstasies over
Some shrill and scrannel voice that sounds like a hen
When the cock gets at her. We can make the same
    compliments, but
It's they who convince. On the stage they remain supreme   110
In female parts, courtesan, matron or slave-girl,
With no concealing cloak: you'd swear it was a genuine
Woman you saw, and not a masked performer.
Look there, beneath that belly: no bulge, all smooth, a neat
Nothingness—even a hint of the Great Divide. Yet back
    home
These queens and dames pass unnoticed. Greece is a
    nation
Of actors. Laugh, and they split their sides. At the sight
Of a friend's tears, they weep too—though quite
    unmoved.
If you ask for a fire in winter, the Greek puts on his cloak;
If you say "I'm hot", *he* starts sweating. So you see   120
We are not on an equal footing: he has the great advantage
Of being able on all occasions, night and day,
To take his cue, his mask, from others. He's always ready
To throw up his hands and applaud when a friend
    delivers

A really resounding belch, or pisses right on the mark,
With a splendid drumming sound from the upturned
    golden basin.
    'Besides, he holds nothing sacred, not a soul is safe
From his randy urges, the lady of the house, her
Virgin daughter, her daughter's still unbearded
Husband-to-be, her hitherto virtuous son—   130
And if none of these are to hand, he'll cheerfully lay
His best friend's grandmother. (Anything to ferret
Domestic secrets out, and get a hold over people.)
    'And while we are on the subject of Greeks, let us
    consider
Academics and their vices—not the gymnasium crowd
But big philosophical wheels, like that Stoic greybeard
Who narked on his friend and pupil, and got him
    liquidated.
He was brought up in Tarsus, by the banks of that river
Where Bellerophon fell to earth from the Gorgon's flying
    nag.
No room for honest Romans when Rome's ruled by a
    junta   140
Of Greek-born secret agents, who—like all their race—
Never share friends or patrons. One small dose of venom
(Half Greek, half personal) dropped in that ready ear
And I'm out, shown the back-door, my years of
    obsequious
Service all gone for nothing. Where can a hanger-on
Be ditched with less fuss than in Rome? Besides (not to
    flatter ourselves)
What use are our poor efforts, where does it all get us,
Dressing up while it's dark still, hurrying along
To pay our morning respects to a couple of wealthy
Maiden aunts? But the praetor's really worked up, his   150
Colleague may get there before him, the ladies have been
    awake
For hours already, the minions catch it—"Get
A *move* on there, can't you?" Here a citizen, free-born,
Must stand aside on the pavement for some wealthy
    tycoon's slave:
He can afford to squander a senior officer's income
On classy amateur harlots, just for the privilege
Of laying them once or twice. But when *you* fancy
A common-or-garden tart, you dither and hesitate:
Can I afford to accost her? With witnesses in court
The same applies. Their morals may be beyond cavil,
    and yet   160
If Scipio took the stand (and he was selected
To escort the Mother Goddess on her journey to Rome)
    or Metellus
Who rescued Minerva's image from her blazing shrine,
    or even
King Numa himself, still the first and foremost question
Would be: *"What's he worth?"* His character would
    command
Little if any respect. "How many slaves does he keep?
What's his acreage? What sort of dinner-service
Appears on his table—how many pieces, how big?"
Each man's word is as good as his bond—or rather,
The number of bonds in his strong-box. A pauper can
    swear by every   170

Altar, and every god between Rome and Samothrace, still
(Though the gods themselves forgive them) he'll pass for
    a perjuror
Defying the wrath of heaven. The poor man's an eternal
Butt for bad jokes, with his torn and dirt-caked top-coat,
His grubby toga, one shoe agape where the leather's
Split—those clumsy patches, that coarse and tell-tale
    stitching
Only a day or two old. The hardest thing to bear
In poverty is the fact that it makes us ridiculous.
"Out of those front-row seats," we're told. "You ought
    to be
Ashamed of yourselves—your incomes are far too small,
    and   180
The law's the law. Make way for some pander's son,
Spawned in an unknown brothel, let your place be
    occupied
By that natty auctioneer's offspring, with his high-class
    companions
The trainer's brat and the son of the gladiator
Applauding beside him." Such were the fruits of that
    pinhead
Otho's Reserved Seat Act. What prospective son-in-law
Ever passed muster here if he was short on cash
To match the girl's dowry? What poor man ever inherits
A legacy, or is granted that meanest of sinecures—
A job with the Office of Works? All lower-income citizens 190
Should have marched out of town, in a body, years ago.
Nobody finds it easy to get to the top if meagre
Resources cripple his talent. But in Rome the problem's
    worse
Than anywhere else. Inflation hits the rental
Of your miserable apartment, inflation distends
The ravenous maws of your slaves; your humble dinner
Suffers inflation too. You feel ashamed to eat
Off earthenware dishes—yet if you were transported
To some rural village, you'd be content enough
And happily wear a cloak of coarse blue broadcloth   200
Complete with hood. Throughout most of Italy—we
Might as well admit it—no one is seen in a toga
Till the day he dies. Even on public holidays,
When the same old shows as last year are cheerfully
    staged
In the grassgrown theatre, when peasant children,
    sitting
On their mothers' laps, shrink back in terror at the sight
Of those gaping, whitened masks, you will still find the
    whole
Audience—top row or bottom—dressed exactly alike;
Even the magistrates need no better badge of status
Than a plain white tunic. But here in Rome we must toe   210
The line of fashion, living beyond our means, and
Often on borrowed credit: every man jack of us
Is keeping up with his neighbours. To cut a long story
    short,
Nothing's for free in Rome. How much does it cost you
To salute our noble Cossus (rare privilege!) or extract
One casual, tight-lipped nod from Veiento the
    honours-broker?
X will be having his beard trimmed, Y just offering up

His boy-friend's kiss-curls: the whole house swarms with
    barbers,
Each of them on the make. You might as well swallow
Your bile, and face the fact that we hangers-on   220
Have to bribe our way, swell some sleek menial's savings.
    'What countryman ever bargained, besides, for his
    house collapsing
About his ears? Such things are unheard-of in cool
Praeneste, or rural Gabii, or Tivoli perched on its hillside,
Or Volsinii, nestling amid its woodland ridges. But here
We live in a city shored up, for the most part, with
    gimcrack
Stays and props: that's how our landlords arrest
The collapse of their property, papering over great cracks
In the ramshackle fabric, reassuring the tenants
They can sleep secure, when all the time the building   230
Is poised like a house of cards. I prefer to live where
Fires and midnight panics are not quite such common
    events.
By the time the smoke's got up to your third-floor
    apartment
(And you still asleep) your downstairs neighbour is
    roaring
For water, and shifting his bits and pieces to safety.
If the alarm goes at ground-level, the last to fry
Will be the attic tenant, way up among the nesting
Pigeons, with nothing but tiles between himself and the
    weather.
What did friend Cordus own? One truckle bed, too short
For even a midget nympho; one marble-topped sideboard   240
On which stood six little mugs; beneath it, a pitcher
And an up-ended bust of Chiron; one ancient settle
Crammed with Greek books (though by now
    analphabetic mice
Had gnawed their way well into his texts of the great
    poets).
Cordus could hardly be called a property-owner, and yet
What little the poor man had, he lost. Today the final
Straw on his load of woe (clothes worn to tatters, reduced
To begging for crusts) is that no one will offer him
    lodging
Or shelter, not even stand him a decent meal. But if
Some millionaire's mansion is gutted, women rend their
    garments,   250
Top people put on mourning, the courts go into recess:
Then you hear endless complaints about the hazards
Of city life, these deplorable outbreaks of fire;
Then contributions pour in while the shell is still
    ash-hot—
Construction materials, marble, fresh-gleaming
    sculptured nudes.
Up come A with bronzes (genuine antique works
By a real Old Master) acquired, as part of his booty,
From their hallowed niche in some Asiatic temple;
B provides bookshelves, books, and a study bust of
    Minerva;
C a sackful of silver. So it goes on, until   260
This dandified bachelor's losses are all recouped—
And more than recouped—with even rarer possessions,
And a rumour (well-founded) begins to circulate

That he fired the place himself, a deliberate piece of arson.
    'If you can face the prospect of no more public games
Purchase a freehold house in the country. What it will
    cost you
Is no more than you pay in annual rent for some shabby
And ill-lit garret here. A garden plot's thrown in
With the house itself, and a well with a shallow basin—
No rope-and-bucket work when your seedlings need
    some water!   270
Learn to enjoy hoeing, work and plant your allotment
Till a hundred vegetarians could feast off its produce.
It's quite an achievement, even out in the backwoods,
To have made yourself master of—well, say one lizard,
    even.
    'Insomnia causes more deaths amongst Roman invalids
Than any other factor (the most common *complaints*, of
    course,
Are heartburn and ulcers, brought on by over-eating).
How much sleep, I ask you, can one get in lodgings here?
Unbroken nights—and this is the root of the trouble—
Are a rich man's privilege. The waggons thundering past   280
Through those narrow twisting streets, the oaths of
    draymen
Caught in a traffic-jam—these alone would suffice
To jolt the doziest sea-cow of an Emperor into
Permanent wakefulness. If a business appointment
Summons the tycoon, *he* gets there fast, by litter,
Tacking above the crowd. There's plenty of room inside:
He can read, or take notes, or snooze as he jogs along—
Those drawn blinds are most soporific. Even so
He outstrips us: however fast we pedestrians hurry
We're blocked by the crowds ahead, while those behind us   290
Tread on our heels. Sharp elbows buffet my ribs,
Poles poke into me; one lout swings a crossbeam
Down on my skull, another scores with a barrel.
My legs are mud-encrusted, big feet kick me, a hobnailed
Soldier's boot lands squarely on my toes. Do you see
All that steam and bustle? The great man's hangers-on
Are getting their free dinner, each with his own
Kitchen-boy in attendance. Those outsize dixies,
And all the rest of the gear one poor little slave
Must balance on his head, while he trots along   300
To keep the charcoal glowing, would tax the strength
Of a musclebound general. Recently-patched tunics
Are ripped to shreds. Here's the great trunk of a fir-tree
Swaying along on its waggon, and look, another dray
Behind it, stacked high with pine-logs, a nodding threat
Over the heads of the crowd. If that axle snapped, and a
Cartload of marble avalanched down on them, what
Would be left of their bodies? Who could identify bits
Of ownerless flesh and bone? The poor man's flattened
    corpse
Would vanish along with his soul. And meanwhile, all
    unwitting,   310
The folk at home are busily scouring dishes,
Blowing the fire to a glow, clattering over greasy
Flesh-scrapers, filling up oil-flasks, laying out clean
    towels.
But all the time, as his houseboys hasten about their
    chores,

Himself is already sitting—the latest arrival—
By the bank of the Styx, and gawping in holy terror
At its filthy old ferryman. No chance of a passage over
That mud-thick channel for him, poor devil, without so
　　much
As a copper stuck in his mouth to pay for the ride.
　'There are other nocturnal perils, of various sorts, 320
Which you should consider. It's a long way up to the
　　rooftops,
And a falling tile can brain you—not to mention all
Those cracked or leaky pots that people toss out through
　　windows.
Look at the way they smash, the weight of them, the
　　damage
They do to the pavement! You'll be thought most
　　improvident,
A catastrophe-happy fool, if you don't make your will
　　before
Venturing out to dinner. Each open upper casement
Along your route at night may prove a death-trap:
So pray and hope (poor you!) that the local housewives
Drop nothing worse on your head than a pailful of slops. 330
　'Then there's the drunken bully, in an agonized state
For lack of a victim, who lies there tossing and turning
The whole night through, like Achilles after the death
Of his boy-friend Patroclus. [This lout is doomed to
　　insomnia
Unless he gets a fight.] Yet however flown with wine
Our young hothead may be, he carefully keeps his
　　distance
From the man in a scarlet cloak, the man surrounded
By torches and big brass lamps and a numerous
　　bodyguard.
But for me, a lonely pedestrian, trudging home by
　　moonlight
Or with hand cupped round the wick of one poor
　　guttering candle, 340
He has no respect whatever. This is the way the wretched
Brawl comes about (if you can term it a brawl
When you do the fighting and I'm just cast as punchbag).
He blocks my way. "Stop," he says. I have no option
But to obey—what else can one do when attacked
By a huge tough, twice one's size and fighting-mad as
　　well?
"Where have *you* sprung from?" he shouts. "Ugh, what a
　　stench
Of beans and sour wine! I know your sort, you've been
　　round

With some cobbler-crony, scoffing a boiled sheep's head
And a dish of spring leeks. What? Nothing to say for
　　yourself? 350
Speak up, or I'll kick your teeth in! Tell me, where's your
　　pitch?
What synagogue do you doss in?" It makes not a jot of
　　difference
Whether you try to answer, or back away from him
Without saying a word, you get beaten up just the
　　same—
And then your irate "victim" takes *you* to court on a
　　charge
Of assault and battery. Such is the poor man's "freedom":
After being slugged to a pulp, he may beg, as a special 360
Favour, to be left with his last few remaining teeth.
　'Nor is this the sum of your terrors: when every house
Is shut up for the night, when shops stand silent, when
　　bolts
Are shot, and doors on the chain, there are still burglars
Lurking around, or maybe some street-apache will settle
Your hash with a knife, the quick way. (Whenever armed
　　detachments
Are patrolling the swamps and forests, Rome becomes
A warren for this sort of scum.) Our furnaces glow, our
　　anvils
Groan everywhere under their output of chains and
　　fetters:
That's where most of our iron goes nowadays: one
　　wonders
Whether ploughshares, hoes and mattocks may not soon
　　be obsolete.
How fortunate they were (you well may think) those
　　early
Forbears of ours, how happy the good old days 370
Of Kings and Tribunes, when Rome made do with one
　　prison only!
　'There are many other arguments I could adduce: but
　　the sun
Slants down, my cattle are lowing, I must be on my
　　way—
The muleteer has been signalling me with his whip
For some while now. So goodbye, and don't forget me—
Whenever you go back home for a break from the City,
　　invite
Me over too, to share your fields and coverts,
Your country festivals: I'll put on my thickest boots
And make the trip to those chilly uplands—and listen
To your *Satires*, if I am reckoned worthy of that honour.' 380

6

JUDAISM AND THE RISE OF CHRISTIANITY

Selections from *The Holy Scriptures*
(The Jewish Bible)

The Jewish Bible (from the Greek *biblia*, "books") is a set of sacred writings for the Jewish faithful, containing thirty-nine books, dating from the tenth to the first centuries B.C. and arranged into three categories: the Torah, the Prophets, and the Writings. Originally written in Hebrew, this book collection became more accessible in the third century B.C. when, as the Septuagint, it was translated into the period's international language, Greek. Later, around A.D. 100, Jewish scholars declared this collection to be the Word of God, hence its title *The Holy Scriptures*.

The most authoritative parts of *The Holy Scriptures* for Jewish readers are the Torah, or Law, which provides rules and instructions for everyday life, and the Prophets, which represents the sayings or writings of seers who were understood to be the voices of God. The Writings, while lacking the force of the Torah and the Prophets, nevertheless contains beautiful prose and poetic works, replete with words of comfort and moral advice, such as the Book of Psalms and the Book of Job.

Genesis, the first book of the Torah, opens with the stories of creation, followed by accounts of Noah, his family, and the flood; then begins the historical narrative of Terah, the father of Abraham, from whom descend the leaders of the Hebrew people. These patriarchal tribal rulers—such as Abraham, Jacob, and Moses—make agreements (covenants) with Yahweh, their deity, to worship him and obey the rules of conduct he has given them. However, throughout their history, the Hebrews do not always live by the covenant; that is, they commit sin, and as a result, Yahweh punishes them.

After their return from exile in Egypt to their former homeland, Palestine, around 1150 B.C., the Hebrews slowly conquer the local tribes and begin to prosper. Their good fortune causes them to forget Yahweh and his moral decrees and to turn more and more away from him and the covenant. At this stage of Hebrew history, God chooses certain persons as prophets to deliver his messages of repentance or consequential destruction. Two of his prophets are Isaiah and Amos. Despite falling away from God, many Hebrews continue to honor Yahweh with songs of praise, as recorded in the Book of Psalms. Yet, other Hebrews question their faith and suffering, as revealed in the Book of Job—a poignant account of the torment experienced by a man who was blameworthy.

Reading the Selections

On the surface the five selections—Genesis, Isaiah, Amos, Psalms, and Job—seem quite different, but all deal with similar and profound issues, such as the nature of God's existence and power, the relationship of God to humans, and the role God plays in the lives of humans and in history. The first three chapters of Genesis offer two accounts of the creation story. In the first, God, as the source of all, creates the universe, the celestial bodies, the earth, and all living things. The second account focuses on God's relationship with his first two human creatures, Adam and Eve. The original covenant—that God will provide for humans if they obey him and not eat of the forbidden fruit—is broken. As a consequence, Adam and Eve and all their descendants will be punished according to their sex; that is, Adam and his male heirs will have to work, while Eve and all other women will suffer pain at childbirth. Both are cast out of the Garden of Eden; ever since, humans have been trying to reenter this paradise by attempting to create utopias on earth.

At some point in history, a portion of the Hebrew tribe moved to Egypt, where they were cast into slavery. Eventually, under the leadership of Moses, they slipped their bondage and were guided to freedom through the desert by God. During years of wandering, they formed the central core of their covenant with God: a set of moral rules, of which the first ten are the Ten Commandments, laid down by Yahweh and to be obeyed by the Hebrew people. Besides the Ten Commandments, these rules included many other guidelines by which the Hebrew people were to regulate their lives as individuals and as a tribe. Later, Christians made the Ten Commandments, along with Christ's teachings, the basis of their moral code.

The excerpts from Isaiah and Amos illustrate how the prophets, as the voices of God, spoke to the Hebrews, warning them to change their sinful ways or suffer punishment. The Isaiah passages—taken from the section known as "Second Isaiah"—forecast the coming of the "Suffering Servant," a sinless deliverer who will be persecuted for the sins of others but who will triumph in the end. Isaiah doesn't reveal the name of this servant, but most Jewish commentators think the reference applies to the Jewish people. Christian scholars, though, equate the Suffering Servant with Jesus Christ. In his prophecy, Amos predicts the destruction of the kingdom of Israel (it was destroyed by Assyria in 722 B.C.) if the populace does not give social justice to the poor, so that justice will "well up like water" and righteousness will be an "unfailing stream." Amos's prophecy, with its rich imagery, was a favorite of the civil rights leader Martin Luther King Jr. (see *Letter from a Birmingham Jail*).

The Book of Psalms, with its prayers, laments, and wisdom, has inspired and comforted both Jews and Christians down through the ages. Psalm 22 is a lament, uttered by the speaker, who, after confessing a sense of having been betrayed by God, resolves to once again trust in the Lord. Its first two lines were spoken by Jesus on the cross. Psalm 23, among the most comforting messages in the Bible, is often recited at funerals or turned to in times of trouble. Psalm 104, in its praise of God, echoes an Egyptian poem (see *The Great Hymn to the Aten*).

The Book of Job rivals *Oedipus the King* in depicting the tragedy of a well-meaning hero. Unlike any other book in *The Holy Scriptures*, Job concentrates on a single theological topic: the question of suffering. In prose form, the Prologue tells of the disasters that befall the blameless Job, the conversation between God and Satan about testing Job's faith, and Job's meeting with friends who offer advice on his plight. Shifting into poetic form, the book next sets forth Job's complaint to God, God's magisterial response, and Job's final reply. The Epilogue, reverting to prose, shows God richly rewarding Job for not renouncing him. The Book of Job steadfastly refuses to answer the bewildering question of why humans suffer, and this silence is part of the work's grandeur.

—⁓—

Genesis
1:1–3:24

1

When God began to create heaven and earth—the earth being unformed and void, with darkness over the surface of the deep and a wind from God sweeping over the water—God said, "Let there be light"; and there was light. God saw that the light was good, and God separated the light from the darkness. God called the light Day, and the darkness He called Night. And there was evening and there was morning, a first day.

God said, "Let there be an expanse in the midst of the water, that it may separate water from water." God made the expanse, and it separated the water which was below the expanse from the water which was above the expanse. And it was so. God called the expanse Sky. And there was evening and there was morning, a second day.

God said, "Let the water below the sky be gathered into one area, that the dry land may appear." And it was so. God called the dry land Earth, and the gathering of waters He called Seas. And God saw that this was good. And God said, "Let the earth sprout vegetation: seed-bearing plants, fruit trees of every kind on earth that bear fruit with the seed in it." And it was so. The earth brought forth vegetation: seed-bearing plants of every kind, and trees of every kind bearing fruit with the seed in it. And God saw that this was good. And there was evening and there was morning, a third day.

God said, "Let there be lights in the expanse of the sky to separate day from night; they shall serve as signs for the set times—the days and the years; and they shall serve as lights in the expanse of the sky to shine upon the earth." And it was so. God made the two great lights, the greater light to dominate the day and the lesser light to dominate the night, and the stars. And God set them in the expanse of the sky to shine upon the earth, to dominate the day and the night, and to separate light from darkness. And God saw that this was good. And there was evening and there was morning, a fourth day.

God said, "Let the waters bring forth swarms of living creatures, and birds that fly above the earth across the expanse of the sky." God created the great sea monsters, and all the living creatures of every kind that creep, which the waters brought forth in swarms, and all the winged birds of every kind. And God saw that this was good. God blessed them, saying, "Be fertile and increase, fill the waters in the seas, and let the birds increase on the earth." And there was evening and there was morning, a fifth day.

God said, "Let the earth bring forth every kind of living creature: cattle, creeping things, and wild beasts of every kind." And it was so. God made wild beasts of every kind and cattle of every kind, and all kinds of creeping things of the earth. And God saw that this was good. And God said, "Let us make man in our image, after our likeness. They shall rule the fish of the sea, the birds of the sky, the cattle, the whole earth, and all the creeping things that creep on earth." And God created man in His image, in the image of God He created him; male and female He created them. God blessed them and God said to them, "Be fertile and increase, fill the earth and master it; and rule the fish of the sea, the birds of the sky, and all the living things that creep on earth."

God said, "See, I give you every seed-bearing plant that is upon all the earth, and every tree that has seed-bearing fruit; they shall be yours for food. And to all the animals on land, to all the birds of the sky, and to everything that creeps on earth, in which there is the breath of life, [I give] all the green plants for food. And it was so. And God saw all that He had made, and found it very good. And there was evening and there was morning, the sixth day.

2

The heaven and the earth were finished, and all their array. On the seventh day God finished the work that He had been doing, and He ceased on the seventh day from all the work that He had done. And God blessed the seventh day and declared it holy, because on it God ceased from all the work of creation that He had done. Such is the story of heaven and earth when they were created.

When the LORD God made earth and heaven—when no shrub of the field was yet one earth and no grasses of the field had yet sprouted, because the LORD God had not sent rain upon the earth and there was no man to till the soil, but a flow would well up from the ground and water the whole surface of the earth—the LORD God formed man from the dust of the earth. He blew into his nostrils the breath of life, and man became a living being.

The LORD God planted a garden in Eden, in the east, and placed there the man whom He had formed. And from the ground the LORD God caused to grow every tree that was pleasing to the sight and good for food, with the tree of life in the middle of the garden, and the tree of knowledge of good and bad.

A river issues from Eden to water the garden, and it then divides and becomes four branches. The name of the first is Pishon, the one that winds through the whole land of Havilah, where the gold is. The gold of that land is good; bdellium is there, and lapis lazuli. The name of the second river is Gihon, the one that winds through the whole land of Cush. The name of the third river is Tigris, the one that flows east of Asshur. And the fourth river is the Euphrates.

The LORD God took the man and placed him in the garden of Eden, to till it and tend it. And the LORD God commanded the man, saying, "Of every tree of the garden you are free to eat; but as for the tree of knowledge of good and bad, you must not eat of it; for as soon as you eat of it, you shall die."

The LORD God said, "It is not good for man to be alone; I will make a fitting helper for him." And the LORD God formed out of the earth all the wild beasts and all the birds of the sky, and brought them to the man to see what he would call them; and whatever the man called each living creature, that would be its name. And the man gave names to all the cattle and to the birds of the sky and to all the wild beasts; but for Adam no fitting helper was found. So the LORD God cast a deep sleep upon the man; and, while he slept, He took one of his ribs and closed up the flesh at that spot. And the LORD God fashioned the rib that He had taken from the man into a woman; and He brought her to the man. Then the man said,

> "This one at last
> Is bone of my bones
> And flesh of my flesh.
> This one shall be called Woman,
> For from man was she taken."

Hence a man leaves his father and mother and clings to his wife, so that they become one flesh.

The two of them were naked, the man and his wife, yet they felt no shame.

3

Now the serpent was the shrewdest of all the wild beasts that the LORD God had made. He said to the woman, "Did God really say: You shall not eat of any tree of the garden?" The woman replied to the serpent, "We may eat of the fruit of the other trees of the garden. It is only about fruit of the tree in the middle of the garden that God said: 'You shall not eat of it or touch it, lest you die.'" And the serpent said to the woman, "You are not going to die, but God knows that as soon as you eat of it your eyes will be opened and you will be like divine beings who know good and bad." When the woman saw that the tree was good for eating and a delight to the eyes, and that the tree was desirable as a source of wisdom, she took of its fruit and ate. She also gave some to her husband, and he ate. Then the eyes of both of them were opened and they perceived that they were naked; and they sewed together fig leaves and made themselves loincloths.

They heard the sound of the Lord God moving about in the garden at the breezy time of day; and the man and his wife hid from the Lord God among the trees of the garden. The Lord God called out to the man and said to him, "Where are you?" He replied, "I heard the sound of You in the garden, and I was afraid because I was naked, so I hid." Then He asked, "Who told you that you were naked? Did you eat of the tree from which I had forbidden you to eat?" The man said, "The woman You put at my side—she gave me of the tree, and I ate." And the Lord God said to the woman, "What is this you have done!" The woman replied, "The serpent duped me, and I ate." Then the Lord God said to the serpent,

> "Because you did this,
> More cursed shall you be
> Than all cattle
> And all the wild beasts:
> On your belly shall you crawl
> And dirt shall you eat
> All the days of your life.
> I will put enmity
> Between you and the woman,
> And between your offspring and hers;

> They shall strike at your head,
> And you shall strike at their heel."

And to the woman He said,

> "I will make most severe
> Your pangs in childbearing;
> In pain shall you bear children.
> Yet your urge shall be for your husband,
> And he shall rule over you."

To Adam He said, "Because you did as your wife said and ate of the tree about which I commanded you, 'You shall not eat of it,'

> Cursed be the ground because of you;
> By toil shall you eat of it
> All the days of your life:
> Thorns and thistles shall it sprout for you.
> But your food shall be the grasses of the field;
> By the sweat of your brow
> Shall you get bread to eat,
> Until you return to the ground—
> For from it you were taken.
> For dust you are,
> And to dust you shall return."

The man named his wife Eve, because she was the mother of all the living. And the Lord God made garments of skins for Adam and his wife, and clothed them.

And the Lord God said, "Now that the man has become like one of us, knowing good and bad, what if he should stretch out his hand and take also from the tree of life and eat, and live forever!" So the Lord God banished him from the garden of Eden, to till the soil from which he was taken. He drove the man out, and stationed east of the garden of Eden the cherubim and the fiery ever-turning sword, to guard the way to the tree of life.

—w—

Exodus
20:1–23

20

God spoke all these words, saying:

I the Lord am your God who brought you out of the land of Egypt, the house of bondage: You shall have no other gods besides Me.

You shall not make for yourself a sculptured image, or any likeness of what is in the heavens above, or on the earth below, or in the waters under the earth. You shall not bow down to them or serve them. For I the Lord your God am an impassioned God, visiting the guilt of the parents upon the children, upon the third and upon the fourth generations of those who reject Me, but showing kindness to the thousandth generation of those who love Me and keep My commandments.

You shall not swear falsely by the name of the Lord your God; for the Lord will not clear one who swears falsely by His name.

Remember the sabbath day and keep it holy. Six days you shall labor and do all your work, but the seventh day is a sabbath of the Lord your God: you shall not do any work—you, your son or daughter, your male or female slave, or your cattle, or the stranger who is within your settlements. For in six days the Lord made heaven and earth and sea, and all that is in them, and He rested on the seventh day; therefore the Lord blessed the sabbath day and hallowed it.

Honor your father and your mother, that you may long endure on the land that the Lord your God is assigning to you.

You shall not murder.

You shall not commit adultery.

You shall not steal.

You shall not bear false witness against your neighbor. 10

You shall not covet your neighbor's house: you shall not covet your neighbor's wife, or his male or female slave, or his ox or his ass, or anything that is your neighbor's.

All the people witnessed the thunder and lightning, the blare of the horn and the mountain smoking; and when the people saw it, they fell back and stood at a distance. "You speak to us," they said to Moses, "and we will obey; but let not God speak to us, lest we die." Moses answered the people, "Be not afraid; for God has come only in order to test you, and in order that the fear of Him may be ever with you, so that you do not go astray." So the people re-mained at a distance, while Moses approached the thick cloud where God was.

The LORD said to Moses:

Thus shall you say to the Israelites: You yourselves saw that I spoke to you from the very heavens: With Me, therefore, you shall not make any gods of silver, nor shall you make for yourselves any gods of gold. Make for Me an alter of earth and sacrifice on it your burnt offerings and your sacrifices of well-being, your sheep and your oxen; in every place where I cause My name to be mentioned I will come to you and bless you. And if you make for Me an altar of stones, do not build it of hewn stones; for by wield-ing your tool upon them you have profaned them. Do not ascend My altar by steps, that your nakedness may not be exposed upon it.

—⁂—

Isaiah
52:13–53:12

"Indeed, My servant shall prosper,   1
Be exalted and raised to great heights.
Just as the many were appalled at him—
So marred was his appearance, unlike that of man,
His form, beyond human semblance—
Just so he shall startle many nations.
Kings shall be silenced because of him,
For they shall see what has not been told them,
Shall behold what they never have heard."

53

"Who can believe what we have heard?   1
Upon whom has the arm of the LORD been revealed?
For he has grown, by His favor, like a tree crown,
Like a tree trunk out of arid ground.
He had no form or beauty, that we should look at him:
No charm, that we should find him pleasing.
He was despised, shunned by men,
A man of suffering, familiar with disease.
As one who hid his face from us,
He was despised, we held him of no account.
Yet it was our sickness that he was bearing,   10
Our suffering that he endured.
We accounted him plagued,
Smitten and afflicted by God;
But he was wounded because of our sins,
Crushed because of our iniquities.
He bore the chastisement that made us whole,
And by his bruises we were healed.
We all went astray like sheep,
Each going his own way;

And the LORD visited upon him   20
The guilt of all of us."

He was maltreated, yet he was submissive,
He did not open his mouth;
Like a sheep being led to slaughter,
Like a ewe, dumb before those who shear her,
He did not open his mouth.
By oppressive judgment he was taken away,
Who could describe his abode?
For he was cut off from the land of the living
Through the sin of my people, who deserved the
        punishment.   30
And his grave was set among the wicked,
And with the rich, in his death—
Though he had done no injustice
And had spoken no falsehood.
But the LORD chose to crush him by disease,
That, if he made himself an offering for guilt,
He might see offspring and have long life,
And that through him the LORD's purpose might
        prosper.
Out of his anguish he shall see it;
He shall enjoy it to the full through his devotion.   40

"My righteous servant makes the many righteous,
It is their punishment that he bears;
Assuredly, I will give him the many as his portion,
He shall receive the multitude as his spoil.
For he exposed himself to death
And was numbered among the sinners,
Whereas he bore the guilt of the many
And made intercession for sinners."

—⁀⁀—

Amos
5:1—27

5

Hear this word which I intone   1
As a dirge over you, O House of Israel:
Fallen, not to rise again,
Is Maiden Israel;
Abandoned on her soil
With none to life her up.
For thus said my LORD God
About the House of Israel:
The town that marches out a thousand strong   10
Shall have a hundred left,
And the one that marches out a hundred strong
Shall have but ten left.

Thus said the LORD
To the House of Israel:
Seek Me, and you will live.
Do not seek Bethel,
Nor go to Gilgal,
Nor cross over to Beer-sheba;
For Gilgal shall go into exile,
And Bethel shall become a delusion.   20
Seek the LORD, and you will live,
Else He will rush like fire upon the House of Joseph
And consume Bethel with none to quench it.

[Ah,] you who turn justice into wormwood
And hurl righteousness to the ground!
[Seek the LORD,]
Who made the Pleiades and Orion,
Who turns deep darkness into dawn
And darkens day into night,
Who summons the waters of the sea   30
And pours them out upon the earth—
His name is the LORD!
It is He who hurls destruction upon strongholds,
So that ruin comes upon fortresses!

They hate the arbiter in the gate,
And detest him whose plea is just.
Assuredly,
Because you impose a tax on the poor
And exact from him a levy of grain,
You have built houses of hewn stone,   40
But you shall not live in them;
You have planted delightful vineyards,
But shall not drink their wine.
For I have noted how many are your crimes,
And how countless your sins—
You enemies of the righteous,
You takers of bribes,
You who subvert in the gate
The cause of the needy!

Assuredly,   50
At such a time the prudent man keeps silent,
For it is an evil time.

Seek good and not evil,
That you may live,
And that the LORD, the God of Hosts,
May truly be with you,
As you think.
Hate evil and love good,
And establish justice in the gate;
Perhaps the LORD, the God of Hosts,   60
Will be gracious to the remnant of Joseph.

Assuredly,
Thus said the LORD,
My Lord, the God of Hosts:
In every square there shall be lamenting,
In every street cries of "Ah, woe!"
And the farm hand shall be
Called to mourn,
And those skilled in wailing
To lament;   70
For there shall be lamenting
In every vineyard, too,
When I pass through your midst

                            —said the LORD.

Ah, you who wish
For the day of the LORD!
Why should you want
The day of the LORD?
It shall be darkness, not light!
—As if a man should run from a lion   80
And be attacked by a bear;
Or if he got indoors,
Should lean his hand on the wall
And be bitten by a snake!
Surely the day of the LORD shall be
Not light, but darkness,
Blackest night without a glimmer.

I loathe, I spurn your festivals,
I am not appeased by your solemn assemblies.
If you offer Me burnt offerings—or your meal offerings—   90
I will not accept them;
I will pay no heed
To your gifts of fatlings.
Spare Me the sound of your hymns,
And let Me not hear the music of your lutes.
But let justice well up like water,
Righteousness like an unfailing stream.
Did you offer sacrifice and oblation to Me
Those forty years in the wilderness,
O House of Israel?   100

And you shall carry off your "king"—
Sikkuth and Kiyyun,
The images you have made for yourselves

Of your astral deity—
As I drive you into exile beyond Damascus
—Said the LORD, whose name is God of Hosts.

—⁓—

Psalms
22

My God, my God,
   why have You abandoned me;
   why so far from delivering me
   and from my anguished roaring?
My God,
   I cry by day—You answer not;
   by night, and have no respite.

But You are the Holy One,
   enthroned,
   the Praise of Israel.   10
In You our fathers trusted;
   they trusted, and You rescued them.
To You they cried out
   and they escaped;
   in You they trusted
   and were not disappointed.

But I am a worm, less than human;
   scorned by men, despised by people.
All who see me mock me;
   they curl their lips,   20
   they shake their heads.
"Let him commit himself to the LORD;
   let Him rescue him,
   let Him save him,
   for He is pleased with him."
You drew me from the womb,
   made me secure at my mother's breast.
I became Your charge at birth;
   from my mother's womb You have been my God.
Do not be far from me,   30
   for trouble is near,
   and there is none to help.
Many bulls surround me,
   mighty ones of Bashan encircle me.
They open their mouths at me
   like tearing, roaring lions.
My life ebbs away:
   all my bones are disjointed;
   my heart is like wax,
   melting within me;   40
   my vigor dries up like a shard;
   my tongue cleaves to my palate;

You commit me to the dust of death.   1
Dogs surround me;
   a pack of evil ones closes in on me,
   like lions [they maul] my hands and feet.
I take the count of all my bones
   while they look on and gloat.
They divide my clothes among themselves,
   casting lots for my garments.   50

But You, O LORD, be not far off;
   my strength, hasten to my aid.
Save my life from the sword,
   my precious life from the clutches of a dog.
Deliver me from a lion's mouth;
   from the horns of wild oxen rescue me.
Then will I proclaim Your fame to my brethren,
   praise You in the congregation.
You who fear the LORD, praise Him!
All you offspring of Jacob, honor Him!   60
Be in dread of Him, all you offspring of Israel!
For He did not scorn, He did not spurn
   the plea of the lowly;
   He did not hide His face from him;
   when he cried out to Him, He listened.
   Because of You I offer praise in the great congregation;
   I pay my vows in the presence of His worshipers.
Let the lowly eat and be satisfied;
   let all who seek the LORD praise Him.
Always be of good cheer!   70
Let all the ends of the earth pay heed and turn to the LORD,
   and the peoples of all nations prostrate themselves
     before You;
   for kingship is the LORD's
   and He rules the nations.
All those in full vigor shall eat and prostrate
     themselves;
   all those at death's door, whose spirits flag,
   shall bend the knee before Him.
Offspring shall serve Him;
   the LORD's fame shall be proclaimed to the generation
     to come;   80
   they shall tell of His beneficence
   to people yet to be born,
   for He has acted.

23

The Lord is my shepherd;
  I lack nothing.
He makes me lie down in green pastures;
  He leads me to water in places of repose;
  He renews my life;
  He guides me in right paths
  as befits His name.

1

Though I walk through a valley of deepest darkness,
  I fear no harm, for You are with me;
  Your rod and Your staff—they comfort me.

10

You spread a table for me in full view of my enemies;
  You anoint my head with oil;
  my drink is abundant.
Only goodness and steadfast love shall pursue me
  all the days of my life,
  and I shall dwell in the house of the Lord
  for many long years.

104

Bless the Lord, O my soul;
O Lord, my God, You are very great;
  You are clothed in glory and majesty,
  wrapped in a robe of light;
  You spread the heavens like a tent cloth.
He sets the rafters of His lofts in the waters,
  makes the clouds His chariot,
  moves on the wings of the wind.
He makes the winds His messengers,
  fiery flames His servants.
He established the earth on its foundations,
  so that it shall never totter.
You made the deep cover it as a garment;
  the waters stood above the mountains.
They fled at Your blast,
  rushed away at the sound of Your thunder,
  —mountains rising, valleys sinking—
  to the place You established for them.
You set bounds they must not pass
  so that they never again cover the earth.

1

10

20

You make springs gush forth in torrents;
  they make their way between the hills,
  giving drink to all the wild beasts;
  the wild asses slake their thirst.
The birds of the sky dwell beside them
  and sing among the foliage.
You water the mountains from Your lofts;
  the earth is sated from the fruit of Your work.
You make the grass grow for the cattle,
  and herbage for man's labor
  that he may get food out of the earth—
  wine that cheers the hearts of men
  oil that make the face shine,
  and bread that sustains man's life.
The trees of the Lord drink their fill,
  the cedars of Lebanon, His own planting,

30

where birds make their nests;
  the stork has her home in the junipers.
The high mountains are for wild goats;
  the crags are a refuge for rock-badgers.

40

He made the moon to mark the seasons;
  the sun knows when to set.
You bring on darkness and it is night,
  when all the beasts of the forests stir.
The lions roar for prey,
  seeking their food from God.
When the sun rises, they come home
  and couch in their dens.
Man then goes out to his work,
  to his labor until the evening.

50

How many are the things You have made, O Lord;
  You have made them all with wisdom;
  the earth is full of Your creations.
There is the sea, vast and wide,
  with its creatures beyond number,
  living things, small and great.
There go the ships,
  and Leviathan that You formed to sport with.
All of them look to You
  to give them their food when it is due.

60

Give it to them, they gather it up;
  open Your hand, they are well satisfied;
  hide Your face, they are terrified;
  take away their breath, they perish
  and turn again into dust;
  send back Your breath, they are created,
  and You renew the face of the earth.
May the glory of the Lord endure forever;
  may the Lord rejoice in His works!
He looks at the earth and it trembles;
  He touches the mountains and they smoke.

70

I will sing to the LORD as long as I live;
    all my life I will chant hymns to my God.
May my prayer be pleasing to Him;
    I will rejoice in the LORD.

May sinners disappear from the earth,
    and the wicked be no more.
Bless the LORD, O my soul.
    Hallelujah.

—✺—

Job
1:1–3:26

1

There was a man in the land of Uz named Job. That man was blameless and upright; he feared God and shunned evil. Seven sons and three daughters were born to him; his possessions were seven thousand sheep, three thousand camels, five hundred yoke of oxen and five hundred she-asses, and a very large household. That man was wealthier than anyone in the East.

It was the custom of his sons to hold feasts, each on his set day in his own home. They would invite their three sisters to eat and drink with them. When a round of feast days was over, Job would send word to them to sanctify themselves, and, rising early in the morning, he would make burnt offerings, one for each of them; for Job thought, "Perhaps my children have sinned and blasphemed God in their thoughts." This is what Job always used to do.

One day the divine beings presented themselves before the LORD, and the Adversary came along with them. The LORD said to the Adversary, "Where have you been?" The Adversary answered the LORD, "I have been roaming all over the earth." The LORD said to the Adversary, "Have you noticed My servant Job? There is no one like him on earth, a blameless and upright man who fears God and shuns evil!" The Adversary answered the LORD, "Does Job not have good reason to fear God? Why, it is You who have fenced him round, him and his household and all that he has. You have blessed his efforts so that his possessions spread out in the land. But lay Your hand upon all that he has and he will surely blaspheme You to Your face." The LORD replied to the Adversary, "See, all that he has is in your power; only do not lay a hand on him." The Adversary departed from the presence of the LORD.

One day, as his sons and daughters were eating and drinking wine in the house of their eldest brother, a messenger came to Job and said, "The oxen were plowing and the she-asses were grazing alongside them when Sabeans attacked them and carried them off, and put the boys to the sword; I alone have escaped to tell you." This one was still speaking when another came and said, "God's fire fell from heaven, took hold of the sheep and the boys, and burned them up; I alone have escaped to tell you." This one was still speaking when another came and said, "A Chaldean formation of three columns made a raid on the camels and carried them off and put the boys to the sword; I alone have escaped to tell you." This one was still speaking when another came and said, "Your sons and daughters were eating and drinking wine in the house of their eldest brother when suddenly a mighty wind came from the wilderness. It struck the four corners of the house so that it collapsed upon the young people and they died; I alone have escaped to tell you."

Then Job arose, tore his robe, cut off his hair, and threw himself on the ground and worshiped. He said, "Naked came I out of my mother's womb, and naked shall I return there; the LORD has given, and the LORD has taken away; blessed be the name of the LORD."

For all that, Job did not sin nor did he cast reproach on God.

2

One day the divine beings presented themselves before the LORD. The Adversary came along with them to present himself before the LORD. The LORD said to the Adversary, "Where have you been?" The Adversary answered the LORD, "I have been roaming all over the earth." The LORD said to the Adversary, "Have you noticed My servant Job? There is no one like him on earth, a blameless and upright man who fears God and shuns evil. He still keeps his integrity; so you have incited Me against him to destroy him for no good reason." The Adversary answered the LORD, "Skin for skin—all that a man has he will give up for his life. But lay a hand on his bones and his flesh, and he will surely blaspheme You to Your face." So the LORD said to the Adversary, "See, he is in your power; only spare his life." The Adversary departed from the presence of the LORD and inflicted a severe inflammation on Job from the sole of his foot to the crown of his head. He took a potsherd to scratch himself as he sat in ashes. His wife said to him, "You still keep your integrity! Blaspheme God and die!" But he said to her, "You talk as any shameless woman might talk! Should we accept only good from God and not accept evil?" For all that, Job said nothing sinful.

When Job's three friends heard about all these calamities that had befallen him, each came from his home—Eliphaz the Temanite, Bildad the Shuhite, and Zophar the Naamathite. They met together to go and console and comfort him. When they saw him from a distance, they could not recognize him, and they broke into loud weeping; each one tore his robe and threw dust into the air onto his head. They sat with him on the ground seven days and seven nights. None spoke a word to him for they saw how very great was his suffering.

3

Afterward, Job began to speak and cursed the day of his birth. Job spoke up and said: 1

> Perish the day on which I was born,
> And the night it was announced,
> "A male has been conceived!"
> May that day be darkness;
> May God above have no concern for it;
> May light not shine on it;
> May darkness and deep gloom reclaim it;
> May a pall lie over it;   10
> May what blackens the day terrify it.
> May obscurity carry off that night;
> May it not be counted among the days of the year;
> May it not appear in any of its months;
> May that night be desolate;
> May no sound of joy be heard in it;
> May those who cast spells upon the day damn it,
> Those prepared to disable Leviathan;
> May its twilight stars remain dark;
> May it hope for light and have none;   20
> May it not see the glimmerings of the dawn—
> Because it did not block my mother's womb,
> And hide trouble from my eyes.

> Why did I not die at birth,
> Expire as I came forth from the womb?
> Why were there knees to receive me,
> Or breasts for me to suck?
> For now would I be lying in repose, asleep and at rest,
> With the world's kings and counselors who rebuild
>   ruins for themselves,
> Or with nobles who possess gold and who fill their
>   houses with silver.   30
> Or why was I not like a buried stillbirth,
> Like babies who never saw the light?
> There the wicked cease from troubling;
> There rest those whose strength is spent.
> Prisoners are wholly at ease;
> They do not hear the taskmaster's voice.
> Small and great alike are there,
> And the slave is free of his master.

> Why does He give light to the sufferer
> And life to the bitter in spirit;   40
> To those who wait for death but it does not come,
> Who search for it more than for treasure,
> Who rejoice to exultation,
> And are glad to reach the grave;
> To the man who has lost his way,
> Whom God has hedged about?

> My groaning serves as my bread;
> My roaring pours forth as water.
> For what I feared has overtaken me;
> What I dreaded has come upon me.   50
> I had no repose, no quiet, no rest,
> And trouble came.

19:1–29

19

Job said in reply: 1

> How long will you grieve my spirit,
> And crush me with words?
> Time and again you humiliate me,
> And are not ashamed to abuse me.
> If indeed I have erred,
> My error remains with me.
> Though you are overbearing toward me,
> Reproaching me with my disgrace,
> Yet know that God has wronged me;   10
> He has thrown up siege works around me.
> I cry, "Violence!" but am not answered;
> I shout, but can get no justice.
> He has barred my way; I cannot pass;
> He has laid darkness upon my path.
> He has stripped me of my glory,
> Removed the crown from my head.

> He tears down every part of me; I perish;
> He uproots my hope like a tree.
> He kindles His anger against me;   20
> He regards me as one of His foes.
> His troops advance together;
> They build their road toward me
> And encamp around my tent.
> He alienated my kin from me;
> My acquaintances disown me.
> My relatives are gone;
> My friends have forgotten me.
> My dependents and maidservants regard me as a
>   stranger;
> I am an outsider to them.   30
> I summon my servant but he does not respond;
> I must myself entreat him.
> My odor is repulsive to my wife;
> I am loathsome to my children.
> Even youngsters disdain me;
> When I rise, they speak against me.

All my bosom friends detest me;
Those I love have turned against me.
My bones stick to my skin and flesh;
I escape with the skin of my teeth.   40

Pity me, pity me! You are my friends;
For the hand of God has struck me!
Why do you pursue me like God,
Maligning me insatiably?
O that my words were written down;
Would they were inscribed in a record,
Incised on a rock forever
With iron stylus and lead!

But I know that my Vindicator lives;
In the end He will testify on earth—   50
This, after my skin will have been peeled off.
But I would behold God while still in my flesh,
I myself, not another, would behold Him;
Would see with my own eyes:
My heart pines within me.
You say, "How do we persecute him?
The root of the matter is in him."
Be in fear of the sword,
For [your] fury is iniquity worthy of the sword;
Know there is a judgment!   60

38:1—42:17

38

Then the Lord replied to Job out of the tempest and
said: 1

Who is this who darkens counsel,
Speaking without knowledge?
Gird your loins like a man;
I will ask and you will inform Me.

Where were you when I laid the earth's foundations?
Speak if you have understanding.
Do you know who fixed its dimensions
Or who measured it with a line?
Onto what were its bases sunk?   10
Who set its cornerstone
When the morning stars sang together
And all the divine beings shouted for joy?

Who closed the sea behind doors
When it gushed forth out of the womb,
When I clothed it in clouds,
Swaddled it in dense clouds,
When I made breakers My limit for it,
And set up its bar and doors,
And said, "You may come so far and no farther;   20
Here your surging waves will stop"?

Have you ever commanded the day to break,
Assigned the dawn its place,
So that it seizes the corners of the earth
And shakes the wicked out of it?
It changes like clay under the seal
Till [its hues] are fixed like those of a garment.
Their light is withheld from the wicked,
And the upraised arm is broken.

Have you penetrated to the sources of the sea,   30
Or walked in the recesses of the deep?
Have the gates of death been disclosed to you?
Have you seen the gates of deep darkness?
Have you surveyed the expanses of the earth?
If you know of these—tell Me.

Which path leads to where light dwells,
And where is the place of darkness,
That you may take it to its domain
And know the way to its home?
Surely you know, for you were born then,   40
And the number of your years is many!

Have you penetrated the vaults of snow,
Seen the vaults of hail,
Which I have put aside for a time of adversity,
For a day of war and battle?
By what path is the west wind dispersed,
The east wind scattered over the earth?
Who cut a channel for the torrents
And a path for the thunderstorms,
To rain down on uninhabited land,   50
On the wilderness where no man is,
To saturate the desolate wasteland,
And make the crop of grass sprout forth?
Does the rain have a father?
Who begot the dewdrops?
From whose belly came forth the ice?
Who gave birth to the frost of heaven?
Water congeals like stone,
And the surface of the deep compacts.

Can you tie cords to Pleiades   60
Or undo the reins of Orion?
Can you lead out Mazzaroth in its season,
Conduct the Bear with her sons?
Do you know the laws of heaven
Or impose its authority on earth?

Can you send up an order to the clouds
For an abundance of water to cover you?
Can you dispatch the lightning on a mission
And have it answer you, "I am ready"?
Who put wisdom in the hidden parts?   70
Who gave understanding to the mind?
Who is wise enough to give an account of the heavens?
Who can tilt the bottles of the sky,
Whereupon the earth melts into a mass,
And its clods stick together.

Can you hunt prey for the lion,
And satisfy the appetite of the king of beasts?
They crouch in their dens,
Lie in ambush in their lairs.
Who provides food for the raven   80
When his young cry out to God
And wander about without food?

39

Do you know the season when the mountain goats
    give birth?   1
Can you mark the time when the hinds calve?
Can you count the months they must complete?
Do you know the season they give birth,
When they couch to bring forth their offspring,
To deliver their young?
Their young are healthy; they grow up in the open;
They leave and return no more.

Who sets the wild ass free?
Who loosens the bonds of the onager,   10
Whose home I have made the wilderness,
The salt land his dwelling-place?
He scoffs at the tumult of the city,
Does not hear the shouts of the driver.
He roams the hills for his pasture;
He searches for any green thing.

Would the wild ox agree to serve you?
Would he spend the night at your crib?
Can you hold the wild ox by ropes to the furrow?
Would he plow up the valleys behind you?   20
Would you rely on his great strength
And leave your toil to him?
Would you trust him to bring in the seed
And gather it in from your threshing floor?

The wing of the ostrich beats joyously;
Are her pinions and plumage like the stork's?
She leaves her eggs on the ground,
Letting them warm in the dirt,
Forgetting they may be crushed underfoot,
Or trampled by a wild beast.   30
Her young are cruelly abandoned as if they were
    not hers;
Her labor is in vain for lack of concern.
For God deprived her of wisdom,
Gave her no share of understanding,
Else she would soar on high,
Scoffing at the horse and its rider.

Do you give the horse his strength?
Do you clothe his neck with a mane?
Do you make him quiver like locusts,
His majestic snorting [spreading] terror?   40
He paws with force, he runs with vigor,
Charging into battle.
He scoffs at fear; he cannot be frightened;

He does not recoil from the sword.
A quiverful of arrows whizzes by him,
And the flashing spear and the javelin.
Trembling with excitement, he swallows the land;
He does not turn aside at the blast of the trumpet.
As the trumpet sounds, he says, "Aha!"
From afar he smells the battle,   50
The roaring and shouting of the officers.

Is it by your wisdom that the hawk grows pinions,
Spreads his wings to the south?
Does the eagle soar at your command,
Building his nest high,
Dwelling in the rock,
Lodging upon the fastness of a jutting rock?
From there he spies out his food;
From afar his eyes see it.
His young gulp blood;   60
Where the slain are, there is he.

40

The LORD said in reply to Job.   1

Shall one who should be disciplined complain
    against Shaddai?
He who arraigns God must respond.

Job said in reply to the LORD:

See, I am of small worth; what can I answer You?
I clap my hand to my mouth.
I have spoken once, and will not reply;
Twice, and will do so no more.

Then the LORD replied to Job out of the tempest and said:

Gird your loins like a man;   10
I will ask, and you will inform Me.
Would you impugn My justice?
Would you condemn Me that you may be right?
Have you an arm like God's?
Can you thunder with a voice like His?
Deck yourself now with grandeur and eminence;
Clothe yourself in glory and majesty.
Scatter wide your raging anger;
See every proud man and bring him low.
See every proud man and humble him,   20
And bring them down where they stand.
Bury them all in the earth;
Hide their faces in obscurity.
Then even I would praise you
For the triumph your right hand won you.

Take now behemoth, whom I made as I did you;
He eats grass, like the cattle.
His strength is in his loins,
His might in the muscles of his belly.
He makes his tail stand up like a cedar;   30
The sinews of his thighs are knit together.

His bones are like tubes of bronze,
His limbs like iron rods.
He is the first of God's works;
Only his Maker can draw the sword against him.
The mountains yield him produce,
Where all the beasts of the field play.
He lies down beneath the lotuses,
In the cover of the swamp reeds.
The lotuses embower him with shade;   40
The willows of the brook surround him.
He can restrain the river from its rushing;
He is confident the stream will gush at his command.
Can he be taken by his eyes?
Can his nose be pierced by hooks?
Can you draw out Leviathan by a fishhook?
Can you press down his tongue by a rope?
Can you put a ring through his nose,
Or pierce his jaw with a barb?
Will he plead with you at length?   50
Will he speak soft words to you?
Will he make an agreement with you
To be taken as your lifelong slave?
Will you play with him like a bird,
And tie him down for your girls?
Shall traders traffic in him?
Will he be divided up among merchants?
Can you fill his skin with darts
Or his head with fish-spears?
Lay a hand on him,   60
And you will never think of battle again.

41

See, any hope [of capturing] him must be
    disappointed;   1
One is prostrated by the very sight of him.
There is no one so fierce as to rouse him;
Who then can stand up to Me?
Whoever confronts Me I will requite,
For everything under the heavens is Mine.
I will not be silent concerning him
Or the praise of his martial exploits.
Who can uncover his outer garment?
Who can penetrate the folds of his jowls?   10
Who can pry open the doors of his face?
His bared teeth strike terror.
His protective scales are his pride,
Locked with a binding seal.
One scale touches the other;
Not even a breath can enter between them.
Each clings to each;
They are interlocked so they cannot be parted.
His sneezings flash lightning,
And his eyes are like the glimmerings of dawn.   20
Firebrands stream from his mouth;
Fiery sparks escape.
Out of his nostrils comes smoke
As from a steaming, boiling cauldron.
His breath ignites coals;

Flames blaze from his mouth.
Strength resides in his neck;
Power leaps before him.
The layers of his flesh stick together;
He is as though cast hard; he does not totter.   30
His heart is cast hard as a stone,
Hard as the nether millstone.
Divine beings are in dread as he rears up;
As he crashes down, they cringe.
No sword that overtakes him can prevail,
Nor spear, nor missile, nor lance.
He regards iron as straw,
Bronze, as rotted wood.
No arrow can put him to flight;
Slingstones turn into stubble for him.   40
Clubs are regarded as stubble;
He scoffs at the quivering javelin.
His underpart is jagged shards;
It spreads a threshing-sledge on the mud.
He makes the depths seethe like a cauldron;
He makes the sea [boil] like an ointment-pot.
His wake is a luminous path;
He makes the deep seem white-haired.
There is no one on land who can dominate him,
Made as he is without fear.   50
He sees all that is haughty;
He is king over all proud beasts.

42

Job said in reply to the Lord: 1

I know that You can do everything,
That nothing you propose is impossible for You.
Who is this who obscures counsel without
    knowledge?
Indeed, I spoke without understanding
Of things beyond me, which I did not know.
Hear now, and I will speak;
I will ask, and You will inform me.
I had heard You with my ears,
But now I see You with my eyes;   10
Therefore, I recant and relent,
Being but dust and ashes.

After the Lord had spoken these words to Job, the Lord said to Eliphaz the Temanite, "I am incensed at you and your two friends, for you have not spoken the truth about Me as did My servant Job. Now take seven bulls and seven rams and go to My servant Job and sacrifice a burnt offering for yourselves. And let Job, My servant, pray for you; for to him I will show favor and not treat you vilely, since you have not spoken the truth about Me as did My servant Job." Eliphaz the Temanite and Bildad the Shuhite and Zophar the Naamathite went and did as the Lord had told them, and the Lord showed favor to Job. The Lord restored Job's fortunes when he prayed on behalf of his friends, and the Lord gave Job twice what he had before.

All his brothers and sisters and all his former friends came to him and had a meal with him in his house. They consoled and comforted him for all the misfortune that the LORD had brought upon him. Each gave him one *kesitah* and each one gold ring. Thus the LORD blessed the latter 30 years of Job's life more than the former. He had fourteen thousand sheep, six thousand camels, one thousand yoke of oxen, and one thousand she-asses. He also had seven sons and three daughters. The first he named Jemimah, the second Keziah, and the third Keren-happuch. Nowhere in the land were women as beautiful as Job's daughters to be found. Their father gave them estates together with their brothers. Afterward, Job lived one hundred and forty years to see four generations of sons and grandsons. So Job died old and contented. 40

Selections from *The Revised Standard Version of the Holy Bible*

Christians adopted the Jewish Bible, *The Holy Scriptures,* renaming it the Old Testament and re-arranging its thirty-nine books into the Pentateuch, the Historical Books, the Wisdom Books, and the Prophetical Books. Christians also developed the New Testament—twenty-seven books about Jesus, grouped into the Gospels, the Acts of the Apostles, Epistles, and Apocalypse. The Christian Bible thus numbers sixty-six books. The books in the New Testament, written between A.D. 50 and 100, were brought together around A.D. 150 as the sacred text for the new religion of Christianity. Greek, the New Testament's language, enabled it to circulate freely in Rome's Greek-speaking eastern provinces. When Christianity triumphed in Rome around A.D. 400, the saintly Jerome rewrote the entire Bible into the ordinary, or common, Latin of that era; thereafter, his work was known as the Vulgate version (from Latin *vulgatus,* "common"). Since then, the Vulgate has been the church's official text, although the Protestants composed vernacular versions after 1500.

From the fall of Rome until recent times, the Holy Bible has been the West's most significant book, touching the lives of everyone in all walks of life. This privileged status rose not simply because the Bible contained God's holy words for Christian and Jewish believers, but most important, because it was the all-encompassing glue that bound the culture together. It influenced every aspect of culture, most notably in the arts, language, and personal behavior. The Bible offered an alternative body of writing to that of Greece and Rome and, as such, inspired artists, writers, and musicians. Its words and rhetoric enriched spoken and written language, and its parables and poems served as a hand-book for moral guidance. Even in today's secular world, biblical knowledge is still indispensable for interpreting Western culture and history.

Reading the Selections

The selections from Matthew's Gospel include key scenes from the life of Jesus, including the virgin birth, the baptism by John the Baptist, the temptation by the devil, and the Sermon on the Mount. Most notably, the Sermon on the Mount presents Jesus' moral teachings. He begins this sermon with the beatitudes—a list of blessings on those who often are at odds with earthly society, such as the poor and the downtrodden. He next reinterprets the Jewish law, pointing out that obedience of rules is never enough; instead, he asks his followers to practice forgiveness even to the extent of loving one's enemies. Jesus expresses his law of love in what Christians later call the Golden Rule: "So whatever you wish that men would do to you, do so to them. . . . (Matthew 7:12). He also describes the correct way to worship God, giving the Lord's Prayer as the best model. Jesus concludes with a caution against false prophets—those who call on the Lord but refuse to obey his will.

The final selection is from the Epistles—the letters written by early Christian leaders to new congregations needing further knowledge of Christ and his teachings, advice on church organization, and help with understanding the rituals and beliefs of the emerging religion. The letters of Paul, the first Christian missionary, make up the largest number of the Epistles—fourteen out of twenty-one. Chapter 13 from Paul's First Letter to the Corinthians [the church in Corinth, Greece] is an exemplary summary of Christian love, which forgives others and asks nothing in return. This expression of un-conditional love, so often read at wedding ceremonies, is more an ideal than a reality.

—⁓—

The Gospel According to Matthew
1:18–4:25
The Coming of Christ

Now the birth of Jesus Christ took place in this way. When his mother Mary had been betrothed to Joseph, before they came together she was found to be with child of the Holy Spirit; and her husband Joseph, being a just man and unwilling to put her to shame, resolved to divorce her quietly. But as he considered this, behold, an angel of the Lord appeared to him in a dream, saying, "Joseph, son of David, do not fear to take Mary your wife, for that which is conceived in her is of the Holy Spirit; she will bear a son, and you shall call his name Jesus, for he will save his people from their sins." All this took place to fulfil what the Lord had spoken by the prophet:

"Behold, a virgin shall conceive and bear a son,
and his name shall be called Emman'u-el"
(which means, God with us).

When Joseph woke from sleep, he did as the angel of the Lord commanded him; he took his wife, but knew her not until she had borne a son; and he called his name Jesus.

2

Now when Jesus was born in Bethlehem of Judea in the days of Herod the king, behold, wise men from the East came to Jerusalem, saying, "Where is he who has been born king of the Jews? For we have seen his star in the East, and have come to worship him." When Herod the king heard this, he was troubled, and all Jerusalem with him; and assembling all the chief priests and scribes of the people, he inquired of them where the Christ was to be born. They told him, "In Bethlehem of Judea; for so it is written by the prophet:

'And you, O Bethlehem, in the land of Judah,
are by no means least among the rulers of Judah;
for from you shall come a ruler
who will govern my people Israel.'"

Then Herod summoned the wise men secretly and ascertained from them what time the star appeared; and he sent them to Bethlehem, saying, "Go and search diligently for the child, and when you have found him bring me word, that I too may come and worship him." When they had heard the king they went their way; and lo, the star which they had seen in the East went before them, till it came to rest over the place where the child was. When they saw the star, they rejoiced exceedingly with great joy; and going into the house they saw the child with Mary his mother, and they fell down and worshiped him. Then, opening their treasures, they offered him gifts, gold and frankincense and myrrh. And being warned in a dream not to return to Herod, they departed to their own country by another way.

Now when they had departed, behold, an angel of the Lord appeared to Joseph in a dream and said, "Rise, take the child and his mother, and flee to Egypt, and remain there till I tell you; for Herod is about to search for the child, to destroy him." And he rose and took the child and his mother by night, and departed to Egypt, and remained there until the death of Herod. This was to fulfil what the Lord had spoken by the prophet, "Out of Egypt have I called my son."

Then Herod, when he saw that he had been tricked by the wise men, was in a furious rage, and he sent and killed all the male children in Bethlehem and in all that region who were two years old or under, according to the time which he had ascertained from the wise men. Then was fulfilled what was spoken by the prophet Jeremiah:

"A voice was heard in Ramah,
wailing and loud lamentation,
Rachel weeping for her children;
she refused to be consoled,
because they were no more."

But when Herod died, behold, an angel of the Lord appeared in a dream to Joseph in Egypt, saying, "Rise, take the child and his mother, and go to the land of Israel, for those who sought the child's life are dead." And he rose and took the child and his mother, and went to the land of Israel. But when he heart that Archela'us reigned over Judea in place of his father Herod, he was afraid to go there, and being warned in a dream he withdrew to the district of Galilee. And he went and dwelt in a city called Nazareth, that what was spoken by the prophets might be fulfilled, "He shall be called a Nazarene."

3

In those days came John the Baptist, preaching in the wilderness of Judea, "Repent, for the kingdom of heaven is at hand." For this is he who was spoken of by the prophet Isaiah when he said,

"The voice of one crying in the wilderness:
Prepare the way of the Lord,
make his paths straight."

Now John wore a garment of camel's hair, and a leather girdle around his waist; and his food was locusts and wild honey. Then went out to him Jerusalem and all Judea and all the region about the Jordan, and they were baptized by him in the river Jordan, confessing their sins.

But when he saw many of the Pharisees and Sad'ducees coming for baptism, he said to them, "You brood of vipers! Who warned you to flee from the wrath to come? Bear fruit that befits repentance, and do not presume to say to yourselves, 'We have Abraham as our father'; for I tell you, God is able from these stones to raise up children to Abraham. Even now the ax is laid to the root of the trees; every tree therefore that does not bear good fruit is cut down and thrown into the fire.

"I baptize you with water for repentance, but he who is coming after me is mightier than I, whose sandals I am not worthy to carry; he will baptize you with the Holy Spirit and with fire. His winnowing fork is in his hand, and he will clear his threshing floor and gather his wheat into the granary, but the chaff he will burn with unquenchable fire."

Then Jesus came from Galilee to the Jordan to John, to be baptized by him. John would have prevented him, saying, "I need to be baptized by you, and do you come to me?" But Jesus answered him, "Let it be so now; for thus it is fitting for us to fulfil all righteousness." Then he consented. And when Jesus was baptized, he went up immediately from the water, and behold, the heavens were opened and he saw the Spirit of God descending like a dove, and alighting on him; and lo, a voice from heaven, saying, "This is my beloved Son, with whom I am well pleased."

4

Then Jesus was led up by the Spirit into the wilderness to be tempted by the devil. And he fasted forty days and forty nights, and afterward he was hungry. And the tempter came and said to him, "If you are the Son of God, command these stones to become loaves of bread." But he answered, "It is written,

'Man shall not live by bread alone,
but by every word that proceeds from the mouth
of God.'"

Then the devil took him to the holy city, and set him on the pinnacle of the temple, and said to him, "If you are the Son of God, throw yourself down; for it is written,

'He will give his angels charge of you,'
and

'On their hands they will bear you up,
lest you strike your foot against a stone.'"

Jesus said to him, "Again it is written, 'You shall not tempt the Lord you God.'" Again, the devil took him to a very high mountain, and showed him all the kingdoms of the world and the glory of them; and he said to him, "All these I will give you, if you will fall down and worship me." Then Jesus said to him, "Begone, Satan! for it is written,

'You shall worship the Lord your God
and him only shall you serve.'"

Then the devil left him, and behold, angels came and ministered to him.

Now when he heard that John had been arrested, he withdrew into Galilee; and leaving Nazareth he went and dwelt in Caper'na-um by the sea, in the territory of Zeb'ulun and Naph'tali, that what was spoken by the prophet Isaiah might be fulfilled:

"The land of Zeb'ulun and the land of Naph'tali,
toward the sea, across the Jordan,
Galilee of the Gentiles—
the people who sat in darkness
have seen a great light,
and for those who sat in the region and shadow
of death
light has dawned."

From that time Jesus began to preach, saying, "Repent, for the kingdom of heaven is at hand."

As he walked by the Sea of Galilee, he saw two brothers, Simon who is called Peter and Andrew his brother, casting a net into the sea; for they were fishermen. And he said to them, "Follow me, and I will make you fishers of men." Immediately they left their nets and followed him. And going on from there he saw two other brothers, James the son of Zeb'edee and John his brother, in the boat with Zeb'edee their father, mending their nets, and he called them. Immediately they left the boat and their father, and followed him.

And he went about all Galilee, teaching in their synagogues and preaching the gospel of the kingdom and healing every disease and every infirmity among the people. So his fame spread throughout all Syria, and they brought him all the sick, those afflicted with various diseases and pains, demoniacs, epileptics, and paralytics, and he healed them. And great crowds followed him from Galilee and the Decap'olis and Jerusalem and Judea and from beyond the Jordan.

5:1–7:29
Sermon on the Mount

5

Seeing the crowds, he went up on the mountain, and when 1 he sat down his disciples came to him. And he opened his mouth and taught them, saying:

"Blessed are the poor in spirit, for theirs is the kingdom of heaven.

"Blessed are those who mourn, for they shall be comforted.

"Blessed are the meek, for they shall inherit the earth.

"Blessed are those who hunger and thirst for righteousness, for they shall be satisfied. 5

"Blessed are the merciful, for they shall obtain mercy.

"Blessed are the pure in heart, for they shall see God.

"Blessed are the peacemakers, for they shall be called sons of God.

"Blessed are those who are persecuted for righteousness' sake, for theirs is the kingdom of heaven.

"Blessed are you when men revile you and persecute 10 you and utter all kinds of evil against you falsely on my account. Rejoice and be glad, for your reward is great in heaven, for so men persecuted the prophets who were before you.

"You are the salt of the earth; but if salt has lost its taste, how shall its saltness be restored? It is no longer good for anything except to be thrown out and trodden under foot by men.

"You are the light of the world. A city set on a hill cannot be hid. Nor do men light a lamp and put it under a bushel, but on a stand, and it gives light to all in the house. Let your light so shine before men, that they may see your good works and give glory to your Father who is in heaven.

"Think not that I have come to abolish the law and the prophets; I have come not to abolish them but to fulfil them. For truly, I say to you, till heaven and earth pass away, not an iota, not a dot, will pass from the law until all is accomplished. Whoever then relaxes one of the least of these commandments and teaches men so, shall be called least in the kingdom of heaven; but he who does them and teaches them shall be called great in the kingdom of heaven. For I tell you, unless your righteousness exceeds that of the scribes and Pharisees, you will never enter the kingdom of heaven.

"You have heard that it was said to the men of old, 'You shall not kill; and whoever kills shall be liable to judgment.' But I say to you that every one who is angry with his brother shall be liable to judgment; whoever insults his brother shall be liable to the council, and whoever says, 'You fool!' shall be liable to the hell of fire. So if you are offering your gift at the altar, and there remember that your brother has something against you, leave your gift there before the altar and go; first be reconciled to your brother, and then come and offer your gift. Make friends quickly with your accuser, while you are going with him to court, lest your accuser hand you over to the judge, and the judge to the guard, and you be put in prison; truly, I

say to you, you will never get out till you have paid the last penny.

"You have heard that it was said, 'You shall not commit adultery.' But I say to you that every one who looks at 15 a woman lustfully has already committed adultery with her in his heart. If your right eye causes you to sin, pluck it out and throw it away; it is better that you lose one of your members than that your whole body be thrown into hell. And if your right hand causes you to sin, cut it off and throw it away; it is better that you lose one of your members than that your whole body go into hell.

"It was also said, 'Whoever divorces his wife, let him give her a certificate of divorce.' But I say to you that every one who divorces his wife, except on the ground of unchastity, makes her an adulteress; and whoever marries a divorced woman commits adultery.

"Again you have heard that it was said to the men of old, 'You shall not swear falsely, but shall perform to the Lord what you have sworn.' But I say to you, Do not swear at all, either by heaven, for it is the throne of God, or by the earth, for it is his footstool, or by Jerusalem, for it is the city of the great King. And do not swear by your head, for you cannot make one hair white or black. Let what you say be simply 'Yes' or 'No'; anything more than this comes from evil.

"You have heard that it was said, 'An eye for an eye and a tooth for a tooth.' But I say to you, Do not resist one who is evil. But if any one strikes you on the right cheek, turn to him the other also; and if any one would sue you and take your coat, let him have your cloak as well; and if any one forces you to go one mile, go with him two miles. Give to him who begs from you, and do not refuse him who would borrow from you.

"You have heard that it was said, 'You shall love your neighbor and hate your enemy.' But I say to you, Love your enemies and pray for those who persecute you, so that you may be sons of your Father who is in heaven; for he makes his sun rise on the evil and on the good, and sends rain on the just and on the unjust. For if you love those who love you, what reward have you? Do not even the tax collectors do the same? And if you salute only your brethren, what more are you doing than others? Do not even the Gentiles do the same? You, therefore, must be perfect, as your heavenly Father is perfect.

6

"Beware of practicing your piety before men in order to be 1 seen by them; for then you will have no reward from your Father who is in heaven.

"Thus, when you give alms, sound no trumpet before you, as the hypocrites do in the synagogues and in the streets, that they may be praised by men. Truly, I say to you, they have their reward. But when you give alms, do not let your left hand know what your right hand is doing, so that your alms may be in secret; and your Father who sees in secret will reward you.

"And when you pray, you must not be like the hypocrites; for they love to stand and pray in the synagogues and at the street corners, that they may be seen by men. Truly, I say to you, they have their reward. But when you pray, go into your room and shut the door and pray to your Father who is in secret; and your Father who sees in secret will reward you.

"And in praying do not heap up empty phrases as the Gentiles do; for they think that they will be heard for their many words. Do not be like them, for your Father knows what you need before you ask him. Pray then like this:

> Our Father who art in heaven,
> Hallowed be thy name.
> Thy kingdom come,
> Thy will be done,
>   On earth as it is in heaven.
> Give us this day our daily bread;
> And forgive us our debts,
>   As we also have forgiven our debtors;
> And lead us not into temptation
>   But deliver us from evil.

For if you forgive men their trespasses, your heavenly Father also will forgive you; but if you do not forgive men their trespasses, neither will your Father forgive your trespasses.

"And when you fast, do not look dismal, like the hypocrites, for they disfigure their faces that their fasting may be seen by men. Truly, I say to you, they have their reward. But when you fast, anoint your head and wash your face, that your fasting may not be seen by men but by your Father who is in secret; and your Father who sees in secret will reward you.

"Do not lay up for yourselves treasures on earth, where moth and rust consume and where thieves break in and steal, but lay up for yourselves treasures in heaven, where neither moth nor rust consumes and where thieves do not break in and steal. For where your treasure is, there will your heart be also.

"The eye is the lamp of the body. So, if your eye is sound, your whole body will be full of light; but if your eye is not sound, your whole body will be full of darkness. If then the light in you is darkness, how great is the darkness!

"No one can serve two masters; for either he will hate the one and love the other, or he will be devoted to the one and despise the other. You cannot serve God and mammon.

"Therefore I tell you, do not be anxious about your life, what you shall eat or what you shall drink, nor about your body, what you shall put on. Is not life more than food, and the body more than clothing? Look at the birds of the air: they neither sow nor reap nor gather into barns, and yet your heavenly Father feeds them. Are you not of more value than they? And which of you by being anxious can add one cubit to his span of life? And why are you anxious about clothing? Consider the lilies of the field, how they grow; they neither toil nor spin; yet I tell you,

even Solomon in all his glory was not arrayed like one of these. But if God so clothes the grass of the field, which today is alive and tomorrow is thrown into the oven, will he not much more clothe you, O men of little faith? Therefore do not be anxious, saying, 'What shall we eat?' or 'What shall we drink?' or 'What shall we wear?' For the Gentiles seek all these things; and your heavenly Father knows that you need them all. But seek first his kingdom and his righteousness, and all these things shall be yours as well.

"Therefore do not be anxious about tomorrow, for tomorrow will be anxious for itself. Let the day's own trouble be sufficient for the day.

7

"Judge not, that you be not judged. For with the judgment you pronounce you will be judged, and the measure you give will be the measure you get. Why do you see the speck that is in your brother's eye, but do not notice the log that is in your own eye? Or how can you say to your brother, 'Let me take the speck out of your eye,' when there is the log in your own eye? You hypocrite, first take the log out of your own eye, and then you will see clearly to take the speck out of your brother's eye.

"Do not give dogs what is holy; and do not throw your pearls before swine, lest they trample them underfoot and turn to attack you.

"Ask, and it will be given you; seek and you will find; knock, and it will be opened to you. For every one who asks receives, and he who seeks finds, and to him who knocks it will be opened. Or what man of you, if his son asks him for a loaf, will give him a stone? Or if he asks for a fish, will give him a serpent? If you then, who are evil, know how to give good gifts to your children, how much more will your Father who is in heaven give good things to those who ask him? So whatever you wish that men would do to you, do so to them; for this is the law and the prophets.

"Enter by the narrow gate; for the gate is wide and the way is easy, that leads to destruction, and those who enter by it are many. For the gate is narrow and the way is hard, that leads to life, and those who find it are few.

"Beware of false prophets, who come to you in sheep's clothing but inwardly are ravenous wolves. You will know them by their fruits. Are grapes gathered from thorns, or figs from thistles? So, every sound tree bears good fruit, but the bad tree bears evil fruit. A sound tree cannot bear evil fruit, nor can a bad tree bear good fruit. Every tree that does not bear good fruit is cut down and thrown into the fire. Thus you will know them by their fruits.

"Not every one who says to me, 'Lord, Lord,' shall enter the kingdom of heaven, but he who does the will of my Father who is in heaven. On that day many will say to me, 'Lord, Lord, did we not prophesy in your name, and cast out demons in your name, and do many mighty works in your name?' And then will I declare to them, 'I never knew you; depart from me, you evildoers.'

"Every one then who hears these words of mine and does them will be like a wise man who built his house upon the rock; and the rain fell, and the floods came, and the winds blew and beat upon that house, but it did not fall, because it had been founded on the rock. And every one who hears these words of mine and does not do them will be like a foolish man who built his house upon the sand; and the rain fell, and the floods came, and the winds blew and beat against that house, and it fell; and great was the fall of it."

And when Jesus finished these sayings, the crowds were astonished at his teaching, for he taught them as one who had authority, and not as their scribes.

—⁓—

1 Corinthians
13:1–13

13

If I speak in the tongues of men and of angels, but have not ₁ love, I am a noisy gong or a clanging cymbal. And if I have prophetic powers, and understand all mysteries and all knowledge, and if I have all faith, so as to remove mountains, but have not love, I am nothing. If I give away all I have, and if I deliver my body to be burned, but have not love, I gain nothing.

Love is patient and kind; love is not jealous or boastful; it is not arrogant or rude. Love does not insist on its own way; it is not irritable or resentful; it does not rejoice at wrong, but rejoices in the right. Love bears all things, believes all things, hopes all things, endures all things.

Love never ends; as for prophecy, it will pass away; as for tongues, they will cease; as for knowledge, it will pass away. For our knowledge is imperfect and our prophecy is imperfect; but when the perfect comes, the imperfect will pass away. When I was a child, I spoke like a child, I thought like a child, I reasoned like a child; when I became a man, I gave up childish ways. For now we see in a mirror dimly, but then face to face. Now I know in part; then I shall understand fully, even as I have been fully understood. So faith, hope, love abide, these three; but the greatest of these is love.

LATE ROMAN CIVILIZATION

ST. AUGUSTINE

Selections from *Confessions* and *The City of God*

St. Augustine (A.D. 354–430) is one of the West's great bridge figures who appear at disjunctures in time and whose mission seems to be to culminate one phase of civilization and point history on a new path. St. Augustine, who lived in the final days of the western Roman Empire (A.D. 476 is the traditional date of its fall), functioned as a bridge between the dying Classical era and the embryonic Christian world. Born in north Africa to a Christian mother (Monica) and pagan father, he was a pagan himself until he joined Christianity at age thirty-three. Later, he became Bishop of Hippo, an ancient city near his birthplace; from that post, through his vast writings, he dominated the Roman world for almost thirty-five years. Fusing his knowledge of Greco-Roman philosophy, especially Platonism (see *The Republic, Phaedo*) and Neoplatonism, with his understanding of Christian beliefs, he developed a theology now called Augustinianism. This theology provided a justification for a religious-centered world—the intellectual framework in which the Christian church operated until about 1300. A controversialist who wrote on every major Christian topic of his day, including original sin, salvation, and God and history, he became an authoritative voice whose influence is still active in Catholic theology.

St. Augustine was possessed of a ferocious vision that saw life on earth as a vale of tears through which humanity must travel. The true meaning of existence would be unveiled in a heavenly future. Within this vale of tears, St. Augustine did not sit idly on the sidelines; he actively engaged in the intellectual wars that consumed this age. Reflecting his self-ascribed natural combativeness, he had, before turning Christian, subscribed for nine years to Manicheanism, a religion that viewed the world as locked in a gigantic struggle between the forces of good and the forces of evil. He relished acrimonious quarrels, notably with fellow churchmen who differed from him on difficult points in theology. A prolific author, he wrote many pamphlets, letters, and essays that belong to Christian theology, as well as two classics of world literature: the *Confessions*, his personal memoirs; and *The City of God*, his Christian-inspired philosophy of history.

Reading the Selection from Confessions

Prior to Book VIII of the *Confessions*, St. Augustine recounted his youth, education, and above all, his search for a final truth, whether philosophical or religious. What fueled his personal search was his longing to feel moral, to gain relief from the guilt that had dogged him since youth, stemming from such sins as stealing pears and, in the main, consorting with mistresses. He often found solutions to his quest in, for example, the writings of Cicero (see *On the Republic*) or the dualistic religion of the Manichees; however, none of these could finally quench his restless spirit.

Book VIII of the *Confessions* concludes Augustine's quest with his conversion to Christianity. The heart of his conversion story occurs in Chapter 12: He hears a child's voice urging him to "Take it and read," a message he interprets as being from God, encouraging him to read at random in the Bible. He follows this mystical advice, and the first passage to greet his eyes is from a letter of Paul's. While reading the passage, St. Augustine feels flooded with light, and his earlier darkness falls away. Now, as a Christian convert, he hurries to tell his mother, who is overjoyed to learn that God has answered her prayers.

Reading the Selections from **The City of God**

In A.D. 410 the Visigoths, a tribe of German invaders, sacked Rome, a calamity that had happened only once before (in about 400 B.C.) in the city's eleven-hundred-year history. Pagans blamed this most recent calamity on, in their eyes, the weak Christian God. To counter this pagan charge, Augustine wrote *The City of God* and in the process also fleshed out a philosophy of history, that was highly influential throughout the Middle Ages.

The City of God numbers about a thousand pages, divided into twenty-two books. Books I through X recount Rome's history and summarize pagan philosophical and religious arguments against Christian beliefs. In Books XI through XXII, Augustine sets forth his main theme about the City of Man and the City of God, which constitutes a belief in predestination: The citizens of the City of Man are doomed to hell, and the citizens of the City of God are destined for heaven.

In Book XIV, Augustine asserts that the two cities may be distinguished from one another by their origins, the City of Man being born of self-love and the City of God from God's love. In Book XIX, Augustine describes the inescapable miseries—in particular, war—that plague the City of Man. Chapter 17 (of Book XIX) points out that the two cities may coexist, except in regard to religious laws. Perhaps fearing a pagan resurgence, which might overthrow Christian dominance of Rome, Augustine maintained that the City of Man and the City of God should *not* have the same religious laws. Here, Augustine laid down the principle of separation of church and state, an issue that became a battleground in medieval Europe and about which skirmishes are still being fought.

—⁓—

Confessions

Book VIII

10

There are many abroad who talk of their own fantasies and lead men's minds astray. They assert that because they have observed that there are two wills at odds with each other when we try to reach a decision, we must therefore have two minds of different natures, one good, the other evil. *Let them vanish at God's presence as the smoke vanishes.* As long as they hold these evil beliefs they are evil themselves, but even they will be good if they see the truth and accept it, so that your apostle may say to them *Once you were all darkness; now, in the Lord you are all daylight.* These people want to be light, not in the Lord, but in themselves, because they think that the nature of the soul is the same as God. In this way their darkness becomes denser still, because in their abominable arrogance they have separated themselves still further from you, who are *the true*

Light which enlightens every soul born into the world. I say to them, 'Take care what you say, and blush for shame. Enter God's presence, and find their enlightenment; *here is no room for downcast looks.*'

When I was trying to reach a decision about serving the Lord my God, as I had long intended to do, it was I who willed to take this course and again it was I who willed not to take it. It was I and I alone. But I neither willed to do it nor refused to do it with my full will. So I was at odds with myself. I was throwing myself into confusion. All this happened to me although I did not want it, but it did not prove that there was some second mind in me besides my own. It only meant that my mind was being punished. *My action did not come from me, but from the sinful principle that dwells in me.* It was part of the punishment of a sin freely committed by Adam, my first father.

If there were as many different natures in us as there are conflicting wills, we should have a great many more natures than merely two. Suppose that someone is trying to decide whether to go to the theatre or to the Manichees' meeting-house. The Manichees will say, 'Clearly he has two natures, the good one bringing him here to us and the bad one leading him away. Otherwise, how can you explain this dilemma of two opposing wills?' I say that the will to attend their meetings is just as bad as the will to go off to the theatre, but in their opinion it can only be a good will that leads a man to come to them. Suppose then that one of us is wavering between two conflicting wills and cannot make up his mind whether to go to the theatre or to our church. Will not the Manichees be embarrassed to know what to say? Either they must admit—which they will not do—that it is a good will which brings a man to our church, just as in their opinion it is a good will which brings their own communicants and adherents to their church; or they must presume that there are two evil natures and two evil minds in conflict in one man. If they think this, they will disprove their own theory that there is one good and one evil will in man. The only alternative is for them to be converted to the truth and to cease to deny that when a man tries to make a decision, he has one soul which is torn between conflicting wills.

So let us hear no more of their assertion, when they observe two wills in conflict in one man, that there are two opposing minds in him, one good and the other bad, and that they are in conflict because they spring from two opposing substances and two opposing principles. For you, O God of truth, prove that they are utterly wrong. You demolish their arguments and confound them completely. It may be that both the wills are bad. For instance, a man may be trying to decide whether to commit murder by poison or by stabbing; whether he should swindle another man out of one part of his property or another, that is, if he cannot obtain both; whether he should spend his money extravagantly on pleasure or hoard it like a miser; or whether he should go to the games in the circus or to the theatre, when there is a performance at both places on the same day. In this case there may be a third possibility, that he should go and rob another person's house, if he has the chance. There may even be a fourth choice open to him, because he may wonder whether to go and commit adultery, if the occasion arises at the same time. These possibilities may all occur at the same moment and all may seem equally desirable. The man cannot do all these things at once, and his mind is torn between four wills which cannot be reconciled—perhaps more than four, because there are a great many things that he might wish to do. But the Manichees do not claim that there are as many different substances in us as this.

It is just the same when the wills are good. If I question the Manichees whether it is good to find pleasure in reading Paul's Epistles or in the tranquil enjoyment of a Psalm or in a discussion of the Gospel, they will reply in each case that it is good. Supposing, then, that a man finds all these things equally attractive and the chance to do all of them occurs at the same time, is it not true that as long as he cannot make up his mind which of them he most

wants to do his heart is torn between several different desires? All these different desires are good, yet they are in conflict with each other until he chooses a single course to which the will may apply itself as a single whole, so that it is no longer split into several different wills.

The same is true when the higher part of our nature aspires after eternal bliss while our lower self is held back by the love of temporal pleasure. It is the same soul that wills both, but it wills neither of them with the full force of the will. So it is wrenched in two and suffers great trials, because while truth teaches it to prefer one course, habit prevents it from relinquishing the other.

11

This was the nature of my sickness. I was in torment, reproaching myself more bitterly than ever as I twisted and turned in my chain. I hoped that my chain might be broken once and for all, because it was only a small thing that held me now. All the same it held me. And you, O Lord, never ceased to watch over my secret heart. In your stern mercy you lashed me with the twin scourge of fear and shame in case I should give way once more and the worn and slender remnant of my chain should not be broken but gain new strength and bind me all the faster. In my heart I kept saying 'Let it be now, let it be now!', and merely by saying this I was on the point of making the resolution. I was on the point of making it, but I did not succeed. Yet I did not fall back into my old state. I stood on the brink of resolution, waiting to take fresh breath. I tried again and came a little nearer to my goal, and then a little nearer still, so that I could almost reach out and grasp it. But I did not reach it. I could not reach out to it or grasp it, because I held back from the step by which I should die to death and become alive to life. My lower instincts, which had taken firm hold of me, were stronger than the higher, which were untried. And the closer I came to the moment which was to mark the great change in me, the more I shrank from its horror. But it did not drive me back or turn me from my purpose: it merely left me hanging in suspense.

I was held back by mere trifles, the most paltry inanities, all my old attachments. They plucked at my garment of flesh and whispered, 'Are you going to dismiss us? From this moment we shall never be with you again, for ever and ever. From this moment you will never again be allowed to do this thing or that, for evermore.' What was it, my God, that they meant when they whispered 'this thing or that'? Things so sordid and so shameful that I beg you in your mercy to keep the soul of your servant free from them! These voices, as I heard them, seemed less than half as loud as they had been before. They no longer barred my way, blatantly contradictory, but their mutterings seemed to reach me from behind, as though they were stealthily plucking at my back, trying to make me turn my head when I wanted to go forward. Yet, in my state of indecision, they kept me from tearing myself away, from shaking myself free of them and leaping across the barrier to the other side, where you were calling me. Habit was too strong for me when it asked 'Do you think you can live without these things?'

But by now the voice of habit was very faint. I had turned my eyes elsewhere, and while I stood trembling at the barrier, on the other side I could see the chaste beauty of Continence in all her serene, unsullied joy, as she modestly beckoned me to cross over and to hesitate no more. She stretched out loving hands to welcome and embrace me, holding up a host of good examples to my sight. With her were countless boys and girls, great numbers of the young and people of all ages, staid widows and women still virgins in old age. And in their midst was Continence herself, not barren but a fruitful mother of children, of joys born of you, O Lord, her Spouse. She smiled at me to give me courage, as though she were saying, 'Can you not do what these men and these women do? Do you think they find the strength to do it in themselves and not in the Lord their God? It was the Lord their God who gave me to them. Why do you try to stand in your own strength and fail? Cast yourself upon God and have no fear. He will not shrink away and let you fall. Cast yourself upon him without fear, for he will welcome you and cure you of your ills.' I was overcome with shame, because I was still listening to the futile mutterings of my lower self and I was still hanging in suspense. And again Continence seemed to say, 'Close your eyes to the unclean whispers of your body, so that it may be mortified. It tells you of things that delight you, but not such things as the law of the Lord your God has to tell.'

In this way I wrangled with myself, in my own heart, about my own self. And all the while Alypius stayed at my side, silently awaiting the outcome of this agitation that was new in me.

12

I probed the hidden depths of my soul and wrung its pitiful secrets from it, and when I mustered them all before the eyes of my heart, a great storm broke within me, bringing with it a great deluge of tears. I stood up and left Alypius so that I might weep and cry to my heart's content, for it occurred to me that tears were best shed in solitude. I moved away far enough to avoid being embarrassed even by his presence. He must have realized what my feelings were, for I suppose I had said something and he had known from the sound of my voice that I was ready to burst into tears. So I stood up and left him where we had been sitting, utterly bewildered. Somehow I flung myself down beneath a fig tree and gave way to the tears which now streamed from my eyes, the sacrifice that is acceptable to you. I had much to say to you, my God, not in these very words but in this strain: *Lord, will you never be content? Must we always taste your vengeance? Forget the long record of our sins.* For I felt that I was still the captive of my sins, and in my misery I kept crying 'How long shall I go on saying "tomorrow, tomorrow"? Why not now? Why not make an end of my ugly sins at this moment?'

I was asking myself these questions, weeping all the while with the most bitter sorrow in my heart, when all at once I heard the sing-song voice of a child in a nearby house. Whether it was the voice of a boy or a girl I cannot say, but again and again it repeated the refrain 'Take it and read, take it and read.' At this I looked up, thinking hard whether there was any kind of game in which children used to chant words like these, but I could not remember ever hearing them before. I stemmed my flood of tears and stood up, telling myself that this could only be a divine command to open my book of Scripture and read the first passage on which my eyes should fall. For I had heard the story of Antony, and I remembered how he had happened to go into a church while the Gospel was being read and had taken it as a counsel addressed to himself when he heard the words *Go home and sell all that belongs to you. Give it to the poor, and so the treasure you have shall be in heaven; then come back and follow me.* By this divine pronouncement he had at once been converted to you.

So I hurried back to the place where Alypius was sitting, for when I stood up to move away I had put down the book containing Paul's Epistles. I seized it and opened it, and in silence I read the first passage on which my eyes fell: *Not in revelling and drunkenness, not in lust and wantonness, not in quarrels and rivalries. Rather, arm yourselves with the Lord Jesus Christ; spend no more thought on nature and nature's appetites.* I had no wish to read more and no need to do so. For in an instant, as I came to the end of the sentence, it was as though the light of confidence flooded into my heart and all the darkness of doubt was dispelled.

I marked the place with my finger or by some other sign and closed the book. My looks now were quite calm as I told Alypius what had happened to me. He too told me what he had been feeling, which of course I did not know. He asked to see what I had read. I showed it to him and he read on beyond the text which I had read. I did not know what followed, but it was this: *Find room among you for a man of over-delicate conscience.* Alypius applied this to himself and told me so. This admonition was enough to give him strength, and without suffering the distress of hesitation he made his resolution and took this good purpose to himself. And it very well suited his moral character, which had long been far, far better than my own.

Then we went in and told my mother, who was overjoyed. And when we went on to describe how it had all happened, she was jubilant with triumph and glorified you, *who are powerful enough, and more than powerful enough, to carry out your purpose beyond all our hopes and dreams.* For she saw that you had granted her far more than she used to ask in her tearful prayers and plaintive lamentations. You converted me to yourself, so that I no longer desired a wife or placed any hope in this world but stood firmly upon the rule of faith, where you had shown me to her in a dream so many years before. And you *turned her sadness into rejoicing,* into joy far fuller than her dearest wish, far sweeter and more chaste than any she had hoped to find in children begotten of my flesh.

The City of God

Book XIV

Chapter 28
The Character of the Two Cities

We see then that the two cities were created by two kinds of love: the earthly city was created by self-love reaching the point of contempt for God, the Heavenly City by the love of God carried as far as contempt of self. In fact, the earthly city glories in itself, the Heavenly City glories in the Lord. The former looks for glory from men, the latter finds its highest glory in God, the witness of a good conscience. The earthly lifts up its head in its own glory, the Heavenly City says to its God: 'My glory; you lift up my head.' In the former, the lust for domination lords it over its princes as over the nations it subjugates; in the other both those put in authority and those subject to them serve one another in love, the rulers by their counsel, the subjects by obedience. The one city loves its own strength shown in its powerful leaders; the other says to its God, 'I will love you, my Lord, my strength.'

Consequently, in the earthly city its wise men who live by men's standards have pursued the goods of the body or of their own mind, or of both. Or those of them who were able to know God 'did not honour him as God, nor did they give thanks to him, but they dwindled into futility in their thoughts, and their senseless heart was darkened: in asserting their wisdom'—that is, exalting themselves in their wisdom, under the domination of pride—'they became foolish, and changed the glory of the imperishable God into an image representing a perishable man, or birds or beasts or reptiles'— for in the adoration of idols of this kind they were either leaders or followers of the general public—'and they worshipped and served created things instead of the Creator, who is blessed for ever.' In the Heavenly City, on the other hand, man's only wisdom is the devotion which rightly worships the true God, and looks for its reward in the fellowship of the saints, not only holy men but also holy angels, 'so that God may be all in all'.

Book XV

Chapter 4
Conflict and Peace in the Earthly City

The earthly city will not be everlasting; for when it is condemned to the final punishment it will no longer be a city. It has its good in this world, and rejoices to participate in it with such gladness as can be derived from things of such a kind. And since this is not the kind of good that causes no frustrations to those enamoured of it, the earthly city is generally divided against itself by litigation, by wars, by battles, by the pursuit of victories that bring death with them or at best are doomed to death. For if any section of that city has risen up in war against another part, it seeks to be victorious over other nations, though it is itself the slave of base passions; and if, when victorious, it is exalted in its arrogance, that victory brings death in its train. Whereas if it considers the human condition and the changes and chances common to mankind, and is more tormented by possible misfortunes than puffed up by its present success, then its victory is only doomed to death. For it will not be able to lord it permanently over those whom it has been able to subdue victoriously.

However, it would be incorrect to say that the goods which this city desires are not goods, since even that city is better, in its own human way, by their possession. For example, that city desires an earthly peace, for the sake of the lowest goods; and it is that peace which it longs to attain by making war. For if it wins the war and no one survives to resist, then there will be peace, which the warring sections did not enjoy when they contended in their unhappy poverty for the things which they could not both possess at the same time. This peace is the aim of wars, with all their hardships; it is this peace that glorious victory (so called) achieves.

Now when the victory goes to those who were fighting for the juster cause, can anyone doubt that the victory is a matter for rejoicing and the resulting peace is something to be desired? These things are goods and undoubtedly they are gifts of God. But if the higher goods are neglected, which belong to the City on high, where victory will be serene in the enjoyment of eternal and perfect peace—if these goods are neglected and those other goods are so desired as to be considered the only goods, or are loved more than the goods which are believed to be higher, the inevitable consequence is fresh misery, and an increase of the wretchedness already there.

—𝑚—

Book XIX

Chapter 7
Human Society Divided by Differences of Language.
The Misery of War, Even When Just

After the city or town comes the world, which the philosophers reckon as the third level of human society. They
begin with the household, proceed to the city, and then arrive at the world. Now the world, being like a confluence
of waters, is obviously more full of danger than the other
communities by reason of its greater size. To begin with,
on this level the diversity of languages separates man
from man. For if two men meet, and are forced by some
compelling reason not to pass on but to stay in company,
then if neither knows the other's language, it is easier for
dumb animals, even of different kinds, to associate together than these men, although both are human beings.
For when men cannot communicate their thoughts to each
other, simply because of difference of language, all the
similarity of their common nature is of no avail to unite
them in fellowship. So true is this that the man would be
more cheerful with his dog for company than with a foreigner. I shall be told that the Imperial City has been at
pains to impose on conquered peoples not only her yoke
but her language also, as a bond of peace and fellowship,
so that there should be no lack of interpreters but even a
profusion of them. True; but think of the cost of this
achievement! Consider the scale of those wars, with all
that slaughter of human beings, all the human blood that
was shed!

Those wars are now past history; and yet the misery
of these evils is not yet ended. For although there has been,
and still is, no lack of enemies among foreign nations,
against whom wars have always been waged, and are still
being waged, yet the very extent of the Empire has given
rise to wars of a worse kind, namely, social and civil wars,
by which mankind is more lamentably disquieted either
when fighting is going on in the hope of bringing hostilities eventually to a peaceful end, or when there are fears
that hostilities will break out again. If I were to try to describe, with an eloquence worthy of the subject, the many
and multifarious disasters, the dour and dire necessities, I
could not possibly be adequate to the theme, and there
would be no end to this protracted discussion. But the
wise man, they say, will wage just wars. Surely, if he remembers that he is a human being, he will rather lament
the fact that he is faced with the necessity of waging just
wars; for if they were not just, he would not have to engage in them, and consequently there would be no wars
for a wise man. For it is the injustice of the opposing side
that lays on the wise man the duty of waging wars; and
this injustice is assuredly to be deplored by a human
being, since it is the injustice of human beings, even
though no necessity for war should arise from it. And so
everyone who reflects with sorrow on such grievous evils,
in all their horror and cruelty, must acknowledge the misery of them. And yet a man who experiences such evils,
or even thinks about them, without heartfelt grief, is
assuredly in a far more pitiable condition, if he thinks himself happy simply because he has lost all human feeling.

Chapter 8
The Friendship of Good Men Can Never Be Carefree,
Because of This Life's Dangers

If we are spared that kind of ignorance, akin to madness,
which is a common affliction in the wretched condition
of this life, an ignorance which leads men to believe an
enemy to be a friend, or a friend an enemy, what consolation have we in this human society, so replete with
mistaken notions and distressing anxieties, except the un-
feigned faith and mutual affections of genuine, loyal
friends? Yet the more friends we have and the more dispersed they are in different places, the further and more
widely extend our fears that some evil may befall them
from among all the mass of evils of this present world. For
not only are we troubled and anxious because they may be
afflicted by famine, war, disease, or captivity, fearing that
in slavery they may suffer evils beyond our powers of
imagination; there is the much more bitter fear, that their
friendship be changed into treachery, malice and baseness.
And when such things do happen (and the more numerous our friends, the more often they happen) and the news
is brought to our ears, who, except one who has this experience, can be aware of the burning sorrow that ravages
our hearts? Certainly we would rather hear that our
friends were dead, although this also we could not hear
without grief.

For if their life brought us the consoling delights of
friendship, how could it be that their death should bring
us no sadness? Anyone who forbids such sadness must
forbid, if he can, all friendly conversation, must lay a ban
on all friendly feeling or put a stop to it, must with a ruthless insensibility break the ties of all human relationships,
or else decree that they must only be engaged upon so
long as they inspire no delight in a man's soul. But if this is
beyond all possibility, how can it be that a man's death
should not be bitter if his life is sweet to us? For this is why
the grief of a heart that has not lost human feeling is a
thing like some wound or ulcer, and our friendly words of
consolation are the healing application. And it does not
follow that there is nothing to be healed simply because
the nobler a man's spirit the quicker and easier the cure.

It is true, then, that the life of mortals is afflicted,
sometimes more gently, sometimes more harshly, by the
death of those most dear to us, and especially the death of
those whose functions are necessary for human society;
and yet we should prefer to hear, or even to witness, the
death of those we love, than to become aware that they
have fallen from faith or from moral conflict—that is, that

they have died in their very soul. The earth is full of this vast mass of evils; that is why we find this in Scripture: 'Is man's life on earth anything but temptation?' And why the Lord himself says, 'Alas for the world, because of these obstacles'; and again, 'Because iniquity will increase beyond measure, the love of many will grow cold.' The result of this situation is that when good men die who are our friends we rejoice for them; and though their death brings us sadness, we find our surer consolation in this, that they have been spared those evils by which in this life even good men are crushed or corrupted, or at least are in danger of both these disasters.

Chapter 17
The Origin of Peace Between the Heavenly Society and the Earthly City, and of Discord Between Them

But a household of human beings whose life is not based on faith is in pursuit of an earthly peace based on the things belonging to this temporal life, and on its advantages, whereas a household of human beings whose life is based on faith looks forward to the blessings which are promised as eternal in the future, making use of earthly and temporal things like a pilgrim in a foreign land, who does not let himself be taken in by them or distracted from his course towards God, but rather treats them as supports which help him more easily to bear the burdens of 'the corruptible body which weighs heavy on the soul'; they must on no account be allowed to increase the load. Thus both kinds of men and both kinds of households alike make use of the things essential for this mortal life; but each has its own very different end in making use of them. So also the earthly city, whose life is not based on faith, aims at an earthly peace, and it limits the harmonious agreement of citizens concerning the giving and obeying of orders to the establishment of a kind of compromise between human wills about the things relevant to mortal life. In contrast, the Heavenly City—or rather that part of it which is on pilgrimage in this condition of mortality, and which lives on the basis of faith—must needs make use of this peace also, until this mortal state, for which this kind of peace is essential, passes away. And therefore, it leads what we may call a life of captivity in this earthly city as in a foreign land, although it has already received the promise of redemption, and the gift of the Spirit as a kind of pledge of it; and yet it does not hesitate to obey the laws of the earthly city by which those things which are designed for the support of this mortal life are regulated; and the purpose of this obedience is that, since this mortal condition is shared by both cities, a harmony may be preserved between them in things that are relevant to this condition.

But this earthly city has had some philosophers belonging to it whose theories are rejected by the teaching inspired by God. Either led astray by their own speculation or deluded by demons, these thinkers reached the belief that there are many gods who must be won over to serve human ends, and also that they have, as it were, different departments with different responsibilities attached. Thus the body is the department of one god, the mind that of another; and within the body itself, one god is in charge of the head, another of the neck and so on with each of the separate members. Similarly, within the mind, one is responsible for natural ability, another for learning, another for anger, another for lust; and in the accessories of life there are separate gods over the departments of flocks, grain, wine, oil, forests, coinage, navigation, war and victory, marriage, birth, fertility, and so on. The Heavenly City, in contrast, knows only one God as the object of worship, and decrees, with faithful devotion, that he only is to be served with that service which the Greeks call *latreia*, which is due to God alone. And the result of this difference has been that the Heavenly City could not have laws of religion common with the earthly city, and in defence of her religious laws she was bound to dissent from those who thought differently and to prove a burdensome nuisance to them. Thus she had to endure their anger and hatred, and the assaults of persecution; until at length that City shattered the morale of her adversaries by the terror inspired by her numbers, and by the help she continually received from God.

While this Heavenly City, therefore, is on pilgrimage in this world, she calls out citizens from all nations and so collects a society of aliens, speaking all languages. She takes on account of any difference in customs, laws, and institutions, by which earthly peace is achieved and preserved—not that she annuls or abolishes any of those, rather, she maintains them and follows them (for whatever divergences there are among the diverse nations, those institutions have one single aim—earthly peace), provided that no hindrance is presented thereby to the religion which teaches that the one supreme and true God is to be worshipped. Thus even the Heavenly City in her pilgrimage here on earth makes use of the earthly peace and defends and seeks the compromise between human wills in respect of the provisions relevant to the mortal nature of man, so far as may be permitted without detriment to true religion and piety. In fact, that City relates the earthly peace to the heavenly peace, which is so truly peaceful that it should be regarded as the only peace deserving the name, at least in respect of the rational creation; for this peace is the perfectly ordered and completely harmonious fellowship in the enjoyment of God, and of each other in God. When we arrive at that state of peace, there will be no longer a life that ends in death, but a life that is life in sure and sober truth; there will be no animal body to 'weigh down the soul' in its process of corruption; there will be a spiritual body with no cravings, a body subdued in every part to the will. This peace the Heavenly City possesses in faith while on its pilgrimage, and it lives a life of righteousness, based on this faith, having the attainment of that peace in view in every good action it performs in relation to God, and in relation to a neighbour, since the life of a city is inevitably a social life.

EUSEBIUS

Selections from *The History of the Church*

Eusebius of Caesarea (about 260–340) wrote a history of the Christian church that covered events from its founding by Christ to the time of Constantine (r. 306–337), the first Christian Roman emperor. Since Eusebius believed that God operated in human affairs and that the future belonged to the Christians, he concluded that a history of the spread of Christianity would disseminate these beliefs to a wider audience. He meant this didactic book for fellow Christians, but he also had in mind Rome's educated elite, most of whom were pagan when he wrote. Recognized today as the "founder of ecclesiastical history," Eusebius set the standard for church history until the Renaissance, when modern research methods, with their human-centered outlook and concern for scientific accuracy, rendered his pious type of history obsolete. Still, his account remains a classic, for it is one of the main sources for events and historical figures in the first years of Christianity.

Eusebius was probably born in Caesarea, in Palestine, an early Christian center under Roman rule. As a young man, he was mentored by Pamphilus, a devout and classically trained Christian whose school awakened Eusebius to the challenge of reconciling Christian thought with Greco-Roman learning. With Pamphilus, he wrote several books—all since lost—with Christian themes. Because of his beliefs, he was imprisoned in 309 and 311 in Rome's empirewide assault on Christianity and its leaders. But in 314 he was made Bishop of Caesarea, a step that reflected Rome's changed policy toward Christians coincident with Constantine's conversion in 312. As Bishop of Caesarea, Eusebius himself baptized the pagan emperor into the new faith. Favored by Constantine, Eusebius grew in reputation to become one of the era's outstanding Christians, playing important roles at the historic Council of Nicaea and other church gatherings.

The History of the Church, arranged in ten books, was written over a sixteen-year period, a time frame based on internal evidence, such as mentions of historic events datable from other sources. Begun during the Great Persecution in 309, this history was completed in 325, when Constantine was presiding over a Christianized imperial court and Eusebius was one of its ornaments. Eusebius's plan for the book embraced a wide range of topics; namely, tracing the "lines of succession" of the first apostles, telling the stories of early Christian leaders, exposing heretics, detailing the calamities suffered by the Jews because of their treatment of Jesus, setting forth Rome's final assault on the Christian faith, and paying homage to the martyrs whose blood was "the seed of the church," in the words of another early Christian writer, Tertullian (about 160–about 230).

Reading the Selections

These passages from Eusebius's work show his method of writing God-centered history. Focusing on a person or event as a framing device, he creates a historical snapshot and at the same time stresses his belief in God's presence everywhere. For example, the treatment of the executions of Peter and Paul dwells on both their martyrdom and the folly of the Emperor Nero, "the first to be heralded as a conspicuous fighter against God." Just so, the narrative of the Great Persecution blends details of Roman atrocities with a moving account of Christians willingly facing martyrdom. Finally, Constantine's triumph is described, although Eusebius makes it clear that the result was because of God, "in fulfillment of His purpose."

The Neronian Persecution, in Which Paul and Peter Died

When Nero's power was now firmly established he gave himself up to unholy practices and took up arms against the God of the universe. To describe the monster of depravity that he became lies outside the scope of the present work. Many writers have recorded the facts about him in minute detail, enabling anyone who wishes to get a complete picture of his perverse and extraordinary madness, which led him to the senseless destruction of innumerable lives, and drove him in the end to such a lust for blood that he did not spare even his nearest and dearest but employed a variety of methods to do away with mother, brothers, and wife alike, to say nothing of countless other members of his family, as if they were personal and public enemies. All this left one crime still to be added to his account—he was the first of the emperors to be the declared enemy of the worship of Almighty God. To this the Roman Tertullian refers in the following terms:

> Study your records: there you will find that Nero was the first to persecute this teaching when, after subjugating the entire East, in Rome especially he treated everyone with savagery. That such a man was author of our chastisement fills us with pride. For anyone who knows him can understand that anything not supremely good would never have been condemned by Nero.

So it came about that this man, the first to be heralded as a conspicuous fighter against God, was led on to murder the apostles. It is recorded that in his reign Paul was beheaded in Rome itself, and that Peter likewise was crucified, and the record is confirmed by the fact that the cemeteries there are still called by the names of Peter and Paul, and equally so by a churchman named Gaius, who was living while Zephyrinus was Bishop of Rome. In his published *Dialogue* with Proclus, the leader of the Phrygian heretics, Gaius has this to say about the places where the mortal remains of the two apostles have been reverently laid:

> I can point out the monuments of the victorious apostles. If you will go as far as the Vatican or the Ostian Way, you will find the monuments of those who founded this church.

That they were both martyred at the same time Bishop Dionysius of Corinth informs us in a letter written to the Romans:

> In this way by your impressive admonition you have bound together all that has grown from the seed which Peter and Paul sowed in Romans and Corinthians alike. For both of them sowed in our Corinth and taught us jointly: in Italy too they taught jointly in the same city, and were martyred at the same time.

These evidences make the truth of my account still more certain.

The Destruction of the Churches

Everything indeed has been fulfilled in my time; I saw with my own eyes the places of worship thrown down from top to bottom, to the very foundations, the inspired holy Scriptures committed to the flames in the middle of the public squares, and the pastors of the churches hiding disgracefully in one place or another, while others suffered the indignity of being held up to ridicule by their enemies—a reminder of another prophetic saying: for contempt was poured on rulers, and He made them wander in a trackless land where there was no road. But it is not for me to describe their wretched misfortunes in the event: nor is it my business to leave on record their quarrels and inhumanity to each other before the persecutions, so I have made up my mind to relate no more about them than enough to justify the divine judgement. I am determined therefore to say nothing even about those who have been tempted by the persecution or have made complete shipwreck of their salvation and of their own accord flung themselves into the depths of the stormy sea; I shall include in my overall account only those things by which first we ourselves, then later generations, may benefit. Let me therefore proceed from this point to describe in outline the hallowed ordeals of the martyrs of God's word.

It was the nineteenth year of Diocletian's reign and the month Dystrus, called March by the Romans, and the festival of the Saviour's Passion was approaching, when an imperial decree was published everywhere, ordering the churches to be razed to the ground and the Scriptures destroyed by fire, and giving notice that those in places of honour would lose their places, and domestic staff, if they continued to profess Christianity, would be deprived of their liberty. Such was the first edict against us. Soon afterwards other decrees arrived in rapid succession, ordering that the presidents of the churches in every place should all be first committed to prison and then coerced by every possible means into offering sacrifice.

—w—

Ordeals Endured in the Persecution: God's Glorious Martyrs

Then, then it was that many rulers of the churches bore up heroically under horrible torments, an object lesson in the endurance of fearful ordeals; while countless others, their souls already numbed with cowardice, promptly succumbed to the first onslaught. Of the rest, each was subjected to a series of different tortures, one flogged unmercifully with the whip, another racked and scraped beyond endurance, so that the lives of some came to a most miserable end. But different people came through the ordeal very differently: one man would be forcibly propelled by others and brought to the disgusting, unholy sacrifices, and dismissed as if he had sacrificed, even if he had done no such thing; another, who had not even approached any abomination, much less touched it, but was said by others to have sacrificed, would go away without attempting to repudiate the baseless charge. Another would be picked up half dead, and thrown away as if already a corpse; and again a man lying on the ground might be dragged a long way by his feet, though included among the willing sacrificers. One man would announce at the top of his voice his determination not to sacrifice, another would shout that he was a Christian, exulting in the confession of the Saviour's Name, while yet another insisted that he had never sacrificed and never would. These were struck on the mouth and silenced by a formidable body of soldiers lined up for the purpose: their faces and cheeks were battered and they were forcibly removed. It was the one object in life of the enemies of true religion to gain credit for having finished the job.

But no such methods could enable them to dispose of the holy martyrs. What could I say that would do full justice to them? I could tell of thousands who showed magnificent enthusiasm for the worship of the God of the universe, not only from the beginning of the general persecution, but much earlier when peace was still secure. For at long last the one who had received the authority was as it were awaking from the deepest sleep, after making attempts—as yet secret and surreptitious—against the churches, in the interval that followed Decius and Valerian. He did not make his preparations all at once for the war against us, but for the time being took action only against members of the legions. In this way he thought that the rest would easily be mastered if he joined battle with these and emerged victorious. Now could be seen large numbers of serving soldiers most happy to embrace civil life, in order to avoid having to repudiate their loyalty to the Architect of the universe. The commander-in-chief, whoever he was, was now first setting about persecuting the soldiery, classifying and sorting those serving in the legions, and allowing them to choose either to obey orders and retain their present rank, or alternatively to be stripped of it if they disobeyed the enactment. But a great many soldiers of Christ's kingdom without hesitation or question chose to confess Him rather than cling to the outward glory and prosperity they enjoyed. Already here and there one or two of them were suffering not only loss of position but even death as the reward of their unshakable devotion: or the time being the man behind the plot was acting cautiously and going as far as bloodshed in a few cases only; he was apparently afraid of the number of believers, and shrank from launching out into war with them all at once. But when he stripped more thoroughly for battle, words are inadequate to depict the host of God's noble martyrs whom the people of every city and every region were privileged to see with their own eyes.

—w—

Victory of Constantine; the Benefits He Conferred on His Subjects

When Licinius had rushed headlong to the limit of madness, this seemed no longer endurable to the emperor, God's friend, who—reasoning along sound lines and tempering the rigidity of justice with humanity—determined to rescue the tyrant's victims, and by putting a few destroyers out of the way made haste to save the bulk of the human race. He had treated Licinius with nothing but kindness hitherto, and had shown mercy where no sympathy was deserved. But Licinius grew no better: his wickedness continued unabated, and he raged more and more madly against his subject peoples; while for his victims there remained no hope of escape, with a wild beast tyrannizing over them.

And so, his love of goodness blended with a hatred of evil, the champion of the good set out with his son Crispus, that most humane emperor, by his side, holding out a saving hand to all who were perishing. Then, taking God the universal King, and God's Son the Saviour of all, as Guide and Ally, father and son together divided their battle array against God's enemies on every side, and easily carried off the victory: every detail of the encounter was made easy for them by God, in fulfilment of His purpose. Suddenly in less time than it takes to say it, those who a day or two before had been breathing death and threats were no more, and even their name was forgotten; their portraits and tributes were swept into merited oblivion;

and the very things that Licinius with his own eyes had seen befall the wicked tyrants who preceded him he underwent himself, because he did not allow himself to be disciplined or learn wisdom from the blows that fell on his neighbours; and having pursued the same path of wickedness as they, he deservedly toppled over the identical cliff.

His adversary thus finally thrown down, the mighty victor Constantine, pre-eminent in every virtue that true religion can confer, with his son Crispus, an emperor most dear to God and in every way resembling his father, won back their own eastern lands and reunited the Roman Empire into a single whole, bringing it all under their peaceful sway, in a wide circle embracing north and south alike from the east to the farthest west. Men had now lost all fear of their former oppressors; day after day they kept dazzling festival; light was everywhere, and men who once dared not look up greeted each other with smiling faces and shining eyes. They danced and sang in city and country alike, giving honour first of all to God our Sovereign Lord, as they had been instructed, and then to the pious emperor with his sons, so dear to God. Old troubles were forgotten, and all irreligion passed into oblivion; good things present were enjoyed, those yet to come eagerly awaited. In every city the victorious emperor published decrees full of humanity and laws that gave proof of munificence and true piety. Thus all tyranny had been purged away, and the kingdom that was theirs was preserved securely and without question for Constantine and his sons alone. They, having made it their first task to wipe the world clean from hatred of God, rejoiced in the blessings that He had conferred upon them, and, by the things they did for all men to see, displayed love of virtue and love of God, devotion and thankfulness to the Almighty.

THE SUCCESSORS OF ROME
Byzantium, Islam, and the Early Medieval West

Selections from the Koran

The Koran (from Arabic, "reading" or "discourse") is the sacred book of Islam, the religion founded by Muhammad (ca. 570–632) in the early seventh century. Even more than the Bible's role in the West (see *The Revised Standard Version of the Holy Bible*), the Koran is at the heart of Islamic culture. Its pages record Muhammad's words, which were dictated to secretaries and preserved as fragments on leaves, on stones, and in followers' memories. After his death, they were compiled into a book. Islamic tradition holds that every one of its words is divinely inspired. Muhammad's work is recognized in Islam's two central beliefs: There is but one God (Allah), and Muhammad is his prophet.

As a book, the Koran has no narrative or chronological structure. It consists of 114 suras ("chapters") arranged not in the order of their composition, which was unknown to its compilers, but in the order of their descending length. Modern studies show that this arrangement contradicts history in that the shorter and more poetic suras appear last, when in fact they were the first.

Although impossible to grasp in totality, the Koran can be known on its own terms. Each sura stands alone and may be understood as a particular response to a specific problem or historic situation. Nearly all suras take the form of discourses by Allah or the angel Gabriel to Muhammad, his followers, or his enemies. The discourses typically announce a doctrine, tell a story, call for holy war ("jihad"), urge charitable giving, regulate trade and finance, or dictate morals and rituals. The best way to approach this book is not to read it from start to finish, but to browse at random and enjoy the richness of its diversity.

The Koran grew in the Arab world of Arabia (Saudi Arabia), but its ideas owed much to Judaism and somewhat less to Christianity. Recognizing Jews and Christians as "People of the Book," it claimed to replace their "books" with God's final word. Like the Jewish-Christian Bible, the Koran taught monotheism; God's total power and knowledge; divine mercy; sin, forgiveness, and faith. Like the Talmud—Jewish writings on the Bible—it stressed the Last Judgment, resurrection, heaven, and hell. Like the New Testament, the Koran accepted Jesus as a prophet, though denies that he is the son of God.

Reading the Selections

Sura 21 is a discourse by Allah, speaking as the divine "We," directed at Muhammad's foes. Like other suras, it begins with the prayer "In the Name of God, the Compassionate, the Merciful." To those who question the Last Judgment ("the Day of Reckoning"), God says he will indeed punish doubters of his word ("blasphemers"), as in the past. To show that he is merciful and not vengeful, he offers a sequence of prophets (Jews, Christians, and Arabs) who prospered because they submitted to his will. (In Arabic, the word *islam* means submission; *muslim* is one who has submitted.)

Sura 24, verses 35–46, is a discourse on God's nature, linking his essence to light, as in "His light is found in temples which God has sanctioned." The theme, God is light, derives from ancient sun worship (see *The Great Hymn to the Aten*) and was a prominent idea in early Christianity. This sura recognizes that such metaphors—as calling God "Light"—are proper for symbolizing Allah. As a result, Islamic mosques—places of worship— were outfitted with ritual lamps. Concerning religious paintings and statues, however, the Koran sided with Judaism and condemned such objects as idolatrous.

—m—

The Prophets

In the Name of God, the Compassionate, the Merciful

21

The Day of Reckoning for mankind is drawing near, yet [1] they blithely persist in unbelief. They listen with ridicule to each fresh warning that their Lord gives them: their hearts are set on pleasure.

In private the wrongdoers say to each other: 'Is this man not a mortal like yourselves? Would you follow witchcraft with your eyes open?'

Say: 'My Lord has knowledge of whatever is said in heaven and earth. He hears all and knows all.'

Some say: 'It is but a medley of dreams.' Others: 'He has invented it himself.' And yet others: 'He is a poet: let him show us some sign, as did the apostles in days gone by.'

Yet though We showed them signs, the nations whom [5] We destroyed before them did not believe either. Will *they* believe?

The apostles We sent before you were but men whom We inspired. Ask the People of the Book if you do not know this. The bodies We gave them could not dispense with food, nor were they immortal. Then We fulfilled Our promise: We delivered them and those We willed, and utterly destroyed the transgressors.

And now We have revealed a Book for your admonishment. Will you not give heed?

We have destroyed many a sinful nation and replaced them by other men. And when they felt Our might they took to their heels and fled. They were told: 'Do not run away. Return to your comforts and to your dwellings. You shall be questioned all.'

'Woe to us, we have done wrong!' was their reply. And this they kept repeating until We mowed them down and put out their light.

It was not in sport that We created the heavens and [10] the earth and all that lies between them. Had it been Our will to find a pastime, We could have found one near at hand.

We will hurl Truth at Falsehood, until Truth shall triumph and Falsehood be no more. Woe shall befall you, for all the falsehoods you have uttered.

His are all who dwell in the heavens and on earth. Those who stand in His presence do not disdain to worship Him, nor are they ever wearied. They praise Him day and night, unflaggingly.

Have they chosen earthly deities? And can these deities restore the dead to life? Were there other gods in heaven or earth besides God, both heaven and earth would be ruined. Exalted be God, Lord of the Throne, above their falsehoods!

None shall question Him about His works, but they shall be questioned. Have they chosen other gods besides Him?

Say: 'Show us your proofs. Here are the Scriptures of [15] today and those of long ago.' But most of them do not know the Truth, and this is why they give no heed.

We inspired all the apostles whom We sent before you, saying: 'There is no god but Me. Therefore serve Me.'

They say: 'The Merciful has begotten children.' God forbid! They are but His honoured servants. They do not speak till He has spoken: they act by His command. He knows what is before them and behind them. They intercede for none save those whom He accepts, and tremble for awe of Him. Whoever of them declares: 'I am a god besides Him,' shall be requited with Hell. Thus shall We reward the wrongdoers.

Are the disbelievers unaware that the heavens and the earth were but one solid mass which We tore asunder, and that We made every living thing of water? Will they not have faith?

We set firm mountains upon the earth lest it should move away with them, and hewed out highways in the rock so that they might be rightly guided.

We spread the heaven like a canopy and provided it [20] with strong support: yet of its signs they are heedless.

It was He who created the night and the day, and the sun and the moon: each moves swiftly in an orbit of its own.

No man before you have We made immortal. If you yourself are doomed to die, will they live for ever?

Every soul shall taste death. We will prove you all with good and evil. To Us you shall return.

When the unbelievers see you, they scoff at you, saying: 'Is this the man who fulminates against your gods?' And they deny all mention of the Merciful.

Impatience is the very stuff man is made of. You shall before long see My signs: you need not ask Me to hasten them.

They say: 'When will this promise be fulfilled, if what you say be true?'

If only the unbelievers knew the day when they shall strive in vain to shield their faces and their backs from the fire of Hell; the day when none shall help them! It will overtake them unawares and stupefy them. They shall have no power to ward it off, nor shall they be reprieved.

Other apostles have been mocked before you; but those who scoffed at them were smitten by the very scourge they mocked.

Say: 'Who will protect you, by night and by day, from the Lord of Mercy?' Yet are they unmindful of their Lord's remembrance.

Have they other gods to defend them? Their idols shall be powerless over their own salvation, nor shall they be protected from Our scourge.

We have bestowed good things upon these men and upon their fathers, and made their lives too long. Can they not see how We invade their land and curtail its borders? Is it they who will triumph?

Say: 'I warn you only by that with which I am inspired.' But the deaf can hear nothing when they are warned.

Yet if the lightest whiff from the vengeance of your Lord touched them, they would say: 'Woe to us: we have done wrong!'

We shall set up just scales on the Day of Resurrection, so that no man shall in the least be wronged. Actions as small as a grain of mustard seed shall be weighed out. Our reckoning shall suffice.

We showed Moses and Aaron the distinction between right and wrong, and gave them a light and an admonition for righteous men: those who truly fear their Lord and dread the terrors of Judgement-day.

And in this We have revealed a blessed counsel. Will you then reject it?

We bestowed guidance on Abraham, for We knew him well. He said to his father and to his people: 'What are these images to which you are so devoted?'

They replied: 'They are the gods our fathers worshipped.'

He said: 'Then you and your fathers are in the grossest error.'

'Is it the truth that you are preaching,' they asked, 'or is this but a jest?'

'Indeed,' he answered, 'your Lord is the Lord of the heavens and the earth. It was He that made them: to this I bear witness. By the Lord, I will overthrow your idols as soon as you have turned your backs.'

He broke them all in pieces, except their supreme god, so that they might return to Him.

'Who has done this to our deities?' asked some. 'He must surely be a wicked man.'

Others replied: 'We have heard a youth called Abraham speak of them.'

They said: 'Then bring him here in sight of all the people, that they may act as witnesses.'

'Abraham,' they said, 'was it you who did this to our deities?'

'No,' he replied. 'It was their chief who smote them. Ask *them*, if they can speak.'

Thereupon they turned their thoughts upon themselves and said to each other: 'Surely you are the ones who have done wrong.'

Confounded as they were, they said to Abraham: 'You know they cannot speak.'

He answered: 'Would you then worship that, instead of God, which can neither help nor harm you? Shame on you and on your idols! Have you no sense?'

They cried: 'Burn him and avenge your gods, if you must punish him!'

'Fire,' We said, 'be cool to Abraham and keep him safe.'

They sought to lay a snare for him, but they themselves were ruined. We delivered him and Lot, and brought them to the land which We had blessed for all mankind.

We gave him Isaac, and then Jacob for a grandson; and We made each a righteous man. We ordained them leaders to guide mankind at Our behest, and enjoined on them charity, prayer and almsgiving. They served none but Ourself.

To Lot We gave wisdom and knowledge and delivered him from the Wicked City; for its inhabitants were men of iniquity and evil. We admitted him to Our mercy: he was a righteous man.

Before him Noah invoked Us, and We heard his prayer. We saved him and all his kinsfolk from the great calamity, and delivered him from those who had denied Our revelations. Evil men they were; We drowned them all.

And tell of David and Solomon: how they passed judgement regarding the cornfield in which strayed lambs had grazed by night. We gave Solomon insight into the case and bore witness to both their judgements.

We bestowed on them wisdom and knowledge, and caused the birds and mountains to join with David in Our praise. All this We have done.

We taught him the armourer's craft, so that you might have protection in your wars. Will you then give thanks?

To Solomon We subjected the raging wind: it sped at his bidding to the land which We had blessed. We have knowledge of all things.

We assigned him devils who dived for him into the sea and who performed other tasks besides. Over them We kept a watchful eye.

And tell of Job: how he called on his Lord, saying: 'I am sorely afflicted: but of all those that show mercy You are the most merciful.'

We heard his prayer and relieved his affliction. We restored to him his family and as many more with them: a blessing from Ourself and an admonition to worshippers.

And you shall also tell of Ishmael, Idis, and Dhūl-Kifl, who all endured with patience. To Our mercy We admitted them, for they were upright men.

And of Dhūl-Nūn: how he went away in anger, thinking We had no power over him. But in the darkness he cried: 'There is no god but You. Glory be to You! I have done wrong.'

We answered his prayer and delivered him from distress. Thus shall We save the true believers.

And of Zacharias, who invoked his Lord, saying: 'Lord, let me not remain childless, though of all heirs You are the best.'

We answered his prayer and gave him John, curing his wife of sterility. They vied with each other in good works and called on Us with piety, fear, and submission.

And of the woman who kept her chastity. We breathed into her of Our spirit, and made her and her son a sign to all men.

Your religion is but one religion, and I am Your only Lord. Therefore serve Me. Men have divided themselves into factions, but to Us they shall all return. He that does good works in the fullness of his faith, his endeavours 70 shall not be lost: We record them all.

It is ordained that no nation We have destroyed shall ever rise again. But when Gog and Magog are let loose and rush headlong down every hill; when the true promise nears its fulfilment; the unbelievers shall stare in amazement, crying: 'Woe to us! Of this we have been heedless. We have done wrong.'

You and your idols shall be the fuel of Hell; therein you shall all go down. Were they true gods, your idols would not go there: but there they shall abide for ever. They shall groan with anguish and be bereft of hearing.

But those to whom We have long since shown Our favour shall be far removed from Hell. They shall not hear its roar, but shall delight for ever in what their souls desire.

The Supreme Terror shall not grieve them, and the angels will receive them, saying: 'This is the day you have been promised.'

On that day We shall roll up the heaven like a scroll of parchment. As We first created man, so will We bring him back to life. This is a promise We shall assuredly 75 fulfil.

We wrote in the Psalms after the Torah was revealed: 'The righteous among My servants shall inherit the earth.' That is an admonition to those who serve Us.

We have sent you forth but as a blessing to mankind. Say: 'It is revealed to me that your God is one God. Will you submit to Him?'

If they give no heed say: 'I have warned you all alike, though I cannot tell whether the scourge you are threatened with is imminent or far off. He knows your spoken words and hidden thoughts. This may be a test for you and a short reprieve.'

Say: 'Lord, judge with fairness. Our Lord is the Merciful, whose help We seek against your blasphemies.'

—◆—

Light
24:35—46

24

God is the light of the heavens and the earth. His light 1 may be compared to a niche that enshrines a lamp, the lamp within a crystal of star-like brilliance. It is lit from a blessed olive tree neither eastern nor western. Its very oil would almost shine forth, though no fire touched it. Light upon light; God guides to His light whom He will.

God speaks in metaphors to men. God has knowledge of all things.

His light is found in temples which God has sanctioned to be built for the remembrance of His name. In them, morning and evening, His praise is sung by men whom neither trade nor profit can divert from remembering Him, from offering prayers, or from giving alms; who dread the day when men's hearts and eyes shall writhe with anguish; who hope that God will requite them for their noblest deeds and lavish His grace upon them. God gives without measure to whom He will.

As for the unbelievers, their works are like a mirage in a desert. The thirsty traveller thinks it is water, but when he comes near he finds that it is nothing. He finds God there, who pays him back in full. Swift is God's reckoning.

Or like darkness on a bottomless ocean spread with 5 clashing billows and overcast with clouds: darkness upon darkness. If he stretches out his hand he can scarcely see it. Indeed the man from whom God withholds His light shall find no light at all.

Do you not see how God is praised by those in heaven and those on earth? The very birds praise Him as they wing their flight. He notes the prayers and praises of all His creatures, and has knowledge of all their actions.

It is God who has sovereignty over the heavens and the earth. To Him shall all things return.

Do you not see how God drives the clouds, then gathers and piles them up in masses which pour down torrents of rain? From heaven's mountains He sends down the hail, pelting with it whom He will and turning it away from whom He pleases. The flash of His lightning almost snatches off men's eyes.

He makes the night succeed the day: surely in this there is a lesson for clear-sighted men.

God created every beast from water. Some creep upon their bellies, others walk on two legs, and others yet on four. God creates what He pleases. He has power over all things.

We have sent down revelations demonstrating the Truth. God guides whom He will to a straight path. . . .

BOETHIUS

Selection from *The Consolation of Philosophy*

Boethius (ca. 480–524), like St. Augustine (see *Confessions*), was a transitional figure who bridged the Classical and Christian worlds. Privileged as an aristocrat and traditionally educated in liberal studies, Boethius, at an early age, came to the attention of Theodoric, the Ostrogoth (German) general who had conquered Italy before 493 and made himself its king. With the king's favor, Boethius rose through the ranks at the royal court, finally becoming, in effect, prime minister. He was made consul in 510.

Despite his administrative duties, Boethius still found time for his studies, writing books on arithmetic, astronomy, and music, and making Latin translations of works by Aristotle and other Greek scholars. His translations of Aristotle laid the foundation for scholasticism and systematized late Classical/Christian philosophy—two of his major contributions to thought during the Middle Ages.

Even though Boethius received royal favor, the king had him arrested as the result of palace intrigue that in turn was part of a conflict between Theodoric and the Byzantine emperor over political and religious issues. While awaiting death, Boethius composed one of the masterpieces of Western thought, *The Consolation of Philosophy*, which reflected his Classical education. He was executed in 524, when his jailers beat him with clubs until he died.

Reading the Selection

Boethius's *The Consolation of Philosophy* is a hybrid work that alternates prose and poetry. The author's mouthpiece in the first three chapters is Dame Philosophy, a personification technique that influenced later medieval writers (see Christine de Pizan's *The Book of the City of Ladies*). Dame Philosophy addresses Boethius and, by extension, the reader, in the ways that philosophy can help mortals face terrible misfortunes. Overall, her advice seems to be one of Stoic resignation to the unaccountable whims of Fortune, an ancient idea of the randomness at work in the world. Dame Philosophy herself does not oppose Fortune. She points out to Boethius that Fortune has been good to him, providing him with a loyal wife, two sons, and true friends; now, however, Fortune's wheel has turned, and he is in prison facing inevitable death. Thus, he must learn to accept life's bitterness with the sweet.

In Book III, Dame Philosophy introduces a new note when she says that there is no true happiness except in union with God. She pledges that she (that is, philosophy) will guide Boethius (the reader) to true happiness, though he must seek help from God.

God, as defined and addressed in this work, is a philosophical concept: "Thou who dost by everlasting reason rule / Creator of the planets and the sky, who time / From timelessness didst bring, unchanging Mover." This language suggests the influence of Plato (see *The Republic* and *Phaedo*) and Aristotle (see *Poetics*). Thus, as Boethius, one of the last Romans but also one of the first medieval Christians, faced death, he expressed no hope in the Christian belief of personal immortality but placed his trust in the truths of Greek philosophy.

Another important point about this selection is the mode of reasoning, which relies on quotations from famous authors and the Bible (appeals to authority), definitions of terms, and summary of all sides to an argument. Because this work was one of the few that was continuously read after the fall of the western Roman Empire, the reasoning methods employed by Boethius were widely imitated until about 1500.

—∿—

Book III

Chapter IX

. . .

'Even a blind man could see it,' I said, 'and you revealed it just now when you were trying to show the causes of false happiness. For unless I'm mistaken, true and perfect happiness is that which makes a man self-sufficient, strong, worthy of respect, glorious and joyful. And to show you that I have more than a superficial understanding, without a shadow of doubt I can see that happiness to be true happiness which, since they are all the same thing, can truly bestow any one of them.'

'You are blessed in this belief, my child, provided you add one thing.'

'What is that?'

'Do you think there is anything among these mortal and degenerate things which could confer such a state?'

'No, I don't, and you have proved it as well as anyone could wish.'

'Clearly, therefore, these things offer man only shadows of the true good, or imperfect blessings, and cannot confer true and perfect good.'

'Yes.'

'Since then you have realized the nature of true happiness and seen its false imitations, what remains now is that you should see where to find this true happiness.'

'Which is the very thing I have long and eagerly been waiting for.'

'But since in the *Timaeus* my servant Plato was pleased to ask for divine help even over small matters, what do you think we ought to do now in order to be worthy of discovering the source of that supreme good?'

'We ought to pray to the Father of all things. To omit to do so would not be laying a proper foundation.'

'Right,' she said, and immediately began the following hymn.

'O Thou who dost by everlasting reason rule,
Creator of the planets and the sky, who time
From timelessness didst bring, unchanging Mover,
No cause drove Thee to mould unstable matter, but
The form benign of highest good within Thee set.
All things Thou bringest forth from Thy high archetype:
Thou, height of beauty, in Thy mind the beauteous world
Dost bear, and in that ideal likeness shaping it,
Dost order perfect parts a perfect whole to frame.
The elements by harmony Thou dost constrain,
That hot to cold and wet to dry are equal made,
That fire grow not too light, or earth too fraught with
*   weight.*
The bridge of threefold nature madest Thou soul, which
*   spreads*
Through nature's limbs harmonious and all things moves.
The soul once cut, in circles two its motion joins,
Goes round and to itself returns encircling mind,

And turns in pattern similar the firmament.
From causes like Thou bringst forth souls and lesser lives,
Which from above in chariots swift Thou dost disperse
Through sky and earth, and by Thy law benign they turn
And back to Thee they come through fire that brings them
*   home.*
Grant, Father, that our minds Thy august seat may scan,
Grant us the sight of true good's source, and grant us light
That we may fix on Thee our mind's unblinded eye.
Disperse the clouds of earthly matter's cloying weight;
Shine out in all Thy glory; for Thou art rest and peace
To those who worship Thee; to see Thee is our end,
Who art our source and maker, lord and path and goal.'

Chapter X

'Since, then, you have seen the form both of imperfect and of perfect good, I think we now have to show where this perfect happiness is to be found.

'The first question to ask is, I think, whether any good of the kind I defined a moment ago can exist in the natural world. This will prevent our being led astray from the truth of the matter before us by false and ill-founded reasoning. But the existence of this good and its function as a kind of fountain-head of all good things cannot be denied; for everything that is said to be imperfect is held to be so by the absence of perfection. So that if a certain imperfection is visible in any class of things, it follows that there is also a proportion of perfection in it. For if you do away with perfection, it is impossible to imagine how that which is held to be imperfect could exist. The natural world did not take its origin from that which was impaired and incomplete, but issues from that which is unimpaired and perfect and then degenerates into this fallen and worn out condition. But we showed just now that there is a certain imperfect happiness in perishable good, so that there can be no doubt that a true and perfect happiness exists.'

'Which is a very sound and true conclusion,' I said.

'As to where it is to be found, then, you should think as follows. It is the universal understanding of the human mind that God, the author of all things, is good. Since nothing can be conceived better than God, everyone agrees that that which has no superior is good. Reason shows that God is so good that we are convinced that His goodness is perfect. Otherwise He couldn't be the author of creation. There would have to be something else possessing perfect goodness over and above God, which would seem to be superior to Him and of greater antiquity. For all perfect things are obviously superior to those that are imperfect. Therefore, to avoid an unending argument, it must be admitted that the supreme God is to the highest degree filled with supreme and perfect goodness. But we have agreed that perfect good is true happiness; so that it follows that true happiness is to be found in the supreme God.'

'I accept that. There is nothing in any way open to contradiction.' 5

'But,' she said, 'I must ask you to make sure that your approval of our statement that the supreme God is to the highest degree filled with supreme good is unqualified and final.'

'How do you mean?' I asked.

'By avoiding the assumption that this Father of creation has received this supreme good with which He is said to be filled from outside Himself, or that He possesses it by nature but in such a way as would lead you to suppose that the substance of God the possessor was a separate thing from the substance of the happiness He possesses. If you thought that He received it from outside Himself, you would be able to count the giver superior to the receiver. But we are in agreement that it is right to consider God the most excellent of things.

'On the other hand, if goodness is a natural property of God, but something logically distinct from Him, whenever we speak of God as the author of creation, an able mind might be able to imagine the existence of a power responsible for bringing together the two that were separate.

'Finally, if one thing is distinct from another, it cannot 10 be the thing from which it is perceived to be distinct. So that which by its own nature is something distinct from supreme good, cannot be supreme good; but this is something we may not hold about Him to whom we agree there is nothing superior. It is impossible for anything to be by nature better than that from which it is derived. I would therefore conclude with perfect logic that that which is the origin of all things is in its own substance supreme good.'

'Perfectly right.'

'But we have agreed that supreme good is the same as happiness.'

'Yes.'

'So that we have to agree that God is the essence of happiness.'

'Your premises are incontestable and I see that this inference follows upon them.' 15

'Then consider whether this, too, can be firmly accepted: that it is impossible for two supreme goods to exist separate from one another. For it is clear that if the two goods are separate, the one cannot be the other, so that neither could be perfect when each is lacking to the other. But that which is not perfect is obviously not supreme. It is therefore impossible for there to be two separate supreme goods. However, we deduced that both happiness and God are supreme goodness, so that it follows that supreme happiness is identical with supreme divinity.'

'There could scarcely be a conclusion more true to reality, or more sure in its reasoning, or more worthy of God.'

'I will add something to it. Just as in geometry some additional inference may be drawn from a theorem that has been proved, called in technical language, in Greek a *porisma* and in Latin a corollary, I too will give you a kind of corollary. Since it is through the possession of happiness that people become happy, and since happiness is in fact divinity, it is clear that it is through the possession of divinity that they become happy. But by the same logic as men become just through the possession of justice, or wise through the possession of wisdom, so those who possess divinity necessarily become divine. Each happy individual is therefore divine. While only God is so by nature, as many as you like may become so by participation.'

'What you say is beautiful and valuable, whether you give it the Greek or the Latin name.'

'But the most beautiful thing is what logic leads us to 20 add to all this.'

'What is that?'

'Are all the many things we see included under the word happiness like parts combining to form a single body, yet separate in their variety, or is there any one of them which can fully supply the essence of happiness and under which the others may be classed?'

'Could you clarify the question by being more specific?'

'Well, we consider happiness something good, don't we?'

'Yes, the supreme good.' 25

'You could say the same of all of them. Absolute sufficiency is judged to be the same as happiness, and so too are power, reverence, glory and pleasure. Well, the question is this, all these things—sufficiency, power and the others—are they good as if happiness were a body of which they were members, or is goodness a kind of heading to which they belong?'

'I understand the question which you are proposing we should ask, but I should like to hear what your answer would be.'

'This is how I would resolve it. If all these were related to happiness like limbs to a body, they would differ from one another, because it is the nature of parts that the body is one, but the parts that make it up are diverse. But all these things have been proved to be identical. So that they are not like limbs. Moreover it would appear that happiness was a body made up of a single limb, which is impossible.'

'There is no doubt of that; but I am eager for what is to come.'

'It is clear that the other properties are classed under 30 good. It is just because sufficiency is judged a good that people want it, and it is just because it too is believed to be a good that power is sought after. And exactly the same conclusion may be reached about reverence, glory and pleasure.

'The chief point and reason, therefore, for seeking all things is goodness. For it is quite impossible for that which contains no good in itself whether real or apparent, to be an object of desire. On the other hand, things which are not good by nature are sought after if they nevertheless seem as if they were truly good.

'The result is, therefore, that there is justice in the belief that goodness is the chief point upon which the pursuit of everything hinges and by which it is motivated. What seems most to be desired is the thing that motivates the pursuit of something, as, for example, if a man wants to go riding for the sake of health; it is not so much the motion of horse-riding he desires as the resultant good health. Since, therefore, all things are desired for the sake of the good in them, no one desires them as much as the good itself. But we are agreed that the reason for desiring things is happiness. So that it is patently obvious that the good itself and happiness are identical.'

'I can see no reason for anyone to disagree.'

'But we have shown that God and happiness are one and the same thing.'

'Yes.'

'We may safely conclude, then, that God is to be found in goodness itself and nowhere else.

'*Come hither now all you who captive are,*
Whom false desire enchains in wicked bonds,
Desire that makes her home in earthly minds;
Here will you find release from grievous toil,
Here find a haven blessed with peaceful calm,
An ever open refuge from distress.

Not all the gold that Tagus' sands bestow,
That Hermus from his glittering banks casts up,
Or Indus, on whose torrid shores are strewn
Green emeralds intermixed with dazzling pearls,
May sharpen and make bright the intellect,
But wealth in its own darkness clouds the thoughts.
For all that thus excites and charms the mind
Dim earth has fostered in her caverns deep;
While that bright light which rules and animates
The sky, will shun such dark and ruined souls:
Whoever once shall see this shining light
Will say the sun's own rays are not so bright.'

35

BEDE

Selection from *A History of the English Church and People*

The English poet and monk known as the Venerable Bede (673–735) spent nearly all his life in the church. At age seven his parents put him under the care of an abbot (the head of a monastery); at nine he was moved to the new monastery at Jarrow, where he remained for the rest of his life. At nineteen he became a deacon, a sign of his worthiness in the eyes of his ecclesiastical superiors, since by law one was not to be made a deacon until age twenty-five. He was ordained a priest at thirty. According to his own account, Bede devoted much of his life to scholarship, writing books on the scriptures, lives of saints and abbots, hymns and epigrams, and above all, *A History of the English Church and People,* his masterpiece. Completed just before his death, this history reflected the recent triumph of Roman Catholicism over Celtic (Irish) Christianity, whose supporters clashed over the right to dominate England in the early eighth century. Indeed, some aspects of Celtic Christianity are apparent in Bede's own life, such as his extreme asceticism and love of learning; still, he was a devout servant of the Pope and supporter of Roman theology.

A History of the English Church and People, consisting of five books, surveys the almost-eight-hundred-year history of Britain from the mid-first century B.C. to events in Bede's day. Book I covers the period from the founding of Roman Britain, under Julius Caesar, to A.D. 596 when St. Augustine (not to be confused with the earlier saint of the same name who wrote the *Confessions*) introduced Roman Catholicism into southeast England. As the first Bishop of Canterbury, St. Augustine converted the king of Kent, ruler of one of the Anglo-Saxon kingdoms into which the land of England was then divided. Books II through V focus on church history, recounting the process by which the north-country Anglo-Saxons, as well as the Scots, were brought into the Christian fold.

Not a mere chronicler of events, Bede was a careful historian who consulted primary sources and took pains to get the dates right. If he has a flaw, it is that he was overly credulous concerning miracles, perhaps reflecting his years in a monastery. Bede believed that miracles did happen and were part of everyday life; as a historian, he simply documented their reported occurrence. Today's readers can thus learn from Bede's account about one of the fundamental ways in which eighth-century and twentieth-century world views differ.

Reading the Selection

This selection from Bede's *History* is famous for being the only existing record of the first English poet, Caedmon, who was also a monk. Caedmon's story, including his call to be a poet and his death, appears in Book IV, Chapter 24, where Bede continues his account of the spread of Christianity among the English people. Caedmon is depicted as a simple man blessed with a genius for poetry, which Bede thinks is a gift from God. In his brief narrative, Bede inserts a few lines of Caedmon's lyrics translated into Latin (Bede's original work was in Latin). These lines constitute all that remains of Caedmon's poetry. Bede's interest in vernacular English poetry is highly unusual during this period and must be remarked upon, for all of his writings were in Latin, the language of the educated throughout medieval times.

―᭱―

Book IV

Chapter 24
A Brother of the Monastery Is Found
to Possess God's Gift of Poetry (A.D. 680)

In this monastery of Streanaeshalch lived a brother singularly gifted by God's grace. So skilful was he in composing religious and devotional songs that, when any passage of Scripture was explained to him by interpreters, he could quickly turn it into delightful and moving poetry in his own English tongue. These verses of his have stirred the hearts of many folk to despise the world and aspire to heavenly things. Others after him tried to compose religious poems in English, but none could compare with him; for he did not acquire the art of poetry from men or through any human teacher but received it as a free gift from God. For this reason he could never compose any frivolous or profane verses; but only such as had a religious theme fell fittingly from his devout lips. He had followed a secular occupation until well advanced in years without ever learning anything about poetry. Indeed it sometimes happened at a feast that all the guests in turn would be invited to sing and entertain the company; then, when he saw the harp coming his way, he would get up from table and go home.

On one such occasion he had left the house in which the entertainment was being held and went out to the stable, where it was his duty that night to look after the beasts. There when the time came he settled down to sleep. Suddenly in a dream he saw a man standing beside him who called him by name. 'Caedmon,' he said, 'sing me a song.' 'I don't know how to sing,' he replied. 'It is because I cannot sing that I left the feast and came here.' The man who addressed him then said: 'But you shall sing to me.' 'What should I sing about?' he replied. 'Sing about the Creation of all things,' the other answered. And Caedmon immediately began to sing verses in praise of God the Creator that he had never heard before, and their theme ran thus:

> Praise we the Fashioner now of Heaven's fabric,
> The majesty of his might and his mind's wisdom,
> Work of the world-warden, worker of all wonders,
> How he the Lord of Glory everlasting,
> Wrought first for the race of men Heaven as a rooftree,
> Then made he Middle Earth to be their mansion.

This is the general sense, but not the actual words that Caedmon sang in his dream; for verses, however masterly, cannot be translated literally from one language into another without losing much of their beauty and dignity. When Caedmon awoke, he remembered everything that he had sung in his dream, and soon added more verses in the same style to a song truly worthy of God.

Early in the morning he went to his superior the reeve, and told him about this gift that he had received. The reeve took him before the abbess, who ordered him to give an account of his dream and repeat the verses in the presence of many learned men, so that a decision might be reached by common consent as to their quality and origin. All of them agreed that Caedmon's gift had been given him by our Lord. And they explained to him a passage of scriptural history or doctrine and asked him to render it into verse if he could. He promised to do this, and returned next morning with excellent verses as they had ordered him. The abbess was delighted that God had given such grace to the man, and advised him to abandon secular life and adopt the monastic state. And when she had admitted him into the Community as a brother, she ordered him to be instructed in the events of sacred history. So Caedmon stored up in his memory all that he learned, and like one of the clean animals chewing the cud, turned it into such melodious verse that his delightful renderings turned his instructors into auditors. He sang of the creation of the world, the origin of the human race, and the whole story of Genesis. He sang of Israel's exodus from Egypt, the entry into the Promised Land, and many other events of scriptural history. He sang of the Lord's Incarnation, Passion, Resurrection, and Ascension into heaven, the coming of the Holy Spirit, and the teaching of the Apostles. He also made many poems on the terrors of the Last Judgement, the horrible pains of Hell, and the joys of the Kingdom of Heaven. In addition to these, he composed several others on the blessings and judgements of God, by which he sought to turn his hearers from delight in wickedness and to inspire them to love and do good. For Caedmon was a deeply religious man, who humbly submitted to regular discipline and hotly rebuked all who tried to follow another course. And so he crowned his life with a happy end.

For, when the time of his death drew near, he felt the onset of physical weakness for fourteen days, but not seriously enough to prevent his walking or talking the whole time. Close by there was a house to which all who were sick or likely to die were taken. Towards nightfall on the day when he was to depart this life, Caedmon asked his attendant to prepare a resting-place for him in this house. The attendant was surprised at this request from a man who did not appear likely to die yet; nevertheless, he did as he was asked. So Caedmon went to the house, and conversed and jested cheerfully with those who were already there; and when it was past midnight, he asked: 'Is the Eucharist in the house?' 'Why do you want the Eucharist?' they enquired; 'you are not likely to die yet, when you are talking so cheerfully to us and seem to be in perfect health.' 'Nevertheless,' he said, 'bring me the Eucharist.' And taking It in his hands, Caedmon asked whether they were all charitably disposed towards him, and whether they had any complaint or ill-feeling against him. They replied that they were all most kindly disposed towards him, and free from all bitterness. Then in turn they asked him to clear his heart of bitterness towards them. At once

he answered: 'Dear sons, my heart is at peace with all the servants of God.' Then, when he had fortified himself with the heavenly Viaticum, he prepared to enter the other life, and asked how long it would be before the brothers were roused to sing God's praises in the Night Office. 'Not long,' they replied. 'Good, then let us wait until then,' he answered; and signing himself with the holy Cross, he laid his head on the pillow and passed away quietly in his sleep. So, having served God with a simple and pure mind, and with tranquil devotion, he left the world and departed to his presence by a tranquil death. His tongue, which had sung so many inspiring verses in praise of his Maker, uttered its last words in his praise as he signed himself with the Cross and commended his soul into his hands. For, as I have already said, Caedmon seems to have had a premonition of his death.

EINHARD

Selection from *The Life of Charlemagne*

The Life of Charlemagne is a precious relic from one of Western civilization's darkest periods, when the fate of culture itself was in doubt. It dates from the Early Middle Ages (500–1000), as Europe, phoenixlike, struggled to rise from the ashes of Rome. Rome's empire in the West had disappeared, its regime wrecked by Germanic invaders, leaving people to either huddle in wooden huts beside armed fortresses or flee to monasteries. For such a masterly work to appear at this time was a sign that Europe's dark night was almost over.

This book is a brief and simple biography of Charlemagne (French, "Charles the Great") (r. 768–814), the ruler of the Germanic Franks; he originated the idea of Europe in his vast multiethnic empire, the first since Rome. In style, the book breaks no new ground but illustrates that this was a timid age, still in the shadow of Rome. Written in Latin and divided into five books, it is modeled on the Roman writer Suetonius's *Lives of the Caesars*, in terms of length and order of material. Passages are even taken from Suetonius and applied to Charlemagne.

The author, Einhard (about 770–840), was a noble-born Frank educated at the monastic school of Fulda, near Frankfurt. From 791 to 814, he served Charlemagne at the Palace School near the imperial court at Aachen, in modern Germany; here he helped train gifted boys of all social ranks for careers in public life. He was among a handful of scholars who made this school the driving force of the Carolingian Renaissance, the cultural rebirth led by Charlemagne, which blended Classical learning and Christian ideals. Einhard became the ruler's trusted adviser, a position that gave him intimate knowledge of the man whose biography he later wrote.

Written between 829 and 836, this biography is essentially a work of praise. At one point Einhard says his purpose was "to describe the life and the day-to-day habits of Charlemagne . . . and to write the public history of this . . . most famous king." He indeed achieves this limited goal, but when the topic touches on dangerous subjects, the text is either silent or veiled. For instance, he writes shyly of scandals involving the imperial daughters: "[Charlemagne] shut his eyes to all that happened, as if no suspicion of any immoral conduct had ever reached him, or as if the rumour was without foundation."

The lasting value of Einhard's work is that it is the fullest eyewitness account of Charlemagne. More then eighty copies of this work survive, attesting to its popularity. Even though Charlemagne's empire fell to pieces after a generation (843), his dream lived on. Today the European Union is a realization of his vision.

Reading the Selection

Book III of Einhard's biography is concerned with Charlemagne's private life, though of necessity it touches on affairs of state in this age when power was so personal and immediate. It covers varied aspects of the emperor's life, including family, guests, appearance, sports, dining habits, learning, and efforts at legal reform.

The most astonishing fact to be gleaned from this life is that Charlemagne was illiterate. "Although he tried very hard [to write], he had begun too late in life and he made little progress." He nevertheless was awed by the written word, as his liberal patronage of scholars proves. He spoke Latin well and understood a little Greek. His own tongue was Frankish, an early form of French. In this chaotic age, literacy was for monastic scholars, such as Einhard; everyone else, like Charlemagne, was illiterate.

—*w*—

Book III
The Emperor's Private Life

. . .

§19.   Charlemagne was determined to give his children, his daughters just as much as his sons, a proper training in the liberal arts which had formed the subject of his own studies. As soon as they were old enough he had his sons taught to ride in the Frankish fashion, to use arms and to hunt. He made his daughters learn to spin and weave wool, use the distaff and spindle, and acquire every womanly accomplishment, rather than fritter away their time in sheer idleness. . . .

When the death of Hadrian, the Pope of Rome and his close friend, was announced to him, he wept as if he had lost a brother or a dearly loved son. He was firm and steady in his human relationships, developing friendship easily, keeping it up with care and doing everything he possibly could for anyone whom he had admitted to this degree of intimacy.

He paid such attention to the upbringing of his sons and daughters that he never sat down to table without them when he was at home, and never set out on a journey without taking them with him. His sons rode at his side and his daughters followed along behind. Hand-picked guards watched over them as they closed the line of march. These girls were extraordinarily beautiful and greatly loved by their father. It is a remarkable fact that, as a result of this, he kept them with him in his household until the very day of his death, instead of giving them in marriage to his own men or to foreigners, maintaining that he could not live without them. The consequence was that he had a number of unfortunate experiences, he who had been so lucky in all else that he undertook. However, he shut his eyes to all that happened, as if no suspicion of any immoral conduct had ever reached him, or as if the rumour was without foundation.

§20.   I did not mention with the others a son called Pepin who was born to Charlemagne by a concubine. He was handsome enough, but a hunchback. At a moment when his father was wintering in Bavaria, soon after the beginning of his campaign against the Huns, this Pepin pretended to be ill and conspired with certain of the Frankish leaders who had won him over to their cause by pretending to offer him the kingship. The plot was discovered and the conspirators were duly punished. Pepin was tonsured and permitted to take up, in the monastery of Prüm, the life of a religious for which he had already expressed a vocation.

Earlier on there had been another dangerous conspiracy against Charlemagne in Germany. All the plotters were exiled, some having their eyes put out first, but the others were not maltreated physically. Only three of them were killed. These resisted arrest, drew their swords and started to defend themselves. They slaughtered a few men in the process and had to be destroyed themselves, as there was no other way of dealing with them.

The cruelty of Queen Fastrada is thought to have been the cause of both these conspiracies, since it was under her influence that Charlemagne seemed to have taken actions which were fundamentally opposed to his normal kindliness and good nature. Throughout the remainder of his life he so won the love and favour of all his fellow human beings, both at home and abroad, that no one ever levelled against him the slightest charge of cruelty or injustice.

§21.   He loved foreigners and took great pains to make them welcome. So many visited him as a result that they were rightly held to be a burden not only to the palace, but to the entire realm. In his magnanimity he took no notice at all of this criticism, for he considered that his reputation for hospitality and the advantage of the good name which he acquired more than compensated for the great nuisance of their being there.

§22.   The Emperor was strong and well built. He was tall in stature, but not excessively so, for his height was just seven times the length of his own feet. The top of his head was round, and his eyes were piercing and unusually large. His nose was slightly longer than normal, he had a fine head of white hair and his expression was gay and good-humoured. As a result, whether he was seated or standing, he always appeared masterful and dignified. His neck was short and rather thick, and his stomach a trifle too heavy, but the proportions of the rest of his body prevented one from noticing these blemishes. His step was firm and he was manly in all his movements. He spoke distinctly, but his voice was thin for a man of his physique. His health was good, except that he suffered from frequent attacks of fever during the last four years of his life, and towards the end he was lame in one foot. Even then he continued to do exactly as he wished, instead of following the advice of his doctors, whom he came positively to dislike after they advised him to stop eating the roast meat to which he was accustomed and to live on stewed dishes.

He spent much of his time on horseback and out hunting, which came naturally to him, for it would be difficult to find another race on earth who could equal the Franks in this activity. He took delight in steam-baths at the thermal springs, and loved to exercise himself in the water whenever he could. He was an extremely strong swimmer and in this sport no one could surpass him. It was for this reason that he built his palace at Aachen and remained continuously in residence there during the last years of his life and indeed until the moment of his death. He would invite not only his sons to bathe with him, but his nobles and friends as well, and occasionally even a crowd of his attendants and bodyguards, so that sometimes a hundred men or more would be in the water together.

§23.   He wore the national dress of the Franks. Next to his skin he had a linen shirt and linen drawers; and then long hose and a tunic edged with silk. He wore shoes on his feet and bands of cloth wound round his legs. In winter he protected his chest and shoulders with a jerkin made of otter skins or ermine. He wrapped himself in a blue cloak and always had a sword strapped to his side, with a hilt and belt of gold or silver. Sometimes he would use a jewelled sword, but this was only on great feast days or when ambassadors came from foreign peoples. He hated the clothes of other countries, no matter how becoming they might be, and he would never consent to wear them. The only exception to this was one day in Rome when Pope Hadrian entreated him to put on a long tunic and a Greek mantle, and to wear shoes made in the Roman fashion; and then a second time, when Leo, Hadrian's successor, persuaded him to do the same thing. On feast days he walked in procession in a suit of cloth of gold, with jewelled shoes, his cloak fastened with a golden brooch and with a crown of gold and precious stones on his head. On ordinary days his dress differed hardly at all from that of the common people.

§24.   He was moderate in his eating and drinking, and especially so in drinking; for he hated to see drunkenness in any man, and even more so in himself and his friends. All the same, he could not go long without food, and he often used to complain that fasting made him feel ill. He rarely gave banquets and these only on high feast days, but then he would invite a great number of guests. His main meal of the day was served in four courses, in addition to the roast meat which his hunters used to bring in on spits and which he enjoyed more than any other food. During his meal he would listen to a public reading or some other entertainment. Stories would be recited for him, or the doings of the ancients told again. He took great pleasure in the books of Saint Augustine and especially in those which are called *The City of God*. . . .

§25.   He spoke easily and fluently, and could express with great clarity whatever he had to say. He was not content with his own mother tongue, but took the trouble to learn foreign languages. He learnt Latin so well that he spoke it as fluently as his own tongue; but he understood Greek better than he could speak it. He was eloquent to the point of sometimes seeming almost garrulous.

He paid the greatest attention to the liberal arts; and he had great respect for men who taught them, bestowing high honours upon them. When he was learning the rules of grammar he received tuition from Peter the Deacon of Pisa, who by then was an old man, but for all other subjects he was taught by Alcuin, surnamed Albinus, another Deacon, a man of the Saxon race who came from Britain and was the most learned man anywhere to be found. Under him the Emperor spent much time and effort in studying rhetoric, dialectic and especially astrology. He applied himself to mathematics and traced the course of the stars with great attention and care. He also tried to learn to write. With this object in view he used to keep writing-tablets and notebooks under the pillows on his bed, so that he could try his hand at forming letters during his leisure moments; but, although he tried very hard, he had begun too late in life and he made little progress. . . .

§29.   Now that he was Emperor, he discovered that there were many defects in the legal system of his own people, for the Franks have two separate codes of law which differ from each other in many points. He gave much thought to how he could best fill the gaps, reconcile the discrepancies, correct the errors and rewrite the laws which were illexpressed. None of this was ever finished; he added a few sections, but even these remained incomplete. What he did do was to have collected together and committed to writing the laws of all the nations under his jurisdiction which still remained unrecorded.

At the same time he directed that the age-old narrative poems, barbarous enough, it is true, in which were celebrated the warlike deeds of the kings of ancient times, should be written out and so preserved. He also began a grammar of his native tongue. . . .

Selection from *Beowulf*

Beowulf is the first great poem in the English tradition. Its language was Anglo-Saxon, or Old English. It was composed orally, probably in England in the eighth century, and is preserved, presumably in complete form, in a single manuscript dating from about 1000. Like *The Epic of Gilgamesh* and Homer's *Iliad*, it is an epic, meant originally to be recited rather than read. Composed anonymously, *Beowulf* gives voice to the creative Anglo-Saxon imagination as it peopled the dark with primordial monsters.

The poem focuses on Beowulf, prince of the Geats (a tribe in Sweden). In the first part Beowulf sails to Denmark to rescue King Hrothgar from Grendel and Grendel's mother, two monsters. Swamp-dwellers, the monsters have been attacking Hrothgar's great hall by night and devouring his people. Beowulf kills the monsters. Back home, he is made king of the Geats and reigns for fifty years. In the second half of the poem, Beowulf faces a dragon. With his comrade Wiglaf's help, Beowulf defeats the dragon, only to die of his wounds.

Woven into *Beowulf* is a chilling theme: the never-ceasing battle of good against evil. The poem shows that evil never sleeps and comes in many forms, demonic and human, and that good, however vigilant, does not always win. Like Greek drama (see Sophocles' *Oedipus the King*), it offers the gloomy message that life is tragic and nothing is guaranteed.

Beowulf was written in alliterative verse, a rhymeless verse characterized by the repetition of consonant sounds, usually at the beginning of words, as in this example from a modern translation:

> *Down off the moorlands' misting fells came*
> *Grendel stalking; God's brand was on him.*
> *The spoiler meant to snatch away*
> *from the high hall some of human race.*

Alliterative verse was typical of Anglo-Saxon poetry and remained an essential feature of English poetry until the Late Middle Ages.

The setting in which Beowulf fights Grendel may be primitive and chaotic, but the society that spawned the poem was not. Modern scholars describe eighth-century England as Christian, law-abiding, and aristocratic. The Anglo-Saxons of the period were civilized, much altered from their pagan ancestors who settled England on the heels of the Roman withdrawal in about A.D. 400.

Reading the Selection

This brief selection from *Beowulf* deals with the defeat of the half-human Grendel. Among other things, it offers some insight into the poet's religious faith. The poet's world is decidedly Christian. It is claimed that [nothing can happen] "without God's willing it." Grendel is "God's enemy"; he is "feuding with God"; he (in a passage not included here) is said to be descended from Cain, the first murderer. Still, the older, primitive world of Anglo-Saxon myth keeps breaking through, in Beowulf's savagery and later in the primordial, nonhuman dragon. This seeming contradiction may be resolved by recognizing that the poem was composed when the Anglo-Saxon conversion to Christianity was only about one century old.

Beowulf's love of fame, or glory, also comes from the pre-Christian, Anglo-Saxon world. Not Christian salvation but desire for glory was his prime motive for living. "To Beowulf the glory of this fight was granted." At the epic's end (not included here), his epitaph reads: "The gentlest and most gracious of men, the kindest to his people and the most desirous of renown."

. . . .

              Gliding through the shadows came   1
the walker in the night; the warriors slept
whose task was to hold the horned building,
all except one. It was well-known to men
that the demon could not drag them to the shades
without God's willing it; yet the one man kept
unblinking watch. He awaited, heart swelling
with anger against his foe, the ordeal of battle.
Down off the moorlands' misting fells came
Grendel stalking; God's brand was on him.   10
The spoiler meant to snatch away
from the high hall some of human race.
He came on under the clouds, clearly saw at last
the gold-hall of men, the mead-drinking place
nailed with gold plates. That was not the first visit
he had paid to the hall of Hrothgar the Dane:
he never before and never after
harder luck nor hall-guards found.

Walking to the hall came this warlike creature
condemned to agony. The door gave way,   20
toughened with iron, at the touch of those hands.
Rage-inflamed, wreckage-bent, he ripped open
the jaws of the hall. Hastening on,
the foe then stepped onto the unstained floor,
angrily advanced: out of his eyes stood
an unlovely light like that of fire.
He saw then in the hall a host of young soldiers,
a company of kinsmen caught away in sleep,
a whole warrior-band. In his heart he laughed then,
horrible monster, his hopes swelling   30
to a gluttonous meal. He meant to wrench
the life from each body that lay in the place
before night was done. It was not to be;
he was no longer to feast on the flesh of mankind
after that night.
             Narrowly the powerful
kinsman of Hygelac kept watch how the ravager
set to work with his sudden catches;
nor did the monster mean to hang back.
As a first step he set his hands on   40
a sleeping soldier, savagely tore at him,
gnashed at his bone-joints, bolted huge gobbets,
sucked at his veins, and had soon eaten
all of the dead man, even down to his
hands and feet.
             Forward he stepped,
stretched out his hands to seize the warrior
calmly at rest there, reached out for him with his
unfriendly fingers: but the faster man
forestalling, sat up, sent back his arm.   50
The upholder of evils at once knew
he had not met, on middle earth's
extremest acres, with any man
of harder hand-grip: his heart panicked.
He was quit of the place no more quickly for that.

Eager to be away, he ailed for his darkness
and the company of devils; the dealings he had there
were like nothing he had come across in his lifetime.
Then Hygelac's brave kinsman called to mind
that evening's utterance, upright he stood,   60
fastened his hold till fingers were bursting.
The monster strained away: the man stepped closer.
The monster's desire was for darkness between them,
direction regardless, to get out and run
for his fen-bordered lair; he felt his grip's strength
crushed by his enemy. It was an ill journey
the rough marauder had made to Heorot.

The crash in the banqueting-hall came to the Danes,
the men of the guard that remained in the building,
with the taste of death. The deepening rage   70
of the claimants to Heorot caused it to resound.
It was indeed wonderful that the wine-supper-hall
withstood the wrestling pair, that the world's palace
fell not to the ground. But it was girt firmly,
both inside and out, by iron braces
of skilled manufacture. Many a figured
gold-worked wine-bench, as we heard it,
started from the floor at the struggles of that pair.
The men of the Danes had not imagined that
any of mankind by what method soever   80
might undo that intricate, antlered hall,
sunder it by strength—unless it were swallowed up in
the embraces of fire.
             Fear entered into
the listening North Danes, as that noise rose up again
strange and strident. It shrilled terror
to the ears that heard it through the hall's side-wall,
the grisly plaint of God's enemy,
his song of ill-success, the sobs of the damned one
bewailing his pain. He was pinioned there   90
by the man of all mankind living
in this world's estate the strongest of his hands.

Not for anything would the earls' guardian
let his deadly guest go living:
he did not count his continued existence
of the least use to anyone. The earls ran
to defend the person of their famous prince;
they drew their ancestral swords to bring
what aid they could to their captain, Beowulf.
They were ignorant of this, when they entered the fight,   100
boldly-intentioned battle-friends,
to hew at Grendel, hunt his life
on every side—that no sword on earth,
not the truest steel, could touch their assailant;
for by a spell he had dispossessed all
blades of their bite on him.
             A bitter parting
from life was that day destined for him;
the eldritch spirit was sent off on his
far faring into the fiends' domain.   110

It was then that this monster, who, moved by spite
against human kind, had caused so much harm
—so feuding with God—found at last
that flesh and bone were to fail him in the end;
for Hygelac's great-hearted kinsman
had him by the hand; and hateful to each
was the breath of the other.
                              A breach in the giant
flesh-frame showed then, shoulder-muscles
sprang apart, there was a snapping of tendons,   120
bone-locks burst. To Beowulf the glory
of this fight was granted; Grendel's lot
to flee the slopes fen-ward with flagging heart,
to a den where he knew there could be no relief,
no refuge for a life at its very last stage,
whose surrender-day had dawned. The Danish hopes
in this fatal fight had found their answer.

He had cleansed Heorot. He who had come from afar,
deep-minded, strong-hearted, had saved the hall
from persecution. He was pleased with his night's work,   130
the deed he had done. Before the Danish people
the Great captain had made good his boast,
had taken away all their unhappiness,

the evil menace under which they had lived,
enduring it by dire constraint,
no slight affliction. As a signal to all
the hero hung up the hand, the arm
and torn-off shoulder, the entire limb,
Grendel's whole grip, below the gable of the roof.

There was, as I heard it, at hall next morning   140
a great gathering in the gift-hall yard
to see the wonder. Along the wide highroads
the chiefs of the clans came from near and far
to see the foe's footprints. It may fairly be said
that his parting from life aroused no pity in any
who tracked the spoor-blood of his blind flight
for the monster's mere-pool; with mood flagging
and strength crushed, he had staggered onwards;
each step evidenced his ebbing life's blood.
The tarn was troubled; a terrible wave-thrash   150
brimmed it, bubbling; black-mingled,
the warm wound-blood welled upwards.
He had dived to his doom, he had died miserably;
here in his fen-lair he had laid aside
his heathen soul. Hell welcomed it.

9

THE HIGH MIDDLE AGES
The Christian Centuries

Selections from the *Song of Roland*

The anonymous poem *Song of Roland* belongs to the literary genre known as *chanson de geste* (from French, "song of deeds"), which dominated medieval literature in the first half of the twelfth century. Based on historical events, it tells of Count Roland, a vassal and knight of Charlemagne, the King of the Franks who ruled the then largest and most centralized state since the fall of Rome. According to medieval records, Roland governed the Breton march (modern Brittany) in the name of Charlemagne and died fighting in Spain in 778. Einhard (see *The Life of Charlemagne*) names Roland as a leader of Charlemagne's rear guard, who was killed by Christian Basques in an ambush in northern Spain while protecting the king and his forward army.

Only a distant echo of these actual events survives in the *Song of Roland*, which glorifies the knight and his sacrificial death. The poem was written down in about 1100, having circulated orally in songs performed by bards (singing poets) for several centuries. By the time it received its final form, what had been a minor skirmish had been transformed by poetic art into a battle of vast proportions. Why Roland, who was only one of the many "brave knights" sung about in the Middle Ages, should have become the focus of so much attention is a mystery. Whatever the cause, he became the central figure in a rousing tale of bravery, treachery, and pride.

The world described in the *Song of Roland* reflects more the time it was finally set in writing (the twelfth century) than the period when Roland lived (the eighth century). Medieval Europe had launched the Crusades (the first began in 1095) against the Muslim world; hence, in the poem, Charlemagne's enemies are changed from Christian Basques to Spanish Saracens (Muslims). France was also in the early stages of becoming a unified state; thus, in the poem, the farflung Frankish kingdom is transformed into France—a sign of embryonic nationalism that French kings wanted to nurture. Finally, the twelfth-century church was more powerful than in Charlemagne's day, and in the poem, this increased power is expressed in the pivotal role played by the warrior Archbishop Turpin.

The *Song of Roland* is typical of *chansons de geste* in that it celebrates a defeat. In an elaborately complicated story set at Charlemagne's court, Roland instigates a possibly deadly mission for his rival, Ganelon. But he suddenly finds the tables turned and himself a victim when Ganelon plots an ambush with the Spanish Saracens. Ultimately, Roland falls prey to his own pride, losing his own life and the lives of the rest of Charlemagne's rear guard.

167

Reading the Selections

These thirteen verses (*laisses*), LXXIX–LXXXVII and CXXIX–CXXXII, depict the doomed Franks as they fall into the trap laid by the Saracens ("Sarrazins"). The turning point of the poem, these verses also set forth the work's theme and moral. Roland ("Rollanz," "Rollant"), in verse LXXIX, gives voice to the anonymous author's chivalric and self-consciously literary theme:

> *Man for his lord should suffer . . .*
> *So evil songs ne'er sung of us shall be.*

The work's moral message emerges in the angry verbal exchanges between Roland and his companion Oliver. Ignoring Oliver's well-considered advice, Roland three times refuses to sound the oliphant (a horn), which would bring Charlemagne ("Carlun," "Charles") to the rescue of his fellow Franks. When Roland does blow the horn (verse CXXXI), it is too late; the outnumbered Franks are soon overwhelmed (not included here). Faced with certain death, the cautious Oliver offers this lesson to Roland (and to readers):

> *Vassalage comes by sense, and not folly;*
> *Prudence more worth is than stupidity.*

—⁓—

LXXIX

Ready they make hauberks Sarrazinese,   1
That folded are, the greater part, in three;
And they lace on good helms Sarragucese;
Gird on their swords of tried steel Viennese;
Fine shields they have, and spears Valentinese,
And white, blue, red, their ensigns take the breeze,
They've left their mules behind, and their palfreys,
Their chargers mount, and canter knee by knee.
Fair shines the sun, the day is bright and clear,
Light burns again from all their polished gear.   10
A thousand horns they sound, more proud to seem;
Great is the noise, the Franks its echo hear.
Says Oliver: "Companion, I believe,
Sarrazins now in battle must we meet."
Answers Rollanz: "God grant us then the fee!
For our King's sake well must we quit us here;
Man for his lord should suffer great disease,
Most bitter cold endure, and burning heat,
His hair and skin should offer up at need.
Now must we each lay on most hardily,   20
So evil songs ne'er sung of us shall be.
Pagans are wrong: Christians are right indeed.
Evil example will never come of me."

LXXX

Oliver mounts upon a lofty peak,   1
Looks to his right along the valley green,
The pagan tribes approaching there appear;
He calls Rollanz, his companion, to see:
"What sound is this, come out of Spain, we hear,
What hauberks bright, what helmets these that gleam?

They'll smite our Franks with fury past belief,
He knew it, Guenes, the traitor and the thief,
Who chose us out before the King our chief."
Answers the count Rollanz: "Olivier, cease.   10
That man is my good-father; hold thy peace."

LXXXI

Upon a peak is Oliver mounted,   1
Kingdom of Spain he sees before him spread,
And Sarrazins, so many gatherèd.
Their helmets gleam, with gold are jewellèd,
Also their shields, their hauberks orfreyèd,
Also their swords, ensigns on spears fixèd.
Rank beyond rank could not be numberèd,
So many there, no measure could he set.
In his own heart he's sore astonishèd,
Fast as he could, down from the peak hath sped,   10
Comes to the Franks, to them his tale hath said.

LXXXII

Says Oliver: "Pagans from there I saw;   1
Never on earth did any man see more.
Gainst us their shields an hundred thousand bore,
That lacèd helms and shining hauberks wore;
And, bolt upright, their bright brown spearheads shone.
Battle we'll have as never was before.
Lords of the Franks, God keep you in valour!
So hold your ground, we be not overborne!"
Then say the Franks: "Shame take him that goes off:
If we must die, then perish one and all."   10

LXXXIII

Says Oliver: "Pagans in force abound,
While of us Franks but very few I count;
Comrade Rollanz, your horn I pray you sound!
If Charlès hear, he'll turn his armies round."
Answers Rollanz: "A fool I should be found;
In France the Douce would perish my renown.
With Durendal I'll lay on thick and stout,
In blood the blade, to its golden hilt, I'll drown.
Felon pagans to th' pass shall not come down;
I pledge you now, to death they all are bound." 10

LXXXIV

"Comrade Rollanz, sound the olifant, I pray;
If Charlès hear, the host he'll turn again;
Will succour us our King and baronage."
Answers Rollanz: "Never, by God, I say,
For my misdeed shall kinsmen hear the blame,
Nor France the Douce fall into evil fame!
Rather stout blows with Durendal I'll lay,
With my good sword that by my side doth sway;
Till bloodied o'er you shall behold the blade.
Felon pagans are gathered to their shame; 10
I pledge you now, to death they're doomed today."

LXXXV

"Comrade Rollanz, once sound your olifant!
If Charlès hear, where in the pass he stands,
I pledge you now, they'll turn again, the Franks."
"Never, by God," then answers him Rollanz,
"Shall it be said by any living man,
That for pagans I took my horn in hand!
Never by me shall men reproach my clan.
When I am come into the battle grand,
And blows lay on, by hundred, by thousand,
Of Durendal bloodied you'll see the brand. 10
Franks are good men; like vassals brave they'll stand;
Nay, Spanish men from death have no warrant."

LXXXVI

Says Oliver: "In this I see no blame;
I have beheld the Sarrazins of Spain;
Covered with them, the mountains and the vales,
The wastes I saw, and all the farthest plains.
A muster great they've made, this people strange;
We have of men a very little tale."
Answers Rollanz: "My anger is inflamed.
Never, please God His Angels and His Saints,
Never by me shall Frankish valour fail!
Rather I'll die than shame shall me attain.
Therefore strike on, the Emperour's love to gain." 10

LXXXVII

Pride hath Rollanz, wisdom Olivier hath;
And both of them shew marvellous courage;
Once they are horsed, once they have donned their arms,
Rather they'ld die than from the battle pass.
Good are the counts, and lofty their language.
Felon pagans come cantering in their wrath.
Says Oliver: "Behold and see, Rollanz,
These are right near, but Charles is very far.
On the olifant deign now to sound a blast;
Were the King here, we should not fear damage. 10
Only look up towards the Pass of Aspre,
In sorrow there you'll see the whole rereward.
Who does this deed, does no more afterward."
Answers Rollanz: "Utter not such outrage!
Evil his heart that is in thought coward!
We shall remain firm in our place installed;
From us the blows shall come, from us the assault."

.   .   .   .

CXXIX

Then says Rollanz: "I'll wind this olifant,
If Charlès hear, where in the pass he stands,
I pledge you now they will return, the Franks."
Says Oliver: "Great shame would come of that;
And a reproach on every one, your clan,
That shall endure while each lives in the land,
When I implored, you would not do this act;
Doing it now, no praise from me you'll have:
So wind your horn, but not by courage rash,
Seeing that both your arms with blood are splashed." 10
Answers that count: "Fine blows I've struck them back."

CXXX

Then says Rollant: "Strong is it now, our battle;
I'll wind my horn, so the King hears it, Charlès."
Says Oliver: "That act were not a vassal's.
When I implored you, comrade, you were wrathful.
Were the King here, we had not borne such damage.
Nor should we blame those with him there, his army."
Says Oliver: "Now by my beard, hereafter
If I may see my gentle sister Alde,
She in her arms, I swear, shall never clasp you."

CXXXI

Then says Rollanz: "Wherefore so wroth with me?"
He answers him: "Comrade, it was your deed:
Vassalage comes by sense, and not folly;
Prudence more worth is than stupidity.
Here are Franks dead, all for your trickery;
No service more to Carlun may we yield.
My lord were here now, had you trusted me,
And fought and won this battle then had we,

Taken or slain were the king Marsilie.
In your prowess, Rollanz, no good we've seen!
Charlès the great in vain your aid will seek—
None such as he till God His Judgement speak;—
Here you must die, and France in shame be steeped;
Here perishes our loyal company,
Before this night great severance and grief."

CXXXII

That Archbishop has heard them, how they spoke,
His horse he pricks with his fine spurs of gold,
Coming to them he takes up his reproach:

"Sir Oliver, and you, Sir Rollant, both,
For God I pray, do not each other scold!
No help it were to us, the horn to blow,
But, none the less, it may be better so;
The King will come, with vengeance that he owes;
These Spanish men never away shall go.
Our Franks here, each descending from his horse,
Will find us dead, and limb from body torn;
They'll take us hence, on biers and litters borne;
With pity and with grief for us they'll mourn;
They'll bury each in some old minster-close;
No wolf nor swine nor dog shall gnaw our bones."
Answers Rollant: "Sir, very well you spoke."

ANNA COMNENA

Selections from *The Alexiad*

The Alexiad, as the first known history written by a woman, is a milestone in world literature. The author was Anna Comnena (1083–1153), the daughter of the Byzantine emperor Alexius I, whose reign (1081–1118) is covered in her book. Ignored by the Byzantines, *The Alexiad* was absorbed into Western culture after being discovered by Renaissance scholars, who translated it from Greek into European languages. Today it is accepted as a valuable historical source, partly as an eyewitness account of Alexius's reign and, equally important, as a sound work of scholarship.

Alexius Comnenus, the subject of *The Alexiad,* ruled Byzantium during a crucial time in its history. His career began as the empire, wracked by internal chaos, faced probable extinction from all sides: Seljuk Turks were on the move through Asia Minor, Normans advanced against Adriatic outposts, and varied tribes from the north menaced Constantinople, the capital. A gifted general and master of intrigue, Alexius seized the throne and, as Alexius I, gave the empire a new lease on life. He conducted winning campaigns against both Turks and Normans and weathered the First Crusade. His political and army reforms allowed the empire to endure until 1204, when soldiers of the Fourth Crusade conquered Constantinople and divided up its lands among themselves.

Anna Comnena's account of Alexius's reign uses the methods of the Greek historian Thucydides (see *History of the Peloponnesian War*). Like him, she writes contemporary history based on personal knowledge, memories of credible witnesses, and study of archival documents and treaties. Unlike him, she concentrates on wars and uprisings, a narrow focus that undoubtedly reflects her troubled age. Told from an insider's point of view and instilled with Christian and Classical learning, hers is a highly readable, persuasive account of Alexius's reign.

The Alexiad is not without flaws. Foremost among these are Anna's biases: She glorifies her father and ignores her brother, John, probably because John succeeded Alexius to the throne (r. 1118–1143), thus ending her hopes of being empress. She was also a religious zealot, gloating over the deaths of heretics. Her love of country led her to overdramatize events. ("They descended on their enemies like lions.") But overall, the book's virtues outweigh these flaws.

Reading the Selections

Anna Comnena, writing in the Preface to *The Alexiad,* echoes Thucydides when she asserts that history is a "bulwark against the stream of Time," thus allowing humans to salvage what is important from "the depths of Oblivion." From this highminded ideal, she descends to the reality of her subject, Alexius's empire as it is simultaneously invaded by Turks and soldiers of the First Crusade

(1097–1104), known variously as Franks, Latins, or Kelts. Books One through Thirteen of *The Alexiad* are filled with military campaigns and governmental crises. The selection taken from Book Fourteen, the next to last chapter, offers a uniquely non-Western view of the crusaders, both as individuals and as a group. Enlisted in Europe's holy war against Middle East Muslims, the crusaders, in Anna's eyes, are nothing but undisciplined and untrustworthy barbarians, greedy for gain. To her, they are no match for her father, despite his declining health.

—m—

Preface

The stream of Time, irresistible, ever moving, carries off and bears away all things that come to birth and plunges them into utter darkness, both deeds of no account and deeds which are mighty and worthy of commemoration; as the playwright says, it 'brings to light that which was unseen and shrouds from us that which was manifiest'. Nevertheless, the science of History is a great bulwark against this stream of Time; in a way it checks this irresistible flood, it holds in a tight grasp whatever it can seize floating on the surface and will not allow it to slip away into the depths of Oblivion.

I, Anna, daughter of the Emperor Alexius and the Empress Irene, born and bred in the Purple, not without some acquaintance with literature—having devoted the most earnest study to the Greek language, in fact, and being not unpractised in Rhetoric and having read thoroughly the treatises of Aristotle and the dialogues of Plato, and having fortified my mind with the Quadrivium of sciences (these things must be divulged, and it is not self-advertisement to recall what Nature and my own zeal for knowledge have given me, nor what God has apportioned to me from above and what has been contributed by Opportunity); I, having realized the effects wrought by Time, desire now by means of my writings to give an account of my father's deeds, which do not deserve to be consigned to Forgetfulness nor to be swept away on the flood of Time into an ocean of Non-Remembrance; I wish to recall everything, the achievements before his elevation to the throne and his actions in the service of others before his coronation.

I approach the task with no intention of flaunting my skill as a writer; my concern is rather that a career so brilliant should not go unrecorded in the future, since even the greatest exploits, unless by some chance their memory is preserved and guarded in history, vanish in silent darkness. My father's actions themselves prove his ability as a ruler and show, too, that he was prepared to submit to authority, within just limits.

Now that I have decided to write the story of his life, I am fearful of an underlying suspicion: someone might conclude that in composing the history of my father I am glorifying myself; the history, wherever I express admiration for any act of his, may seem wholly false and mere panegyric. On the other hand, if he himself should ever lead me, under the compulsion of events, to criticize some action taken by him, not because of what he decided but because of the circumstances, here again I fear the cavillers: in their all-embracing jealousy and refusal to accept what is right, because they are malicious and full of envy, they may cast in my teeth the story of Noah's son Ham and, as Homer says, 'blame the guiltless'.

Whenever one assumes the role of historian, friendship and enmities have to be forgotten; often one has to bestow on adversaries the highest commendation (where their deeds merit it); often, too, one's nearest relatives, if their pursuits are in error and suggest the desirability of reproach, have to be censured. The historian, therefore, must shirk neither remonstrance with his friends, nor praise of his enemies. For my part, I hope to satisfy both parties, both those who are offended by us and those who accept us, by appealing to the evidence of the actual events and of eye-witnesses. The fathers and grandfathers of some men living today saw these things.

—m—

Book XIV

One day he was exercising at polo, his partner being the Taticius I have often mentioned. Taticius was carried away by his horse and fell on the emperor, whose knee-cap was injured by the impact (Taticius was a heavy man). The pain affected the whole of his foot and although he did not show that he was in distress—he was used to bearing pain—he did receive some minor treatment. Little by little the trouble wore off and disappeared, so that his normal habits were resumed. That was the prime origin of his gout, for the painful areas attracted rheumatism. There was a second, more obvious cause of all this illness. Everyone knows that countless multitudes of Kelts came to the imperial city, having migrated from their own lands and hurried from all directions to us. It was then that the emperor was plunged into a vast ocean of worries. He had long been aware of their dream of Empire; he was aware too of their overwhelming numbers—more than the grains of sand on the sea-shore or all the stars of heaven; the sum total of Roman forces would equal not one tiny part of their multitudes, even if they were concentrated in one place—much less when they were dissipated over wide areas, for some were on guard in the valleys of Serbia and in Dalmatia, others keeping watch near the Danube against Cuman and Dacian incursions, and many had been entrusted with the task of saving Dyrrachium from a second Keltic victory. Under the circumstances he devoted his whole attention now to these Kelts and all else was considered of secondary importance. The barbarian world on our borders, which was restless but had not yet broken out into open hostility, he kept in check by granting honours and presents, while the ambition of the Kelts was confined by all possible means. The rebellious spirit of his own subjects caused no less trouble—in fact he suspected them even more and hastened to protect himself as best he could. Their plots were skilfully averted. But no one could adequately describe the ferment of troubles which descended on him at this period. It compelled him to become all things to all men, to accommodate himself as far as he could to circumstances. Like a trained physician (following the rules of his craft) he had to apply himself to the most pressing need. At daybreak, as soon as the sun leapt up over the eastern horizon, he took his seat on the imperial throne and every day on his orders all Kelts were freely admitted to his presence. The purpose of this was twofold: he liked them to make their own requests, and he strove by various arguments to reconcile them to his wishes. The Keltic counts are brazen-faced, violent men, money-grubbers and where their personal desires are concerned quite immoderate. These are natural characteristics of the race. They also surpass all other nations in loquacity. So when they came to the palace they did so in an undisciplined fashion, every count bringing with him as many comrades as he wished; after him, without interruption, came another and then a third—an endless queue. Once there they did not limit the conversation by the water-clock, like the orators of ancient times, but each, whoever he was, enjoyed as much time as he wanted for the interview with the emperor. Men of such character, talkers so exuberant, had neither respect for his feelings nor thought for the passing of time nor any idea of the by-standers' wrath; instead of giving way to those coming behind them, they talked on and on with an incessant stream of petitions. Every student of human customs will be acquainted with Frankish verbosity and their pettifogging love of detail; but the audience on these occasions learnt the lesson more thoroughly—from actual experience. When evening came, after remaining without food all through the day, the emperor would rise from his throne and retire to his private apartment, but even then he was not free from the importunities of the Kelts. They came one after another, not only those who had failed to obtain a hearing during the day, but those who had already been heard returned as well, putting forward this or that excuse for more talk. In the midst of them, calmly enduring their endless chatter stood the emperor. One could see them there, all asking questions, and him, alone and unchanging, giving them prompt replies. But there was no limit to their foolish babbling, and if a court official did try to cut them short, he was himself interrupted by Alexius. He knew the traditional pugnacity of the Franks and feared that from some trivial pretext a mighty blaze of trouble might spring up, resulting in serious harm to the prestige of Rome. It was really a most extraordinary sight. Like a statue wrought by the hammer, made perhaps of bronze or cold-forged iron, the emperor would sit through the night, often from evening till midnight, often till third cock-crow, sometimes almost until the sun was shining clearly. The attendants were all worn out, but by frequently retiring had a rest and then came back again—in bad humour. Thus not one of them would stay motionless as long as he did; all in one way or another kept changing position: one would sit down, another turned his head away and rested it on something, another propped himself against a wall. Only one man, the emperor, faced this tremendous task without weakening. His endurance was truly remarkable. Hundreds of people were talking, each one prattling on at length, 'brawling away unbridled of tongue' as Homer says. As one stood aside he passed the conversation on to another, and he to the next, and so on and on. They stood only in these intervals but he all the time, up to first or even second cock-crow. After a brief rest, when the sun rose he was again seated on his throne and once more fresh labours and twofold troubles succeeded those of the night. It was for this reason, then, that the emperor was attacked by the pain in his feet. From that time to the end of his life the rheumatism came on at regular intervals and caused him dreadful pain. Despite this he bore it so well that not once did he murmur in complaint; all he said was, 'I deserve to suffer. This happens to me justly because of the multitude of my sins.' And if by chance a cross word did escape his lips he immediately made the sign of the Cross against the assault of the evil demon. 'Flee from me, wicked one,' he would say. 'A curse on you and your tempting of Christians!' I will say no more now about the pain that afflicted him. Maybe there was someone who contributed to this malady of his and increased the sufferings he bore (and surely his cup of bitterness was already full). I will give a brief outline of the story, not the full details. The empress smeared the rim of the cup with honey, as it were, and contrived that he should avoid most of his troubles, for she unceasingly watched over him. The man I am speaking of must be introduced at this point and considered a third reason of the emperor's illness, not merely as the immediate cause, but also the most effective cause (to use the doctors' terms). He did not attack once and for all and then disappear, but remained with him, a constant companion like the most pernicious humours in the veins. Worse than that, if one reflects on the man's character, he was not only a cause of the disease, but he was himself a malady and its most troublesome symptom. But I must bite my tongue and say no more. However eager I may be to jump on these scoundrels, I must not run off the main highway. I will reserve what I have to say about him to the appropriate time.

CHRÈTIEN DE TROYES

Selection from *Arthurian Romances*

Lancelot belongs to the legendary world of King Arthur and his knights, which gripped the imagination of writers and public alike in the twelfth and thirteenth centuries. Chrètien de Troyes's *Lancelot, or the Knight of the Cart,* was one of the works that put the Arthurian tradition on the map. This tradition has lived on in the popular consciousness for centuries, as evidenced by modern films and fiction on Arthurian themes.

The Arthurian legends sprang from the history of the Celts, ancient peoples (Gauls and Britons) who dominated western and central Europe until Germanic invaders pushed them to the continent's fringes of Ireland, Scotland, Wales, and Brittany. The historic Arthur ruled probably in sixth-century Wales, where his wars against both Romans and Germans made him a figure larger than life. Over the next six hundred years, the historic Arthur gave way to the Arthur of legend; in 1125 a writer could comment on the "idle fictions" and "wild tales" then circulating about the Welsh king. Little remains of these works, which were recited by wandering storytellers; but they form the background for Chrètien's writing.

Chrètien places the spotlight not on Arthur but on the court and the knights. The Arthurian court is depicted as the epitome of civilization. To be received there is joy; banishment is misery. The stories of the knights express the ideals of courtly love, the code that made duty to women a higher good than personal honor.

Chrètien de Troyes (flourished 1170) composed works for the feudal courts of northern France. Chrètien credits one patron, Countess Marie of Champagne, as inspiring *Lancelot.* Written in French, these poems are long narratives of fantastic adventures of knights and ladies. They are the first romances, the genre that replaced the *chansons de geste* (see the *Song of Roland*) in popularity after 1150. The romances, with their ideal of love as an ennobling passion, helped raise women's status, especially among the feudal elite.

Reading the Selection

The plot of *Lancelot* is typical of Chrètien's romances. It is organized around a quest—Lancelot's search for Guinevere, Arthur's queen, who is abducted by the evil Meleagant, Prince of Gorre. The plot is complicated by Lancelot's initial and almost unforgivable sin: He hesitates for two steps to mount into the shameful cart. Lancelot's "sin" against the courtly code is that he chose even for an instant personal honor before love.

To redeem himself, Lancelot goes through a series of tests meant to teach him to serve women unhesitatingly. This selection includes four of these episodes. In the first, he shows ignorance when he disobeys a damsel and is wounded for his pride. Next, when a subdued Lancelot says to a second damsel that "without hesitation he will promise her anything she desires," he is soon rewarded. Meeting a third damsel, he instantly obeys her though it means going back on his word. In the last episode, confronted by still another damsel, he has not yet learned his lesson: "The knight hesitated at the door, and thought: 'God, what can I do?'"

Only in the poem's climax (not included here) does Lancelot reach the courtly ideal: He obeys the queen's every whim, even shaming himself in public. The final meaning of the two lovers' passion is hotly debated today. Was it meant to glorify adultery, or was it a traitorous love to be condemned by a courtly audience?

—ᴍ—

Lancelot

· · ·

Late in the afternoon they arrive at a town, which, you must know, was very rich and beautiful. All three entered through the gate; the people are greatly amazed to see the knight borne upon the cart, and they take no pains to conceal their feelings, but small and great and old and young shout taunts at him in the streets, so that the knight hears many vile and scornful words at his expense. They all inquire: "To what punishment is this knight to be consigned? Is he to be flayed, or hanged, or drowned, or burned upon a fire of thorns? Tell us, thou dwarf, who art driving him, in what crime was he caught? Is he convicted of robbery? Is he a murderer, or a criminal?" And to all this the dwarf made no response, vouchsafing to them no reply. He conducts the knight to a lodging-place; and Gawain follows the dwarf closely to a tower, which stood on the same level over against the town. Beyond there stretched a meadow, and the tower was built close by, upon a lofty eminence of rock, whose face formed a sharp precipice. Following the horse and cart, Gawain entered the tower. In the hall they met a damsel elegantly attired, than whom there was none fairer in the land, and with her they saw coming two fair and charming maidens. As soon as they saw my lord Gawain, they received him joyously and saluted him, and then asked news about the other knight: "Dwarf, of what crime is this knight guilty, whom thou dost drive like a lame man?" He would not answer her question, but he made the knight get out of the cart, and then he withdrew, without their knowing whither he went. Then my lord Gawain dismounts, and valets come forward to relieve the two knights of their armour. The damsel ordered two green mantles to be brought, which they put on. When the hour for supper came, a sumptuous repast was set. The damsel sat at table beside my lord Gawain. They would not have changed their lodging-place to seek any other, for all that evening the damsel showed them great honour, and provided them with fair and pleasant company.

Vv. 463–538.—When they had sat up long enough, two long, high beds were prepared in the middle of the hall; and there was another bed alongside, fairer and more splendid than the rest; for, as the story testifies, it possessed all the excellence that one could think of in a bed. When the time came to retire, the damsel took both the guests to whom she had offered her hospitality; she shows them the two fine, long, wide beds, and says: "These two beds are set up here for the accommodation of your bodies; but in that one yonder no one ever lay who did not merit it: it was not set up to be used by you." The knight who came riding on the cart replies at once: "Tell me," he says, "for what cause this bed is inaccessible." Being thoroughly informed of this, she answers unhesitatingly: "It is not your place to ask or make such an inquiry. Any knight is disgraced in the land after being in a cart, and it is not fitting that he should concern himself with the matter

upon which you have questioned me; and most of all it is not right that he should lie upon the bed, for he would soon pay dearly for his act. So rich a couch has not been prepared for you, and you would pay dearly for ever harbouring such a thought." He replies: "You will see about that presently." . . . "Am I to see it?" . . . "Yes." . . . "It will soon appear." . . . "By my head," the knight replies, "I know not who is to pay the penalty. But whoever may object or disapprove, I intend to lie upon this bed and repose there at my ease." Then he at once disrobed in the bed, which was long and raised half an ell above the other two, and was covered with a yellow cloth of silk and a coverlet with gilded stars. The furs were not of skinned vair but of sable; the covering he had on him would have been fitting for a king. The mattress was not made of straw or rushes or of old mats. At midnight there descended from the rafters suddenly a lance, as with the intention of pinning the knight through the flanks to the coverlet and the white sheets where he lay. To the lance there was attached a pennon all ablaze. The coverlet, the bedclothes, and the bed itself all caught fire at once. And the tip of the lance passed so close to the knight's side that it cut the skin a little, without seriously wounding him. Then the knight got up, put out the fire and, taking the lance, swung it in the middle of the hall, all this without leaving his bed; rather did he lie down again and slept as securely as at first.

Vv. 539–982.—In the morning, at daybreak, the damsel of the tower had Mass celebrated on their account, and had them rise and dress. When Mass had been celebrated for them, the knight who had ridden in the cart sat down pensively at a window, which looked out upon the meadow, and he gazed upon the fields below. The damsel came to another window close by, and there my lord Gawain conversed with her privately for a while about something, I know not what. I do not know what words were uttered, but while they were leaning on the window-sill they saw carried along the river through the fields a bier, upon which there lay a knight, and alongside three damsels walked, mourning bitterly. Behind the bier they saw a crowd approaching, with a tall knight in front, leading a fair lady by the horse's rein. The knight at the window knew that it was the Queen. He continued to gaze at her attentively and with delight as long as she was visible. And when he could no longer see her, he was minded to throw himself out and break his body down below. And he would have let himself fall out had not my lord Gawain seen him, and drawn him back, saying: "I beg you, sire, be quiet now. For God's sake, never think again of committing such a mad deed. It is wrong for you to despise your life." "He is perfectly right," the damsel says; "for will not the news of his disgrace be known everywhere? Since he has been upon the cart, he has good reason to wish to die, for he would be better dead than alive. His life henceforth is sure to be one of shame, vexation, and unhappiness." Then the knights asked for their armour, and armed themselves, the damsel treating them courteously, with distinction and generosity; for when she had joked with the knight and ridiculed him enough, she presented him with a horse and lance as a token of her goodwill. The knights then courteously and politely took leave of the damsel, first saluting her, and then going off in the direction taken by the crowd they had seen. Thus they rode out from the town without addressing them. They proceeded quickly in the direction they had seen taken by the Queen, but they did not overtake the procession, which had advanced rapidly. After leaving the fields, the knights enter an enclosed place, and find a beaten road. They advanced through the woods until it might be six o'clock, and then at a crossroads they met a damsel, whom they both saluted, each asking and requesting her to tell them, if she knows, whither the Queen has been taken. Replying intelligently, she said to them: "If you would pledge me your word, I could set you on the right road and path, and I would tell you the name of the country and of the knight who is conducting her; but whoever would essay to enter that country must endure sore trials, for before he could reach there he must suffer much." Then my lord Gawain replies: "Damsel, so help me God, I promise to place all my strength at your disposal and service, whenever you please, if you will tell me now the truth." And he who had been on the cart did not say that he would pledge her all his strength; but he proclaims, like one whom love makes rich, powerful and bold for any enterprise, that at once and without hesitation he will promise her anything she desires, and he puts himself altogether at her disposal. "Then I will tell you the truth," says she. Then the damsel relates to them the following story: "In truth, my lords, Meleagant, a tall and powerful knight, son of the King of Gorre, has taken her off into the kingdom whence no foreigner returns, but where he must perforce remain in servitude and banishment." Then they ask her: "Damsel, where is this country? Where can we find the way thither?" She replies: "That you shall quickly learn; but you may be sure that you will meet with many obstacles and difficult passages, for it is not easy to enter there except with the permission of the king, whose name is Bademagu; however, it is possible to enter by two very perilous paths and by two very difficult passage-ways. One is called 'the water-bridge,' because the bridge is under water, and there is the same amount of water beneath it as above it, so that the bridge is exactly in the middle; and it is only a foot and a half in width and in thickness. This choice is certainly to be avoided, and yet it is the less dangerous of the two. In addition there are a number of other obstacles of which I will say nothing. The other bridge is still more impracticable and much more perilous, never having been crossed by man. It is just like a sharp sword, and therefore all the people call it 'the sword-bridge.' Now I have told you all the truth I know." But they ask of her once again: "Damsel, deign to show us these two passages." To which the damsel makes reply: "This road here is the most direct to the water-bridge, and that one yonder leads straight to the sword-bridge." Then the knight, who had been on the cart, says: "Sire, I am ready to share with you without prejudice: take one of these two routes, and leave the other one to me; take whichever you

prefer." "In truth," my lord Gawain replies, "both of them are hard and dangerous: I am not skilled in making such a choice, and hardly know which of them to take; but it is not right for me to hesitate when you have left the choice to me: I will choose the water-bridge." The other answers: "Then I must go uncomplainingly to the sword-bridge, which I agree to do." Thereupon, they all three part, each one commending the others very courteously to God. And when she sees them departing, she says: "Each one of you owes me a favour of my choosing, whenever I may choose to ask it. Take care not to forget that." "We shall surely not forget it, sweet friend," both the knights call out. Then each one goes his own way, and he of the cart is occupied with deep reflections, like one who has no strength or defence against love which holds him in its sway. His thoughts are such that he totally forgets himself, and he knows not whether he is alive or dead, forgetting even his own name, not knowing whether he is armed or not, or whither he is going or whence he came. Only one creature he has in mind, and for her his thought is so occupied that he neither sees nor hears aught else. And his horse bears him along rapidly, following no crooked road, but the best and the most direct; and thus proceeding unguided, he brings him into an open plain. In this plain there was a ford, on the other side of which a knight stood armed, who guarded it, and in his company there was a damsel who had come on a palfrey. By this time the afternoon was well advanced, and yet the knight, unchanged and unwearied, pursued his thoughts. The horse, being very thirsty, sees clearly the ford, and as soon as he sees it, hastens toward it. Then he on the other side cries out: "Knight, I am guarding the ford, and forbid you to cross." He neither gives him heed, nor hears his words, being still deep in thought. In the meantime, his horse advanced rapidly toward the water. The knight calls out to him that he will do wisely to keep at a distance from the ford, for there is no passage that way; and he swears by the heart within his breast that he will smite him if he enters the water. But his threats are not heard, and he calls out to him a third time: "Knight, do not enter the ford against my will and prohibition; for, by my head, I shall strike you as soon as I see you in the ford." But he is so deep in thought that he does not hear him. And the horse, quickly leaving the bank, leaps into the ford and greedily begins to drink. And the knight says he shall pay for this, that his shield and the hauberk he wears upon his back shall afford him no protection. First, he puts his horse at a gallop, and from a gallop he urges him to a run, and he strikes the knight so hard that he knocks him down flat in the ford which he had forbidden him to cross. His lance flew from his hand and the shield from his neck. When he feels the water, he shivers, and though stunned, he jumps to his feet, like one aroused from sleep, listening and looking about him with astonishment, to see who it can be who has struck him. Then face to face with the other knight, he said: "Vassal, tell me why you have struck me, when I was not aware of your presence, and when I had done you no harm." "Upon my word, you had wronged me," the other says; "did you not treat me disdainfully when I forbade you three times to cross the ford, shouting at you as loudly as I could? You surely heard me challenge you at least two or three times, and you entered in spite of me, though I told you I should strike you as soon as I saw you in the ford." Then the knight replies to him: "Whoever heard you or saw you, let him be damned, so far as I am concerned. I was probably deep in thought when you forbade me to cross the ford. But be assured that I would make you regret it, if I could just lay one of my hands on your bridle." And the other replies: "Why, what of that? If you dare, you may seize my bridle here and now. I do not esteem your proud threats so much as a handful of ashes." And he replies: "That suits me perfectly. However the affair may turn out, I should like to lay my hands on you." Then the other knight advances to the middle of the ford, where the other lays his left hand upon his bridle, and his right hand upon his leg, pulling, dragging and pressing him so roughly that he remonstrates, thinking that he would pull his leg out of his body. Then he begs him to let go, saying: "Knight, if it please thee to fight me on even terms, take thy shield and horse and lance, and joust with me." He answers: "That will I not do, upon my word; for I suppose thou wouldst run away as soon as thou hadst escaped my grip." Hearing this, he was much ashamed, and said: "Knight, mount thy horse, in confidence for I will pledge thee loyally my word that I shall not flinch or run away." Then once again he answers him: "First, thou wilt have to swear to that, and I insist upon receiving thy oath that thou wilt neither run away nor flinch, nor touch me, nor come near me until thou shalt see me on my horse; I shall be treating thee very generously, if, when thou art in my hands, I let thee go." He can do nothing but give his oath; and when the other hears him swear, he gathers up his shield and lance which were floating in the ford and by this time had drifted well downstream; then he returns and takes his horse. After catching and mounting him, he seizes the shield by the shoulderstraps and lays his lance in rest. Then each spurs toward the other as fast as their horses can carry them. And he who had to defend the ford first attacks the other, striking him so hard that his lance is completely splintered. The other strikes him in return so that he throws him prostrate into the ford, and the water closes over him. Having accomplished that, he draws back and dismounts, thinking he could drive and chase away a hundred such. While he draws from the scabbard his sword of steel, the other jumps up and draws his excellent flashing blade. Then they clash again, advancing and covering themselves with the shields which gleam with gold. Ceaselessly and without repose they wield their swords; they have the courage to deal so many blows that the battle finally is so protracted that the Knight of the Cart is greatly ashamed in his heart, thinking that he is making a sorry start in the way he has undertaken, when he has spent so much time in defeating a single knight. If he had met yesterday a hundred such, he does not think or believe that they could have withstood him; so now he is much grieved and wroth to be in such an exhausted state that he is missing his strokes and losing time. Then he runs at him and presses him so hard that the other knight gives way and flees. However reluctant he may be, he leaves the ford and crossing free. But the other follows him in pursuit until he falls forward upon his hands; then he of the cart runs up to him, swearing by all

he sees that he shall rue the day when he upset him in the ford and disturbed his revery. The damsel, whom the knight had with him, upon hearing the threats, is in great fear, and begs him for her sake to forbear from killing him; but he tells her that he must do so, and can show him no mercy for her sake, in view of the shameful wrong that he has done him. Then, with sword drawn, he approaches the knight who cries in sore dismay: "For God's sake and for my own, show me the mercy I ask of you." And he replies: "As God may save me, no one ever sinned so against me that I would not show him mercy once, for God's sake as is right, if he asked it of me in God's name. And so on thee I will have mercy; for I ought not to refuse thee when thou hast besought me. But first, thou shalt give me thy word to constitute thyself my prisoner whenever I may wish to summon thee." Though it was hard to do so, he promised him. At once the damsel said: "O knight, since thou hast granted the mercy he asked of thee, if ever thou hast broken any bonds, for my sake now be merciful and release this prisoner from his parole. Set him free at my request, upon condition that when the time comes, I shall do my utmost to repay thee in any way that thou shalt choose." Then he declares himself satisfied with the promise she has made, and sets the knight at liberty. Then she is ashamed and anxious, thinking that he will recognise her, which she did not wish. But he goes away at once, the knight and the damsel commending him to God, and taking leave of him. He grants them leave to go, while he himself pursues his way, until late in the afternoon he met a damsel coming, who was very fair and charming, well attired and richly dressed. The damsel greets him prudently and courteously, and he replies: "Damsel, God grant you health and happiness." Then the damsel said to him: "Sire, my house is prepared for you, if you will accept my hospitality; but you shall find shelter there only on condition that you will lie with me; upon these terms I propose and make the offer." Not a few there are who would have thanked her five hundred times for such a gift; but he is much displeased, and made a very different answer: "Damsel, I thank you for the offer of your house, and esteem it highly; but, if you please, I should be very sorry to lie with you." "By my eyes," the damsel says, "then I retract my offer." And he, since it is unavoidable, lets her have her way, though his heart grieves to give consent. He feels only reluctance now; but greater distress will be his when it is time to go to bed. The damsel, too, who leads him away, will pass through sorrow and heaviness. For it is possible that she will love him so that she will not wish to part with him. As soon as he had granted her wish and desire, she escorts him to a fortified place, than which there was none fairer in Thessaly; for it was entirely enclosed by a high wall and a deep moat, and there was no man within except him whom she brought with her.

Vv. 983–1042.—Here she had constructed for her residence a quantity of handsome rooms, and a large and roomy hall. Riding along a river bank, they approached their lodging-place, and a drawbridge was lowered to allow them to pass. Crossing the bridge, they entered in, and found the hall open with its roof of tiles. Through the open door they pass, and see a table laid with a broad white cloth, upon which the dishes were set, and the candles burning in their stands, and the gilded silver drinking-cups, and two pots of wine, one red and one white. Standing beside the table, at the end of a bench, they found two basins of warm water in which to wash their hands, with a richly embroidered towel, all white and clean, with which to dry their hands. No valets, servants, or squires were to be found or seen. The knight, removing his shield from about his neck, hangs it upon a hook, and, taking his lance, lays it above upon a rack. Then he dismounts from his horse, as does the damsel from hers. The knight, for his part, was pleased that she did not care to wait for him to help her to dismount. Having dismounted, she runs directly to a room and brings him a short mantle of scarlet cloth which she puts on him. The hall was by no means dark; for beside the light from the stars, there were many large twisted candles lighted there, so that the illumination was very bright. When she had thrown the mantle about his shoulders, she said to him: "Friend, here is the water and the towel; there is no one to present or offer it to you except me whom you see. Wash your hands, and then sit down, when you feel like doing so. The hour and the meal, as you can see, demand that you should do so." He washes, and then gladly and readily takes his seat, and she sits down beside him, and they eat and drink together, until the time comes to leave the table.

Vv. 1043–1206.—When they had risen from the table, the damsel said to the knight: "Sire, if you do not object, go outside and amuse yourself; but, if you please, do not stay after you think I must be in bed. Feel no concern or embarrassment; for then you may come to me at once, if you will keep the promise you have made." And he replies: "I will keep my word, and will return when I think the time has come." Then he went out, and stayed in the courtyard until he thought it was time to return and keep the promise he had made. Going back into the hall, he sees nothing of her who would be his mistress; for she was not there. Not finding or seeing her, he said: "Wherever she may be, I shall look for her until I find her." He makes no delay in his search, being bound by the promise he had made her. Entering one of the rooms, he hears a damsel cry aloud, and it was the very one with whom he was about to lie. At the same time, he sees the door of another room standing open, and stepping toward it, he sees right before his eyes a knight who had thrown her down, and was holding her naked and prostrate upon the bed. She, thinking that he had come of course to help her, cried aloud: "Help, help, thou knight, who art my guest. If thou dost not take this man away from me, I shall find no one to do so; if thou dost not succour me speedily, he will wrong me before thy eyes. Thou art the one to lie with me, in accordance with thy promise; and shall this man by force accomplish his wish before thy eyes? Gentle knight, exert thyself, and make haste to bear me aid." He sees that the other man held the damsel brutally uncovered to the waist, and he is ashamed and angered to see him assault her so; yet it is not jealousy he feels, nor will he be made a cuckold by him. At the door there stood as guards two knights completely armed and with swords drawn. Be-

hind them there stood four men-at-arms, each armed with an axe—the sort with which you could split a cow down the back as easily as a root of juniper or broom. The knight hesitated at the door, and thought: "God, what can I do? I am engaged in no less an affair than the quest of Queen Guinevere. I ought not to have the heart of a hare, when for her sake I have engaged in such a quest. If cowardice puts its heart in me, and if I follow its dictates, I shall never attain what I seek. I am disgraced, if I stand here; indeed, I am ashamed even to have thought of holding back. My heart is very sad and oppressed: now I am so ashamed and distressed that I would gladly die for having hesitated here so long. I say it not in pride: but may God have mercy on me if I do not prefer to die honourably rather than live a life of shame! If my path were unobstructed, and if these men gave me leave to pass through without restraint, what honour would I gain? Truly, in that case the greatest coward alive would pass through; and all the while I hear this poor creature calling for help constantly, and reminding me of my promise, and reproaching me with bitter taunts." Then he steps to the door, thrusting in his head and shoulders; glancing up, he sees two swords descending. He draws back, and the knights could not check their strokes: they had wielded them with such force that the swords struck the floor, and both were broken in pieces. When he sees that the swords are broken, he pays less attention to the axes, fearing and dreading them much less. Rushing in among them, he strikes first one guard in the side and then another. The two who are nearest him he jostles and thrusts aside, throwing them both down flat; the third missed his stroke at him, but the fourth, who attacked him, strikes him so that he cuts his mantle and shirt, and slices the white flesh on his shoulder so that the blood trickles down from the wound. But he, without delay, and without complaining of his wound, presses on more rapidly, until he strikes between the temples him who was assaulting his hostess. Before he departs, he will try to keep his pledge to her. He makes him stand up reluctantly. Meanwhile, he who had missed striking him comes at him as fast as he can, and, raising his arm again, expects to split his head to the teeth with the axe. But the other, alert to defend himself, thrusts the knight toward him in such a way that he receives the axe just where the shoulder joins the neck, so that they are cleaved apart. Then the knight seizes the axe, wresting it quickly from him who holds it; then he lets go the knight whom he still held, and looks to his own defence; for the knights from the door, and the three men with axes are all attacking him fiercely. So he leaped quickly between the bed and the wall, and called to them: "Come on now, all of you. If there were thirty-seven of you, you would have all the fight you wish, with me so favourably placed; I shall never be overcome by you." And the damsel watching him, exclaimed: "By my eyes, you need have no thought of that henceforth where I am." Then at once she dismisses the knights and the men-at-arms, who retire from there at once, without delay or objection. And the damsel continues: "Sire you have well defended me against the men of my household. Come now, and I'll lead you on.". . .

MARIE DE FRANCE

The Lay of the Dolorous Knight

After 1150, Marie de France originated the narrative lay, a short poem telling a story and meant to be sung to the accompaniment of a musical instrument, such as a harp. (Lyrical lays were begun somewhat later [early thirteenth century] by a French poet and have a history different from that of narrative lays.) Like the romance (see Chrètien de Troyes's *Arthurian Romances*), with which it was contemporary, the narrative lay tells a courtly love tale based on Celtic sources. The narrative lay had a short life and vanished around 1300. After 1600 the term "lay" came to denote any simple song or narrative of adventure. The lay genre enjoyed a brief comeback in the Neo-Gothic revival of the 1800s.

Marie de France wrote in Old French; she was part of the so-called twelfth-century renaissance, centered in France, which produced scholastic philosophy (Abelard), the Gothic church (Suger), the universities (Bologna and Paris), polyphonic music, liturgical drama, and most especially, vernacular literature, including the *chansons de geste,* Arthurian romances, and love lyrics. De France contributed to this movement by being the first known European woman to write successfully in the vernacular.

Of Marie de France (flourished 1160–1190) very little is known for certain. She was probably French, working as a professional writer at the English royal court. It was only after 1880 that scholars firmly linked de France with these lays. Even so, one expert claims her name is used "since [it is] convenient and attractive."

The mystery surrounding de France extends to her works. Her lays are preserved in five manuscripts, the earliest dating from about fifty years after she wrote. Each of these contains several lays in varied groupings, with some found in two or more manuscripts and a few, like *The Lay of the Dolorous Knight*, appearing only once.

The general Prologue (not included here) to the manuscript containing *The Dolorous Knight* offers insight into de France's literary habits. In it she speaks of not being bullied into giving up her work because of gossip and threats. Whatever provoked these remarks, it seems that de France valued her reputation and literary gifts. She dedicated these short tales to a "noble king," probably Henry II (1133–1189), the husband of Eleanor of Aquitaine (about 1122–1204), herself reputedly the founder of courtly love. De France also spoke of her literary work: "I have often stayed awake at night working on them."

Reading the Selection

The selection is the full text of *The Lay of the Dolorous Knight,* rendered here in prose. The word *dolorous* (from Latin *dolor,* "pain") means sorrowful. This lay is set in Brittany, thus suggesting it may have been written in France. Typical of her lays, it is a moral tale rather than a love story with a happy ending. Its moral is highly ironic: Excessive virtue can lead to disaster.

This story is about a lady totally devoted to courtly love. Faced with four worthy suitors, she encourages each while deftly rejecting them all, "for she would not slay three lovers . . . so that one might have content." Even when three are slain, she refuses the survivor, though she nurses him to health.

Irony is stressed in the lay's two titles. The virtuous lady calls it "the Lay of the Four Sorrows," symbolizing her agony, while the survivor prefers "the Lay of the Dolorous Knight," highlighting his anguish. Refusing to take sides, de France says, "Either name befits it well," leaving it to the reader to decide.

Hearken now to the Lay that once I heard a minstrel chanting to his harp. In surety of its truth I will name the city where this story passed. The Lay of the Dolorous Knight, my harper called his song, but of those who hearkened, some named it rather, The Lay of the Four Sorrows.

In Nantes, of Brittany, there dwelt a dame who was dearly held of all, for reason of the much good that was found in her. This lady was passing fair of body, apt in book as any clerk, and meetly schooled in every grace that it becometh dame to have. So gracious of person was this damsel, that throughout the realm there was no knight could refrain from setting his heart upon her, though he saw her but one only time. Although the demoiselle might not return the love of so many, certainly she had no wish to slay them all. Better by far that a man pray and require in love all the dames of his country, than run mad in woods for the bright eyes of one. Therefore this dame gave courtesy and good will to each alike. Even when she might not hear a lover's words, so sweetly she denied his wish that the more he held her dear and was the more her servant for that fond denial. So because of her great riches of body and of heart, this lady of whom I tell, was prayed and required in love by the lords of her country, both by night and by day.

Now in Brittany lived four young barons, but their names I cannot tell. It is enough that they were desirable in the eyes of maidens for reason of their beauty, and that men esteemed them because they were courteous of manner and open of hand. Moreover they were stout and hardy knights amongst the spears, and rich and worthy gentlemen of those very parts. Each of these four knights had set his heart upon the lady, and for love of her pained himself mightily, and did all that he was able, so that by any means he might gain her favour. Each prayed her privily for her love, and strove all that he could to make him worthy of the gift, above his fellows. For her part the lady was sore perplexed, and considered in her mind very earnestly, which of these four knights she should take as friend. But since they all were loyal and worthy gentlemen, she durst not choose amongst them; for she would not slay three lovers with her hand so that one might have content. Therefore to each and all, the dame made herself fair and sweet of semblance. Gifts she gave to all alike. Tender messages she sent to each. Every knight deemed himself esteemed and favoured above his fellows, and by soft words and fair service diligently strove to please. When the knights gathered together for the games, each of these lords contended earnestly for the prize, so that he might be first, and draw on him the favour of his dame. Each held her for his friend. Each bore upon him her gift—pennon, or sleeve, or ring. Each cried her name within the lists.

Now when Eastertide was come, a great tournament was proclaimed to be held beyond the walls of Nantes, that rich city. The four lovers were the appellants in this tourney, and from every realm knights rode to break a lance in honour of their dame. Frenchman and Norman and Fleming; the hardiest knights of Brabant, Boulogne and Anjou; each came to do his devoir in the field. Nor was the chivalry of Nantes backward in this quarrel, but till the vespers of the tournament was come, they stayed themselves within the lists, and struck stoutly for their lord. After the four lovers had laced their harness upon them, they issued forth from the city, followed by the knights who were of their company in this adventure. But upon the four fell the burden of the day, for they were known of all by the embroidered arms upon their surcoat, and the device fashioned on the shield. Now against the four lovers arrayed themselves four other knights, armed altogether in coats of mail, and helmets and gauntlets of steel. Of these stranger knights two were of Hainault, and the two others were Flemings. When the four lovers saw their adversaries prepare themselves for the combat, they had little desire to flee, but hastened to join them in battle. Each lowered his spear, and choosing his enemy, met him so eagerly that all men wondered, for horse and man fell to the earth. The four lovers recked little of their destriers, but freeing their feet from the stirrups bent over the fallen foe, and called on him to yield. When the friends of the vanquished knights saw their case, they hastened to their succour; so for their rescue there was a great press, and many a mighty stroke with the sword.

The damsel stood upon a tower to watch these feats of arms. By their blazoned coats and shields she knew her knights; she saw their marvellous deeds, yet might not say who did best, nor give to one the praise. But the tournament was no longer a seemly and ordered battle. The ranks of the two companies were confused together, so that every man fought against his fellow, and none might tell whether he struck his comrade or his foe. The four lovers did well and worshipfully, so that all men deemed them worthy of the prize. But when evening was come, and the sport drew to its close, their courage led them to folly. Having ventured too far from their companions, they were set upon by their adversaries, and assailed so fiercely that three were slain outright. As to the fourth he yet lived, but altogether mauled and shaken, for his thigh was broken, and a spear head remained in his side. The four bodies were fallen on the field, and lay with those who had perished in that day. But because of the great mischief these four lovers had done their adversaries, their shields were cast despitefully without the lists; but in this their foemen did wrongfully, and all men held them in sore displeasure.

Great were the lamentation and the cry when the news of this mischance was noised about the city. Such a tumult of mourning was never before heard, for the whole city was moved. All men hastened forth to the place where the lists were set. Meetly to mourn the dead there rode nigh upon two thousand knights, with hauberks unlaced, and uncovered heads, plucking upon their beards. So the four lovers were placed each upon his shield, and being brought back in honour to Nantes, were carried to the house of that dame, whom so greatly they had loved.

When the lady knew this distressful adventure, straightway she fell to the ground. Being returned from her swoon, she made her complaint, calling upon her lovers each by his name.

"Alas," she said, "what shall I do, for never shall I know happiness again. These four knights had set their hearts upon me, and despite their great treasure, esteemed my love as richer than all their wealth. Alas, for the fair and valiant knight! Alas, for the loyal and generous man! By gifts such as these they sought to gain my favour, but how might lady bereave three of life, so as to cherish one. Even now I cannot tell for whom I have most pity, or who was closest to my mind. But three are dead, and one is sore stricken; neither is there anything in the world which can bring me comfort. Only this is there to do—to give the slain men seemly burial, and, if it may be, to heal their comrade of his wounds."

So, because of her great love and nobleness, the lady caused these three distressful knights to be buried well and worshipfully in a rich abbey. In that place she offered their Mass penny, and gave rich offerings of silver and of lights besides. May God have mercy on them in that day. As for the wounded knight she commanded him to be carried to her own chamber. She sent for surgeons, and gave him into their hands. These searched his wounds so skilfully, and tended him with so great care, that presently his hurt commenced to heal. Very often was the lady in the chamber, and very tenderly she cherished the stricken man. Yet ever she felt pity for the three Knights of the Sorrows, and ever she went heavily by reason of their deaths.

Now on a summer's day, the lady and the knight sat together after meat. She called to mind the sorrow that was hers; so that, in a space, her head fell upon her breast, and she gave herself altogether to her grief. The knight looked earnestly upon his dame. Well he might see that she was far away, and clearly he perceived the cause.

"Lady," said he, "you are in sorrow. Open now your grief to me. If you tell me what is in your heart perchance I may find you comfort." 10

"Fair friend," replied she, "I think of what is gone, and remember your companions, who are dead. Never was lady of my peerage, however fair and good and gracious, ever loved by four such valiant gentlemen, nor ever lost them in one single day. Save you—who were so maimed and in such peril—all are gone. Therefore I call to mind those who loved me so dearly, and am the saddest lady beneath the sun. To remember these things, of you four I shall make a Lay, and will call it the Lay of the Four Sorrows."

When the knight heard these words he made answer very swiftly,

"Lady, name it not the Lay of the Four Sorrows, but, rather, the Lay of the Dolorous Knight. Would you hear the reason why it should bear this name? My three comrades have finished their course; they have nothing more to hope of their life. They are gone, and with them the pang of their great sorrow, and the knowledge of their enduring love for you. I alone have come, all amazed and fearful, from the net wherein they were taken, but I find my life more bitter than my comrades found the grave. I see you on your goings and comings about the house. I may speak with you both matins and vespers. But no other joy do I get—neither clasp nor kiss, nothing but a few empty, courteous words. Since all these evils are come upon me because of you, I choose death rather than life. For this reason your Lay should bear my name, and be called the Lay of the Dolorous Knight. He who would name it the Lay of the Four Sorrows would name it wrongly, and not according to the truth."

"By my faith," replied the lady, "this is a fair saying. So shall the song be known as the Lay of the Dolorous Knight."

Thus was the Lay conceived, made perfect, and brought to a fair birth. For this reason it came by its name; though to this day some call it the Lay of the Four Sorrows. Either name befits it well, for the story tells of both these matters, but it is the use and wont in this land to call it the Lay of the Dolorous Knight. Here it ends; no more is there to say. I heard no more, and nothing more I know. Perforce I bring my story to a close. 15

ST. THOMAS AQUINAS

Selection from *Summa theologica*

Thomas Aquinas's (1226–1274) theology, called Thomism, is the climax of the key intellectual trend that characterized the High Middle Ages (1000–1300). Thomism uniquely embodies the age's spirit, which tried to harmonize the opposing domains of philosophy and theology, reason and faith. Thomas performed this feat with two vast *summas* (from Latin, a comprehensive treatise), namely the *Summa theologica* and the *Summa contra gentiles*. In these works, he founded a rational theology that aligned Aristotle's thought with Christian principles. Some of Thomas's ideas (on, for example, the Trinity) were called into question after his death, but his reputation steadily grew; in 1874 the papacy declared Thomism to be the official basis of Roman Catholic beliefs.

In order to develop a rational theology along the lines laid down by Aristotle, Thomas had to come to terms with the pessimistic thought of Augustine (see *Confessions*), which had dominated Christian discourse since the fifth century. To Augustine, reason is helpless because it cannot operate apart from the human will, which has lost its freedom because of original sin. In reply, Thomas held that the will is free, and reason, while spoiled by sin, is yet able to discover much about the world; reason, even if limited, must be obeyed as far as it goes. Augustine further claimed that true knowledge can arise only if God implants it in the mind, either slowly or all at once. In contrast, Thomas was more hopeful, saying that all knowledge begins in the senses, even of things that lie beyond the senses. Finally, Augustine thought that not only was human nature impaired, but so was the world of nature. Thomas's opposing view was that the natural world, though necessarily incomplete because it is created, is nonetheless good since it reflects God as its creator. Thus, Thomism ranged widely over human concerns, covering topics such as justice, fair prices, usury, and good government.

Reading the Selection

This selection from the *Summa theologica* deals with faith, or belief. Faith, to Thomas, is one of the three theological virtues—the others are hope and charity—which have God as their object and bring eternal life to those who obey them. In discussing the theological, or spiritual, virtues, St. Thomas was inspired by the Greek thinker Aristotle, who had identified the four cardinal virtues of secular life: wisdom, courage, justice, and temperance. Thomist thought eventually embraced both the theological and the cardinal virtues, maintaining that both were essential to a Christian.

The Fifth Article from the *Summa theologica* deals with the question, Should matters of faith be tested by the rules of science? After a full discussion, Thomas concludes that faith and science (reason) are two separate domains and should not be intermingled: "[T]he object of science is something seen, whereas the object of faith is the unseen."

Thomas's argument is typical of the medieval style of reasoning, which included a question, discussion, and resolution. The opening question is followed by a series of arguments, pro and con, drawn from the Bible (*I Timothy, II Corinthians*), the church fathers (Gregory), Aristotle ("the Philosopher"), and logic. Thomas gives the resolution in the first person ("I answer that"), though his presence is ever felt, shaping the argument as he replies to both the pro and con sides of the debate. Because of its give-and-take format, this method is believed to have begun in the classroom practices of schools and universities, hence the name *scholasticism*.

—w—

Fifth Article

Whether Those Things That Are of Faith Can Be an Object of Science?

We proceed thus to the Fifth Article:—Objection 1. It would seem that those things that are of faith can be an object of science. For where science is lacking there is ignorance, since ignorance is the opposite of science. Now we are not in ignorance of those things we have to believe, since ignorance of such things savors of unbelief, according to 1 Tim. i. 13: *I did it ignorantly in unbelief.* Therefore things that are of faith can be an object of science.

Obj. 2. Further, science is acquired by reasons. Now sacred writers employ reasons to inculcate things that are of faith. Therefore such things can be an object of science.

Obj. 3. Further, things which are demonstrated are an object of science, since a *demonstration is a syllogism that produces science.* Now certain matters of faith have been demonstrated by the philosophers, such as the Existence

and Unity of God, and so forth. Therefore things that are of faith can be an object of science.

Obj. 4. Further, opinion is further from science than faith is, since faith is said to stand between opinion and science. Now opinion and science can, in a way, be about the same object, as stated in *Poster.* i. Therefore faith and science can be about the same object also.

On the contrary, Gregory says (*Hom.* xxvi *in Ev.*) that *when a thing is manifest, it is the object, not of faith, but of perception.* Therefore things that are of faith are not the object of perception, whereas what is an object of science is the object of perception. Therefore there can be no faith about things which are an object of science.

I answer that, All science is derived from self-evident and therefore *seen* principles; wherefore all objects of science must needs be, in a fashion, seen.

Now as stated above (A. 4) it is impossible that one and the same thing should be believed and seen by the same person. Hence it is equally impossible for one and the same thing to be an object of science and of belief for the same person. It may happen, however, that a thing which is an object of vision or science for one, is believed by another: since we hope to see some day what we now believe about the Trinity, according to 1 Cor. xiii. 12: *We see now through a glass in a dark manner; but then face to face:* which vision the angels possess already; so that what we believe, they see. In like manner it may happen that what is an object of vision or scientific knowledge for one man, even in the state of a wayfarer, is, for another man, an object of faith, because he does not know it by demonstration.

Nevertheless, that which is proposed to be believed equally by all, is equally unknown by all as an object of science: such are the things which are of faith simply. Consequently faith and science are not about the same things.

Reply Obj. 1. Unbelievers are in ignorance of things that are of faith, for neither do they see or know them in themselves, nor do they know them to be credible. The faithful, on the other hand, know them, not as by demonstration, but by the light of faith which makes them see that they ought to believe them, as stated above (A. 4, *ad* 2, 3).

Reply Obj. 2. The reasons employed by holy men to prove things that are of faith, are not demonstrations; they are either persuasive arguments showing that what is proposed to our faith is not impossible, or else they are proofs drawn from the principles of faith, i.e. from the authority of Holy Writ, as Dionysius declares (*Div. Nom.* ii). Whatever is based on these principles is as well proved in the eyes of the faithful, as a conclusion drawn from self-evident principles is in the eyes of all. Hence again, theol-

ogy is a science, as we stated at the outset of this work (P. I, Q. 1, A. 2).

Reply Obj. 3. Things which can be proved by demonstration are reckoned among the articles of faith, not because they are believed simply by all, but because they are a necessary presupposition to matters of faith, so that those who do not know them by demonstration must know them first of all by faith.

Reply Obj. 4. As the Philosopher says (*loc. cit.*), *science and opinion about the same object can certainly be in different men,* as we have stated above about science and faith; yet it is possible for one and the same man to have science and faith about the same thing relatively, i.e. in relation to the object, but not in the same respect. For it is possible for the same person, about one and the same object, to know one thing and to think another: and, in like manner, one may know by demonstration the unity of the Godhead, and, by faith, the Trinity. On the other hand, in one and the same man, about the same object, and in the same respect, science is incompatible with either opinion or faith, yet for different reasons. Because science is incompatible with opinion about the same object simply, for the reason that science demands that its object should be deemed impossible to be otherwise, whereas it is essential to opinion, that its object should be deemed possible to be otherwise. Yet that which is the object of faith, on account of the certainty of faith, is also deemed impossible to be otherwise: and the reason why science and faith cannot be about the same object and in the same respect is because the object of science is something seen, whereas the object of faith is the unseen, as stated above.

DANTE ALIGHIERI

Selections from *The Divine Comedy*

Few writers of any time have had such an impact on Western culture as the medieval writer Dante Alighieri (1265–1321) of Florence. So great were his gifts that the world was not the same after he wrote. His works in Italian had such broad appeal that the geographic focus of Europe's culture shifted from France to Italy, where it stayed until about 1600. His poetry affected all of Europe and changed the terms in which poets wrote. Dante, for example, composed lyrics celebrating his undying love for the beautiful Beatrice; later poets, enchanted by these poems, followed his lead, with Petrarch writing verses to Laura (see *Canzoniere*), Shakespeare to the Dark Lady, and so on. Scholars often link Dante to the Renaissance, but this surely is an exaggeration, given his religious views. He is better understood as the culmination of the medieval spirit, as he balances the secular and the spiritual, the ancient and the new.

Of Dante's works, *The Divine Comedy* (about 1314) is his enduring masterpiece. In form, this long narrative poem belongs to the epic genre with its hero of superhuman caliber, dangerous journey, misadventures, divine dimension, digressions, long speeches, vivid descriptions, and general lofty tone (see *The Epic of Gilgamesh*, Homer's *Iliad* and *Odyssey*, and Vergil's *Aeneid*). But *The Divine Comedy* is *much* more than an epic, because Dante worked into the poem anything he felt like including. It is an allegory of great complexity, meant by Dante to be interpreted on many levels, such as depicting the way to God or the way of the artist. It is a hymn to the Middle Ages, including scholastic reasoning, mysticism, numerology, Thomism (see St. Thomas Aquinas's *Summa theologica*), Aristotelianism, and Italian history. Above all, it is a vision of Christianity and Classicism reconciled.

The elaborate framework is built over a fairly simple plot. The hero, Dante himself, goes on a journey of self-discovery through hell, purgatory, and heaven, led first by Vergil, the Latin poet, and later by Beatrice, his human muse. The time is Easter 1300. The perennial appeal of this plot is that Dante becomes a stand-in for readers, virtually all of whom have been prey to self-doubts similar to those driving this hero on his life-or-death voyage.

Reading the Selections

The selections include four cantos (chapters) from the *Inferno* portion of *The Divine Comedy*. The Inferno, or hell, is the realm of sinners who suffer not because of predestined fate but because of their own bad choices. Here are found those who rejected spiritual values and yielded to animal appetites or violence, or perverted their human reason to fraud or malice against other human beings.

Canto I introduces Dante, who is tortured by self-doubts: "I went astray . . . and woke to find myself alone in a dark wood." He learns that two guides will lead him back to "the straight road."

Dante and Vergil enter hell in Canto III and are instantly greeted by the cries of the Opportunists, those sinners who chose to sit on the fence rather than side with evil or good. Dante begins to understand that God's justice reigns even in hell, as the Opportunists are punished in a manner appropriate to their sin; namely, they spend eternity chasing ever-shifting banners.

In Canto V, Dante and Vergil encounter the Carnal, those who succumbed to lust. Their eternal punishment is to be swept along in a whirlwind, just as their passions carried them to doom.

The *Inferno*'s last canto, XXXIV, describes the center of hell, where a mindless Satan (called Dis)—a three-faced fallen angel, representative of the anti-Trinity and characterized by impotence, ignorance, and hatred—sits enthroned in ice. Dis's three mouths chew eternally on those ultimate rebels who betrayed church and state.

—⟋⟍—

Inferno, Canto I

The Dark Wood of Error

Midway in his allotted threescore years and ten, Dante comes to himself with a start and realizes that he has strayed from the True Way into the Dark Wood of Error (Worldliness). As soon as he has realized his loss, Dante lifts his eyes and sees the first light of the sunrise (the Sun is the Symbol of Divine Illumination) lighting the shoulders of a little hill (The Mount of Joy). It is the Easter Season, the time of resurrection, and the sun is in its equinoctial rebirth. This juxtaposition of joyous symbols fills Dante with hope and he sets out at once to climb directly up the Mount of Joy, but almost immediately his way is blocked by the Three Beasts of Worldliness: THE LEOPARD OF MALICE AND FRAUD, THE LION OF VIOLENCE AND AMBITION, and THE SHE-WOLF OF INCONTINENCE. These beasts, and especially the She-Wolf, drive him back despairing into the darkness of error. But just as all seems lost, a figure appears to him. It is the shade of VERGIL, Dante's symbol of HUMAN REASON.

Vergil explains that he has been sent to lead Dante from error. There can, however, be no direct ascent past the beasts: the man who would escape them must go a longer and harder way. First he must descend through Hell (The Recognition of Sin), then he must ascend through Purgatory (The Renunciation of Sin), and only then may he reach the pinnacle of joy and come to the Light of God. Vergil offers to guide Dante, but only as far as Human Reason can go. An-

other guide (BEATRICE, symbol of DIVINE LOVE) must take over for the final ascent, for Human Reason is self-limited. Dante submits himself joyously to Vergil's guidance and they move off.

Midway in our life's journey, I went astray   1
    from the straight road and woke to find myself
    alone in a dark wood. How shall I say

what wood that was! I never saw so drear,
    so rank, so arduous a wilderness!
    Its very memory gives a shape to fear.

Death could scarce be more bitter than that place!
    But since it came to good, I will recount
    all that I found revealed there by God's grace.

How I came to it I cannot rightly say,   10
    so drugged and loose with sleep had I become
    when I first wandered there from the True Way.

But at the far end of that valley of evil
    whose maze had sapped my very heart with fear!
    I found myself before a little hill

and lifted up my eyes. Its shoulders glowed
  already with the sweet rays of that planet
  whose virtue leads men straight on every road,

and the shining strengthened me against the fright
  whose agony had wracked the lake of my heart   20
  through all the terrors of that piteous night.

Just as a swimmer, who with his last breath
  flounders ashore from perilous seas, might turn
  to memorize the wide water of his death—

so did I turn, my soul still fugitive
  from death's surviving image, to stare down
  that pass that none had ever left alive.

And there I lay to rest from my heart's race
  till calm and breath returned to me. Then rose
  and pushed up that dead slope at such a pace   30

each footfall rose above the last. And lo!
  almost at the beginning of the rise
  I faced a spotted Leopard, all tremor and flow

and gaudy pelt. And it would not pass, but stood
  so blocking my every turn that time and again
  I was on the verge of turning back to the wood.

This fell at the first widening of the dawn
  as the sun was climbing Aries with those stars
  that rode with him to light the new creation.

Thus the holy hour and the sweet season   40
  of commemoration did much to arm my fear
  of that bright murderous beast with their good omen.

Yet not so much but what I shook with dread
  at sight of a great Lion that broke upon me
  raging with hunger, its enormous head

held high as if to strike a mortal terror
  into the very air. And down his track,
  a She-Wolf drove upon me, a starved horror

ravening and wasted beyond all belief.
  She seemed a rack for avarice, gaunt and craving. 50
  Oh many the souls she has brought to endless grief!

She brought such heaviness upon my spirit
  at sight of her savagery and desperation,
  I died from every hope of that high summit.

And like a miser—eager in acquisition
  but desperate in self-reproach when Fortune's wheel
  turns to the hour of his loss—all tears and attrition

I wavered back; and still the beast pursued,
  forcing herself against me bit by bit
  till I slid back into the sunless wood.   60

And as I fell to my soul's ruin, a presence
  gathered before me on the discolored air,
  the figure of one who seemed hoarse from long
    silence.

At sight of him in that friendless waste I cried:
  "Have pity on me, whatever thing you are,
  whether shade or living man." And it replied:

"Not man, though man I once was, and my blood
  was Lombard, both my parents Mantuan.
  I was born, though late, *sub Julio,* and bred

in Rome under Augustus in the noon   70
  of the false and lying gods. I was a poet
  and sang of old Anchises' noble son

who came to Rome after the burning of Troy.
  But you—why do *you* return to these distresses
  instead of climbing that shining Mount of Joy

which is the seat and first cause of man's bliss?"
  "And are you then that Vergil and that fountain
  of purest speech?" My voice grew tremulous:

"Glory and light of poets! now may that zeal
  and love's apprenticeship that I poured out   80
  on your heroic verses serve me well!

For you are my true master and first author,
  the sole maker from whom I drew the breath
  of that sweet style whose measures have brought me
    honor.

See there, immortal sage, the beast I flee.
  For my soul's salvation, I beg you, guard me from her,
  for she has struck a mortal tremor through me."

And he replied, seeing my soul in tears:
  "He must go by another way who would escape
  this wilderness, for that mad beast that fleers   90

before you there, suffers no man to pass.
  She tracks down all, kills all, and knows no glut,
  but, feeding, she grows hungrier than she was.

She mates with any beast, and will mate with more
  before the Greyhound comes to hunt her down.
  He will not feed on lands nor loot, but honor

and love and wisdom will make straight his way.
  He will rise between Feltro and Feltro, and in him
  shall be the resurrection and new day

of that sad Italy for which Nisus died,   100
  and Turnus, and Euryalus, and the maid Camilla.
  He shall hunt her through every nation of sick pride

till she is driven back forever to Hell
　　whence Envy first released her on the world.
　　Therefore, for your own good, I think it well

you follow me and I will be your guide
　　and lead you forth through an eternal place.
　　There you shall see the ancient spirits tried

in endless pain, and hear their lamentation
　　as each bemoans the second death of souls.　110
　　Next you shall see upon a burning mountain

souls in fire and yet content in fire,
　　knowing that whensoever it may be
　　they yet will mount into the blessed choir.

To which, if it is still your wish to climb,
　　a worthier spirit shall be sent to guide you.
　　With her shall I leave you, for the King of Time,

who reigns on high, forbids me to come there
　　since, living, I rebelled against his law.
　　He rules the waters and the land and air　120

and there holds court, his city and his throne.
　　Oh blessed are they he chooses!" And I to him:
　　"Poet, by that God to you unknown,

lead me this way. Beyond this present ill
　　and worse to dread, lead me to Peter's gate
　　and be my guide through the sad halls of Hell."

And he then: "Follow." And he moved ahead
in silence, and I followed where he led.

—w—

Inferno, Canto III

The Vestibule of Hell

The Opportunists

The Poets pass the Gate of Hell and are immediately assailed by cries of anguish. Dante sees the first of the souls in torment. They are THE OPPORTUNISTS, those souls who in life were neither for good nor evil but only for themselves. Mixed with them are those outcasts who took no sides in the Rebellion of the Angels. They are neither in Hell nor out of it. Eternally unclassified, they race round and round pursuing a wavering banner that runs forever before them through the dirty air; and as they run they are pursued by swarms of wasps and hornets, who sting them and produce a constant flow of blood and putrid matter which trickles down the bodies of the sinners and is feasted upon by loathsome worms and maggots who coat the ground.

The law of Dante's Hell is the law of symbolic retribution. As they sinned so are they punished. They took no sides, therefore they are given no place. As they pursued the ever-shifting illusion of their own advantage, changing their courses with every changing wind, so they pursue eternally an elusive, ever-shifting banner. As their sin was a darkness, so they move in darkness. As their own guilty conscience pursued them, so they are pursued by swarms of wasps and hornets. And as their actions were a moral filth, so they run eternally through the filth of worms and maggots which they themselves feed.

Dante recognizes several, among them POPE CELESTINE V, but without delaying to speak to any of these souls, the Poets move on to ACHERON, the first of the rivers of Hell. Here the newly-arrived souls of the damned gather and wait for monstrous CHARON to ferry them over to punishment. Charon recognizes Dante as a living man and angrily refuses him passage. Vergil forces Charon to serve them, but Dante swoons with terror, and does not reawaken until he is on the other side.

I AM THE WAY INTO THE CITY OF WOE.　　　1
I AM THE WAY TO A FORSAKEN PEOPLE.
I AM THE WAY INTO ETERNAL SORROW.

SACRED JUSTICE MOVED MY ARCHITECT.
I WAS RAISED HERE BY DIVINE OMNIPOTENCE,
PRIMORDIAL LOVE AND ULTIMATE INTELLECT.

ONLY THOSE ELEMENTS TIME CANNOT WEAR
WERE MADE BEFORE ME, AND BEYOND TIME I
　　STAND.
ABANDON ALL HOPE YE WHO ENTER HERE.

These mysteries I read cut into stone　　　10
　　above a gate. And turning I said: "Master,
　　what is the meaning of this harsh inscription?"

And he then as initiate to novice:
　　"Here must you put by all division of spirit
　　and gather your soul against all cowardice.

This is the place I told you to expect.
　　Here you shall pass among the fallen people,
　　souls who have lost the good of intellect."

So saying, he put forth his hand to me,
　　and with a gentle and encouraging smile　20
　　he led me through the gate of mystery.

Here sighs and cries and wails coiled and recoiled
　　on the starless air, spilling my soul to tears.
　　A confusion of tongues and monstrous accents toiled

in pain and anger. Voices hoarse and shrill
and sounds of blows, all intermingled, raised
tumult and pandemonium that still

whirls on the air forever dirty with it
as if a whirlwind sucked at sand. And I,
holding my head in horror, cried: "Sweet Spirit,   30

what souls are these who run through this black haze?"
And he to me: "These are the nearly soulless
whose lives concluded neither blame nor praise.

They are mixed here with that despicable corps
of angels who were neither for God nor Satan,
but only for themselves. The High Creator

scourged them from Heaven for its perfect beauty,
and Hell will not receive them since the wicked
might feel some glory over them." And I:

"Master, what gnaws at them so hideously   40
their lamentation stuns the very air?"
"They have no hope of death," he answered me,

"and in their blind and unattaining state
their miserable lives have sunk so low
that they must envy every other fate.

No word of them survives their living season.
Mercy and Justice deny them even a name.
Let us not speak of them: look, and pass on."

I saw a banner there upon the mist.
Circling and circling, it seemed to scorn all pause.   50
So it ran on, and still behind it pressed

a never-ending rout of souls in pain.
I had not thought death had undone so many
as passed before me in that mournful train.

And some I knew among them; last of all
I recognized the shadow of that soul
who, in his cowardice, made the Great Denial.

At once I understood for certain: these
were of that retrograde and faithless crew
hateful to God and to His enemies.   60

These wretches never born and never dead
ran naked in a swarm of wasps and hornets
that goaded them the more they fled,

and made their faces stream with bloody gouts
of pus and tears that dribbled to their feet
to be swallowed there by loathsome worms and
maggots.

Then looking onward I made out a throng
assembled on the beach of a wide river,
whereupon I turned to him: "Master, I long

to know what souls these are, and what strange usage   70
makes them as eager to cross as they seem to be
in this infected light." At which the Sage:

"All this shall be made known to you when we stand
on the joyless beach of Acheron." And I
cast down my eyes, sensing a reprimand

in what he said, and so walked at his side
in silence and ashamed until we came
through the dead cavern to that sunless tide.

There, steering toward us in an ancient ferry
came an old man with a white bush of hair,   80
bellowing: "Woe to you depraved souls! Bury

here and forever all hope of Paradise:
I come to lead you to the other shore,
into eternal dark, into fire and ice.

And you who are living yet, I say begone
from these who are dead." But when he saw me
stand
against his violence he began again:

"By other windings and by other steerage
shall you cross to that other shore. Not here! Not
here!
A lighter craft than mine must give you passage."   90

And my Guide to him: "Charon, bite back your spleen:
this has been willed where what is willed must be,
and is not yours to ask what it may mean."

The steersman of that marsh of ruined souls,
who wore a wheel of flame around each eye,
stifled the rage that shook his woolly jowls.

But those unmanned and naked spirits there
turned pale with fear and their teeth began to
chatter
at sound of his crude bellow. In despair

they blasphemed God, their parents, their time on
earth,   100
the race of Adam, and the day and the hour
and the place and the seed and the womb that gave
them birth.

But all together they drew to that grim shore
where all must come who lose the fear of God.
Weeping and cursing they come for evermore,

and demon Charon with eyes like burning coals
herds them in, and with a whistling oar
flails on the stragglers to his wake of souls.

As leaves in autumn loosen and stream down
until the branch stands bare above its tatters   110
spread on the rustling ground, so one by one

the evil seed of Adam in its Fall
  cast themselves, at his signal, from the shore
  and streamed away like birds who hear their call.

So they are gone over that shadowy water,
  and always before they reach the other shore
  a new noise stirs on this, and new throngs gather.

"My son," the courteous Master said to me,
  "all who die in the shadow of God's wrath
  converge to this from every clime and country.   120

And all pass over eagerly, for here
  Divine Justice transforms and spurs them so
  their dread turns wish: they yearn for what they fear.

No soul in Grace comes ever to this crossing;
  therefore if Charon rages at your presence
  you will understand the reason for his cursing."

When he had spoken, all the twilight country
  shook so violently, the terror of it
  bathes me with sweat even in memory:

the tear-soaked ground gave out a sigh of wind   130
  that spewed itself in flame on a red sky,
  and all my shattered senses left me. Blind,

like one whom sleep comes over in a swoon,
  I stumbled into darkness and went down.

Inferno, Canto V

Circle Two

THE CARNAL

*The Poets leave Limbo and enter the SECOND CIRCLE. Here
begin the torments of Hell proper, and here, blocking the way, sits
MINOS, the dread and semi-bestial judge of the damned who as-
signs to each soul its eternal torment. He orders the Poets back;
but Vergil silences him as he earlier silenced Charon, and the Poets
move on.*
  *They find themselves on a dark ledge swept by a great whirl-
wind, which spins within it the souls of the CARNAL, those who
betrayed reason to their appetites. Their sin was to abandon themselves to the tempest of their passions: so they are swept forever in
the tempest of Hell, forever denied the light of reason and of God.
Vergil identifies many among them. SEMIRAMIS is there, and
DIDO, CLEOPATRA, HELEN, ACHILLES, PARIS, and TRIS-
TAN. Dante sees PAOLO and FRANCESCA swept together, and
in the name of love he calls to them to tell their sad story. They
pause from their eternal flight to come to him, and Francesca tells
their history while Paolo weeps at her side. Dante is so stricken by
compassion at their tragic tale that he swoons once again.*

So we went down to the second ledge alone;   1
  a smaller circle of so much greater pain
  the voice of the damned rose in a bestial moan.

There Minos sits, grinning, grotesque, and hale.
  He examines each lost soul as it arrives
  and delivers his verdict with his coiling tail.

That is to say, when the ill-fated soul
  appears before him it confesses all,
  and that grim sorter of the dark and foul

decides which place in Hell shall be its end,   10
  then wraps his twitching tail about himself
  one coil for each degree it must descend.

The soul descends and others take its place:
  each crowds in its turn to judgment, each confesses,
  each hears its doom and falls away through space.

"O you who come into this camp of woe,"
  cried Minos when he saw me turn away
  without awaiting his judgment, "watch where you go

once you have entered here, and to whom you turn!
  Do not be misled by that wide and easy passage!"   20
  And my Guide to him: "That is not your concern;

it is his fate to enter every door.
  This has been willed where what is willed must be,
  and is not yours to question. Say no more."

Now the choir of anguish, like a wound,
  strikes through the tortured air. Now I have come
  to Hell's full lamentation, sound beyond sound.

I came to a place stripped bare of every light
  and roaring on the naked dark like seas
  wracked by a war of winds. Their hellish flight   30

of storm and counterstorm through time foregone,
  sweeps the souls of the damned before its charge.
  Whirling and battering it drives them on,

and when they pass the ruined gap of Hell
  through which we had come, their shrieks begin anew.
  There they blaspheme the power of God eternal.

And this, I learned, was the never ending flight
  of those who sinned in the flesh, the carnal and lusty
  who betrayed reason to their appetite.

As the wings of wintering starlings bear them on   40
   in their great wheeling flights, just so the blast
   wherries these evil souls through time foregone.

Here, there, up, down, they whirl and, whirling, strain
   with never a hope of hope to comfort them,
   not of release, but even of less pain.

As cranes go over sounding their harsh cry,
   leaving the long streak of their flight in air,
   so come these spirits, wailing as they fly.

And watching their shadows lashed by wind, I cried:
   "Master, what souls are these the very air   50
   lashes with its black whips from side to side?"

"The first of these whose history you would know,"
   he answered me, "was Empress of many tongues.
   Mad sensuality corrupted her so

that to hide the guilt of her debauchery
   she licensed all depravity alike,
   and lust and law were one in her decree.

She is Semiramis of whom the tale is told
   how she married Ninus and succeeded him
   to the throne of that wide land the Sultans hold.   60

The other is Dido; faithless to the ashes
   of Sichaeus, she killed herself for love.
   The next whom the eternal tempest lashes

is sense-drugged Cleopatra. See Helen there,
   from whom such ill arose. And great Achilles,
   who fought at last with love in the house of prayer.

And Paris. And Tristan." As they whirled above
   he pointed out more than a thousand shades
   of those torn from the mortal life by love.

I stood there while my Teacher one by one   70
   named the great knights and ladies of dim time;
   and I was swept by pity and confusion.

At last I spoke: "Poet, I should be glad
   to speak a word with those two swept together
   so lightly on the wind and still so sad."

And he to me: "Watch them. When next they pass,
   call to them in the name of love that drives
   and damns them here. In that name they will pause."

Thus, as soon as the wind in its wild course
   brought them around, I called: "O wearied souls!   80
   if none forbid it, pause and speak to us."

As mating doves that love calls to their nest
   glide through the air with motionless raised wings,
   borne by the sweet desire that fills each breast—

Just so those spirits turned on the torn sky
   from the band where Dido whirls across the air;
   such was the power of pity in my cry.

"O living creature, gracious, kind, and good,
   going this pilgrimage through the sick night,
   visiting us who stained the earth with blood,   90

were the King of Time our friend, we would pray His peace
   on you who have pitied us. As long as the wind
   will let us pause, ask of us what you please.

The town where I was born lies by the shore
   where the Po descends into its ocean rest
   with its attendant streams in one long murmur.

Love, which in gentlest hearts will soonest bloom
   seized my lover with passion for that sweet body
   from which I was torn unshriven to my doom.

Love, which permits no loved one not to love,   100
   took me so strongly with delight in him
   that we are one in Hell, as we were above.

Love led us to one death. In the depths of Hell
   Caïnä waits for him who took our lives."
   This was the piteous tale they stopped to tell.

And when I had heard those world-offended lovers
   I bowed my head. At last the Poet spoke:
   "What painful thoughts are these your lowered brow
     covers?"

When at length I answered, I began: "Alas!
   What sweetest thoughts, what green and young desire   110
   led these two lovers to this sorry pass."

Then turning to those spirits once again,
   I said: "Francesca, what you suffer here
   melts me to tears of pity and of pain.

But tell me: in the time of your sweet sighs
   by what appearances found love the way
   to lure you to his perilous paradise?"

And she: "The double grief of a lost bliss
   is to recall its happy hour in pain.
   Your Guide and Teacher knows the truth of this.   120

But if there is indeed a soul in Hell
   to ask of the beginning of our love
   out of his pity, I will weep and tell:

On a day for dalliance we read the rhyme
   of Lancelot, how love had mastered him.
   We were alone with innocence and dim time.

Pause after pause that high old story drew
   our eyes together while we blushed and paled;
   but it was one soft passage overthrew

our caution and our hearts. For when we read   130
   how her fond smile was kissed by such a lover,
   he who is one with me alive and dead

breathed on my lips the tremor of his kiss.
   That book, and he who wrote it, was a pander.
   That day we read no further." As she said this,

the other spirit, who stood by her, wept
   so piteously, I felt my senses reel
   and faint away with anguish. I was swept

by such a swoon as death is, and I fell,
   as a corpse might fall, to the dead floor of Hell.   140

—⚏—

Inferno, Canto XXXIV

NINTH CIRCLE: *Cocytus*	*Compound Fraud*
ROUND FOUR: *Judecca*	*The Treacherous to Their Masters*
THE CENTER	*Satan*

"On march the banners of the King," Virgil begins as the Poets face the last depth. He is quoting a medieval hymn, and to it he adds the distortion and perversion of all that lies about him. "On march the banners of the King—of Hell." And there before them, in an infernal parody of Godhead, they see Satan in the distance, his great wings beating like a windmill. It is their beating that is the source of the icy wind of Cocytus, the exhalation of all evil.

All about him in the ice are strewn the sinners of the last round, JUDECCA, named for Judas Iscariot. These are the TREACHEROUS TO THEIR MASTERS. They lie completely sealed in the ice, twisted and distorted into every conceivable posture. It is impossible to speak to them, and the Poets move on to observe Satan.

He is fixed into the ice at the center to which flow all the rivers of guilt; and as he beats his great wings as if to escape, their icy wind only freezes him more surely into the polluted ice. In a grotesque parody of the Trinity, he has three faces, each a different color, and in each mouth he clamps a sinner whom he rips eternally with his teeth. JUDAS ISCARIOT is in the central mouth: BRUTUS and CASSIUS in the mouths on either side.

Having seen all, the Poets now climb through the center, grappling hand over hand down the hairy flank of Satan himself—a last supremely symbolic action—and at last, when they have passed the center of all gravity, they emerge from Hell. A long climb from the earth's center to the Mount of Purgatory awaits them, and they push on without rest, ascending along the sides of the river Lethe, till they emerge once more to see the stars of Heaven, just before dawn on Easter Sunday.

"On march the banners of the King of Hell,"   1
   my Master said. "Toward us. Look straight ahead:
   can you make him out at the core of the frozen shell?"

Like a whirling windmill seen afar at twilight,
   or when a mist has risen from the ground—
   just such an engine rose upon my sight

stirring up such a wild and bitter wind
   I cowered for shelter at my Master's back,
   there being no other windbreak I could find.

I stood now where the souls of the last class   10
   (with fear my verses tell it) were covered wholly;
   they shone below the ice like straws in glass.

Some lie stretched out; others are fixed in place
   upright, some on their heads, some on their soles;
   another, like a bow, bends foot to face.

When we had gone so far across the ice
   that it pleased my Guide to show me the foul creature
   which once had worn the grace of Paradise,

he made me stop, and, stepping aside, he said:
   "Now see the face of Dis! This is the place   20
   where you must arm your soul against all dread."

Do not ask, Reader, how my blood ran cold
   and my voice choked up with fear. I cannot write it:
   this is a terror that cannot be told.

I did not die, and yet I lost life's breath:
   imagine for yourself what I became,
   deprived at once of both my life and death.

The Emperor of the Universe of Pain
   jutted his upper chest above the ice;
   and I am closer in size to the great mountain   30

the Titans make around the central pit,
   than they to his arms. Now, starting from this part,
   imagine the whole that corresponds to it!

If he was once as beautiful as now
   he is hideous, and still turned on his Maker,
   well may he be the source of every woe!

With what a sense of awe I saw his head
   towering above me! for it had three faces:
   one was in front, and it was fiery red;

the other two, as weirdly wonderful,   40
   merged with it from the middle of each shoulder
   to the point where all converged at the top of the skull;

the right was something between white and bile;
  the left was about the color that one finds
  on those who live along the banks of the Nile.

Under each head two wings rose terribly,
  their span proportioned to so gross a bird:
  I never saw such sails upon the sea.

They were not feathers—their texture and their form
  were like a bat's wings—and he beat them so   50
  that three winds blew from him in one great storm:

it is these winds that freeze all Cocytus.
  He wept from his six eyes, and down three chins
  the tears ran mixed with bloody froth and pus.

In every mouth he worked a broken sinner
  between his rake-like teeth. Thus he kept three
  in eternal pain at his eternal dinner.

For the one in front the biting seemed to play
  no part at all compared to the ripping: at times
  the whole skin of his back was flayed away.   60

"That soul that suffers most," explained my Guide,
  "is Judas Iscariot, he who kicks his legs
  on the fiery chin and has his head inside.

Of the other two, who have their heads thrust forward,
  the one who dangles down from the black face
  is Brutus: note how he writhes without a word.

And there, with the huge and sinewy arms, is the soul
  of Cassius.—But the night is coming on
  and we must go, for we have seen the whole."

Then, as he bade, I clasped his neck, and he,   70
  watching for a moment when the wings
  were opened wide, reached over dexterously

and seized the shaggy coat of the king demon;
  then grappling matted hair and frozen crusts
  from one tuft to another, clambered down.

When we had reached the joint where the great thigh
  merges into the swelling of the haunch,
  my Guide and Master, straining terribly,

turned his head to where his feet had been
  and began to grip the hair as if he were climbing;   80
  so that I thought we moved toward Hell again.

"Hold fast!" my Guide said, and his breath came shrill
  with labor and exhaustion. "There is no way
  but by such stairs to rise above such evil."

At last he climbed out through an opening
  in the central rock, and he seated me on the rim;
  then joined me with a nimble backward spring.

I looked up, thinking to see Lucifer
  as I had left him, and I saw instead
  his legs projecting high into the air.   90

Now let all those whose dull minds are still vexed
  by failure to understand what point it was
  I had passed through, judge if I was perplexed.

"Get up. Up on your feet," my Master said.
  "The sun already mounts to middle tierce,
  and a long road and hard climbing lie ahead."

It was no hall of state we had found there,
  but a natural animal pit hollowed from rock
  with a broken floor and a close and sunless air.

"Before I tear myself from the Abyss,"   100
  I said when I had risen, "O my Master,
  explain to me my error in all this:

where is the ice? and Lucifer—how has he
  been turned from top to bottom: and how can the sun
  have gone from night to day so suddenly?"

And he to me: "You imagine you are still
  on the other side of the center where I grasped
  the shaggy flank of the Great Worm of Evil

which bores through the world—you *were* while I
    climbed down,
  but when I turned myself about, you passed   110
  the point to which all gravities are drawn.

You are under the other hemisphere where you stand;
  the sky above us is the half opposed
  to that which canopies the great dry land.

Under the mid-point of that other sky
  the Man who was born sinless and who lived
  beyond all blemish, came to suffer and die.

You have your feet upon a little sphere
  which forms the other face of the Judecca.
  There it is evening when it is morning here.   120

And this gross Fiend and Image of all Evil
  who made a stairway for us with his hide
  is pinched and prisoned in the ice-pack still.

On this side he plunged down from heaven's height,
  and the land that spread here once hid in the sea
  and fled North to our hemisphere for fright;

and it may be that moved by that same fear,
  the one peak that still rises on this side
  fled upward leaving this great cavern here.

Down there, beginning at the further bound   130
  of Beelzebub's dim tomb, there is a space
  not known by sight, but only by the sound

of a little stream descending through the hollow
  it has eroded from the massive stone
  in its endlessly entwining lazy flow."

My Guide and I crossed over and began
  to mount that little known and lightless road
  to ascend into the shining world again.

He first, I second, without thought of rest
  we climbed the dark until we reached the point
  where a round opening brought in sight the blest   140

and beauteous shining of the Heavenly cars.
  And we walked out once more beneath the Stars.

HILDEGARD OF BINGEN

Selections from *Scivias* (*May You Know* or *Know the Ways*)

Hildegard of Bingen (1098–1179) is a rare female voice from the Middle Ages. Indeed, in an era defined by a hierarchical male-dominated political, religious, and cultural system, she stands out as a remarkable individual. In particular, she expressed her most intimate feelings in books and participated in the period's major debates through public discourses and correspondence with leading figures. Today, as her reputation is on the rise, she has become a protean figure viewed from myriad angles, some contradictory, but all of them pioneering. Some admirers claim her as the first in a long line of visionary women who offer guidance to souls in distress. Others place her in the tradition of Christian thinkers who focus on Divine Wisdom, as evidenced by her stress on creation and redemption. Modern feminists salute her as a role model, for her managerial skills and willingness to confront patriarchal power. Traditionalists also admire her for her strong papalist politics, as a supporter of the church's hierarchy and the conservative reforms of Pope Gregory VII. Musicians and musicologists are now beginning to recognize her as an innovative composer of hymns and sacred songs. Historians study her letters for clues to the personalities of the period and for insight into medieval problems. Historians of science believe she broke new ground with her works on nature and medicine, especially regarding diagnosis and treatment of diseases. Finally, literary scholars identify her as a master of medieval prose with her prodigious and varied writings; they also marvel at the secret language she created, composed of nearly nine hundred words, to disguise her most confidential writing.

From the age of five to her last days, Hildegard experienced visions of God, in which she claimed she was directed to write down the details of her encounters as an aid to others. At first skeptical of her mystical writings, the church investigated but ultimately was satisfied and thereafter encouraged her in this path. Over the course of her life, she wrote three visionary books that are still considered classics of this genre. The first book dealt with religious beliefs, the second was concerned with virtue and vice, and the third summarized her theological ideas.

Scivias, or *May You Know* or *Know the Ways*, the first of her visionary books, set the pattern for the other two. Divided into three parts, it comprises a series of visions, each accompanied by a long commentary. The book's topics are far-ranging, including the nature of the universe, the relation between the macrocosm and the microcosm, birth, death, and the nature of the human soul.

Reading the Selections

In the first selection, the opening part of *Scivias*, Hildegard describes her encounter with the "heavenly voice." In obedience to its urgings, she writes down and interprets the mystical encounter. She concludes with an account of a mysterious illness, which probably caused her to take ten years to complete the book.

In the other selection, taken from the second part of *Scivias*, Hildegard recounts a vision that she explains is a symbol of the omnipotence of God. She reinforces this interpretation by citing a verse from the Book of Job. She then asks a theological question—Is the word of God indivisible and eternal?—and answers it in the affirmative. Next she observes that the human race has been given new life through the promise of salvation. Finally, using a variation of the argument from design, she affirms God's power based on his creation of the world and all its creatures.

—*w*—

Part I

Here begins the Book:
May you know of upright humanity.
Here begins the First Part of the Book:
May you know proof of the truthfulness of
the Visions flowing from God.

Behold, in the forty-third year of my passing journey, when I clung to a heavenly vision with fear and trembling, I saw a very great light from which a heavenly voice spoke and said to me:

> *O weak person, both ashes of ashes, and decaying of the decaying, speak and write what you see and hear. Because you are timid about speaking and simple about explaining and unskilled about writing those things, speak and write those things not according to the mouth of a person nor according to the perception of human inventiveness nor according to the wishes of human arrangement. But according to the extent that you see and hear those things in the heavens above in the marvelousness of God, bring to light those things by way of explanation, just as even a listener, understanding the words of a teacher, explains those things according to the course of the teacher's speech—willingly, plainly, and instructively. So therefore even you, o person, speak those things which you see and hear; and write those things not according to yourself nor according to another person, but according to the will of the one knowing, see and arrange all things in the secrets of the divinity's own mysteries.*

A second time I heard a heavenly voice speak and say to me:

> *Speak therefore these marvelous things and write and speak those things taught in this manner.*

In the year 1141 of the incarnation of Jesus Christ, the Word of God, when I was forty-two years and seven months old, a burning light coming from heaven poured into my mind. Like a flame which does not burn but rather enkindles, it inflamed my heart and my breast, just as the sun warms something with its rays. And I was able to understand books suddenly, the psaltery clearly, the evangelists and the volumes of the Old and New Testament, but I did not have the interpretation of the words of their texts nor the division of their syllables nor the knowledge of their grammar. Previously though, I had felt within myself the gift of secret mysteries and wondrous visions from the time I was a little girl, certainly from the time I was five years old right up to the present time. I revealed my gift to no one except to a select few and some religious who were living in my area, and I concealed my gift continuously in quiet silence until God wished it to be manifest by God's own grace. I truly saw those visions; I did not perceive them in dreams, nor while sleeping, nor in a frenzy, nor with the human eyes or with the external ears of a person, nor in remote places; but I received those visions according to the will of God while I was awake and alert with a clear mind, with the innermost eyes and ears of a person, and in open places. There may be a reason why I received those visions in this manner, but it is difficult for a human person to understand why. But after I had passed through the turning point of young womanhood, when I had arrived at the beginning of the age of perfect fortitude, I again heard a heavenly voice speaking to me:

> *I, the living light and the obscured illumination, appointed the person whom I wished, and I drove out the person whom I wished, wondrously according to what pleased me, with great wonders across the boundary of ancient people, who have seen many secrets in me; indeed I struck people down on earth, so that they might not lift themselves up in any exaltation of their own minds. The world also had no joy in it nor playfulness nor practice in those things which belong to the world, because I restrained it from stubborn daring, having fear and quaking in its own labors. People indeed suffered pain in their hearts and in the veins of their flesh, having bound together soul and senses, and sustaining the many passions of the body, so that diverse peace of mind was not concealed in them, but they judged themselves blameworthy in all their motives. For I surrounded the fissures of their hearts, lest their minds might raise themselves up through pride or through glory, but that they might have in all these things fear and sorrow rather than delight and wantonness. Whence they searched through my love in their own souls, where they came upon the one who hastened the way of salvation. And the one came upon those people and loved them, acknowledging that they had been faithful and similar to the one in some part of that labor which they had done for me. And holding themselves together with that one, they strained in all these things with heavenly zeal, so that my hidden miracles might be revealed. And the same people did not place themselves above that one, but when they came to that one with an ascent of humility and with the intention of good will, the one bent over them with warm protection. You therefore, o person, who receive these things not in the turmoil of deceit, but in the purity of simplicity, who receive these things straight for the manifestation of the things concealed, write what you see and hear.*

Although I saw and heard these things, I nevertheless refused to write them because of doubt and evil opinion and because of the diversity of other people's words, not so much out of stubbornness, but out of humility, until I became sick, pressed down by the scourge of God. I was sick for a long time with many different illnesses. Eventually, with the testimony of a certain noble man and a young woman of good wishes, I started to write what I had searched out and come upon secretly. As soon as I did that, I became healthy with a received strength, and knowing—as I said—the profoundness of the narration of books, I was able to bring my work to completion with difficulty, taking ten years.

These visions were written in the days of Henry Moguntin, archbishop, and Conrad, king of the Romans, and Cunon, abbot of the mountain, and blessed Disibod, high priest, under Pope Eugene.

And I spoke and wrote these things not according to the invention of my or any other person's heart, but as I saw, heard, and perceived them in the heavens through the hidden mysteries of God.

And again I heard a heavenly voice speaking to me:

Proclaim and write thus.

—⁓—

Part II

Vision One: 1

The very bright fire which you see stands for the omnipotent and living God. In the clarity of peacefulness, God has never been blackened by any evil—which is the fire being incomprehensible. God is divided by no divisions, either in the beginning or at the end. God is to be understood just as God is by all of God's thinking creatures—which is the fire being inextinguishable. God is that fullness which is not touched by any end—the fire being wholly living. No thing which God may know has ever been completely hidden from God—the fire being totally alive. Everything which lives, chooses to live from God. Job, who has been inspired, shows this through me when he speaks.

Vision One: 2

Who does not know that the hand of the Lord has done all these things? The soul of every living thing and the spirit of the body of every person is in the hand of God. (Job 12:9–10) What does this mean? No creature is so dull in its nature that is does not know the completeness of its cause. What does this mean? The sky has light, the light air, and the air winged creatures. The earth nourishes greenness, the greenness fruit, and the fruit animals. All things bear witness to this order because the strongest of all possible hands ordered these things. Such is the very great power of the ruler of all things who did all these things with such strength that there were no mistakes in their doing. The movement of all living things is from the omnipotence of the same creator. This is true of all the things of the earth—such as flocks of birds—who do not have the power of reason. It is also true of those who dwell in human flesh who do have the power of reason, discretion, and wisdom. What does this mean?

The soul goes around in its earthly conditions, laboring among many changes, according to whatever fleshly ways demand. The spirit truly sets itself up in two ways: clearly sighing, groaning, and longing for God; but seeking the power or the guidance or the choice to command things because it has the discretion of reason. Therefore, a person contains both the likeness of heaven and of earth in himself or herself. What does this mean? A person has a head in which there is clarity, inspiration and reason—just as the sky contains light-giving things, air and winged creatures. A person also has the means to bring forth new life and the desire to do so—just as the earth has the means to bring forth greenness, fruitfulness, and animals. What does this mean? O person, you are complete in every way, but do not forget your creator. Obey your creator as your creator arranged for you to do. Will you break the commandments of your creator?

Vision One: 3

The flame of the fire was an airy color, and it was blazing violently in a gentle wind. This flame was inseparable from the fire, just as the entrails are to a person. This signifies that the infinite Word was in the Creator before the time of any creature had been arranged. And the infinite Word was wondrously made incarnate without the filth or heaviness of any sin. This was done through the Holy Spirit in the dawn of blessed virginity. Nevertheless, just as the Word was indivisible from the Creator before taking on flesh, the Word was still inseparable from the Creator after taking on flesh. A person is not without life on the journey of the flesh; likewise, the Word was not completely without the Creator.

Vision One: 4

Why is the Son spoken of as the Word? Just as the orders of a teacher are prudently understood in the passing words of the teacher—because people know and foresee with the power of reason—so likewise the power of the Creator is truly known by the various creatures of the world in the Word which is not transitory but eternal. As the power and honor of a person is known through the person's word, so the holiness and goodness of the Creator is gleamed through the complete Word.

Vision One: 5

And I saw this flame lighten in color and give forth a bolt of lightning. This signifies that the Word of God, blazing as it were, shows strong virtues. When all the creatures were stirred up, began to lighten as it were, the Word was made flesh in the dawn and whiteness of virginity. As a result, all the virtues came from the Word in recognition of God. The Word came to life again for the salvation of souls.

Vision One: 6

Behold, the air—round and of great size—suddenly rose up. The air is the raw material which is still in the darkness of imperfection. The air certainly has not yet been made bright with the fullness of creation. It is round: this signifies the incomprehensible power of God. God's divinity does not lack anything in any way. The air suddenly rose up by the very great power of God's will, as if in the blink of an eye. And the flame sent sparks into the air, thereby leading the air to perfection. The air sparkled and was put in order, just as heaven and earth. The flame is like a worker. The heavenly Word showed the power of strength by creating creation. The Word brought forth various species of creatures from the air. These species shone with excitement because of the wondrousness of their origin. These creatures sparkled in the beauty of their perfection, just as when a worker makes something out of copper. These creatures sparkled in every direction, just as higher things shine forth from lower things and lower things from higher things.

Vision One: 7

After that, this flame sent forth some of its fire to a little clod of muddy earth which was lying on the ground. This means that after all the creatures had been created, the Word of God—because of the will of God and because of heavenly sweetness of love—saw the poor and fragile material of humanity as both soft and firm, that is, as both evil and good. This material of humanity was insensible and weighed down because the sharp and vital wind of perfection had not reached it yet. Then this flame made this little clod warm so that a body and blood were brought forth. The flame is making the clod warm because the earth is the material from which the flesh of people is made. The flame is nourishing the clod, just as a mother nurses her child. This flame breathed into this body and blood, and a person was brought forth. Through heavenly power, the human race was brought forth in body and soul.

Vision One: 8

With this finished, the bright fire—blazing violently in a gentle wind—brought the whitest of flowers to this person. This flower hung down from the flame just as the dew hangs down from the grass. This signifies that after Adam had been created, God—the greatest peacefulness—gave Adam the command to be fruitful through the Word and in the Holy Spirit. Through the Word, the sweet moisture of holiness fell from God and in the Holy Spirit. This is just like the dew falling from the blade of grass to the ground and thereby making the grass sprout. The person did not smell the flower with his or her nose, nor taste it with his or her mouth, nor touch it with his or her hands. This means that the person followed God's command with the understanding of wisdom—as if with the nose, but the person did not allow the strength of God's command to

enter him or her completely—as if in the mouth. Nor did the person do his or her work with the fullness of blessedness—as if with the hands. But this person left and fell into a very dense darkness. And this person was not strong enough to raise up out of this darkness. This person turned his or her back on the command of the Divinity on the advice of the devil. This person did not look for God with faith or in work. As a result of being weighed down with sin, this person was not able to rise up to the true knowledge until the one who was obedient to God came completely without any sin.

The darkness increased in size and spread itself out more and more in the air. This means that the power of death has always increased in the world by increasing the different kinds of faults. And people surround themselves with a large number of these faults and fall into bristling, breaking, and stinking sins.

Vision One: 9

Then three large stars—all of the same size—moved into the air. These stars—all of the same brightness—appeared in the darkness together with other stars. Some of the other stars were large and some small, but they were all very bright. These stars are three great persons—Abraham, Isaac, and Jacob—who were figurative of the Trinity. Abraham, Isaac, and Jacob performed faithful works, but they also gave birth to children. They drove the darkness of the world back by doing both. And many other minor and major prophets followed them, shining forth with many and astonishing miracles.

Vision One: 10

Finally, a very large star appeared which radiated light with wonderful clearness. This very large star directed its brightness toward the previously mentioned flame. This star is, of course, the distinguished prophet, John the Baptist. John worked rapidly with faithful and peaceful miracles. He prophesied the coming of the true Word of God. John did not fall into any evil, but he quickly and strongly cast all evil aside with his works of justice.

Vision One: 11

On earth, however, a certain brightness appeared as the dawn from this flame even though the previously mentioned bright fire had not been separated from the flame. This means that God sent the greatest brightness of light—the Word. God was not separated from the Word though, but sent the Word as if the Word were a great fountain from which every faithful person could drink so that his or her throat would not be thirsty and dry. In the brightness of this dawn, the greatest of all wills has been raised up. In the clarity of this great peacefulness, all the legions who had come earlier admired the great counsel of the Word.

Vision One: 12

Nevertheless, o person, even though you want to know this great counsel while you are human, you cannot because a bolt of concealment has been put in place. You are not supposed to understand the mysteries of the Divinity more than God wishes you to understand.

Vision One: 13

Next I saw a very peaceful person going out from the brightness of the previously mentioned dawn. This person poured light into the darkness. With the redness of blood and in the whiteness of paleness, this person drove this darkness upward with great strength. This person—having been hurled through the darkness and having touched it—became visible, was bright, was lifted up, and went forth. This person signifies the Word of God. Although the Word was made flesh in the whiteness of unspotted virginity and was born without any pain, the Word was not separated from God. How is this possible? When the Word was born into the world from a mother, the Word still appeared in heaven with God where the angels quaked and rejoiced, singing the sweetest of praises. The Word lived in time without any stain of sin and sent forth the light-giving blessedness of learning and of salvation into the darkness of unfaithfulness. For the Word was cast aside by an unbelieving people and was led to the passion where the Word poured out the fairest of blood and tasted the mist of death. By doing this, the Word conquered the devil and freed from the lower world the chosen ones who had been led astray by the devil, taking them to their inheritance which they had lost through Adam. When those chosen ones received their inheritance again, tambourines and lutes and songs of various musicians were played very elaborately because the Word, having been cast down in destruction, was lifted up in blessedness. The Word went forth, having freed death through heavenly virtues.

Vision One: 17

This person brought forth endless glory on high and sent forth a wondrous fruitfulness and odor. This means that the Word ascended to the Creator who is one with the Word and with the Holy Spirit. All are on high with indescribable joy and gladness. The Word also appeared gloriously in the fullness of peacefulness and blessedness to the faithful who believed with pure and simple hearts that the Word was truly God and human. At the same time, the new bride of this lamb was showered with various beautiful gifts. She was adorned with all kinds of virtues because of the faithful fighting strongly against the sly serpent.

Whereupon whoever sees with watchful eyes and hears with listening ears, this one may offer a kiss of love to my secret words, which flow from me, the living one

10

THE LATE MIDDLE AGES
1300–1500

PETRARCH
Selections from the *Canzoniere*

Francesco Petrarch (in Italian, "Petrarca") (1304–1374) is another of the West's great bridge figures (see St. Augustine's *Confessions*), whose careers straddle historical periods with opposing cultural tendencies. He lived in the Late Middle Ages, a period dominated by Gothic forms and ideals; yet, he was a founder of the Renaissance, for he was the first author to make his writing task the recovery and updating of the Classical literary tradition. He is particularly noted for his reintroduction of lost or neglected texts from antiquity into European culture. Inspired by Classicism, he placed the natural before the supernatural, thus reversing the judgment of his age; and he was the first European writer to defend secular culture and earthly fame. Despite his modern outlook, he saw some merit in the medieval view, as in the dialogue *Secretum* (or *My Secret*), in which he gives St. Augustine some of the best lines.

Despite being born in Italy and residing there, notably in Rome and Florence, for much of his life, Petrarch was a true European. Widely traveled, in part because of his studies and in part because his patrons required that he act as a diplomat, he spent months in France, Flanders, and the Rhineland. During these travels, he searched for and found old manuscripts (for example, some letters of Cicero), revised earlier works, and began new tasks. His most famous visit was to Avignon, a papal territory, where the worldliness of the papal court led him to coin the famous phrase "the Babylonian Captivity of the Papacy" to denote the seventy-year period when the popes lived in Avignon instead of Rome. His works, regardless of where written, reflect his impressions of daily life and his drive for self-understanding.

Reading the Selections

Besides being devoted to Classicism and Latin literature, Petrarch was equally famed as a master of Italian poetry, as shown in the *Canzoniere* (*Songbook* or *Rhymes*), his masterpiece in his native tongue. Drawing on Classical models and the ethos of the troubadour poets of southern France, these poems were inspired by the living woman he called Laura, whom he first saw in Avignon in 1327. Though she was married to someone else and completely uninterested in the poet's attentions, Laura personified beauty and truth for Petrarch. Nevertheless, in private life he wooed other women and fathered two children. When Laura was carried off by the Black Death in 1348, Petrarch turned to God, struggling with his sense of sin and the fate of his soul.

Seven of the 366 poems in the *Canzoniere* are presented here. All were composed in the form of sonnets, the fourteen-line verse form that Petrarch inherited from Italian predecessors and brought to perfection. The Petrarchan sonnet is divided into two parts: The first eight lines usually rhyme ab-baabba; the following six lines usually rhyme cdecde. This verse form was imported into England in the sixteenth century, where it enjoyed great vogue.

These sonnets show typical themes in the *Canzoniere*. The opening four poems, in the category of *in vita* (on life), recall Petrarch's introduction to Laura, who ignored him; they dwell on the pain of unrequited love. The last three poems, in the category of *in morte* (on death), show stoic acceptance of the loss of his "goddess," as he is forced to recognize that nothing lasts forever.

—✻—

3

It was the day the sun's ray had turned pale   1
with pity for the suffering of his Maker
when I was caught, and I put up no fight,
my lady, for your lovely eyes had bound me.

It seemed no time to be on guard against
Love's blows; therefore, I went my way
secure and fearless—so, all my misfortunes
began in midst of universal woe.

Love found me all disarmed and found the way
was clear to reach my heart down through the eyes   10
which have become the halls and doors of tears.

It seems to me it did him little honour
to wound me with his arrow in my state
and to you, armed, not show his bow at all.

—✻—

61

Oh blessèd be the day, the month, the year,   1
the season and the time, the hour, the instant,
the gracious countryside, the place where I
was struck by those two lovely eyes that bound me;

and blessèd be the first sweet agony
I felt when I found myself bound to Love,
the bow and all the arrows that have pierced me,
the wounds that reach the bottom of my heart.

And blessèd be all of the poetry
I scattered, calling out my lady's name,   10
and all the sighs, and tears, and the desire;

blessèd be all the paper upon which
I earn her fame, and every thought of mine,
only of her, and shared with no one else.

—✻—

132

If it's not love, then what is it I feel?   1
But if it's love, by God, what is this thing?
If good, why then the bitter mortal sting?
If bad, then why is every torment sweet?

If I burn willingly, why weep and grieve?
And if against my will, what good lamenting?
O living death, O pleasurable harm,
how can you rule me if I not consent?

And if I do consent, it's wrong to grieve.
Caught in contrasting winds in a frail boat   10
on the high seas I am without a helm,

so light of wisdom, so laden of error,
that I myself do not know what I want,
and shiver in midsummer, burn in winter.

—w—

134

I find no peace, and I am not at war,   1
I fear and hope, and burn and I am ice;
I fly above the heavens, and lie on earth,
and I grasp nothing and embrace the world.

One keeps me jailed who neither locks nor opens,
nor keeps me for her own nor frees the noose;
Love does not kill, nor does he loose my chains;
he wants me lifeless but won't loosen me.

I see with no eyes, shout without a tongue;
I yearn to perish, and I beg for help;   10
I hate myself and love somebody else.

I thrive on pain and laugh with all my tears;
I dislike death as much as I do life:
because of you, lady, I am this way.

—w—

272

Life runs away and never rests a moment   1
and death runs after it with mighty stride,
and present things and things back from the past
and from the future, too, wage war on me:

anticipation, memory weigh down
my heart on either side so that, in truth,
if I did not take pity on myself,
I would, by now, be free of all such thoughts.

What little sweetness my sad heart once felt
comes back to me; but from the other side   10
I see turbulent winds blowing my sails;

I see a storm in port, and weary now
my helmsman, and my masts and lines destroyed,
and the fair stars I loved to look at, dead.

—w—

311

That nightingale so tenderly lamenting   1
perhaps his children or his cherished mate,
in sweetness fills the sky and countryside
with many notes of grief skilfully played,

and all night long he stays with me it seems,
reminding me of my harsh destiny;
I have no one to blame except myself
for thinking that Death could not take a goddess.

How easy to deceive one who is sure!
Those two lights, lovely, brighter than the sun,   10
whoever thought would turn the earth so dark?

And now I know what this fierce fate of mine
would have me learn as I live on in tears:
that nothing here can please and also last.

365

I go my way regretting those past times
I spent in loving something which was mortal
instead of soaring high, since I had wings
that might have taken me to higher levels.

You who see all my shameful, wicked errors,
King of all Heaven, invisible, immortal,
help this frail soul of mine for she has strayed,
and all her emptiness fill up with grace,

so that, having once lived in storms, at war,
I may now die in peace, in port; and if my stay
was vain, at least let my departure count.

Over that little life that still remains to me,
and at my death, deign that your hand be present:
You know You are the only hope I have.

GIOVANNI BOCCACCIO

Selections from *The Decameron*

The Decameron is one of the most important works of European literature. It was written by Giovanni Boccaccio (1313–1375), the contemporary of his fellow humanist and friend, Petrarch (see *Canzoniere*), in turbulent fourteenth-century Italy. Like Petrarch, he was devoted to Classicism, especially to reading and translating the great works of Latin literature. Boccaccio, too, was attracted to the world's delights, recognizing that life was to be experienced and, for the most part, enjoyed. He also suffered the pangs of guilt for his sins and expressed regrets about his earlier life in his old age.

The illegitimate son of a successful Florentine financier, Boccaccio prepared for a banking career and studied law before turning to a life of letters. Awakened to the possibility of a literary career while attached to the court of the well-educated king of Naples, Robert the Wise (r. 1309–1343), he became enamored of a court lady whom he christened Fiammetta (Little Flame) and wrote sonnets to her in the style of Petrarch. Removed to Florence, where his literary fame and fortune soared, he lived an active life engaged in diplomatic missions that took him up and down the Italian peninsula. In Florence, he survived the devastation of the Black Death, which, by one estimate, killed nearly half the population in 1348.

Boccaccio's Classical scholarship, medieval romances in both poetry and prose, and Italian love lyrics would have ensured him an honored place in Western letters; however, *The Decameron* has made him one of the literary immortals. Composed between 1349 and 1353, *The Decameron* presents this chaotic age in microcosm, showing the good and evil therein. It contains a rich collection of folk tales, parables, romances, and stories from Italian, French, Near Eastern, Classical, and biblical sources. The work's realism, secular spirit, and frank probing of the human heart had an immediate impact on European fiction, leading ultimately to the modern novel. In later years, Boccaccio expressed regret about his most famous work, deploring its lighthearted style.

Reading the Selections

The Decameron (from the Greek for "ten") is a tale within a tale, an old genre most famously realized in the *Arabian Nights*. In Boccaccio's work, this structure unfolds as ten young Florentines—seven ladies and three gentlemen—escape the plague that is ravaging their city and take refuge in a country palace. There, they pass the time, each telling a story a day for ten days, hence one hundred tales total.

The first selection, taken from the author's introduction to *The Decameron*, opens with Boccaccio addressing female readers, the audience for vernacular literature in the Middle Ages because male readers supposedly were only interested in works in Latin. He advises these "fairest ladies" not to give up too soon on his book, though he knows that the details of the plague, which of necessity he must include in his story, may be unappetizing to them. After this warning, he describes the plague, showing how it disrupted Florentine life at every level—one of the most valuable aspects of this work for modern scholars. The details of the disease's symptoms and the victims' suffering—verified as accurate by medical historians—vividly portray the conditions under which people died or survived. He also discusses varied responses to the plague, ranging from self-imposed isolation to riotous living to even abandoning loved ones, including spouses and children.

The second selection (from First Day, Third Story) contains the philosophical tale known as "the legend of the three rings." In it, Melchisedech, a Jew, escapes a trap set by Saladin, a Muslim warrior whose deeds made him a hero to medieval Europeans even though his reputation came from fighting Christians during the Crusades. Saladin, needing money, invites the rich Melchisedech to dinner and asks which of the three faiths—Christianity, Judaism, or Islam—is best. Aware that this is a trick question, Melchisedech replies with an allegorical fable that artfully avoids calling one religion the best. Saladin, recognizing Melchisedech's wisdom, adopts him as a close friend. Such a tale suggests that Boccaccio was freer of religious bigotry than most Europeans of the time.

—m—

Introduction

. . .

Whenever, fairest ladies, I pause to consider how compassionate you all are by nature, I invariably become aware that the present work will seem to you to possess an irksome and ponderous opening. For it carries at its head the painful memory of the deadly havoc wrought by the recent plague, which brought so much heartache and misery to those who witnessed, or had experience of it. But I do not want you to be deterred, for this reason, from reading any further, on the assumption that you are to be subjected, as you read, to an endless torrent of tears and sobbing. You will be affected no differently by this grim beginning than walkers confronted by a steep and rugged hill, beyond which there lies a beautiful and delectable plain. The degree of pleasure they derive from the latter will correspond directly to the difficulty of the climb and the descent. And just as the end of mirth is heaviness, so sorrows are dispersed by the advent of joy.

This brief unpleasantness (I call it brief, inasmuch as it is contained within few words) is quickly followed by the sweetness and the pleasure which I have already promised you, and which, unless you were told in advance, you would not perhaps be expecting to find after such a beginning as this. Believe me, if I could decently have taken you whither I desire by some other route, rather than along a path so difficult as this, I would gladly have done so. But since it is impossible without this memoir to show the origin of the events you will read about later, I really have no alternative but to address myself to its composition.

I say, then, that the sum of thirteen hundred and forty-eight years had elapsed since the fruitful Incarnation of the Son of God, when the noble city of Florence, which for its great beauty excels all others in Italy, was visited by the deadly pestilence. Some say that it descended upon the human race through the influence of the heavenly bodies, others that it was a punishment signifying God's righteous anger at our iniquitous way of life. But whatever its cause, it had originated some years earlier in the East, where it had claimed countless lives before it unhappily spread westward, growing in strength as it swept relentlessly on from one place to the next.

In the face of its onrush, all the wisdom and ingenuity of man were unavailing. Large quantities of refuse were cleared out of the city by officials specially appointed for the purpose, all sick persons were forbidden entry, and numerous instructions were issued for safeguarding the people's health, but all to no avail. Nor were the countless petitions humbly directed to God by the pious, whether by means of formal processions or in any other guise, any less ineffectual. For in the early spring of the year we have mentioned, the plague began, in a terrifying and extraordinary manner, to make its disastrous effects apparent. It did not take the form it had assumed in the East, where if anyone bled from the nose it was an obvious portent of certain death. On the contrary, its earliest symptom, in men and women alike, was the appearance of certain swellings in the groin or the armpit, some of which were egg-shaped whilst others were roughly the size of the common apple. Sometimes the swellings were large, sometimes not so large, and they were referred to by the populace as *gavòccioli*. From the two areas already mentioned, this deadly *gavòcciolo* would begin to spread, and within a short time it would appear at random all over the body. Later on, the symptoms of the disease changed, and many people began to find dark blotches and bruises on their arms, thighs, and other parts of the body, sometimes large and few in number, at other times tiny and closely spaced. These, to anyone unfortunate enough to contract them, were just as infallible a sign that he would die as the *gavòcciolo* had been earlier, and as indeed it still was.

Against these maladies, it seemed that all the advice of physicians and all the power of medicine were profitless and unavailing. Perhaps the nature of the illness was such that it allowed no remedy: or perhaps those people who were treating the illness (whose numbers had increased enormously because the ranks of the qualified were invaded by people, both men and women, who had never received any training in medicine), being ignorant of its causes, were not prescribing the appropriate cure. At all events, few of those who caught it ever recovered, and in most cases death occurred within three days from the appearance of the symptoms we have described, some people dying more rapidly than others, the majority without any fever or other complications.

But what made this pestilence even more severe was that whenever those suffering from it mixed with people who were still unaffected, it would rush upon these with the speed of a fire racing through dry or oily substances that happened to be placed within its reach. Nor was this the full extent of its evil, for not only did it infect healthy persons who conversed or had any dealings with the sick, making them ill or visiting an equally horrible death upon them, but it also seemed to transfer the sickness to anyone touching the clothes or other objects which had been handled or used by its victims.

It is a remarkable story that I have to relate. And were it not for the fact that I am one of many people who saw it with their own eyes, I would scarcely dare to believe it, let alone commit it to paper, even though I had heard it from a person whose word I could trust. The plague I have been describing was of so contagious a nature that very often it visibly did more than simply pass from one person to another. In other words, whenever an animal other than a human being touched anything belonging to a person who had been stricken or exterminated by the disease, it not only caught the sickness, but died from it almost at once. To all of this, as I have just said, my own eyes bore witness on more than one occasion. One day, for instance, the rags of a pauper who had died from the disease were thrown into the street, where they attracted the attention of two pigs. In their wonted fashion, the pigs first of all gave the rags a thorough mauling with their snouts after which they took them between their teeth and shook them against their cheeks. And within a short time they began to writhe as though they had been poisoned, then they both dropped dead to the ground, spreadeagled upon the rags that had brought about their undoing.

These things, and many others of a similar or even worse nature, caused various fears and fantasies to take root in the minds of those who were still alive and well. And almost without exception, they took a single and very inhuman precaution, namely to avoid or run away from the sick and their belongings, by which means they all thought that their own health would be preserved.

Some people were of the opinion that a sober and abstemious mode of living considerably reduced the risk of infection. They therefore formed themselves into groups and lived in isolation from everyone else. Having withdrawn to a comfortable abode where there were no sick persons, they locked themselves in and settled down to a peaceable existence, consuming modest quantities of delicate foods and precious wines and avoiding all excesses. They refrained from speaking to outsiders, refused to receive news of the dead or the sick, and entertained themselves with music and whatever other amusements they were able to devise.

Others took the opposite view, and maintained that an infallible way of warding off this appalling evil was to drink heavily, enjoy life to the full, go round singing and merrymaking, gratify all of one's cravings whenever the opportunity offered, and shrug the whole thing off as one enormous joke. Moreover, they practised what they preached to the best of their ability, for they would visit one tavern after another, drinking all day and night to immoderate excess; or alternatively (and this was their more frequent custom), they would do their drinking in various private houses, but only in the ones where the conversation was restricted to subjects that were pleasant or entertaining. Such places were easy to find, for people behaved as though their days were numbered, and treated their belongings and their own persons with equal abandon. Hence most houses had become common property, and any passing stranger could make himself at home as naturally as though he were the rightful owner. But for all their riotous manner of living, these people always took good care to avoid any contact with the sick.

In the face of so much affliction and misery, all respect for the laws of God and man had virtually broken down and been extinguished in our city. For like everybody else, those ministers and executors of the laws who were not either dead or ill were left with so few subordinates that they were unable to discharge any of their duties. Hence everyone was free to behave as he pleased.

There were many other people who steered a middle course between the two already mentioned, neither restricting their diet to the same degree as the first group, nor indulging so freely as the second in drinking and other forms of wantonness, but simply doing no more than satisfy their appetite. Instead of incarcerating themselves, these people moved about freely, holding in their hands a posy of flowers, or fragrant herbs, or one of a wide range of spices, which they applied at frequent intervals to their nostrils, thinking it an excellent idea to fortify the brain with smells of that particular sort; for the stench of dead bodies, sickness, and medicines seemed to fill and pollute the whole of the atmosphere.

Some people, pursuing what was possibly the safer alternative, callously maintained that there was no better or more efficacious remedy against a plague than to run away from it. Swayed by this argument, and sparing no thought for anyone but themselves, large numbers of men and women abandoned their city, their homes, their relatives, their estates and their belongings, and headed for the countryside, either in Florentine territory or, better still, abroad. It was as though they imagined that the wrath of God would not unleash this plague against men for their iniquities irrespective of where they happened to be, but would only be aroused against those who found themselves within the city walls; or possibly they assumed that the whole of the population would be exterminated and that the city's last hour had come.

Of the people who held these various opinions, not all of them died. Nor, however, did they all survive. On the contrary, many of each different persuasion fell ill here, there, and everywhere, and having themselves, when they were fit and well, set an example to those who were as yet unaffected, they languished away with virtually no one to nurse them. It was not merely a question of one citizen avoiding another, and of people almost invariably neglecting their neighbours and rarely or never visiting their relatives, addressing them only from a distance; this scourge had implanted so great a terror in the hearts of men and women that brothers abandoned brothers, uncles their nephews, sisters their brothers, and in many cases wives deserted their husbands. But even worse, and almost incredible, was the fact that fathers and mothers refused to nurse and assist their own children, as though they did not belong to them.

Hence the countless numbers of people who fell ill, both male and female, were entirely dependent upon either the charity of friends (who were few and far between) or the greed of servants, who remained in short supply despite the attraction of high wages out of all proportion to the services they performed. Furthermore, these latter were men and women of coarse intellect and the majority were unused to such duties, and they did little more than hand things to the invalid when asked to do so and watch over him when he was dying. And in performing this kind of service, they frequently lost their lives as well as their earnings.

As a result of this wholesale desertion of the sick by neighbours, relatives and friends, and in view of the scarcity of servants, there grew up a practice almost never previously heard of, whereby when a woman fell ill, no matter how gracious or beautiful or gently bred she might be, she raised no objection to being attended by a male servant, whether he was young or not. Nor did she have any scruples about showing him every part of her body as freely as she would have displayed it to a woman, provided that the nature of her infirmity required her to do so; and this explains why those women who recovered were possibly less chaste in the period that followed.

Moreover a great many people died who would perhaps have survived had they received some assistance. And hence, what with the lack of appropriate means for tending the sick, and the virulence of the plague, the number of deaths reported in the city whether by day or night was so enormous that it astonished all who heard tell of it, to say nothing of the people who actually witnessed the carnage. And it was perhaps inevitable that among the citizens who survived there arose certain customs that were quite contrary to established tradition.

It had once been customary, as it is again nowadays, for the women relatives and neighbours of a dead man to assemble in his house in order to mourn in the company of the women who had been closest to him; moreover his kinfolk would forgather in front of his house along with his neighbours and various other citizens, and there would be a contingent of priests, whose numbers varied according to the quality of the deceased; his body would be taken thence to the church in which he had wanted to be buried, being borne on the shoulders of his peers amidst the funeral pomp of candles and dirges. But as the ferocity of the plague began to mount, this practice all but disappeared entirely and was replaced by different customs. For not only did people die without having many

women about them, but a great number departed this life without anyone at all to witness their going. Few indeed were those to whom the lamentations and bitter tears of their relatives were accorded; on the contrary, more often than not bereavement was the signal for laughter and witticisms and general jollification—the art of which the women, having for the most part suppressed their feminine concern for the salvation of the souls of the dead, had learned to perfection. Moreover it was rare for the bodies of the dead to be accompanied by more than ten or twelve neighbours to the church, nor were they borne on the shoulders of worthy and honest citizens, but by a kind of gravedigging fraternity, newly come into being and drawn from the lower orders of society. These people assumed the title of sexton, and demanded a fat fee for their services, which consisted in taking up the coffin and hauling it swiftly away, not to the church specified by the dead man in his will, but usually to the nearest at hand. They would be preceded by a group of four or six clerics, who between them carried one or two candles at most, and sometimes none at all. Nor did the priests go to the trouble of pronouncing solemn and lengthy funeral rites, but, with the aid of these so-called sextons, they hastily lowered the body into the nearest empty grave they could find.

As for the common people and a large proportion of the bourgeoisie, they presented a much more pathetic spectacle, for the majority of them were constrained, either by their poverty or the hope of survival, to remain in their houses. Being confined to their own parts of the city, they fell ill daily in their thousands, and since they had no one to assist them or attend to their needs, they inevitably perished almost without exception. Many dropped dead in the open streets, both by day and by night, whilst a great many others, though dying in their own houses, drew their neighbours' attention to the fact more by the smell of their rotting corpses than by any other means. And what with these, and the others who were dying all over the city, bodies were here, there and everywhere.

Whenever people died, their neighbours nearly always followed a single, set routine, prompted as much by their fear of being contaminated by the decaying corpse as by any charitable feelings they may have entertained towards the deceased. Either on their own, or with the assistance of bearers whenever these were to be had, they extracted the bodies of the dead from their houses and left them lying outside their front doors, where anyone going about the streets, especially in the early morning, could have observed countless numbers of them. Funeral biers would then be sent for, upon which the dead were taken away, though there were some who, for lack of biers, were carried off on plain boards. It was by no means rare for more than one of these biers to be seen with two or three bodies upon it at a time; on the contrary, many were seen to contain a husband and wife, two or three brothers and sisters, a father and son, or some other pair of close relatives. And times without number it happened that two priests would be on their way to bury someone, holding a cross before them, only to find that bearers carrying three or four additional biers would fall in behind them; so that whereas the priests had thought they had only one burial to attend to, they in fact had six or seven, and sometimes more. Even in these circumstances, however, there were no tears or candles or mourners to honour the dead; in fact, no more respect was accorded to dead people than would nowadays be shown towards dead goats. For it was quite apparent that the one thing which, in normal times, no wise man had ever learned to accept with patient resignation (even though it struck so seldom and unobtrusively), had now been brought home to the feeble-minded as well, but the scale of the calamity caused them to regard it with indifference.

Such was the multitude of corpses (of which further consignments were arriving every day and almost by the hour at each of the churches), that there was not sufficient consecrated ground for them to be buried in, especially if each was to have its own plot in accordance with long-established custom. So when all the graves were full, huge trenches were excavated in the churchyards, into which new arrivals were placed in their hundreds, stowed tier upon tier like ships' cargo, each layer of corpses being covered over with a thin layer of soil till the trench was filled to the top.

But rather than describe in elaborate detail the calamities . . . experienced in the city at that time, I must mention that, whilst an ill wind was blowing through Florence itself, the surrounding region was no less badly affected. In the fortified towns, conditions were similar to those in the city itself on a minor scale; but in the scattered hamlets and the countryside proper, the poor unfortunate peasants and their families had no physicians or servants whatever to assist them, and collapsed by the wayside, in their fields, and in their cottages at all hours of the day and night, dying more like animals than human beings. Like the townspeople, they too grew apathetic in their ways, disregarded their affairs, and neglected their possessions. Moreover they all behaved as though each day was to be their last, and far from making provision for the future by tilling their lands, tending their flocks, and adding to their previous labours, they tried in every way they could think of to squander the assets already in their possession. Thus it came about that oxen, asses, sheep, goats, pigs, chickens, and even dogs (for all their deep fidelity to man) were driven away and allowed to roam freely through the fields, where the crops lay abandoned and had not even been reaped, let alone gathered in. And after a whole day's feasting, many of these animals, as though possessing the power of reason, would return glutted in the evening to their own quarters, without any shepherd to guide them.

But let us leave the countryside and return to the city. What more remains to be said, except that the cruelty of heaven (and possibly, in some measure, also that of man) was so immense and so devastating that between March and July of the year in question, what with the fury of the pestilence and the fact that so many of the sick were inadequately cared for or abandoned in their hour of need because the healthy were too terrified to approach them, it is reliably thought that over a hundred thousand human lives were extinguished within the walls of the city of Florence? Yet before this lethal catastrophe fell upon the city, it is doubtful whether anyone would have guessed it contained so many inhabitants.

Ah, how great a number of splendid palaces, fine houses, and noble dwellings, once filled with retainers, with lords and with ladies, were bereft of all who had lived there, down to the tiniest child! How numerous were the famous families, the vast estates, the notable fortunes, that were seen to be left without a rightful successor! How many gallant gentlemen, fair ladies, and sprightly youths, who would have been judged hale and hearty by Galen, Hippocrates and Aesculapius (to say nothing of others), having breakfasted in the morning with their kinsfolk, acquaintances and friends, supped that same evening with their ancestors in the next world! . . .

—⁓—

First Day, Third Story

Melchisedech, a Jew, by means of a short story about three rings, escapes from a trap set for him by Saladin.

Neifile's tale was praised by all, and when she had finished talking, at the queen's command, Filomena began to speak in this fashion.

The tale that Neifile told brings back to my memory a dangerous incident that once happened to a Jew; and since God and the truth of our faith have already been well dealt with by us, we should not be forbidden to descend to the acts of men from now on. Now, I shall tell you this story and when you have heard it, perhaps you will become more cautious when you reply to questions put to you.

You should know, my dear companions, that just as stupidity can often remove one from a state of happiness and place him in the greatest misery, so, too, intelligence can rescue the wise man from the gravest of dangers and restore him to his secure state. The fact that stupidity leads one from a state of happiness to one of misery is shown by many examples which, at present, I do not intend to relate, since thousands of clear illustrations of this appear every day; but, as I promised, I shall demonstrate briefly in a little story how intelligence may be the cause of some consolation.

Saladin, whose worth was such that from humble beginnings he became Sultan of Babylon and won many victories over Christian and Saracen kings, discovered one day that he had consumed, in his various wars and his displays of grandiose magnificence, all his treasury, while the occasion arose in which he needed a large amount of money. Not being able to envision a means of obtaining what he needed in a short time, he happened to recall a rich Jew, whose name was Melchisedech, who loaned money at usurious rates in Alexandria, and he thought that this man might be able to assist him, if only he would agree to. But this Jew was so avaricious that he would not do so of his own free will, and the Sultan did not wish to have recourse to force; therefore, as his need was pressing, he thought of nothing but finding a means of getting the Jew to help him, and he decided to use some colorful pretext to accomplish this. He had him summoned, and after welcoming him in a friendly manner, he had him sit beside him and said to him:

"Worthy man, I have heard from many people that you are very wise and most versed in the affairs of God; because of this, I should like to know from you which of the three Laws you believe to be the true one: the Jewish, the Saracen, or the Christian."

The Jew, who really was a wise man, realized too well that Saladin was trying to catch him with his words in order to accuse him of something, and he understood that he could not praise any of the three Laws more than the other without Saladin achieving his goal; therefore, he sharpened his wits, like one who seems to need an answer in order not to be entrapped, and knew well what he had to say before he had to, and said:

"My Lord, the question which you have put to me is a good one, and in order to give you an answer, I shall have to tell you a little story which you shall now hear. If I am not mistaken, I remember having heard many times that there once was a great and wealthy man who had a most beautiful and precious ring among the many precious jewels in his treasury. Because of its worth and its beauty, he wanted to honor it by bequeathing it to his descendants forever, and he ordered that whichever of his sons would be found in possession of this ring, which he would have left him, should be honored and revered as his true heir and head of the family by all the others. The man to whom he left the ring did the same as his predecessor had, hav-

ing left behind the same instructions to his descendants; in short, this ring went from hand to hand through many generations, and finally it came into the hands of a man who had three handsome and virtuous sons, all of whom were obedient to their father, and for this reason, all three were equally loved by him. Since the father was growing old and they knew about the tradition of the ring, each of the three men was anxious to be the most honored among his sons, and each one, as best he knew how, begged the father to leave the ring to him when he died. The worthy man, who loved them all equally, did not know himself which of the three he would choose to leave the ring, and since he had promised it to each of them, he decided to try and satisfy all three: he had a good jeweler secretly make two more rings which were so much like the first one that he himself, who had had them made, hardly could tell which was the real one. When the father was dying, he gave a ring to each of his sons in secret, and after he died each son claimed the inheritance and position and one son denied the claims of the other, each bringing forth his ring to prove his case; when they discovered the rings were so much alike that they could not recognize the true one, they put aside the question of who the true heir was and left it undecided as it is to this day.

"And let me say the same thing to you, my lord, concerning the three Laws given to three peoples by God our Father which are the subject of the question you posed to me: each believes itself to be the true heir, to possess the true Law, and to follow the true commandments, but whoever is right, just as in the case of the rings, is still undecided."

Saladin realized how the man had most cleverly avoided the trap which he had set to snare him, and for that reason he decided to make his needs known openly to him and to see if he might wish to help him; and he did so, revealing to him what he had in mind to do if the Jew had not replied to his question as discreetly as he had. The Jew willingly gave Saladin as much money as he desired, and Saladin later repaid him in full; in fact, he more than repaid him: he gave him great gifts and always esteemed him as his friend and kept him near at court in a grand and honorable fashion.

GEOFFREY CHAUCER

Selections from *The Canterbury Tales*

The Canterbury Tales by Geoffrey Chaucer (about 1340–1400) is generally recognized as the earliest masterpiece in English. Its popularity helped assure the triumph of the native tongue over Anglo-Norman, the French spoken in England after the Norman conquest (1066). Recited perhaps as court entertainment and circulated privately in manuscript, it quickly established Chaucer as a master storyteller and a melodious poet, a judgment shared by generations of readers. Today, it is among the best loved works in English; its lively tales are enjoyed by children and adults alike, and its unique characters are a part of popular culture. For scholars, the poem is a treasure trove for the social attitudes of its day.

The literary form of *The Canterbury Tales* (about 1385–1400) is beautifully simple, a tale within a tale, a genre inspired by Boccaccio's *Decameron*. For plot, Chaucer introduces himself as a traveler who joins a motley band of English men and women at the Tabard Inn in Southwark (south London); he rides horseback with them on their partly religious, partly diverting pilgrimage to the shrine of St. Thomas à Becket at Canterbury. On the journey, he put into their mouths the tales and learning that he had acquired during his lifetime. For reasons unknown, Chaucer left the work unfinished; he completed only twenty-three tales of the more than 120 projected.

For the modern reader, much of the interest of this work lies in the full-blooded description of the pilgrims. Together, the thirty-one pilgrims constitute a cross-section of Late Medieval English society. Especially in the "end-bits" linking the tales, he presents the pilgrims in their own words, as they joke, quarrel, and philosophize. The frank, sometimes obscene language spoken by a few low characters (e.g., the Miller) reflects the open speech of England before the advent of Puritanism in the late 1500s.

Reading the Selections

The Prologue—the opening section of the poem—introduces each pilgrim with a pithy description full of telling detail. Chaucer's method is to blend random data of physical traits, personal and work habits, clothing features, and speech patterns in order to create memorable characters. The unforgettable portrait of the Wife of Bath is one such character—a talented weaver in her native town, with her wide-spaced teeth, large hips, even larger hat, vulgar taste for red clothes, roving eye, and skill at "wandering by the way." Moral yet forgiving of the vices that he sees in church, state, and society, Chaucer unfailingly pokes fun at the foibles of his contemporaries. His insight into personality proves he was a keen psychologist, perhaps the finest in European letters prior to Machiavelli.

The Wife of Bath's Tale is typical of Chaucer's comical-moral tales. Originating the literary device that each tale should morally suit its teller, he presents the domineering Wife of Bath as she recounts a tale whose theme is that happy wives need henpecked husbands. Even more to the Wife's discredit, her tale is thoroughly immoral, as the knight-rapist in the story escapes death and wins true love by solving a riddle. The tale is a reworking of a common folk story ("The Loathly Lady"), which Chaucer embellishes with magnificently irrelevant references to Ovid (see *Metamorphoses*), Dante (see *The Divine Comedy*), Boethius (see *The Consolation of Philosophy*), and Juvenal (see *Satire III*). Beneath the sexual politics, however, Chaucer offers a revolutionary moral: Gentility comes from God alone, not from social breeding.

—ᴍ—

The Prologue

When in April the sweet showers fall   1
And pierce the drought of March to the root, and all
The veins are bathed in liquor of such power
As brings about the engendering of the flower,
When also Zephyrus with his sweet breath
Exhales an air in every grove and heath
Upon the tender shoots, and the young sun
His half-course in the sign of the *Ram* has run,
And the small fowl are making melody
That sleep away the night with open eye   10
(So nature pricks them and their heart engages)
Then people long to go on pilgrimages
And palmers long to seek the stranger strands
Of far-off saints, hallowed in sundry lands,
And specially, from every shire's end
Of England, down to Canterbury they wend

To seek the holy blissful martyr, quick
To give his help to them when they were sick.
    It happened in that season that one day
In Southwark, at *The Tabard,* as I lay   20
Ready to go on pilgrimage and start
For Canterbury, most devout at heart,
At night there came into that hostelry
Some nine and twenty in a company
Of sundry folk happening then to fall
In fellowship, and they were pilgrims all
That towards Canterbury meant to ride.
The rooms and stables of the inn were wide;
They made us easy, all was of the best.
And, briefly, when the sun had gone to rest,   30
I'd spoken to them all upon the trip
And was soon one with them in fellowship,

Pledged to rise early and to take the way
To Canterbury, as you heard me say.
   But none the less, while I have time and space,
Before my story takes a further pace,
It seems a reasonable thing to say
What their condition was, the full array
Of each of them, as it appeared to me,
According to profession and degree,   40
And what apparel they were riding in;
And at a Knight I therefore will begin.
There was a *Knight*, a most distinguished man,
Who from the day on which he first began
To ride abroad had followed chivalry,
Truth, honour, generousness and courtesy.
He had done nobly in his sovereign's war
And ridden into battle, no man more,
As well in Christian as in heathen places,
And ever honoured for his noble graces.   50
   When we took Alexandria, he was there.
He often sat at table in the chair
Of honour, above all nations, when in Prussia.
In Lithuania he had ridden, and Russia,
No Christian man so often, of his rank.
When, in Granada, Algeciras sank
Under assault, he had been there, and in
North Africa, raiding Benamarin;
In Anatolia he had been as well
And fought when Ayas and Attalia fell,   60
For all along the Mediterranean coast
He had embarked with many a noble host.
In fifteen mortal battles he had been
And jousted for our faith at Tramissene
Thrice in the lists, and always killed his man.
This same distinguished knight had led the van
Once with the Bey of Balat, doing work
For him against another heathen Turk;
He was of sovereign value in all eyes.
And though so much distinguished, he was wise   70
And in his bearing modest as a maid.
He never yet a boorish thing had said
In all his life to any, come what might;
He was a true, a perfect gentle-knight.
   Speaking of his equipment, he possessed
Fine horses, but he was not gaily dressed.
He wore a fustian tunic stained and dark
With smudges where his armour had left mark;
Just home from service, he had joined our ranks
To do his pilgrimage and render thanks.   80
   He had his son with him, a fine young *Squire*,
A lover and cadet, a lad of fire
With locks as curly as if they had been pressed.
He was some twenty years of age, I guessed.
In stature he was of a moderate length,
With wonderful agility and strength.
He'd seen some service with the cavalry
In Flanders and Artois and Picardy
And had done valiantly in little space
Of time, in hope to win his lady's grace.   90
He was embroidered like a meadow bright
And full of freshest flowers, red and white.

Singing he was, or fluting all the day;
He was as fresh as is the month of May.
Short was his gown, the sleeves were long and wide;
He knew the way to sit a horse and ride.
He could make songs and poems and recite,
Knew how to joust and dance, to draw and write.
He loved so hotly that till dawn grew pale
He slept as little as a nightingale.   100
Courteous he was, lowly and serviceable,
And carved to serve his father at the table.
   There was a *Yeoman* with him at his side,
No other servant; so he chose to ride.
This Yeoman wore a coat and hood of green,
And peacock-feathered arrows, bright and keen
And neatly sheathed, hung at his belt the while
—For he could dress his gear in yeoman style,
His arrows never dropped their feathers low—
And in his hand he bore a mighty bow.   110
His head was like a nut, his face was brown.
He knew the whole of woodcraft up and down.
A saucy brace was on his arm to ward
It from the bow-string, and a shield and sword
Hung at one side, and at the other slipped
A jaunty dirk, spear-sharp and well-equipped.
A medal of St Christopher he wore
Of shining silver on his breast, and bore
A hunting-horn, well slung and burnished clean,
That dangled from a baldrick of bright green.   120
He was a proper forester, I guess.
   There also was a *Nun*, a Prioress,
Her way of smiling very simple and coy.
Her greatest oath was only 'By St Loy!'
And she was known as Madam Eglantyne.
And well she sang a service, with a fine
Intoning through her nose, as was most seemly,
And she spoke daintily in French, extremely,
After the school of Stratford-atte-Bowe;
French in the Paris style she did not know.   130
At meat her manners were well taught withal;
No morsel from her lips did she let fall,
Nor dipped her fingers in the sauce too deep;
But she could carry a morsel up and keep
The smallest drop from falling on her breast.
For courtliness she had a special zest,
And she would wipe her upper lip so clean
That not a trace of grease was to be seen
Upon the cup when she had drunk; to eat,
She reached a hand sedately for the meat.   140
She certainly was very entertaining,
Pleasant and friendly in her ways, and straining
To counterfeit a courtly kind of grace,
A stately bearing fitting to her place,
And to seem dignified in all her dealings.
As for her sympathies and tender feelings,
She was so charitably solicitous
She used to weep if she but saw a mouse
Caught in a trap, if it were dead or bleeding.
And she had little dogs she would be feeding   150
With roasted flesh, or milk, or fine white bread.
And bitterly she wept if one were dead

Or someone took a stick and made it smart;
She was all sentiment and tender heart.
Her veil was gathered in a seemly way,
Her nose was elegant, her eyes glass-grey;
Her mouth was very small, but soft and red,
Her forehead, certainly, was fair of spread,
Almost a span across the brows, I own;
She was indeed by no means undergrown.   160
Her cloak, I noticed, had a graceful charm.
She wore a coral trinket on her arm,
A set of beads, the gaudies tricked in green,
Whence hung a golden brooch of brightest sheen
On which there first was graven a crowned A,
And lower, *Amor vincit omnia.*
    Another *Nun,* the secretary at her cell,
Was riding with her, and *three Priests* as well.
    A *Monk* there was, one of the finest sort
Who rode the country; hunting was his sport.   170
A manly man, to be an Abbot able;
Many a dainty horse he had in stable.
His bridle, when he rode, a man might hear
Jingling in a whistling wind as clear,
Aye, and as loud as does the chapel bell
Where my lord Monk was Prior of the cell.
The Rule of good St Benet or St Maur
As old and strict he tended to ignore;
He let go by the things of yesterday
And took the modern world's more spacious
        way.   180
He did not rate that text at a plucked hen
Which says that hunters are not holy men
And that a monk uncloistered is a mere
Fish out of water, flapping on the pier,
That is to say a monk out of his cloister.
That was a text he held not worth an oyster;
And I agreed and said his views were sound;
Was he to study till his head went round
Poring over books in cloisters? Must he toil
As Austin bade and till the very soil?   190
Was he to leave the world upon the shelf?
Let Austin have his labour to himself.
    This Monk was therefore a good man to horse;
Greyhounds he had, as swift as birds, to course.
Hunting a hare or riding at a fence
Was all his fun, he spared for no expense.
I saw his sleeves were garnished at the hand
With fine grey fur, the finest in the land,
And on his hood, to fasten it at his chin
He had a wrought-gold cunningly fashioned pin;   200
Into a lover's knot it seemed to pass.
His head was bald and shone like looking-glass;
So did his face, as if it had been greased.
He was a fat and personable priest;
His prominent eyeballs never seemed to settle.
They glittered like the flames beneath a kettle;
Supple his boots, his horse in fine condition.
He was a prelate fit for exhibition,
He was not pale like a tormented soul.
He liked a fat swan best, and roasted whole.   210
His palfrey was as brown as is a berry.

    There was a *Friar,* a wanton one and merry,
A Limiter, a very festive fellow.
In all Four Orders there was none so mellow,
So glib with gallant phrase and well-turned speech.
He'd fixed up many a marriage, giving each
Of his young women what he could afford her.
He was a noble pillar to his Order.
Highly beloved and intimate was he
With County folk within his boundary,   220
And city dames of honour and possessions;
For he was qualified to hear confessions,
Or so he said, with more than priestly scope;
He had a special licence from the Pope.
Sweetly he heard his penitents at shrift
With pleasant absolution, for a gift.
He was an easy man in penance-giving
Where he could hope to make a decent living;
It's a sure sign whenever gifts are given
To a poor Order that a man's well shriven,   230
And should he give enough he knew in verity
The penitent repented in sincerity.
For many a fellow is so hard of heart
He cannot weep, for all his inward smart.
Therefore instead of weeping and of prayer
One should give silver for a poor Friar's care.
He kept his tippet stuffed with pins for curls,
And pocket-knives, to give to pretty girls.
And certainly his voice was gay and sturdy,
For he sang well and played the hurdy-gurdy.   240
At sing-songs he was champion of the hour.
His neck was whiter than a lily-flower
But strong enough to butt a bruiser down.
He knew the taverns well in every town
And every innkeeper and barmaid too
Better than lepers, beggars and that crew,
For in so eminent a man as he
It was not fitting with the dignity
Of his position, dealing with a scum
Of wretched lepers; nothing good can come   250
Of commerce with such slum-and-gutter dwellers,
But only with the rich and victual-sellers.
But anywhere a profit might accrue
Courteous he was and lowly of service too.
Natural gifts like his were hard to match.
He was the finest beggar of his batch,
And, for his begging-district, paid a rent;
His brethren did no poaching where he went.
For though a widow mightn't have a shoe,
So pleasant was his holy how-d'ye-do   260
He got his farthing from her just the same
Before he left, and so his income came
To more than he laid out. And how he romped,
Just like a puppy! He was ever prompt
To arbitrate disputes on settling days
(For a small fee) in many helpful ways,
Not then appearing as your cloistered scholar
With threadbare habit hardly worth a dollar,
But much more like a Doctor or a Pope.
Of double-worsted was the semi-cope   270
Upon his shoulders, and the swelling fold

About him, like a bell about its mould
When it is casting, rounded out his dress.
He lisped a little out of wantonness
To make his English sweet upon his tongue.
When he had played his harp, or having sung,
His eyes would twinkle in his head as bright
As any star upon a frosty night.
This worthy's name was Hubert, it appeared.
    There was a *Merchant* with a forking beard 280
And motley dress; high on his horse he sat,
Upon his head a Flemish beaver hat
And on his feet daintily buckled boots.
He told of his opinions and pursuits
In solemn tones, he harped on his increase
Of capital; there should be sea-police
(He thought) upon the Harwich-Holland ranges;
He was expert at dabbling in exchanges.
This estimable Merchant so had set
His wits to work, none knew he was in debt, 290
He was so stately in administration,
In loans and bargains and negotiation.
He was an excellent fellow all the same;
To tell the truth I do not know his name.
    An *Oxford Cleric*, still a student though,
One who had taken logic long ago,
Was there; his horse was thinner than a rake,
And he was not too fat, I undertake,
But had a hollow look, a sober stare;
The thread upon his overcoat was bare. 300
He had found no preferment in the church
And he was too unworldly to make search
For secular employment. By his bed
He preferred having twenty books in red
And black, of Aristotle's philosophy,
Than costly clothes, fiddle or psaltery.
Though a philosopher, as I have told,
He had not found the stone for making gold.
Whatever money from his friends he took
He spent on learning or another book 310
And prayed for them most earnestly, returning
Thanks to them thus for paying for his learning.
His only care was study, and indeed
He never spoke a word more than was need,
Formal at that, respectful in the extreme,
Short, to the point, and lofty in his theme.
A tone of moral virtue filled his speech
And gladly would he learn, and gladly teach.
    A *Serjeant at the Law* who paid his calls,
Wary and wise, for clients at St Paul's 320
There also was, of noted excellence.
Discreet he was, a man to reverence,
Or so he seemed, his sayings were so wise.
He often had been Justice of Assize
By letters patent, and in full commission.
His fame and learning and his high position
Had won him many a robe and many a fee.
There was no such conveyancer as he;
All was fee-simple to his strong digestion,
Not one conveyance could be called in question. 330
Though there was nowhere one so busy as he,

He was less busy than he seemed to be.
He knew of every judgement, case and crime
Ever recorded since King William's time.
He could dictate defences or draft deeds;
No one could pinch a comma from his screeds
And he knew every statute off by rote.
He wore a homely parti-coloured coat,
Girt with a silken belt of pin-stripe stuff;
Of his appearance I have said enough. 340
    There was a *Franklin* with him, it appeared;
White as a daisy-petal was his beard.
A sanguine man, high-coloured and benign,
He loved a morning sop of cake in wine.
He lived for pleasure and had always done,
For he was Epicurus' very son,
In whose opinion sensual delight
Was the one true felicity in sight.
As noted as St Julian was for bounty
He made his household free to all the County. 350
His bread, his ale were finest of the fine
And no one had a better stock of wine.
His house was never short of bake-meat pies,
Of fish and flesh, and these in such supplies
It positively snowed with meat and drink
And all the dainties that a man could think.
According to the seasons of the year
Changes of dish were ordered to appear.
He kept fat partridges in coops, beyond,
Many a bream and pike were in his pond. 360
Woe to the cook unless the sauce was hot
And sharp, or if he wasn't on the spot!
And in his hall a table stood arrayed
And ready all day long, with places laid.
As Justice at the Sessions none stood higher;
He often had been Member for the Shire.
A dagger and a little purse of silk
Hung at his girdle, white as morning milk.
As Sheriff he checked audit, every entry.
He was a model among landed gentry. 370
    A *Haberdasher*, a *Dyer*, a *Carpenter*,
A *Weaver* and a *Carpet-maker* were
Among our ranks, all in the livery
Of one impressive guild-fraternity.
They were so trim and fresh their gear would pass
For new. Their knives were not tricked out with brass
But wrought with purest silver, which avouches
A like display on girdles and on pouches.
Each seemed a worthy burgess, fit to grace
A guild-hall with a seat upon the dais. 380
Their wisdom would have justified a plan
To make each one of them an alderman;
They had the capital and revenue,
Besides their wives declared it was their due.
And if they did not think so, then they ought;
To be called '*Madam*' is a glorious thought,
And so is going to church and being seen
Having your mantle carried, like a queen.
    They had a *Cook* with them who stood alone
For boiling chicken with a marrow-bone, 390
Sharp flavouring-powder and a spice for savour.

He could distinguish London ale by flavour,
And he could roast and seethe and broil and fry,
Make good thick soup and bake a tasty pie.
But what a pity—so it seemed to me,
That he should have an ulcer on his knee.
As for blancmange, he made it with the best.

There was a *Skipper* hailing from far west;
He came from Dartmouth, so I understood.
He rode a farmer's horse as best he could, 400
In a woollen gown that reached his knee.
A dagger on a lanyard falling free
Hung from his neck under his arm and down.
The summer heat had tanned his colour brown,
And certainly he was an excellent fellow.
Many a draught of vintage, red and yellow,
He'd drawn at Bordeaux, while the trader snored.
The nicer rules of conscience he ignored.
If, when he fought, the enemy vessel sank,
He sent his prisoners home; they walked the plank. 410
As for his skill in reckoning his tides,
Currents and many another risk besides,
Moons, harbours, pilots, he had such dispatch
That none from Hull to Carthage was his match.
Hardy he was, prudent in undertaking;
His beard in many a tempest had its shaking,
And he knew all the heavens as they were
From Gottland to the Cape of Finisterre,
And every creek in Brittany and Spain;
The barge he owned was called *The Maudelayne*. 420

A *Doctor* too emerged as we proceeded;
No one alive could talk as well as he did
On points of medicine and of surgery,
For, being grounded in astronomy,
He watched his patient closely for the hours
When, by his horoscope, he knew the powers
Of favourable planets, then ascendent,
Worked on the images for his dependent.
The cause of every malady you'd got
He knew, and whether dry, cold, moist or hot; 430
He knew their seat, their humour and condition.
He was a perfect practising physician.
These causes being known for what they were,
He gave the man his medicine then and there.
All his apothecaries in a tribe
Were ready with the drugs he would prescribe
And each made money from the other's guile;
They had been friendly for a goodish while.
He was well-versed in Aesculapius too
And what Hippocrates and Rufus knew 440
And Dioscorides, now dead and gone,
Galen and Rhazes, Hali, Serapion,
Averroes, Avicenna, Constantine,
Scotch Bernard, John of Gaddesden, Gilbertine.
In his own diet he observed some measure;
There were no superfluities for pleasure,
Only digestives, nutritives and such.
He did not read the Bible very much.
In blood-red garments, slashed with bluish grey
And lined with taffeta, he rode his way; 450
Yet he was rather close as to expenses

And kept the gold he won in pestilences.
Gold stimulates the heart, or so we're told.
He therefore had a special love of gold.

A worthy *woman* from beside *Bath* city
Was with us, somewhat deaf, which was a pity.
In making cloth she showed so great a bent
She bettered those of Ypres and of Ghent.
In all the parish not a dame dared stir
Towards the altar steps in front of her, 460
And if indeed they did, so wrath was she
As to be quite put out of charity.
Her kerchiefs were of finely woven ground;
I dared have sworn they weighed a good ten pound,
The ones she wore on Sunday, on her head.
Her hose were of the finest scarlet red
And gartered tight; her shoes were soft and new.
Bold was her face, handsome, and red in hue.
A worthy woman all her life, what's more
She'd had five husbands, all at the church door, 470
Apart from other company in youth;
No need just now to speak of that, forsooth.
And she had thrice been to Jerusalem,
Seen many strange rivers and passed over them;
She'd been to Rome and also to Boulogne,
St James of Compostella and Cologne,
And she was skilled in wandering by the way.
She had gap-teeth, set widely, truth to say.
Easily on an ambling horse she sat
Well wimpled up, and on her head a hat 480
As broad as is a buckler or a shield;
She had a flowing mantle that concealed
Large hips, her heels spurred sharply under that.
In company she liked to laugh and chat
And knew the remedies for love's mischances,
An art in which she knew the oldest dances.

A holy-minded man of good renown
There was, and poor, the *Parson* to a town,
Yet he was rich in holy thought and work.
He also was a learned man, a clerk, 490
Who truly knew Christ's gospel and would preach it
Devoutly to parishioners, and teach it.
Benign and wonderfully diligent,
And patient when adversity was sent
(For so he proved in much adversity)
He hated cursing to extort a fee,
Nay rather he preferred beyond a doubt
Giving to poor parishioners round about
Both from church offerings and his property;
He could in little find sufficiency. 500
Wide was his parish, with houses far asunder,
Yet he neglected not in rain or thunder,
In sickness or in grief, to pay a call
On the remotest, whether great or small,
Upon his feet, and in his hand a stave.
This noble example to his sheep he gave
That first he wrought, and afterwards he taught;
And it was from the Gospel he had caught
Those words, and he would add this figure too,
That if gold rust, what then will iron do? 510
For if a priest be foul in whom we trust

No wonder that a common man should rust;
And shame it is to see—let priests take stock—
A shitten shepherd and a snowy flock.
The true example that a priest should give
Is one of cleanness, how the sheep should live.
He did not set his benefice to hire
And leave his sheep encumbered in the mire
Or run to London to earn easy bread
By singing masses for the wealthy dead,   520
Or find some Brotherhood and get enrolled.
He stayed at home and watched over his fold
So that no wolf should make the sheep miscarry.
He was a shepherd and no mercenary.
Holy and virtuous he was, but then
Never contemptuous of sinful men,
Never disdainful, never too proud or fine,
But was discreet in teaching and benign.
His business was to show a fair behaviour
And draw men thus to Heaven and their Saviour,   530
Unless indeed a man were obstinate;
And such, whether of high or low estate,
He put to sharp rebuke, to say the least.
I think there never was a better priest.
He sought no pomp or glory in his dealings,
No scrupulosity had spiced his feelings.
Christ and His Twelve Apostles and their lore
He taught, but followed it himself before.
    There was a *Plowman* with him there, his brother;
Many a load of dung one time or other   540
He must have carted through the morning dew.
He was an honest worker, good and true,
Living in peace and perfect charity,
And, as the gospel bade him, so did he,
Loving God best with all his heart and mind
And then his neighbour as himself, repined
At no misfortune, slacked for no content,
For steadily about his work he went
To thrash his corn, to dig or to manure
Or make a ditch; and he would help the poor   550
For love of Christ and never take a penny
If he could help it, and, as prompt as any,
He paid his tithes in full when they were due
On what he owned, and on his earnings too.
He wore a tabard smock and rode a mare.
    There was a *Reeve*, also a *Miller*, there,
A College *Manciple* from the Inns of Court,
A papal *Pardoner* and, in close consort,
A Church-Court *Summoner*, riding at a trot,
And finally myself—that was the lot.   560
    The *Miller* was a chap of sixteen stone,
A great stout fellow big in brawn and bone.
He did well out of them, for he could go
And win the ram at any wrestling show.
Broad, knotty and short-shouldered, he would boast
He could heave any door off hinge and post,
Or take a run and break it with his head.
His beard, like any sow or fox, was red
And broad as well, as though it were a spade;
And, at its very tip, his nose displayed   570
A wart on which there stood a tuft of hair
Red as the bristles in an old sow's ear.

His nostrils were as black as they were wide.
He had a sword and buckler at his side,
His mighty mouth was like a furnace door.
A wrangler and buffoon, he had a store
Of tavern stories, filthy in the main.
His was a master-hand at stealing grain.
He felt it with his thumb and thus he knew
Its quality and took three times his due—   580
A thumb of gold, by God, to gauge an oat!
He wore a hood of blue and a white coat.
He liked to play his bagpipes up and down
And that was how he brought us out of town.
    The *Manciple* came from the Inner Temple;
All caterers might follow his example
In buying victuals; he was never rash
Whether he bought on credit or paid cash.
He used to watch the market most precisely
And got in first, and so he did quite nicely.   590
Now isn't it a marvel of God's grace
That an illiterate fellow can outpace
The wisdom of a heap of learned men?
His masters—he had more than thirty then—
All versed in the abstrusest legal knowledge,
Could have produced a dozen from their College
Fit to be stewards in land and rents and game
To any Peer in England you could name,
And show him how to live on what he had
Debt-free (unless of course the Peer were mad)   600
Or be as frugal as he might desire,
And make them fit to help about the Shire
In any legal case there was to try;
And yet this Manciple could wipe their eye.
    The *Reeve* was old and choleric and thin;
His beard was shaven closely to the skin,
His shorn hair came abruptly to a stop
Above his ears, and he was docked on top
Just like a priest in front; his legs were lean,
Like sticks they were, no calf was to be seen.   610
He kept his bins and garners very trim;
No auditor could gain a point on him.
And he could judge by watching drought and rain
The yield he might expect from seed and grain.
His master's sheep, his animals and hens,
Pigs, horses, dairies, stores and cattle-pens
Were wholly trusted to his government.
He had been under contract to present
The accounts, right from his master's earliest years.
No one had ever caught him in arrears.   620
No bailiff, serf or herdsman dared to kick,
He knew their dodges, knew their every trick;
Feared like the plague he was, by those beneath.
He had a lovely dwelling on a heath,
Shadowed in green by trees above the sward.
A better hand at bargains than his lord,
He had grown rich and had a store of treasure
Well tucked away, yet out it came to pleasure
His lord with subtle loans or gifts of goods,
To earn his thanks and even coats and hoods.   630
When young he'd learnt a useful trade and still
He was a carpenter of first-rate skill.
The stallion-cob he rode at a slow trot

Was dapple-grey and bore the name of Scot.
He wore an overcoat of bluish shade
And rather long; he had a rusty blade
Slung at his side. He came, as I heard tell,
From Norfolk, near a place called Baldeswell.
His coat was tucked under his belt and splayed.
He rode the hindmost of our cavalcade.   640

    There was a *Summoner* with us at that Inn,
His face on fire, like a cherubin,
For he had carbuncles. His eyes were narrow,
He was as hot and lecherous as a sparrow.
Black scabby brows he had, and a thin beard.
Children were afraid when he appeared.
No quicksilver, lead ointment, tartar creams,
No brimstone, no boracic, so it seems,
Could make a salve that had the power to bite,
Clean up or cure his whelks of knobby white   650
Or purge the pimples sitting on his cheeks.
Garlic he loved, and onions too, and leeks,
And drinking strong red wine till all was hazy.
Then he would shout and jabber as if crazy,
And wouldn't speak a word except in Latin
When he was drunk, such tags as he was pat in;
He had only a few, say two or three,
That he had mugged up out of some decree;
No wonder, for he heard them every day.
And, as you know, a man can teach a jay   660
To call out 'Walter' better than the Pope.
But had you tried to test his wits and grope
For more, you'd have found nothing in the bag.
Then *'Questio quid juris'* was his tag.
He was a noble varlet and a kind one,
You'd meet none better if you went to find one.
Why, he'd allow—just for a quart of wine—
Any good lad to keep a concubine
A twelvemonth and dispense him altogether!
And he had finches of his own to feather: 670
And if he found some rascal with a maid
He would instruct him not to be afraid
In such a case of the Archdeacon's curse
(Unless the rascal's soul were in his purse)
For in his purse the punishment should be.
'Purse is the good Archdeacon's Hell,' said he.
But well I know he lied in what he said;
A curse should put a guilty man in dread,
For curses kill, as shriving brings, salvation.
We should beware of excommunication.   680
Thus, as he pleased, the man could bring duress
On any young fellow in the diocese.
He knew their secrets, they did what he said.
He wore a garland set upon his head
Large as the holly-bush upon a stake
Outside an ale-house, and he had a cake,
A round one, which it was his joke to wield
As if it were intended for a shield.

    He and a gentle *Pardoner* rode together,
A bird from Charing Cross of the same feather,   690
Just back from visiting the Court of Rome.
He loudly sang *'Come hither, love, come home!'*
The Summoner sang deep seconds to this song,
No trumpet ever sounded half so strong.

This Pardoner had hair as yellow as wax,
Hanging down smoothly like a hank of flax.
In driblets fell his locks behind his head
Down to his shoulders which they overspread;
Thinly they fell, like rat-tails, one by one.
He wore no hood upon his head, for fun;   700
The hood inside his wallet had been stowed,
He aimed at riding in the latest mode;
But for a little cap his head was bare
And he had bulging eye-balls, like a hare.
He'd sewed a holy relic on his cap;
His wallet lay before him on his lap,
Brimful of pardons come from Rome, all hot.
He had the same small voice a goat has got.
His chin no beard had harboured, nor would harbour,
Smoother than ever chin was left by barber.   710
I judge he was a gelding, or a mare.
As to his trade, from Berwick down to Ware
There was no pardoner of equal grace,
For in his trunk he had a pillow-case
Which he asserted was Our Lady's veil.
He said he had a gobbet of the sail
Saint Peter had the time when he made bold
To walk the waves, till Jesu Christ took hold.
He had a cross of metal set with stones
And, in a glass, a rubble of pigs' bones.   720
And with these relics, any time he found
Some poor up-country parson to astound,
In one short day, in money down, he drew
More than the parson in a month or two,
And by his flatteries and prevarication
Made monkeys of the priest and congregation.
But still to do him justice first and last
In church he was a noble ecclesiast.
How well he read a lesson or told a story!
But best of all he sang an Offertory,   730
For well he knew that when that song was sung
He'd have to preach and tune his honey-tongue
And (well he could) win silver from the crowd.
That's why he sang so merrily and loud.

    Now I have told you shortly, in a clause,
The rank, the array, the number and the cause
Of our assembly in this company
In Southwark, at that high-class hostelry
Known as *The Tabard*, close beside *The Bell*.
And now the time has come for me to tell   740
How we behaved that evening; I'll begin
After we had alighted at the Inn,
Then I'll report our journey, stage by stage,
All the remainder of our pilgrimage.
But first I beg of you, in courtesy,
Not to condemn me as unmannerly
If I speak plainly and with no concealings
And give account of all their words and dealings,
Using their very phrases as they fell.
For certainly, as you all know so well,   750
He who repeats a tale after a man
Is bound to say, as nearly as he can,
Each single word, if he remembers it,
However rudely spoken or unfit,
Or else the tale he tells will be untrue,

The things pretended and the phrases new.
He may not flinch although it were his brother,
He may as well say one word as another.
And Christ Himself spoke broad in Holy Writ,
Yet there is no scurrility in it,
And Plato says, for those with power to read,

'The word should be as cousin to the deed.'
Further I beg you to forgive it me
If I neglect the order and degree
And what is due to rank in what I've planned.   760
I'm short of wit as you will understand. . . .

—m—

The Wife of Bath's Tale

When good King Arthur ruled in ancient days,   1
(A king that every Briton loves to praise.)
This was a land brim-full of fairy folk.
The Elf-Queen and her courtiers joined and broke
Their elfin dance on many a green mead,
Or so was the opinion once, I read,
Hundreds of years ago, in days of yore.
But no one now sees fairies any more,
For now the saintly charity and prayer
Of holy friars seem to have purged the air;   10
They search the countryside through field and
    stream
As thick as motes that speckle a sun-beam,
Blessing the halls, the chambers, kitchens, bowers,
Cities and boroughs, castles, courts and towers,
Thorpes, barns and stables, outhouses and dairies,
And that's the reason why there are no fairies.
Wherever there was wont to walk an elf
To-day there walks the holy friar himself
As evening falls or when the daylight springs,
Saying his mattins and his holy things,   20
Walking his limit round from town to town.
Women can now go safely up and down.
By every bush or under every tree;
There is no other incubus but he,
So there is really no one else to hurt you
And he will do no more than take your virtue.
    Now it so happened, I began to say,
Long, long ago in good King Arthur's day,
There was a knight who was a lusty liver.
One day as he came riding from the river   30
He saw a maiden walking all forlorn
Ahead of him, alone as she was born.
And of that maiden, spite of all she said,
By very force he took her maidenhead.
    This act of violence made such a stir,
So much petitioning of the king for her,
That he condemned the knight to lose his head
By course of law. He was as good as dead
(It seems that then the statutes took that view)
But that the queen, and other ladies too,   40
Implored the king to exercise his grace
So ceaselessly, he gave the queen the case
And granted her his life, and she could choose
Whether to show him mercy or refuse.

    The queen returned him thanks with all her might,
And then she sent a summons to the knight
At her convenience, and expressed her will:
'You stand, for such is the position still,
In no way certain of your life,' said she,
'Yet you shall live if you can answer me: 50
What is the thing that women most desire?
Beware the axe and say as I require.
    'If you can't answer on the moment, though,
I will concede you this: you are to go
A twelvemonth and a day to seek and learn
Sufficient answer, then you shall return.
I shall take gages from you to extort
Surrender of your body to the court.'
    Sad was the knight and sorrowfully sighed,
But there! All other choices were denied,   60
And in the end he chose to go away
And to return after a year and day
Armed with such answer as there might be sent
To him by God. He took his leave and went.
    He knocked at every house, searched every place,
Yes, anywhere that offered hope of grace.
What could it be that women wanted most?
But all the same he never touched a coast,
Country or town in which there seemed to be
Any two people willing to agree.   70
    Some said that women wanted wealth and
        treasure,
'Honour,' said some, some 'Jollity and pleasure,'
Some 'Gorgeous clothes' and others 'Fun in bed,'
'To be oft widowed and remarried,' said
Others again, and some that what most mattered
Was that we should be cosseted and flattered.
That's very near the truth, it seems to me;
A man can win us best with flattery.
To dance attendance on us, make a fuss,
Ensnares us all, the best and worst of us.   80
    Some say the things we most desire are these:
Freedom to do exactly as we please,
With no one to reprove our faults and lies,
Rather to have one call us good and wise.
Truly there's not a woman in ten score
Who has a fault, and someone rubs the sore,
But she will kick if what he says is true;
You try it out and you will find so too.

However vicious we may be within
We like to be thought wise and void of sin.   90
Others assert we women find it sweet
When we are thought dependable, discreet
And secret, firm of purpose and controlled,
Never betraying things that we are told.
But that's not worth the handle of a rake;
Women conceal a thing? For Heaven's sake!
Remember Midas? Will you hear the tale?

    Among some other little things, now stale,
Ovid relates that under his long hair
The unhappy Midas grew a splendid pair   100
Of ass's ears; as subtly as he might,
He kept his foul deformity from sight;
Save for his wife, there was not one that knew.
He loved her best, and trusted in her too.
He begged her not to tell a living creature
That he possessed so horrible a feature.
And she—she swore, were all the world to win,
She would not do such villainy and sin
As saddle her husband with so foul a name;
Besides to speak would be to share the shame.   110
Nevertheless she thought she would have died
Keeping this secret bottled up inside;
It seemed to swell her heart and she, no doubt,
Thought it was on the point of bursting out.

    Fearing to speak of it to woman or man,
Down to a reedy marsh she quickly ran
And reached the sedge. Her heart was all on fire
And, as a bittern bumbles in the mire,
She whispered to the water, near the ground,
'Betray me not, O water, with thy sound!   120
To thee alone I tell it: it appears
My husband has a pair of ass's ears!
Ah! My heart's well again, the secret's out!
I could no longer keep it, not a doubt.'
And so you see, although we may hold fast
A little while, it must come out at last,
We can't keep secrets; as for Midas, well,
Read Ovid for his story; he will tell.

    This knight that I am telling you about
Perceived at last he never would find out   130
What it could be that women loved the best.
Faint was the soul within his sorrowful breast
As home he went, he dared no longer stay;
His year was up and now it was the day.

    As he rode home in a dejected mood,
Suddenly, at the margin of a wood,
He saw a dance upon the leafy floor
Of four and twenty ladies, nay, and more.
Eagerly he approached, in hope to learn
Some words of wisdom ere he should return;   140
But lo! Before he came to where they were,
Dancers and dance all vanished into air!
There wasn't a living creature to be seen
Save one old woman crouched upon the green.
A fouler-looking creature I suppose
Could scarcely be imagined. She arose
And said, 'Sir knight, there's no way on from here.
Tell me what you are looking for, my dear,

For peradventure that were best for you;
We old, old women know a thing or two.'   150
    'Dear Mother,' said the knight, 'alack the day!
I am as good as dead if I can't say
What thing it is that women most desire;
If you could tell me I would pay your hire.'
'Give me your hand,' she said, 'and swear to do
Whatever I shall next require of you
—If so to do should lie within your might—
And you shall know the answer before night.'
'Upon my honour,' he answered, 'I agree.'
'Then,' said the crone, 'I dare to guarantee   160
Your life is safe; I shall make good my claim.
Upon my life the queen will say the same.
Show me the very proudest of them all
In costly coverchief or jewelled caul
That dare say no to what I have to teach.
Let us go forward without further speech.'
And then she crooned her gospel in his ear
And told him to be glad and not to fear.

    They came to court. This knight, in full array,
Stood forth and said, 'O Queen, I've kept my day   170
And kept my word and have my answer ready.'

    There sat the noble matrons and the heady
Young girls, and widows too, that have the grace
Of wisdom, all assembled in that place,
And there the queen herself was throned to hear
And judge his answer. Then the knight drew near
And silence was commanded through the hall.

    The queen then bade the knight to tell them all
What thing it was that women wanted most.
He stood not silent like a beast or post,   180
But gave his answer with the ringing word
Of a man's voice and the assembly heard:

    'My liege and lady, in general,' said he,
'A woman wants the self-same sovereignty
Over her husband as over her lover,
And master him; he must not be above her.
That is your greatest wish, whether you kill
Or spare me; please yourself. I wait your will.'

    In all the court not one that shook her head
Or contradicted what the knight had said;   190
Maid, wife and widow cried, 'He's saved his life!'

    And on the word up started the old wife,
The one the knight saw sitting on the green,
And cried, 'Your mercy, sovereign lady queen!
Before the court disperses, do me right!
'Twas I who taught this answer to the knight,
For which he swore, and pledged his honour to it,
That the first thing I asked of him he'd do it,
So far as it should lie within his might.
Before this court I ask you then, sir knight,   200
To keep your word and take me for your wife;
For well you know that I have saved your life.
If this be false, deny it on your sword!'

    'Alas!' he said, 'Old lady, by the Lord
I know indeed that such was my behest,
But for God's love think of a new request,
Take all my goods, but leave my body free.'
'A curse on us,' she said, 'if I agree!

I may be foul, I may be poor and old,
Yet will not choose to be, for all the gold   210
That's bedded in the earth or lies above,
Less than your wife, nay, than your very love!'
    'My love?' said he. 'By Heaven, my damnation!
Alas that any of my race and station
Should ever make so foul a misalliance!'
Yet in the end his pleading and defiance
All went for nothing, he was forced to wed.
He takes his ancient wife and goes to bed.
    Now peradventure some may well suspect
A lack of care in me since I neglect   220
To tell of the rejoicings and display
Made at the feast upon their wedding-day.
I have but a short answer to let fall;
I say there was no joy or feast at all,
Nothing but heaviness of heart and sorrow.
He married her in private on the morrow
And all day long stayed hidden like an owl,
It was such torture that his wife looked foul.
    Great was the anguish churning in his head
When he and she were piloted to bed;   230
He wallowed back and forth in desperate style.
His ancient wife lay smiling all the while;
At last she said 'Bless us! Is this, my dear,
How knights and wives get on together here?
Are these the laws of good King Arthur's house?
Are knights of his all so contemptuous?
I am your own beloved and your wife,
And I am she, indeed, that saved your life;
And certainly I never did you wrong.
Then why, this first of nights, so sad a song?   240
You're carrying on as if you were half-witted!
Say, for God's love, what sin have I committed?
I'll put things right if you will tell me how.'
    'Put right?' he cried. 'That never can be now!
Nothing can ever be put right again!
You're old, and so abominably plain,
So poor to start with, so low-bred to follow!
It's little wonder if I twist and wallow!
God, that my heart would burst within my breast!'
    'Is that,' said she, 'the cause of your unrest?'   250
    'Yes, certainly,' he said, 'and can you wonder?'
    'I could set right what you suppose a blunder,
That's if I cared to, in a day or two,
If I were shown more courtesy by you.
Just now,' she said, 'you spoke of gentle birth,
Such as descends from ancient wealth and worth.
If that's the claim you make for gentlemen
Such arrogance is hardly worth a hen.
Whoever loves to work for virtuous ends,
Public and private, and who most intends   260
To do what deeds of gentleness he can,
Take him to be the greatest gentleman.
Christ wills we take our gentleness from Him,
Not from a wealth of ancestry long dim,
Though they bequeath their whole establishment
By which we claim to be of high descent.
Our fathers cannot make us a bequest
Of all those virtues that became them best

And earned for them the name of gentleman,
But bade us follow them as best we can.   270
    'Thus the wise poet of the Florentines,
Dante by name, has written in these lines,
For such is the opinion Dante launches:
"Seldom arises by these slender branches
Prowess of men, for it is God, no less,
Wills us to claim of Him our gentleness."
For of our parents nothing can we claim
Save temporal things, and these may hurt and maim.
    'But everyone knows this as well as I;
For if gentility were implanted by   280
The natural course of lineage down the line,
Public or private, could it cease to shine
In doing the fair work of gentle deed?
No vice or villainy could then bear seed.
    'Take fire and carry it to the darkest house
Between this kingdom and the Caucasus,
And shut the doors on it and leave it there,
It will burn on, and it will burn as fair
As if ten thousand men were there to see,
For fire will keep its nature and degree,   290
I can assure you, sir, until it dies.
    'But gentleness, as you will recognize,
Is not annexed in nature to possessions,
Men fail in living up to their professions;
But fire never ceases to be fire.
God knows you'll often find, if you enquire,
Some lording full of villainy and shame.
If you would be esteemed for the mere name
Of having been by birth a gentleman
And stemming from some virtuous, noble clan,   300
And do not live yourself by gentle deed
Or take your fathers' noble code and creed,
You are no gentleman, though duke or earl.
Vice and bad manners are what make a churl.
    'Gentility is only the renown
For bounty that your fathers handed down,
Quite foreign to your person, not your own;
Gentility must come from God alone.
That we are gentle comes to us by grace
And by no means is it bequeathed with place.   310
    'Reflect how noble (says Valerius)
Was Tullius surnamed Hostilius,
Who rose from poverty to nobleness.
And read Boethius, Seneca no less,
Thus they express themselves and are agreed:
"Gentle is he that does a gentle deed."
And therefore, my dear husband, I conclude
That even if my ancestors were rude,
Yet God on high—and so I hope He will—
Can grant me grace to live in virtue still,   320
A gentlewoman only when beginning
To live in virtue and to shrink from sinning.
    'As for my poverty which you reprove,
Almighty God Himself in whom we move,
Believe and have our being, chose a life
Of poverty, and every man or wife
Nay, every child can see our Heavenly King
Would never stoop to choose a shameful thing.

No shame in poverty if the heart is gay,
As Seneca and all the learned say.
He who accepts his poverty unhurt
I'd say is rich although he lacked a shirt.
But truly poor are they who whine and fret
And covet what they cannot hope to get.
And he that, having nothing, covets not,
Is rich, though you may think he is a sot.
    'True poverty can find a song to sing.
Juvenal says a pleasant little thing:
"The poor can dance and sing in the relief
Of having nothing that will tempt a thief."
Though it be hateful, poverty is good,
A great incentive to a livelihood,
And a great help to our capacity
For wisdom, if accepted patiently.
Poverty is, though wanting in estate,
A kind of wealth that none calumniate.
Poverty often, when the heart is lowly,
Brings one to God and teaches what is holy,
Gives knowledge of oneself and even lends
A glass by which to see one's truest friends.
And since it's no offence, let me be plain;
Do not rebuke my poverty again.
    'Lastly you taxed me, sir, with being old.
Yet even if you never had been told
By ancient books, you gentlemen engage
Yourselves in honour to respect old age.
To call an old man "father" shows good breeding,
And this could be supported from my reading.
    'You say I'm old and fouler than a fen.
You need not fear to be a cuckold, then.
Filth and old age, I'm sure you will agree,
Are powerful wardens upon chastity.
Nevertheless, well knowing your delights,
I shall fulfil your worldly appetites.
    'You have two choices; which one will you try?
To have me old and ugly till I die,
But still a loyal, true and humble wife
That never will displease you all her life,
Or would you rather I were young and pretty

330

340

350

360

And chance your arm what happens in a city
Where friends will visit you because of me,
Yes, and in other places too, maybe.
Which would you have? The choice is all your own.'
    The knight thought long, and with a piteous groan
At last he said, with all the care in life,
'My lady and my love, my dearest wife,
I leave the matter to your wise decision.
You make the choice yourself, for the provision
Of what may be agreeable and rich
In honour to us both, I don't care which;
Whatever pleases you suffices me.'
    'And have I won the mastery?' said she,
'Since I'm to choose and rule as I think fit?'
'Certainly, wife,' he answered her, 'that's it.'
'Kiss me,' she cried. 'No quarrels! On my oath
And word of honour, you shall find me both,
That is, both fair and faithful as a wife;
May I go howling mad and take my life
Unless I prove to be as good and true
As ever wife was since the world was new!
And if to-morrow when the sun's above
I seem less fair than any lady-love,
Than any queen or empress east or west,
Do with my life and death as you think best.
Cast up the curtain, husband. Look at me!'
    And when indeed the knight had looked to see,
Lo, she was young and lovely, rich in charms.
In ecstasy he caught her in her arms,
His heart went bathing in a bath of blisses
And melted in a hundred thousand kisses,
And she responded in the fullest measure
With all that could delight or give him pleasure.
    So they lived ever after to the end
In perfect bliss; and may Christ Jesus send
Us husbands meek and young and fresh in bed,
And grace to overbid them when we wed.
And—Jesu hear my prayer!—cut short the lives
Of those who won't be governed by their wives;
And all old, angry niggards of their pence,
God send them soon a very pestilence!

370

380

390

400

410

CHRISTINE DE PIZAN

Selections from *The Book of the City of Ladies*

History pretty much overlooked Christine de Pizan's *The Book of the City of Ladies* (1405) for almost 550 years, until the upsurge of feminism after World War II. While the author was recognized as a minor poet, this book, existing in four manuscript copies, remained almost unknown. Recently, because of its topical theme—the problem of female authority—feminists have rescued the book from oblivion. Today, it is accepted as one of the earliest feminist texts, and its author is hailed as the first to identify the "woman question"—a central concern in the West's ongoing intellectual debate.

Christine's *City of Ladies* was a late medieval salvo fired in the perennial battle of the sexes. It was meant to counter the misogyny (hatred of women) of men who claimed that women were innately inferior because female frailty descended from Eve, the first mother. It avoided the thorny debate over Eve and, forecasting a modern view, assumed woman's basic morality and goodness. While medieval in its reasoning style and antidemocratic ideas, this book is a seminal work of Western literature.

In form, the *City of Ladies* is an allegorical debate modeled on Boethius's *Consolation of Philosophy.* The debate members are Christine herself and the three Virtues who appear in a waking dream. Dressed as goddesses, the Virtues are Lady Reason, carrying a mirror, who shows viewers their true images; Lady Rectitude, carrying a ruler, who divides good from evil; and Lady Justice, holding a measuring cup, who sets limits to earthly things. They offer Christine moral guidance as she frames an ideal city where women will be safe for all time from misogynist attack.

The Book of the City of Ladies consists of three "books," or chapters. Lady Reason dominates the first book, praising women who founded cities and cultural institutions. Lady Rectitude holds forth in the second book, telling stories of female seers and offering insight into mother-child and husband-wife relations. The third book features Lady Justice's tales of saints' lives, mainly of martyrs.

Christine de Pizan's (1364–ca. 1430) sensitivity to women's issues sprang from her marginal status as an Italian at the French court. She was moved there by her Venetian father, who served as court astrologer, and she later wed a court secretary. Marginalized even more by her husband's death in 1389, she supported her family through writing, with patronage from the French kings and the dukes of Burgundy. She was France's first professional woman of letters.

Reading the Selections

These selections are taken from Books I and II of *City of Ladies.* In section I.1, Christine explains her book's purpose: to reject the misogynist's view that "women [are] inclined to and full of every vice." While once sharing this view, she now abhors it, believing instead in the innate goodness of God and woman herself.

In section I.27, Lady Reason advances the radical notion that women and men, though unequal physically, are equal mentally, if given equal access to education and public careers. Sections I.30 and I.34 show Lady Reason detailing the cultural achievements of the Greek poet Sappho (see "To a Soldier's Wife in Sardis: Anactoria," etc.) and the Greek goddess Minerva (Athena).

In section II.36, Dame Rectitude argues that the sexes should have the same education, especially in morality. She reasons that such parity would make women virtuous as well as satisfy their natural bent toward learning.

—w—

Book I

1. Here Begins the Book of the City of Ladies, Whose First Chapter Tells Why and for What Purpose This Book Was Written.

One day as I was sitting alone in my study surrounded by books on all kinds of subjects, devoting myself to literary studies, my usual habit, my mind dwelt at length on the weighty opinions of various authors whom I had studied for a long time. I looked up from my book, having decided to leave such subtle questions in peace and to relax by reading some light poetry. With this in mind, I searched for some small book. By chance a strange volume came into my hands, not one of my own, but one which had been given to me along with some others. When I held it open and saw from its title page that it was by Mathéolus, I smiled, for though I had never seen it before, I had often heard that like other books it discussed respect for women. I thought I would browse through it to amuse myself. I

had not been reading for very long when my good mother called me to refresh myself with some supper, for it was evening. Intending to look at it the next day, I put it down. The next morning, again seated in my study as was my habit, I remembered wanting to examine this book by Mathéolus. I started to read it and went on for a little while. Because the subject seemed to me not very pleasant for people who do not enjoy lies, and of no use in developing virtue or manners, given its lack of integrity in diction and theme, and after browsing here and there and reading the end, I put it down in order to turn my attention to more elevated and useful study. But just the sight of this book, even though it was of no authority, made me wonder how it happened that so many different men—and learned men among them—have been and are so inclined to express both in speaking and in their treatises and writings so many wicked insults about women and their behavior. Not only one or two and not even just this

Mathéolus (for this book had a bad name anyway and was intended as a satire) but, more generally, judging from the treatises of all philosophers and poets and from all the orators—it would take too long to mention their names—it seems that they all speak from one and the same mouth. They all concur in one conclusion: that the behavior of women is inclined to and full of every vice. Thinking deeply about these matters, I began to examine my character and conduct as a natural woman and, similarly, I considered other women whose company I frequently kept, princesses, great ladies, women of the middle and lower classes, who had graciously told me of their most private and intimate thoughts, hoping that I could judge impartially and in good conscience whether the testimony of so many notable men could be true. To the best of my knowledge, no matter how long I confronted or dissected the problem, I could not see or realize how their claims could be true when compared to the natural behavior and character of women. Yet I still argued vehemently against women, saying that it would be impossible that so many famous men—such solemn scholars, possessed of such deep and great understanding, so clear-sighted in all things, as it seemed—could have spoken falsely on so many occasions that I could hardly find a book on morals where, even before I had read it in its entirety, I did not find several chapters or certain sections attacking women, no matter who the author was. This reason alone, in short, made me conclude that, although my intellect did not perceive my own great faults and, likewise, those of other women because of its simpleness and ignorance, it was however truly fitting that such was the case. And so I relied more on the judgment of others than on what I myself felt and knew. I was so transfixed in this line of thinking for such a long time that it seemed as if I were in a stupor. Like a gushing fountain, a series of authorities, whom I recalled one after another, came to mind, along with their opinions on this topic. And I finally decided that God formed a vile creature when He made woman, and I wondered how such a worthy artisan could have deigned to make such an abominable work which, from what they say, is the vessel as well as the refuge and abode of every evil and vice. As I was thinking this, a great unhappiness and sadness welled up in my heart, for I detested myself and the entire feminine sex, as though we were monstrosities in nature. And in my lament I spoke these words:

"Oh, God, how can this be? For unless I stray from my faith, I must never doubt that Your infinite wisdom and most perfect goodness ever created anything which was not good. Did You yourself not create woman in a very special way and since that time did You not give her all those inclinations which it pleased You for her to have? And how could it be that You could go wrong in anything? Yet look at all these accusations which have been judged, decided, and concluded against women. I do not know how to understand this repugnance. If it is so, fair Lord God, that in fact so many abominations abound in the female sex, for You Yourself say that the testimony of two or three witnesses lends credence, why shall I not doubt that this is true? Alas, God, why did You not let me be born in the world as a man, so that all my inclinations would be to

serve You better, and so that I would not stray in anything and would be as perfect as a man is said to be? But since Your kindness has not been extended to me, then forgive my negligence in Your service, most fair Lord God, and may it not displease You, for the servant who receives fewer gifts from his lord is less obliged in his service." I spoke these words to God in my lament and a great deal more for a very long time in sad reflection, and in my folly I considered myself most unfortunate because God had made me inhabit a female body in this world. . . .

27. Christine Asks Reason Whether God Has Ever Wished to Ennoble the Mind of Woman With the Loftiness of the Sciences; and Reason's Answer.

After hearing these things, I replied to the lady who spoke infallibly: "My lady, truly has God revealed great wonders in the strength of these women whom you describe. But please enlighten me again, whether it has ever pleased this God, who has bestowed so many favors on women, to honor the feminine sex with the privilege of the virtue of high understanding and great learning, and whether women ever have a clever enough mind for this. I wish very much to know this because men maintain that the mind of women can learn only a little."

She answered, "My daughter, since I told you before, you know quite well that the opposite of their opinion is true, and to show you this even more clearly, I will give you proof through examples. I tell you again—and don't doubt the contrary—if it were customary to send daughters to school like sons, and if they were then taught the natural sciences, they would learn as thoroughly and understand the subtleties of all the arts and sciences as well as sons. And by chance there happen to be such women, for, as I touched on before, just as women have more delicate bodies than men, weaker and less able to perform many tasks, so do they have minds that are freer and sharper whenever they apply themselves."

"My lady, what are you saying? With all due respect, could you dwell longer on this point, please. Certainly men would never admit this answer is true, unless it is explained more plainly, for they believe that one normally sees that men know more than women do."

She answered, "Do you know why women know less?"

"Not unless you tell me, my lady."

"Without the slightest doubt, it is because they are not involved in many different things, but stay at home, where it is enough for them to run the household, and there is nothing which so instructs a reasonable creature as the exercise and experience of many different things."

"My lady, since they have minds skilled in conceptualizing and learning, just like men, why don't women learn more?"

She replied, "Because, my daughter, the public does not require them to get involved in the affairs which men are commissioned to execute, just as I told you before. It is enough for women to perform the usual duties to which they are ordained. As for judging from experience, since one sees that women usually know less than men, that therefore their capacity for understanding is less, look at men who farm the flatlands or who live in the mountains. You will find that in many countries they seem completely savage because they are so simple-minded. All the same, there is no doubt that Nature provided them with the qualities of body and mind found in the wisest and most learned men. All of this stems from a failure to learn, though, just as I told you, among men and women, some possess better minds than others. Let me tell you about women who have possessed great learning and profound understanding and treat the question of the similarity of women's minds to men's."

30. Here She Speaks of Sappho, That Most Subtle Woman, Poet, and Philosopher.

"The wise Sappho, who was from the city of Mytilene, was no less learned than Proba. This Sappho had a beautiful body and face and was agreeable and pleasant in appearance, conduct, and speech. But the charm of her profound understanding surpassed all the other charms with which she was endowed, for she was expert and learned in several arts and sciences, and she was not only well-educated in the works and writings composed by others but also discovered many new things herself and wrote many books and poems. Concerning her, Boccaccio has offered these fair words couched in the sweetness of poetic language: 'Sappho, possessed of sharp wit and burning desire for constant study in the midst of bestial and ignorant men, frequented the heights of Mount Parnassus, that is, of perfect study. Thanks to her fortunate boldness and daring, she kept company with the Muses, that is, the arts and sciences, without being turned away. She entered the forest of laurel trees filled with may boughs, greenery, and different colored flowers, soft fragrances and various aromatic spices, where Grammar, Logic, noble Rhetoric, Geometry, and Arithmetic live and take their leisure. She went on her way until she came to the deep grotto of Apollo, god of learning, and found the brook and conduit of the fountain of Castalia, and took up the plectrum and quill of the harp and played sweet melodies, with the nymphs all the while leading the dance, that is, following the rules of harmony and musical accord.' From what Boccaccio says about her, it should be inferred that the profundity of both her understanding and of her learned books could only be known and understood by men of great perception and learning, according to the testimony of the ancients. Her writings and poems have survived to this day, most remarkably constructed and composed, and they serve as illumination and models of consummate poetic craft and composition to those who have come afterward. She invented different genres of lyric and poetry, short narratives, tearful laments and strange lamentations about love and other emotions, and these were so well made and so well ordered that they were named 'Sapphic' after her. Horace recounts, concern-

ing her poems, that when Plato, the great philosopher who was Aristotle's teacher, died, a book of Sappho's poems was found under his pillow.

"In brief this lady was so outstanding in learning that in the city where she resided a statue of bronze in her image was dedicated in her name and erected in a prominent place so that she would be honored by all and be remembered forever. This lady was placed and counted among the greatest and most famous poets, and, according to Boccaccio, the honors of the diadems and crowns of kings and the miters of bishops are not any greater, nor are the crowns of laurel and victor's palm.

"I could tell you a great deal about women of great learning. Leontium was a Greek woman and also such a great philosopher that she dared, for impartial and serious reasons, to correct and attack the philosopher Theophrastus, who was quite famous in her time."

34. Here She Speaks of Minerva, Who Invented Many Sciences and the Technique of Making Armor from Iron and Steel.

"Minerva, just as you have written elsewhere, was a maiden of Greece and surnamed Pallas. This maiden was of such excellence of mind that the foolish people of that time, because they did not know who her parents were and saw her doing things which had never been done before, said she was a goddess descended from Heaven; for the less they knew about her ancestry, the more marvelous her great knowledge seemed to them, when compared to that of the women of her time. She had a subtle mind, of profound understanding, not only in one subject but also generally, in every subject. Through her ingenuity she invented a shorthand Greek script in which a long written narrative could be transcribed with far fewer letters, and which is still used by the Greeks today, a fine invention whose discovery demanded great subtlety. She invented numbers and a means of quickly counting and adding sums. Her mind was so enlightened with general knowledge that she devised various skills and designs which had never before been discovered. She developed the entire technique of gathering wool and making cloth and was the first who ever thought to shear sheep of their wool and then to pick, comb, and card it with iron spindles and finally to spin it with a distaff, and then she invented the tools needed to make the cloth and also the method by which the wool should finally be woven.

"Similarly she initiated the custom of extracting oil from different fruits of the earth, also from olives, and of squeezing and pressing juice from other fruits. At the same time she discovered how to make wagons and carts to transport things easily from one place to another.

"This lady, in a similar manner, did even more, and it seems all the more remarkable because it is far removed from a woman's nature to conceive of such things; for she invented the art and technique of making harnesses and armor from iron and steel, which knights and armed soldiers employ in battle and with which they cover their bodies, and which she first gave to the Athenians whom she taught how to deploy an army and battalions and how to fight in organized ranks.

"Similarly she was the first to invent flutes and fifes, trumpets and wind instruments. With her considerable force of mind, this lady remained a virgin her entire life. Because of her outstanding chastity, the poets claimed in their fictions that Vulcan, the god of fire, wrestled with her for a long time and that finally she won and overcame him, which is to say that she overcame the ardor and lusts of the flesh which so strongly assail the young. The Athenians held this maiden in such high reverence that they worshiped her as a goddess and called her the goddess of arms and chivalry because she was the first to devise their use, and they also called her the goddess of knowledge because of her learnedness.

"After her death they erected a temple in Athens dedicated to her, and there they placed a statue of her, portraying a maiden, as a representation of wisdom and chivalry. This statue had terrible and cruel eyes because chivalry has been instituted to carry out rigorous justice; they also signified that one seldom knows toward what end the meditation of the wise man tends. She wore a helmet on her head which signified that a knight must have strength, endurance, and constant courage in the deeds of arms, and further signified that the counsels of the wise are concealed, secret, and hidden. She was dressed in a coat of mail which stood for the power of the estate of chivalry and also taught that the wise man is always armed against the whims of Fortune, whether good or bad. She held some kind of spear or very long lance, which meant that the knight must be the rod of justice and also signified that the wise man casts his spears from great distances. A buckler or shield of crystal hung at her neck, which meant that the knight must always be alert and oversee everywhere the defense of his country and people and further signified that things are open and evident to the wise man. She had portrayed in the middle of this shield the head of a serpent called Gorgon, which teaches that the knight must always be wary and watchful over his enemies like the serpent, and furthermore, that the wise man is aware of all the malice which can hurt him. Next to this image they also placed a bird that flies by night, named the owl, as if to watch over her, which signified that the knight must be ready by night as well as by day for civil defense, when necessary, and also that the wise man should take care at all times to do what is profitable and fitting for him. For a long time this lady was held in such high regard and her great fame spread so far that in many places temples were founded to praise her. Even long afterward, when the Romans were at the height of their power, they included her image among their gods."

—⟨⟩—

Book II

36. Against Those Men Who Claim It Is Not Good for Women to Be Educated.

Following these remarks, I, Christine, spoke, "My lady, I realize that women have accomplished many good things and that even if evil women have done evil, it seems to me, nevertheless, that the benefits accrued and still accruing because of good women—particularly the wise and literary ones and those educated in the natural sciences whom I mentioned above—outweigh the evil. Therefore, I am amazed by the opinion of some men who claim that they do not want their daughters, wives, or kinswomen to be educated because their mores would be ruined as a result."

She responded, "Here you can clearly see that not all opinions of men are based on reason and that these men are wrong. For it must not be presumed that mores necessarily grow worse from knowing the moral sciences, which teach the virtues, indeed, there is not the slightest doubt that moral education amends and ennobles them. How could anyone think or believe that whoever follows good teaching or doctrine is the worse for it? Such an opinion cannot be expressed or maintained. I do not mean that it would be good for a man or a woman to study the art of divination or those fields of learning which are forbidden—for the holy Church did not remove them from common use without good reason—but it should not be believed that women are the worse for knowing what is good.

"Quintus Hortensius, a great rhetorician and consumately skilled orator in Rome, did not share this opinion. He had a daughter, named Hortensia, whom he greatly loved for the subtlety of her wit. He had her learn letters and study the science of rhetoric, which she mastered so thoroughly that she resembled her father Hortensius not only in wit and lively memory but also in her excellent delivery and order of speech—in fact, he surpassed her in nothing. As for the subject discussed above, concerning the good which comes about through women, the benefits realized by this woman and her learning were, among others, exceptionally remarkable. That is, during the time when Rome was governed by three men, this Hortensia began to support the cause of women and to undertake what no man dared to undertake. There was a question whether certain taxes should be levied on women and on their jewelry during a needy period in Rome. This woman's eloquence was so compelling that she was listened to, no less readily than her father would have been, and she won her case.

"Similarly, to speak of more recent times, without searching for examples in ancient history, Giovanni Andrea, a solemn law professor in Bologna not quite sixty years ago, was not of the opinion that it was bad for women to be educated. He had a fair and good daughter, named Novella, who was educated in the law to such an advanced degree that when he was occupied by some task and not at leisure to present his lectures to his students, he would send Novella, his daughter, in his place to lecture to the students from his chair. And to prevent her beauty from distracting the concentration of her audience, she had a little curtain drawn in front of her. In this manner she could on occasion supplement and lighten her father's occupation. He loved her so much that, to commemorate her name, he wrote a book of remarkable lectures on the law which he entitled *Novella super Decretalium*, after his daughter's name.

"Thus, not all men (and especially the wisest) share the opinion that it is bad for women to be educated. But it is very true that many foolish men have claimed this because it displeased them that women knew more than they did. Your father, who was a great scientist and philosopher, did not believe that women were worth less by knowing science; rather, as you know, he took great pleasure from seeing your inclination to learning. The feminine opinion of your mother, however, who wished to keep you busy with spinning and silly girlishness, following the common custom of women, was the major obstacle to your being more involved in the sciences. But just as the proverb already mentioned above says, 'No one can take away what Nature has given,' your mother could not hinder in you the feeling for the sciences which you, through natural inclination, had nevertheless gathered together in little droplets. I am sure that, on account of these things, you do not think you are worth less but rather that you consider it a great treasure for yourself; and you doubtless have reason to."

And I, Christine, replied to all of this, "Indeed, my lady, what you say is as true as the Lord's Prayer."

11

THE EARLY RENAISSANCE
Return to Classical Roots
1400–1494

LEON BATTISTA ALBERTI

Selection from *On Painting*

Alberti's *On Painting* helped ensure the triumph of the new Renaissance style over older medieval art. Published in Latin (1435) and Italian (1436) just as the Renaissance was picking up steam, this was the first modern treatise on the theory of painting. It became the era's authoritative guide for painters, both within and outside Florence, including Fra Angelico (about 1400–1455), Piero della Francesca (1420–1492), and perhaps Leonardo da Vinci (1452–1519). From 1600 until 1800, Alberti's treatise was invoked as an authority for painting practices approved by Europe's art academies. Today's historians still find this work invaluable, for it prepared the way for the art, the artist, and the patron of the Renaissance.

Alberti wrote his treatise "as a painter speaking to painters." The work is divided into three "books," or parts. Book I presents a mathematical method for creating perspective—the illusion of depth on a flat surface. Some perspectival ideas had long been used in Italy, but he was the first to codify them into an accessible work. Book II deals with painterly matters, such as color, drawing, and grace and beauty in poses and movements. Book III sets forth a type of humanist painting that uses Greco-Roman themes and depicts the soul's condition through bodily gestures and facial expressions.

Leon Battista Alberti (1404–1472) was the "universal man," the beau ideal of the age, and his achievements rivaled those of the later Leonardo da Vinci. Besides painting, Alberti also mastered music, mathematics, engineering, architecture, sculpture, poetry, drama, and civil and canon law, and he wrote books on most of these fields. A friend of Cosimo de' Medici (1389–1464), the merchant-banker who dominated Florence, Alberti was active in Cosimo's Platonic Academy, the club of artists and thinkers who studied Plato (see *Phaedo* and *The Republic*). Alberti's spirit had such force that his friends called him the complete genius, hence the authority attributed to his works.

Reading the Selection

This selection from Book II of *On Painting* shows Alberti as a Renaissance humanist, making the case for a radical new role for the age's painters. These painters are characterized by intellect, with the ascendancy of mind over hand visible in their art. Humanism is the theme: "[P]ainting contributes to the most honorable delights of the soul." This argument echoes the familiar rationale of humanists that studying and practicing grammar, rhetoric, logic, arithmetic, geometry, music, and astronomy—the seven liberal arts—are good exercises for the soul. What is radical in Alberti's claim is the ranking of painting with the liberal arts. In fact, in the Middle Ages, painting ranked low, on a par with crafts (shoemaking, weaving, and such). The favorable reception of this treatise encouraged the rise of independent artists, as evidenced around 1500 in the careers of Michelangelo, Leonardo da Vinci, and Raphael.

Alberti also argued that painting should be part of the core curriculum of the schools. To prove his case, he used examples from antiquity showing that the best families required that painting be taught to their sons and daughters. By 1513, Alberti's hope was realized in the well-rounded backgrounds of the idealized lady and gentleman of Castiglione's highly influential *The Book of the Courtier*.

Finally, Alberti was a pioneer in his claim for the sovereign power of painting: "Who can doubt that painting is the master art?" A generation later Leonardo gave voice to the identical claim.

—꿔—

Book II

Because this [process of] learning may perhaps appear a fatiguing thing to young people, I ought to prove here that painting is not unworthy of consuming all our time and study.

Painting contains a divine force which not only makes absent men present, as friendship is said to do, but moreover makes the dead seem almost alive. Even after many centuries they are recognized with great pleasure and with great admiration for the painter. Plutarch says that Cassander, one of the captains of Alexander, trembled through all his body because he saw a portrait of his King. Agesilaos, the Lacedaemonian, never permitted anyone to paint him or to represent him in sculpture; his own form so displeased him that he avoided being known by those who would come after him. Thus the face of a man who is already dead certainly lives a long life through painting. Some think that painting shaped the gods who were adored by the nations. It certainly was their greatest gift to mortals, for painting is most useful to that piety which joins us to the gods and keeps our souls full of religion. They say that Phidias made in Aulis a god Jove so beautiful that it considerably strengthened the religion then current.

The extent to which painting contributes to the most honourable delights of the soul and to the dignified beauty of things can be clearly seen not only from other things but especially from this: you can conceive of almost nothing so precious which is not made far richer and much more beautiful by association with painting. Ivory, gems and similar expensive things become more precious when worked by the hand of the painter. Gold worked by the art of painting outweighs an equal amount of unworked gold. If figures were made by the hand of Phidias or Praxiteles from lead itself—the lowest of metals—they would be valued more highly than silver. The painter, Zeuxis, began to give away his things because, as he said, they could not be bought. He did not think it possible to come to a just price which would be satisfactory to the painter, for in painting animals he set himself up almost as a god.

Therefore, painting contains within itself this virtue that any master painter who sees his works adored will feel himself considered another god. Who can doubt that painting is the master art or at least not a small ornament of things? The architect, if I am not mistaken, takes from the painter architraves, bases, capitals, columns, façades and other similar things. All the smiths, sculptors, shops and guilds are governed by the rules and art of the painter. It is scarcely possible to find any superior art which is not concerned with painting, so that whatever beauty is found can be said to be born of painting. *But also this, a dignified painting is held in high honour by many so that among all artists some smiths are named, only this is not the rule among smiths.* For this reason, I say among my friends that Narcissus who was changed into a flower, according to the poets, was the inventor of painting. Since painting is already the flower of every art, the story of Narcissus is most to the point. What else can you call painting but a similar embracing with art of what is presented on the surface of the water in the fountain?

Quintilian said that the ancient painters used to circumscribe shadows cast by the sun, and from this our art has grown. There are those who say that a certain Philocles, an Egyptian, and a Cleantes were among the first inventors of this art. The Egyptians affirm that painting was in use among them a good 6000 years before it was carried into Greece. They say that painting was brought to us from Greece after the victory of Marcellus over Sicily. But we are not interested in knowing who was the inventor of the art or the first painter, since we are not telling stories like Pliny. We are, however, building anew an art of painting about which nothing, as I see it, has been written in this age. They say that Euphranor of Isthmus wrote something about measure and about colours, that Antigonos and Xenocrates exchanged something in their letters about painting, and that Apelles wrote to Pelleus about painting. Diogenes Laertius recounts that Demetrius made commentaries on painting. Since all the other arts were recommended in letters by our great men, and since painting was not neglected by our Latin writers, I believe that our ancient Tuscan [ancestors] were already most expert masters in painting.

Trismegistus, an ancient writer, judged that painting and sculpture were born at the same time as religion, *for thus he answered Aesclepius: mankind portrays the gods in his own image from his memories of nature and his own origins.* Who can here deny that in all things public and private, profane and religious, painting has taken all the most honourable parts to itself so that nothing has ever been so esteemed by mortals?

The incredible prices of painted pictures have been recorded. Aristides the Theban sold a single picture for one hundred talents. They say that Rhodes was not burned by King Demetrius for fear that a painting of Protogenes' should perish. It could be said that the city of Rhodes was ransomed from the enemy by a single painting. Pliny collected many other such things in which you can see that good painters have always been greatly honoured by all. The most noble citizens, philosophers and quite a few kings not only enjoyed painted things but also painted with their own hands. Lucius Manilius, Roman citizen, and Fabius, a most noble man, were painters. Turpilius, a Roman knight, painted at Verona. Sitedius, praetor and proconsul, acquired renown as a painter. Pacuvius, tragic poet and nephew of the poet Ennius, painted Hercules in the Roman forum. Socrates, Plato, Metrodorus, Pyrrho were connoisseurs of painting. The emperors Nero, Valentinian, and Alexander Severus were most devoted to painting. It would be too long, however, to recount here how many princes and kings were pleased by painting. Nor does it seem necessary to me to recount all the throng of ancient painters. Their number is seen in the fact that 360 statues, part on horseback and part in chariots, were completed in four hundred days for Demetrius Phalerius, son of Phanostratus. In a land in which there was such a great number of sculptors, can you believe that painters were lacking? I am certain that both these arts are related and nurtured by the same genius, painting with sculpture. But I always give higher rank to the genius of the painter because he works with more difficult things.

However, let us return to our work. Certainly the number of sculptors and painters was great in those times when princes and plebeians, learned and unlearned enjoyed painting, and when painted panels and portraits, considered the choicest booty from the provinces, were set up in the theatres. Finally L. Paulus Aemilius and not a few other Roman citizens taught their sons painting along with the fine arts and the art of living piously and well.

This excellent custom was frequently observed among the Greeks who, because they wished their sons to be well educated, taught them painting along with geometry and music. It was also an honour among women to know how to paint. Martia, daughter of Varro, is praised by the writers because she knew how to paint. Painting had such reputation and honour among the Greeks that laws and edicts were passed forbidding slaves to learn painting. It was certainly well that they did this, for the art of painting has always been most worthy of liberal minds and noble souls.

As for me, I certainly consider a great appreciation of painting to be the best indication of a most perfect mind, even though it happens that this art is pleasing to the uneducated as well as to the educated. It occurs rarely in any other art that what delights the experienced also moves the inexperienced. In the same way you will find that many greatly desire to be well versed in painting. Nature herself seems to delight in painting, for in the cut faces of marble she often paints centaurs and faces of bearded and curly headed kings. It is said, moreover, that in a gem from Pyrrhus all nine Muses, each with her symbol, are to be found clearly painted by nature. Add to this that in no other art does it happen that both the experienced and the inexperienced of every age apply themselves so voluntarily to the learning and exercising of it. Allow me to speak of myself here. Whenever I turn to painting for my recreation, which I frequently do when I am tired of more pressing affairs, I apply myself to it with so much pleasure that I am surprised that three or four hours have passed. Thus this art gives pleasure and praise to whoever is skilled in it; riches and perpetual fame to one who is master of it. Since these things are so, since painting is the best and most ancient ornament of things, worthy of free men, pleasing to learned and unlearned, I greatly encourage our studious youth to exert themselves as much as possible in painting.

Therefore, I recommend that he who is devoted to painting should learn this art. The first great care of one who seeks to obtain eminence in painting is to acquire the fame and renown of the ancients. It is useful to remember that avarice is always the enemy of virtue. Rarely can anyone given to acquisition of wealth acquire renown. I have seen many in the first flower of learning suddenly sink to money-making. As a result they acquire neither riches nor praise. However, if they had increased their talent with study, they would have easily soared into great renown. Then they would have acquired much riches and pleasure. . . .

—m—

GIOVANNI PICO DELLA MIRANDOLA
Selections from *On the Dignity of Man*

The Latin oration *On the Dignity of Man* is a tour de force by Pico (1463–1494), a son of the noble house of Mirandola (Italy). Written when Pico was twenty-four, the oration is a mixture of Aristotelian, Hebraic, Arabic, Persian, and Aramaic notions held together by Neo-Platonism—a blend of Plato's ideas and Christian beliefs. Its central Neo-Platonic motif is that love is the divine glue unifying the universe. Christian in structure, this heady synthesis of ideas breaks free of its frame to become a non-sectarian philosophy.

Pico's oration embodies the Renaissance spirit. In its appeal to wide-ranging sources, it expresses Renaissance zeal for the Classic texts of Greece and Rome as well as hitherto ignored ancient sources. Its theme is the Renaissance belief that the findings of reason and the truths of the Bible share a basic unity that is reflected in the history of thought. Most of all, its view that human nature has no limits is the prototype of the Renaissance idea of unlimited possibility. Today this idea, with its corollary of free expression, is a defining trait of Western culture.

The oration was composed to introduce a debate Pico scheduled for Rome in 1487. In this debate, Pico proposed to defend nine hundred theses gleaned from his vast readings; he even offered to pay his potential opponents' travel expenses. The debate, however, did not take place because Pope Innocent VIII forbade it. The pope also appointed a commission to examine the debate topics, with the result that seven theses were condemned as heretical, and six more were suspect. Threatened by church officials, Pico subsequently settled in Florence, where he was caught up in the anti-Renaissance crusade of the monk Savonarola. Pico's plan to wander as an evangelist was cut short in 1494, when he suddenly died at age thirty-one.

Reading the Selections

The first selection from the oration *On the Dignity of Man* begins with a greeting—"Most venerable fathers"—thus establishing that the work was meant to be recited orally, ostensibly before a group of clergy. The major insights to be gained from this selection are Pico's concept of human nature and his style of reasoning.

Pico's concept of human nature is his major contribution to Western thought. For him, human nature is not fixed, and the will is perfectly free. In a burst of lyricism he claimed that human beings are shape-shifting creatures who may be vegetative, bestial, rational, divine, or even co-equal with God: When humanity's quest ends, "We shall . . . not be ourselves, but He himself who made us." Brushing aside medieval ideas, Pico expresses the radiant faith of Renaissance humanism, that human beings are not flawed by original sin but are capable of becoming godlike.

Pico's style of reasoning reflects the Renaissance trend of treating old problems in new ways. To deal with the question of human nature, he takes the Platonic concept of the Great Chain of Being, which maintains that creation is a linked cord reaching step-by-step from the simplest life to God, and gives it a modern twist. Ancient thinkers had used the Great Chain of Being to argue that human potential is limited, since the place of human beings in the chain is fixed, and that change would destroy the whole creation. In contrast, Pico claimed that human beings may make of themselves anything they please, because as hybrids of the whole creation, they exist both outside and above the Great Chain of Being.

Most venerable fathers, I have read in the records of the
Arabians that Abdul the Saracen, on being asked what
thing on, so to speak, the world's stage, he viewed as most
greatly worthy of wonder, answered that he viewed nothing more wonderful than man. And Mercury's, "a great
wonder, Asclepius, is man!" agrees with that opinion. On
thinking over the reason for these sayings, I was not satisfied by the many assertions made by many men concerning the outstandingness of human nature: that man is the
messenger between creatures, familiar with the upper and
king of the lower; by the sharpsightedness of the senses,
by the hunting-power of reason, and by the light of intelligence, the interpreter of nature; the part in between the
standstill of eternity and the flow of time, and, as the Persians say, the bond tying the world together, nay, the nuptial bond; and, according to David, "a little lower than the
angels." These reasons are great but not the chief ones,
that is, they are not reasons for a lawful claim to the highest wonder as to a prerogative. Why should we not wonder more at the angels themselves and at the very blessed
heavenly choirs?

Finally, it seemed to me that I understood why man is
the animal that is most happy, and is therefore worthy of
all wonder; and lastly, what the state is that is allotted to
man in the succession of things, and that is capable of
arousing envy not only in the brutes but also in the stars
and even in minds beyond the world. It is wonderful and
beyond belief. For this is the reason why man is rightly
said and thought to be a great marvel and the animal really worthy of wonder. Now hear what it is, fathers; and
with kindly ears and for the sake of your humanity, give
me your close attention:

Now the highest Father, God the master-builder, had,
by the laws of his secret wisdom, fabricated this house,
this world which we see, a very superb temple of divinity.
He had adorned the super-celestial region with minds. He
had animated the celestial globes with eternal souls; he
had filled with a diverse throng of animals the cast-off and
residual parts of the lower world. But, with the work finished, the Artisan desired that there be someone to reckon
up the reason of such a big work, to love its beauty, and to
wonder at its greatness. Accordingly, now that all things
had been completed, as Moses and Timaeus testify, He
lastly considered creating man. But there was nothing in
the archetypes from which He could mold a new sprout,
nor anything in His storehouses which He could bestow
as a heritage upon a new son, nor was there an empty ju-
diciary seat where this contemplator of the universe could
sit. Everything was filled up; all things had been laid out
in the highest, the lowest, and the middle orders. But it
did not belong to the paternal power to have failed in the
final parturition, as though exhausted by child-bearing; it
did not belong to wisdom, in a case of necessity, to have
been tossed back and forth through want of a plan; it did
not belong to the loving-kindness which was going to
praise divine liberality in others to be forced to condemn
itself. Finally, the best of workmen decided that that to

which nothing of its very own could be given should be,
in composite fashion, whatsoever had belonged individu-
ally to each and every thing. Therefore He took up man, a
work of indeterminate form; and, placing him at the mid-
point of the world, He spoke to him as follows:

"We have given to thee, Adam, no fixed seat, no form
of thy very own, no gift peculiarly thine, that thou mayest
feel as thine own, have as thine own, possess as thine own
the seat, the form, the gifts which thou thyself shalt desire.
A limited nature in other creatures is confined within the
laws written down by Us. In conformity with thy free
judgment, in whose hand We have placed thee, thou art
confined by no bounds; and thou wilt fix limits of nature
for thyself. I have placed thee at the center of the world,
that from there thou mayest more conveniently look
around and see whatsoever is in the world. Neither heavenly nor earthly, neither mortal nor immortal have We
made thee. Thou, like a judge appointed for being honorable, art the molder and maker of thyself; thou mayest
sculpt thyself into whatever shape thou dost prefer. Thou
canst grow downward into the lower natures which are
brutes. Thou canst again grow upward from thy soul's
reason into the higher natures which are divine."

O great liberality of God the Father! O great and wonderful happiness of man. It is given him to have that
which he chooses and to be that which he wills. As soon as
brutes are born, they bring with them, "from their dam's
bag," as Lucilius says, what they are going to possess.
Highest spirits have been, either from the beginning or
soon after, that which they are going to be throughout
everlasting eternity. At man's birth the Father placed in
him every sort of seed and sprouts of every kind of life.
The seeds that each man cultivates will grow and bear
their fruit in him. If he cultivates vegetable seeds, he will
become a plant. If the seeds of sensation, he will grow into
brute. If rational, he will come out a heavenly animal. If
intellectual, he will be an angel, and a son of God. And if
he is not contented with the lot of any creature but takes
himself up into the center of his own unity, then, made
one spirit with God and settled in the solitary darkness of
the Father, who is above all things, he will stand ahead of
all things. Who does not wonder at this chameleon which
we are? Or who at all feels more wonder at anything else
whatsoever? It was not unfittingly that Asclepius the
Athenian said that man was symbolized by Prometheus in
the secret rites, by reason of our nature sloughing its skin
and transforming itself; hence metamorphoses were popular among the Jews and the Pythagoreans. For the more
secret Hebrew theology at one time reshapes holy Enoch
into an angel of divinity, whom they call *malach hashechina*,
and at other times reshapes other men into other divinities. According to the Pythagoreans, wicked men are de-
formed into brutes and, if you believe Empedocles, into
plants too. And copying them, Maumeth [Mohammed]
often had it on his lips that he who draws back from
divine law becomes a brute. And his saying so was reasonable: for it is not the rind which makes the plant, but a

dull and non-sentient nature; not the hide which makes a beast of burden, but a brutal and sensual soul; not the spherical body which makes the heavens, but right reason; and not a separateness from the body but a spiritual intelligence which makes an angel. For example, if you see a man given over to his belly and crawling upon the ground, it is a bush not a man that you see. If you see anyone blinded by the illusions of his empty and Calypso-like imagination, seized by the desire of scratching, and delivered over to the senses, it is a brute not a man that you see. If you come upon a philosopher winnowing out all things by right reason, he is a heavenly not an earthly animal. If you come upon a pure contemplator, ignorant of the body, banished to the innermost places of the mind, he is not an earthly, not a heavenly animal; he more superbly is a divinity clothed with human flesh.

Who is there that does not wonder at man? And it is not unreasonable that in the mosaic and Christian holy writ man is sometimes denoted by the name "all flesh" and at other times by that of "every creature"; and man fashions, fabricates, transforms himself into the shape of all flesh, into the character of every creature. Accordingly, where Evantes the Persian tells of the Chaldaean theology, he writes that man is not any inborn image of himself, but many images coming in from the outside: hence that say-

ing of the Chaldaeans: *enosh hu shinuy vekamah tevaoth baal chayim,* that is, man is an animal of diverse, multiform, and destructible nature.

But why all this? In order for us to understand that, after having been born in this state so that we may be what we will to be, then, since we are held in honor, we ought to take particular care that no one may say against us that we do not know that we are made similar to brutes and mindless beasts of burden. But rather, as Asaph the prophet says: "Ye are all gods, and sons of the most high," unless by abusing the very indulgent liberality of the Father, we make the free choice, which he gave to us, harmful to ourselves instead of helpful toward salvation. Let a certain holy ambition invade the mind, so that we may not be content with mean things but may aspire to the highest things and strive with all our forces to attain them: for if we will to, we can. Let us spurn earthly things; let us struggle toward the heavenly. Let us put in last place whatever is of the world; and let us fly beyond the chambers of the world to the chamber nearest the most lofty divinity. There, as the sacred mysteries reveal, the seraphim, cherubim, and thrones occupy the first places. Ignorant of how to yield to them and unable to endure the second places, let us compete with the angels in dignity and glory. When we have willed it, we shall be not at all below them. . . .

—⁂—

. . . Not only the Mosaic or Christian mysteries but also the theology of the ancients show the advantages for us and the dignity of these liberal arts about which I have come here to dispute. For what else is meant by the degrees of initiation that are customary in the secret rites of Greeks? First, to those who had been purified by moral and dialectic arts, which we have called, as it were, purgative, befell the reception of the mysteries. And what else can this reception be but the interpretation of more hidden nature by means of philosophy? Then lastly, to those who had been thus prepared, came that ἐποπτεία, that is, a vision of divine things by means of the light of theology. Who does not seek to be initiated into such rites? Who does not set all human things at a lower value and, contemning the goods of fortune and neglecting the body, does not desire, while still continuing on earth, to become the drinking-companion of the gods; and, drunken with the nectar of eternity, to bestow the gift of immortality upon the mortal animal? Who does not wish to have breathed into him the Socratic frenzies sung by Plato in the *Phaedrus,* that by the oarlike movement of wings and feet he may quickly escape from here, that is, from this world where he is laid down as in an evil place, and be carried in speediest flight to the heavenly Jerusalem. We shall be possessed, fathers,

we shall be possessed by these Socratic frenzies, which will so place us outside of our minds that they will place our mind and ourselves in God. We shall be possessed by them if we have first done what is in us to do. For if through morality the forces of the passions will have been so stretched to the [proper] measure, through due proportions, that they sound together in fixed concord, and if through dialectic, reason will have moved, keeping time in her forward march, then, aroused by the frenzy of the muses, we shall drink in the heavenly harmony of our ears. Then Bacchus the leader of the muses, in his own mysteries, that is, in the visible signs of nature, will show the invisible things of God to us as we philosophize, and will make us drunk with the abundance of the house of God. In this house, if we are faithful like Moses, holiest theology will approach, and will inspire us with a twofold frenzy. We, raised up into the loftiest watchtower of theology, from which, measuring with indivisible eternity the things that are, will be, and shall have been, and looking at their primeval beauty, shall be prophets of Phoebus, his winged lovers, and finally, aroused with ineffable charity as with fire, placed outside of ourselves like burning Seraphim, filled with divinity, we shall now not be ourselves, but He himself who made us.

12

THE HIGH RENAISSANCE AND EARLY MANNERISM

1494–1564

NICCOLÒ MACHIAVELLI

Selections from *The Prince*

The Prince is a short and strikingly honest handbook on how to win power and keep it. Based on Niccolò Machiavelli's (1469–1527) personal experiences as diplomat and government employee (in the service of his beloved Florence), the book has become the foundation of modern political theory. In his other works, in particular his histories of Italy and Florence, Machiavelli drew upon his Classical education and personal experiences to develop this message: Learn from the past what works and what does not. But nowhere else does Machiavelli express his thesis so boldly and succinctly as in *The Prince:* "The end justifies any means."

The Prince's harsh and amoral attitude toward politics sparked controversies when first published. Many of Machiavelli's contemporaries, who were witnessing the end of the medieval Age of Faith and experiencing the dawn of a more secular time, were sharply divided over the meaning of his writings. Especially damaging to the book's reputation was its persistent low opinion of human nature. Succeeding generations have debated his analysis of human behavior and his consequent rationale for a strong government. In modern secular society, many readers have come to accept Machiavelli's view that political power, driven by personal or group interests, must be understood in utilitarian and practical terms.

The Prince, a treatise on the art of successful governing, is composed of three parts. The first part, comprising eleven chapters, categorizes and describes the various types of existing governments. The second part, which consists of fourteen chapters, offers advice and examples on winning and maintaining political power. In these fourteen chapters, Machiavelli instructs the ruler on how to raise and organize armies, how to keep subjects loyal, and how to avoid the pitfalls of overconfidence and flattery. Throughout *The Prince*, the author compares and contrasts key traits that make a ruler a success or a failure. He also addresses the issue of fortune—what is now called opportunity—and emphasizes how often it affects a ruler. In the third part—the concluding chapter—Machiavelli calls upon "the prince" to unite the Italians against foreign oppressors and drive them from Italy.

Reading the Selections

Chapters XV, XVI, and XVII appear in the second part of *The Prince,* in which Machiavelli discusses the most effective way for a ruler to govern his subjects. He points out that his discussion is rooted in practical politics, rather than based on imaginary regimes created by writers—a reference to the idealized commonwealths of Plato and medieval Christian authors. In Chapter XV, Machiavelli lists traits for which rulers are praised or blamed—such as being called stubborn or flexible, religious or skeptical—and notes that no ruler could continuously practice the best of these without damaging his ability to govern. Thus, in a crisis the ruler should not shrink from being blamed for vices if they are needed to safeguard the state, though most of the time, the prince should pretend to be what he is not in order to keep his subjects' loyalty.

In Chapter XVI, Machiavelli focuses on the traits of generosity and miserliness and shows, through ancient and current examples, the consequences for rulers who practiced one or the other of them. He concludes, given his dark view of human nature, that a ruler is better to be miserly than generous. In Chapter XVII, Machiavelli raises perhaps the most controversial question in the treatise: Is it better for the ruler to be loved or feared? Ideally, the ruler should be both loved and feared, but as this is nearly impossible, then the ruler should be feared. Machiavelli, realizing that fear has its limits, ends on a cautionary note: The "wise prince" must avoid being hated by his subjects, for hatred is the soil out of which rebellions grow.

—⁂—

Chapter XV
The Things for Which Men, and Especially Princes, are Praised or Blamed

It now remains for us to see how a prince should govern his conduct towards his subjects or his friends. I know that this has often been written about before, and so I hope it will not be thought presumptuous for me to do so, as, especially in discussing this subject, I draw up an original set of rules. But since my intention is to say something that will prove of practical use to the inquirer, I have thought it proper to represent things as they are in real truth, rather than as they are imagined. Many have dreamed up republics and principalities which have never in truth been known to exist; the gulf between how one should live and how one does live is so wide that a man who neglects what is actually done for what should be done learns the way to self-destruction rather than self-preservation. The fact is that a man who wants to act virtuously in every way necessarily comes to grief among so many who are not virtuous. Therefore if a prince wants to maintain his rule he must learn how not to be virtuous, and to make use of this or not according to need.

So leaving aside imaginary things, and referring only to those which truly exist, I say that whenever men are discussed (and especially princes, who are more exposed to view), they are noted for various qualities which earn them either praise or condemnation. Some, for example, are held to be generous, and others miserly (I use the Tuscan word rather than the word avaricious: we call a man who is mean with what he possesses, miserly, and a man who wants to plunder others, avaricious). Some are held to be benefactors, others are called grasping; some cruel, some compassionate; one man faithless, another faithful; one man effeminate and cowardly, another fierce and courageous; one man courteous, another proud; one man lascivious, another pure; one guileless, another crafty; one stubborn, another flexible; one grave, another frivolous; one religious, another sceptical; and so forth. I know everyone will agree that it would be most laudable if a prince possessed all the qualities deemed to be good among those I have enumerated. But, human nature being what it is, princes cannot possess those qualities, or rather they cannot always exhibit them. So a prince should be so prudent that he knows how to escape the evil reputation attached to those vices which could lose him his state, and how to avoid those vices which are not so dangerous, if he possibly can; but, if he cannot, he need not worry so much about the latter. And then, he must not flinch from being blamed for vices which are necessary for safeguarding the state. This is because, taking everything into account, he will find that some of the things that appear to be virtues will, if he practises them, ruin him, and some of the things that appear to be wicked will bring him security and prosperity.

—⁓—

Chapter XVI
Generosity and Parsimony

So, starting with the first of the qualities I enumerated above, I say it would be splendid if one had a reputation for generosity; nonetheless if your actions are influenced by the desire for such a reputation you will come to grief. This is because if your generosity is good and sincere it may pass unnoticed and it will not save you from being reproached for its opposite. If you want to acquire a reputation for generosity, therefore, you have to be ostentatiously lavish; and a prince acting in that fashion will soon squander all his resources, only to be forced in the end, if he wants to maintain his reputation, to lay excessive burdens on the people, to impose extortionate taxes, and to do everything else he can to raise money. This will start to make his subjects hate him, and, since he will have impoverished himself, he will be generally despised. As a result, because of this generosity of his, having injured many and rewarded few, he will be vulnerable to the first minor setback, and the first real danger he encounters will bring him to grief. When he realizes this and tries to retrace his path he will immediately be reputed a miser.

So as a prince cannot practise the virtue of generosity in such a way that he is noted for it, except to his cost, he should if he is prudent not mind being called a miser. In time he will be recognized as being essentially a generous man, seeing that because of his parsimony his existing revenues are enough for him, he can defend himself against an aggressor, and he can embark on enterprises without burdening the people. So he proves himself generous to all those from whom he takes nothing, and they are innumerable, and miserly towards all those to whom he gives nothing, and they are few. In our own times great things have been accomplished only by those who have been held miserly, and the others have met disaster. Pope Julius II made use of a reputation for generosity to win the papacy, but subsequently he made no effort to maintain this reputation, because he wanted to be able to finance his wars. The present king of France has been able to wage so many wars without taxing his subjects excessively only because his long-standing parsimony enabled him to meet the additional expenses involved. Were the present king of Spain renowned for his generosity he would not have started and successfully concluded so many enterprises.

So if a prince does not have to rob his subjects, if he can defend himself, if he is not plunged into poverty and shame, if he is not forced to become rapacious, he ought not to worry about being called a miser. Miserliness is one of those vices which sustain his rule. Someone may object: Caesar came to power by virtue of his generosity, and many others, because they practised and were known for their generosity, have risen to the very highest positions. My answer to this is as follows. Either you are already a prince, or you are on the way to becoming one. In the first case, your generosity will be to your cost; in the second, it is certainly necessary to have a reputation for generosity. Caesar was one of those who wanted to establish his own rule over Rome; but if, after he had established it, he had remained alive and not moderated his expenditure he would have fallen from power.

Again, someone may retort: there have been many princes who have won great successes with their armies, and who have had the reputation of being extremely generous. My reply to this is: the prince gives away what is his own or his subjects', or else what belongs to others. In the first case he should be frugal; in the second, he should indulge his generosity to the full. The prince who campaigns with his armies, who lives by pillaging, sacking, and extortion, disposes of what belongs to aliens; and he must be open-handed, otherwise the soldiers would refuse to follow him. And you can be more liberal with what does not belong to you or your subjects, as Caesar, Cyrus, and Alexander were. Giving away what belongs to strangers in no way affects your standing at home; rather it increases it. You hurt yourself only when you give away what is your own. There is nothing so self-defeating as generosity: in the act of practising it, you lose the ability to do so, and you become either poor and despised or, seeking to escape poverty, rapacious and hated. A prince should try to avoid, above all else, being despised and hated; and generosity results in your being both. Therefore it is wiser to incur the reputation of being a miser, which invites ignominy but not hatred, than to be forced by seeking a name for generosity to incur a reputation for rapacity, which brings you hatred as well as ignominy.

—ᴍ—

Chapter XVII
Cruelty and Compassion; and Whether It Is Better to Be Loved Than Feared, or the Reverse

Taking others of the qualities I enumerated above, I say that a prince should want to have a reputation for compassion rather than for cruelty: nonetheless, he should be careful that he does not make bad use of compassion. Cesare Borgia was accounted cruel; nevertheless, this cruelty of his reformed the Romagna, brought it unity, and restored order and obedience. On reflection, it will be seen that there was more compassion in Cesare than in the Florentine people, who, to escape being called cruel, allowed Pistoia to be devastated.* So a prince should not worry if he incurs reproach for his cruelty so long as he keeps his subjects united and loyal. By making an example or two he will prove more compassionate than those who, being too compassionate, allow disorders which lead to murder and rapine. These nearly always harm the whole community, whereas executions ordered by a prince only affect individuals. A new prince, of all rulers, finds it impossible to avoid a reputation for cruelty, because of the abundant dangers inherent in a newly won state. Vergil, through the mouth of Dido, says:

> Res dura, et regni novitas me talia cogunt
> Moliri, et late fines custode tueri.†

Nonetheless, a prince should be slow to take action, and should watch that he does not come to be afraid of his own shadow; his behaviour should be tempered by humanity and prudence so that over-confidence does not make him rash or excessive distrust make him unbearable.

From this arises the following question: whether it is better to be loved than feared, or the reverse. The answer is that one would like to be both the one and the other; but because it is difficult to combine them, it is far better to be feared than loved if you cannot be both. One can make this generalization about men: they are ungrateful, fickle, liars, and deceivers, they shun danger and are greedy for profit; while you treat them well, they are yours. They would shed their blood for you, risk their property, their lives, their children, so long, as I said above, as danger is remote; but when you are in danger they turn against you. Any prince who has come to depend entirely on promises and has taken no other precautions ensures his own ruin; friendship which is bought with money and not with greatness and nobility of mind is paid for, but it does not last and it yields nothing. Men worry less about doing an injury to one who makes himself loved than to one who

makes himself feared. The bond of love is one which men, wretched creatures that they are, break when it is to their advantage to do so; but fear is strengthened by a dread of punishment which is always effective.

The prince should nonetheless make himself feared in such a way that, if he is not loved, at least he escapes being hated. For fear is quite compatible with an absence of hatred; and the prince can always avoid hatred if he abstains from the property of his subjects and citizens and from their women. If, even so, it proves necessary to execute someone, this should be done only when there is proper justification and manifest reason for it. But above all a prince should abstain from the property of others; because men sooner forget the death of their father than the loss of their patrimony. It is always possible to find pretexts for confiscating someone's property; and a prince who starts to live by rapine always finds pretexts for seizing what belongs to others. On the other hand, pretexts for executing someone are harder to find and they are less easily sustained.

However, when a prince is campaigning with his soldiers and is in command of a large army then he need not worry about having a reputation for cruelty; because, without such a reputation, he can never keep his army united and disciplined. Among the admirable achievements of Hannibal is included this: that although he led a huge army, made up of countless different races, on foreign campaigns, there was never any dissension, either among the troops themselves or against their leader, whether things were going well or badly. For this, his inhuman cruelty was wholly responsible. It was this, along with his countless other qualities, which made him feared and respected by his soldiers. If it had not been for his cruelty, his other qualities would not have been enough. The historians, having given little thought to this, on the one hand admire what Hannibal achieved, and on the other condemn what made his achievements possible.

That his other qualities would not have been enough by themselves can be proved by looking at Scipio, a man unique in his own time and through all recorded history. His armies mutinied against him in Spain, and the only reason for this was his excessive leniency, which allowed his soldiers more licence than was good for military discipline. Fabius Maximus reproached him for this in the Senate and called him a corrupter of the Roman legions. Again, when the Locri were plundered by one of Scipio's officers, he neither gave them satisfaction nor punished his officer's insubordination; and this was all because of his having too lenient a nature. By way of excuse for him some senators argued that many men were better at not making mistakes themselves than at correcting them in others. But in time Scipio's lenient nature would have spoilt his fame and glory had he continued to indulge it during his command; when he lived under orders from

---

*Pistoia was a subject-city of Florence, which forcibly restored order there when conflict broke out between two rival factions in 1501–2. Machiavelli was concerned with this business at first hand.

†'Harsh necessity, and the newness of my kingdom, force me to do such things and to guard my frontiers everywhere.' *Aeneid* i, 563.

the Senate, however, this fatal characteristic of his was not only concealed but even brought him glory.

So, on this question of being loved or feared, I conclude that since some men love as they please but fear when the prince pleases, a wise prince should rely on what he controls, not on what he cannot control. He should only endeavour, as I said, to escape being hated.

BALDASSARE CASTIGLIONE
Selections from *The Book of the Courtier*

The Book of the Courtier (*courtier* being a "gentleman") belongs to the genre of etiquette books that flourished in Renaissance Europe as a religious-based culture gave way to a more humanistic world. Books of this type were much in evidence, in response to this period's ideal that secular life in the upper levels of society should be marked by reserved grace, especially between the sexes. Court life, whether in the royal or aristocratic domain, already had well-established rules of behavior derived from the medieval chivalric code; however, courts were still dominated by a male ethos, manifested in rough speech, crude manners, and general lack of refinement between men and women. Whereas most Renaissance etiquette books were meant to correct crude behavior and speech, *The Courtier* took a broader view by offering an idealized vision of court life in which courteous ladies became the arbiters of society. Published in 1528 and translated into most Western languages by 1600, this work became the bible of politeness for Europe's upper classes, and its rules were formalized into strict expectations. This Renaissance book is the source from which modern notions of "lady" and "gentleman" descend.

The Courtier's author, Baldassare Castiglione (1478–1529), was himself a polished courtier, growing up among the Italian nobility and studying the Classics at the University of Milan. Later, he was attached to various northern Italian ducal courts (Milan, Urbino, and Mantua), for whose rulers he performed military and diplomatic missions. While serving as the Duke of Mantua's ambassador to Rome, he was brought by his duties into the cultivated court of the Medici pope, Leo X. A later pope, Clement VII, made Castiglione the papal representative to Spain, a post he held until he died.

The Courtier, Castiglione's only publication, was his life's work. He was moved to write it during his eleven years at the ducal court of Urbino, which was the center of an accomplished circle of artists, writers, and intellectuals presided over by the old duke and his young wife, Elisabetta. This Urbino circle, with its witty talk, integrity, and grace, came to embody Castiglione's social ideal. When he wrote *The Courtier*, he tried to capture the conversational tone of this circle by making the work a dialogue, divided into four books, set during an evening in the ducal palace. In his book, as in life, Duchess Elisabetta is the playful leader of the group.

Reading the Selections

These selections from *The Book of the Courtier* are excerpts from Books I and III, dealing respectively with the qualities that define a courtier and a lady. Not based on real life, these attributes are ideals meant as a guide for correct deportment and had been gleaned from Castiglione's readings in medieval and Classical literature. Of the ideal courtier, the participants agree that he should be both a soldier trained in the bearing of arms and a scholar skilled in the liberal arts and social graces; however, they are of two minds as to which role should dominate.

No such dispute divides Castiglione's participants over the ideal lady: All concur that she should be the consummate hostess—charming, witty, graceful, physically attractive, and utterly feminine. An innovative aspect of this idealized model is the insistence that a lady be educated in the liberal arts in the same way as a gentleman. This idea swept away the barrier that, since the Middle Ages, had excluded women from higher learning. However, women remained barred from universities until the nineteenth century.

—*w*—

Book I

. . .

'But to come to specific details, I judge that the first and true profession of the courtier must be that of arms; and this above everything else I wish him to pursue vigorously. Let him also stand out from the rest as enterprising, bold, and loyal to whomever he serves. And he will win a good reputation by demonstrating these qualities whenever and wherever possible, since failure to do so always incurs the gravest censure. Just as once a woman's reputation for purity has been sullied it can never be restored, so once the reputation of a gentleman-at-arms has been stained through cowardice or some other reproachful behaviour, even if only once, it always remains defiled in the eyes of the world and covered with ignominy. The more our courtier excels in this art, therefore, the more praise he will deserve, although I do not think he needs to have the professional knowledge of such things and the other qualities appropriate to a military commander. However, since the subject of what constitutes a great captain takes us into very deep waters, we shall be content, as we said, for the courtier to show complete loyalty and an undaunted spirit, and for these to be always in evidence. For men demonstrate their courage far more often in little things than in great. Very often in the face of appalling danger but where there are numerous witnesses one will find those who, though ready to drop dead with fear, driven on by shame or the presence of others, will press forward, with their eyes closed, and do their duty; and only God knows how. But in things of trifling importance, when they believe they can avoid danger without its being noticed, they are only too willing to play for safety. As for those who, even when they are sure they are not being observed or seen or recognized by anyone, are full of ardour and avoid doing anything, no matter how trivial, for which they would incur reproach, they possess the temper and quality we are looking for in our courtier. All the same, we do not wish the courtier to make a show of being so fierce that he is always blustering and bragging, declaring that he is married to his cuirass, and glowering with the haughty looks that we know only too well in Berto. To these may very fairly be said what a worthy lady once remarked jokingly, in polite company, to a certain man (I don't want just now to mention him by name) whom she had honoured by asking him to dance and who not only refused but would not listen to music or take part in the many other entertainments offered, protesting all the while that such frivolities were not his business. And when at length the lady asked what his business was, he answered with a scowl: "Fighting . . ."

"'Well then," the lady retorted, "I should think that since you aren't at war at the moment and you are not engaged in fighting, it would be a good thing if you were to have yourself well greased and stowed away in a cupboard with all your fighting equipment, so that you avoid getting rustier than you are already."

'And of course everyone burst out laughing at the way she showed her contempt for his stupid presumption.

'Therefore,' Count Lodovico went on, 'the man we are seeking should be fierce, rough and always to the fore, in the presence of the enemy; but anywhere else he should be kind, modest, reticent and anxious above all to avoid ostentation or the kind of outrageous self-glorification by which a man always arouses loathing and disgust among those who have to listen to him. . . .

'I should like our courtier to be a more than average scholar, at least in those studies which we call the humanities; and he should have a knowledge of Greek as well as Latin, because of the many different things that are so beautifully written in that language. He should be very well acquainted with the poets, and no less with the orators and historians, and also skilled at writing both verse and prose, especially in our own language; for in addition to the satisfaction this will give him personally, it will enable him to provide constant entertainment for the ladies, who are usually very fond of such things. But if because of his other activities or through lack of study he fails to achieve a commendable standard in his writing, then he should take pains to suppress his work, to avoid ridicule, and he should show it only to a friend he can trust. And the exercise of writing will be profitable for him at least to the extent that it will teach him how to judge the work of others. For it is very unusual for someone who is not a practised writer, however erudite he may be, to understand completely the demanding work done by writers, or appreciate their stylistic accomplishments and triumphs and those subtle details characteristic of the writers of the ancient world. Moreover, these studies will make our courtier well informed and eloquent and (as Aristippus said to the tyrant) self-confident and assured no matter whom he is talking to. However, I should like our courtier to keep one precept firmly in mind: namely, that in what I have just discussed and in everything else he should always be diffident and reserved rather than forward, and he should be on his guard against assuming that he knows what he does not know. For we are instinctively all too greedy for praise, and there is no sound or song that comes sweeter to our ears; praise, like Sirens' voices, is the kind of music that causes shipwreck to the man who does not stop his ears to its deceptive harmony. Recognizing this danger, some of the philosophers of the ancient world wrote books giving advice on how a man can tell the difference between a true friend and a flatterer. Even so, we may well ask what use is this, seeing that there are so many who realize perfectly well that they are listening to flattery, and yet love the flatterer and detest the one who tells them the truth. Indeed, very often, deciding that the one who praises them is not being fulsome enough, they lend him a hand themselves and say such things that even the most outrageous flatterer feels ashamed. Let us leave these blind fools to their errors and decide that our courtier should possess such good judgement that he will not be told that black is white or presume anything of himself unless he is certain that it is true, and especially in regard to those flaws which, if you remember, when he was suggesting his game for the evening Cesare recalled we had often used to demonstrate the particular folly of this person or another. To make no mistake at all, the courtier should, on the contrary, when he knows the praises he receives are deserved, not assent to them too openly nor let them pass without some protest. Rather he should tend to disclaim them modestly, always giving the impression that arms are, as indeed they should be, his chief profession, and that all his other fine accomplishments serve merely as adornments; and this should especially be his attitude when he is in the company of soldiers, lest he behave like those who in the world of scholarship want to be taken for warriors and among warriors want to seem men of letters. In this way, as we have said, he will avoid affectation, and even his modest achievements will appear great.'

At this point, Pietro Bembo interrupted: 'I cannot see, my dear Count, why you wish this courtier, who is so literate and so well endowed with other worthy qualities, to regard everything as serving to adorn the profession of arms, and not arms and the rest as serving to adorn the profession of letters, which, taken by themselves, are as superior in dignity to arms as is the soul to the body, since letters are a function of the soul, just as arms are of the body.'

Then the Count answered: 'On the contrary, the profession of arms pertains both to the soul and to the body. But I should not want you to be the judge of this, Pietro, because by one of the parties concerned it would be assumed that you were prejudiced. And as this is a controversy that the wisest men have already thrashed out, there is no call to re-open it. As it is, I consider that it has been settled in favour of arms; and since I may form our courtier as I wish, I want him to be of the same opinion. If you think the contrary, wait until you hear of a contest in which the man who defends the cause of arms is allowed to use them, just as those who defend the cause of letters make use of letters in their defence; for if each one uses his own weapons, you will see that the men of letters will lose.'

'Ah,' said Pietro Bembo, 'you were only too ready earlier on to damn the French for their scant appreciation of letters, and you mentioned the glory that they bring to men and the way they make a man immortal. And now you seem to have changed your mind. Do you not remember that:

> *Giunto Alessandro alla famosa tomba*
> *del fero Achille, sospirando disse:*
> *O fortunato, che sì chiara tromba*
> *trovasti, e chi di te sì alto scrisse!**

*The first quatrain of a sonnet by Petrarch, literally: 'When Alexander reached the famous tomb of fierce Achilles, he sighed and said: O happy man, who found so illustrious a trumpet, and one to write of you so nobly!'

And if Alexander was envious of Achilles not because of what he had done himself but because of the way he was blessed by fortune in having his deeds celebrated by Homer, we must conclude that he put a higher value on the writings of Homer than on the arms of Achilles. What other judge do you want, or what other verdict on the relative worth of arms and letters than the one delivered by one of the greatest commanders that has ever lived?'

The Count replied: 'I blame the French for believing [10] that letters are harmful to the profession of arms, and I maintain myself that it is more fitting for a warrior to be educated than for anyone else; and I would have these two accomplishments, the one helping the other, as is most fitting, joined together in our courtier. I do not think that this means I have changed my opinion. But, as I said, I do not wish to argue which of them is more praiseworthy. Let it be enough that men of letters hardly ever choose to praise other than great men and glorious deeds, which deserve praise both on their own account and because, in addition, they provide writers with a truly noble theme. And this subject-matter embellishes what is written and, no doubt, is the reason why such writings endure, for otherwise, if they dealt not with noble deeds but with vain and trivial subjects, they would surely be read and appreciated less. And if Alexander was envious of Achilles because he was praised by Homer, it still does not necessarily follow that he thought more of letters than of arms; and if he had thought that he was as inferior to Achilles as a soldier as he believed that all those who would write about him were inferior to Homer as writers, he would, I am sure, have far preferred brave exploits on his own part to brave talk from others. Therefore I believe that when he said what he did, Alexander was tacitly praising himself, and expressing a desire for what he thought he lacked, namely supreme ability as a writer, rather than for what he took for granted he already had, namely prowess as a warrior, in which he was far from acknowledging Achilles as his superior. So when he called Achilles fortunate he meant that if so far his own fame did not rival that of Achilles (which had been made bright and illustrious through so inspired a poem) this was not because his valour and merits were less notable or less deserving of the highest praise but because of the way fortune had granted Achilles a born genius to be his herald and to trumpet his deeds to the world. Moreover, perhaps Alexander wanted to encourage some gifted person to write about him, showing that his pleasure in this would be as great as his love and respect for the sacred monuments of literature. And now we have said enough about this subject.'

'Indeed, far too much,' remarked signor Lodovico, 'for I don't think that one could discover anywhere in the world a vessel big enough to hold all the things you want to put into our courtier.' . . .

—⁂—

Book III

. . .

Thus just as it is very fitting that a man should display a certain robust and sturdy manliness, so it is well for a woman to have a certain soft and delicate tenderness, with an air of feminine sweetness in her every movement, which, in her going and staying and whatsoever she does, always makes her appear a woman, without any resemblance to a man. If this precept be added to the rules that these gentlemen have taught the courtier, then I think that she ought to be able to make use of many of them, and adorn herself with the finest accomplishments, as signor Gaspare says. For I consider that many virtues of the mind are as necessary to a woman as to a man; as it is to be of good family; to shun affectation: to be naturally graceful; to be well mannered, clever and prudent; to be neither proud, envious or evil-tongued, nor vain, contentious or clumsy; to know how to gain and keep the favour of her mistress and of everyone else; to perform well and gracefully the sports suitable for women. It also seems to me that good looks are more important to her than to the courtier, for much is lacking to a woman who lacks beauty. She must also be more circumspect and at greater pains to avoid giving an excuse for someone to speak ill of her; she should not only be beyond reproach but also beyond even suspicion, for a woman lacks a man's resources when it comes to defending herself. And now, seeing that Count Lodovico has explained in great detail what should be the principal occupation of a courtier, namely, to his mind, the profession of arms, it seems right for me to say what I consider ought to be that of the lady at Court. And when I have done this, then I shall believe that most of my task has been carried out.

'Leaving aside, therefore, those virtues of the mind which she must have in common with the courtier, such as prudence, magnanimity, continence and many others besides, and also the qualities that are common to all kinds of women, such as goodness and discretion, the ability to take good care, if she is married, of her husband's belongings and house and children, and the virtues belonging to a good mother, I say that the lady who is at Court should properly have, before all else, a certain pleasing affability whereby she will know how to entertain graciously every kind of man with charming and honest conversation, suited to the time and the place and the rank of the person with whom she is talking. And her serene and modest behaviour, and the candour that ought to inform all her actions, should be accompanied by a quick and vivacious spirit by which she shows her freedom from boorishness; but with such a virtuous manner that she makes herself thought no less chaste, prudent and benign than she is pleasing, witty and discreet. Thus she must observe a certain difficult mean, composed as it were of contrasting qualities, and take care not to stray beyond certain fixed limits. . . .

'Now since signor Gaspare also asks what are the many things a lady at Court should know about, how she ought to converse, and whether her virtues should be such as to contribute to her conversation, I declare that I want her to understand what these gentlemen have said the courtier himself ought to know; and as for the activities we have said are unbecoming to her, I want her at least to have the understanding that people can have of things they do not practise themselves; and this so that she may know how to value and praise the gentlemen concerned in all fairness, according to their merits. And, to repeat in just a few words something of what has already been said, I want this lady to be knowledgeable about literature and painting, to know how to dance and play games, adding a discreet modesty and the ability to give a good impression of herself to the other principles that have been taught the courtier. And so when she is talking or laughing, playing or jesting, no matter what, she will always be most graceful, and she will converse in a suitable manner with whomever she happens to meet, making use of agreeable witticisms and jokes. And although continence, magnanimity, temperance, fortitude of spirit, prudence and the other virtues may not appear to be relevant in her social encounters with others, I want her to be adorned with these as well, not so much for the sake of good company, though they play a part in this too, as to make her truly virtuous, and so that her virtues, shining through everything she does, make her worthy of honour.'

'I am quite surprised,' said signor Gaspare with a laugh, 'that since you endow women with letters, continence, magnanimity and temperance, you do not want them to govern cities as well, and to make laws and lead armies, while the men stay at home to cook and spin.'

The Magnifico replied, also laughing: 'Perhaps that would not be so bad, either.'

Then he added: 'Do you not know that Plato, who was certainly no great friend of women, put them in charge of the city and gave all the military duties to the men? Don't you think that we might find many women just as capable of governing cities and armies as men? But I have not imposed these duties on them, since I am fashioning a Court lady and not a queen. I'm fully aware that you would like by implication to repeat the slander that signor Ottaviano made against women yesterday, namely, that they are most imperfect creatures, incapable of any virtuous act, worth very little and quite without dignity compared with men. But truly both you and he would be very much in error if you really thought this.' . . .

CREDITS

LEON BATTISTA ALBERTI, *On Painting*. Translated by Cecil Grayson. Translation copyright © 1972 Cecil Grayson. Reprinted by permission of the translator.

DANTE ALIGHIERI, *The Divine Comedy*. Translated by John Ciardi. Translation copyright © 1954, 1957, 1959, 1960, 1961, 1967, 1970 by the Ciardi Family Publishing Trust. Reprinted by permission of W. W. Norton & Company, Inc.

ST. THOMAS AQUINAS, *Summa theologica*, Volume II, Fifth Article. Translated by Fathers of the English Dominican Province. Benzinger Publishing Company. Copyright © 1947 Benzinger Publishing Company.

ARISTOPHANES, *Lysistrata* from *Five Comedies of Aristophanes*. Translated by Benjamin Bickley Rogers. Copyright © 1955 Doubleday & Co. Reprinted by permission of Doubleday Anchor Books, Garden City, NY.

ARISTOTLE, *Poetics* from *Classical Literary Criticism*. Translated by T. S. Dorsch (Penguin Classics, 1965). Copyright © 1985 T. S. Dorsch.

ST. AUGUSTINE, *Confessions*. Translated by R. S. Pine-Coffin (Penguin Classics, 1961). Copyright © 1961 R. S. Pine-Coffin, 1961. *The City of God*. Translated by Henry Bettenson (Penguin Classics, 1972). Translation copyright © 1972 Henry Bettenson, 1972.

BEDE, *A History of the English Church and People*. Translated by Leo Sherley-Price (Penguin Classics, 1955, revised edition 1968). Copyright © 1955, 1968 Leo Sherley-Price.

Beowulf. Translated by Michael Alexander (Penguin Classics, 1973). Copyright © 1973 Michael Alexander.

GIOVANNI BOCCACCIO, "Filomena's Tale" from *The Decameron*. Translated by Mark Musa and Peter Bondanella. Copyright © 1982 by Mark Musa and Peter Bondanella. Used by permission of Dutton Signet, a division of Penguin Books USA, Inc.

BOETHIUS, *The Consolation of Philosophy*. Translated by V. E. Watts (Penguin Classics, 1969). Copyright © 1969 V. E. Watts.

BALDASSARE CASTIGLIONE, *The Book of the Courtier*. Translated by George Bull (Penguin Classics 1967, revised edition 1975). Copyright © 1967 George Bull.

CATULLUS, *The Poems of Catullus*. Translated by Peter Whigham (Penguin Classics, 1966). Translation copyright © 1966 Peter Whigham.

GEOFFREY CHAUCER, "The Prologue" and "The Wife of Bath's Tale" from *The Canterbury Tales*. Translated by Nevill Coghill (Penguin Classics, 1951, fourth revised edition, 1977). Copyright © 1958, 1960, 1975, 1977 Nevill Coghill.

CICERO, "The Dream of Scipio" from *On the Good Life*. Translated by Michael Grant (Penguin Classics, 1971). Translation copyright © 1971 Michael Grant Publications Ltd.

ANNA COMNENA, T*he Alexiad of Anna Comnena*. Translated by E. R. A. Sewter (Penguin Classics, 1969). Copyright © 1969 E. R. A. Sewter.

CHRISTINE DE PIZAN, *The Book of the City of Ladies*. Translated by Earl Jeffrey Richards. Copyright © 1982 by Persea Books, Inc. Reprinted by permission of Persea Books, Inc.

The Dispute of a Man with His Soul from *Wings of the Falcon: Life and Thought in Ancient Egypt*. Translation by Joseph Kaster. Copyright © 1968 by Joseph Kaster. Reprinted by permission of Henry Holt and Co., Inc.

EINHARD AND NOTKER THE STAMMERER, *Two Lives of Charlemagne*. Translated by Lewis Thorpe (Penguin Classics, 1969). Copyright © 1969 Lewis Thorpe.

ENHEDUANNA, *The Exaltation of Inanna*. Translated by William P. Hallo & J. J. A. VanDijk. Yale University Press. Copyright © 1968 by Yale University Press. Reprinted by permission of the publisher.

The Epic of Gilgamesh. Translated by N. K. Sandars (Penguin Classics 1960, second revised edition 1972). Copyright © 1960, 1964, 1972 N. K. Sandars.

EPICURUS, "Letter to Menoeceus" from *Hellenistic Philosophy*. By Herman Shapiro & Edwin M. Curley. Copyright © 1965 by Herman Shapiro & Edwin M. Curley. Reprinted by permission of Random House, Inc.

EUSEBIUS, *The History of the Church*. Translated by G. A. Williamson (Penguin Classics, 1965, revised edition, 1989). Copyright © 1965 G. A. Williamson, revisions copyright © 1989 Andrew Louth.

The Great Hymn to the Aten from *Wings of the Falcon: Life and Thought in Ancient Egypt*. Translation by Joseph Kaster.

INDEX

—⟊—